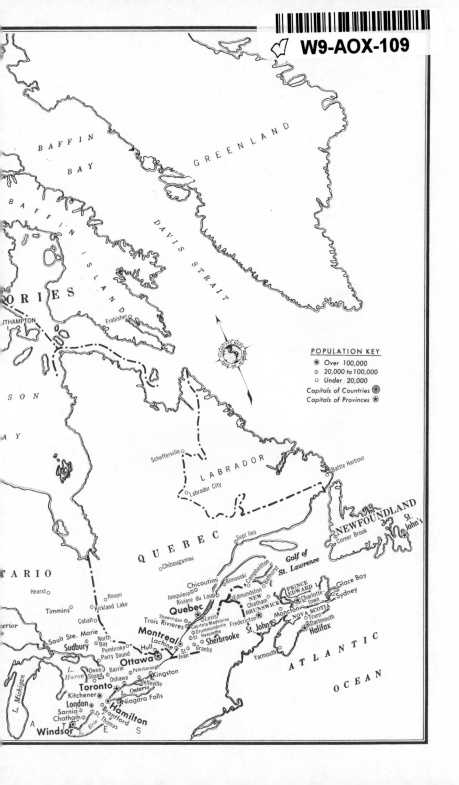

W9-AOX-109

POPULATION KEY

⊛ Over 100,000
⊙ 20,000 to 100,000
○ Under 20,000
Capitals of Countries ⊛
Capitals of Provinces ⊕

Conflict and Language Planning in Quebec

Multilingual Matters

Please contact us for the latest information on recent and forthcoming books in the series.
Derrick Sharp, General Editor, Multilingual Matters,
Bank House, 8a Hill Road, Clevedon, Avon BS21 7HH, England.

MULTILINGUAL MATTERS 5

Conflict and Language Planning in Quebec

Edited by
Richard Y. Bourhis

MULTILINGUAL
MATTERS LTD

P119.32.C65B68 1984t

British Library Cataloguing in Publication Data

Bourhis, Richard Y.
  Conflict and language planning in Quebec –
  (Multilingual matters; 5)
  1. Language policy — Québec (Province)
  2. French language — Social aspects — Québec (Province)
  306.4   P119.32.C3

  ISBN 0-905028-16-3
  ISBN 0-905028-25-2 Pbk

Multilingual Matters Ltd,
Bank House, 8a Hill Road,
Clevedon, Avon BS21 7HH,
England.

Typeset by Wayside Graphics, Clevedon, Avon.
Printed and bound in Great Britain by
Short Run Press Ltd, Exeter EX2 7LW.

A Louise, Chantal et Gisèle

Contents

Preface

This book should be of interest to a wide audience since it deals with language planning efforts aimed at regulating the use of two major world languages: French and English. Current estimates rank English as the second most widely used language in the world with an estimated 325 million speakers while French ranks 12th with approximately 75 million speakers. The aim of this multidisciplinary book is to present a coherent picture of Quebec's efforts to make French the only official language of Quebec society through the adoption in 1977 of the *Charter of the French Language*. Also known as Bill 101, the *Charter* has been well received in francophone Quebec but is still viewed as quite a controversial measure in the anglophone communities of Quebec and Canada. This book provides numerous answers as to why Bill 101 was implemented by the Quebec Government but it raises as many questions as it answers when it comes time to evaluate the impact of the *Charter* on different sectors of Quebec society. For instance has Bill 101 achieved its goal of promoting the use of French in Quebec and if so at what cost? Was the *Office de la langue française*, the government body in charge of implementing Bill 101, succeeded in its task of enforcing the Francization of Quebec business firms? How have Canadian and American business firms responded to the Francization process? Whose interests has the passage of Bill 101 really served in Quebec society and does the *Charter* really promote the cause of Quebec Independence? What have been the effects of Bill 101 on French/English relations in the Province? What strategic options are open to Quebec anglophones faced as they are with a drop from majority to minority status? Finally, how do the education provisions of Bill 101 dealing with Quebec anglophone minorities compare with those found for francophone minorities across Anglo-Canada?

Each chapter of this edited volume deals with one or more of these questions and many more. The issues raised by each of these questions should be of concern not only to Quebec and Canadian readers but also to all those involved in fields such as political science, sociology, public policy, education, sociolinguistics, language planning and social psychology. If this volume helps readers better appreciate the issues raised by language planning decisions such as Bill 101 in Quebec, then this volume will have achieved its purpose. Above all, this volume shows that as with other aspects of human activity language too can be planned.

Finally, a brief note about the origin of this volume. The original plan for this project was to edit a special issue of the *Journal of Multilingual and Multicultural Development* on Language Planning in Quebec. However, the publishers and editors of *Multilingual Matters* suggested that an edited book in their series would be a better format for such a project. I am glad I followed their advice and I wish to thank Mike Grover, Derrick Sharp and Howard Giles for their advice and encouragement in completing this project. I also wish to thank all my chapter contributors for believing in the project and for providing their respective chapters. A special "thank you" is also due to William F. Mackey who so kindly agreed to write the *Foreword* to this volume. I also wish to thank the clerical staff of the Psychology Department of McMaster University who provided superb support in typing and preparing final manuscripts. In this regard I wish to convey my thanks to Beverly Pitt, Wendy Selbie and Joyce Litster. Finally, I wish to thank the Canadian *Multiculturalism Directorate* for agreeing to re-direct some of my research funds to help the completion of this volume.

Richard Y. Bourhis
Fern Cottage,
Dundas, Ontario
June, 1983

Foreword

William F. Mackey, FRSC
International Centre for Research on Bilingualism
Université Laval

No country has invested more in language policy than has Canada, and particularly Quebec. If one counts only the commissioned research of the royal commissions investigating bilingualism, biculturalism, multicultural-ism, the state of the French language, the bilingual districts, bilingualization of the public service and the numerous federal and provincial internal government reports, the resulting publications would cover the four walls of a large living room library.

The focus of all this attention both at the Canadian federal and the Quebec provincial levels is Canada's French-speaking people, most of whom — some six million — inhabit the valley of the St. Lawrence, where the large urban centres of the cities of Montreal and Quebec are located. Yet the French-speaking areas of Canada overflow the political boundaries of the Province of Quebec and extend into the neighboring provinces of New Brunswick (Acadia) to the east, Ontario to the west and parts of the upper fringe of the United States to the south (Maine and Vermont).

As can be seen in Figure 1, a language map of French Canada includes as a continuing land mass all of Quebec, Acadia and Northern Ontario. Within this area are to be found more than 96% of all Canadians whose mother tongue is French (Mackey, 1978). Although many French speakers are able to understand and speak English with various degrees of compe-tence, these bilinguals are distributed in such a way as to form a bilingual belt around Quebec (Vallee & Dufour, 1974). Nearly all French speakers out-side Quebec, with the exception of a few isolated communities, are to a certain degree bilingual. And this is not surprising, since their only language of schooling for generations past has been English. Within Quebec, bilingual communities are limited to those areas of language contact with monolingual English-speaking areas near the western boundary of Quebec (including Montreal) and to the south between the St. Lawrence and the United States frontier (the Eastern Townships). Apart from these areas, Quebec is a French-speaking society. For example, the great hydro-electric and metallurgical developments in the Saguenay and along the north shore of the St. Lawrence support a population which is about 94% unilingual in French.

If one considers these geolinguistic realities, it is not really surprising that Quebec has tended toward a policy of French unilingualism, while the central government in Ottawa has been committed to a policy of official bilingualism (Mackey, 1973). Each of these divergent policies was developed on the basis of many years of painstaking research under independent commissions of investigation which spared no expense to gather, at home and abroad, the best ideas and the most complete data.

In the case of Quebec, there now exists a body of knowledge on the implementation of language policy which is unique. So is the administrative structure, both in variety and in scope. One of the five government bodies responsible for language policy implementation (l'Office de la langue française) counted in 1983 some four hundred full-time language workers who within a period of a few years were responsible for producing a regular flow of policy studies, bibliographies, glossaries, surveys, language tests, and the proceedings of their frequent international conferences on such topics as the languages of science, language and the law, and the computerization of word-banks. For all these reasons, it is understandable that the Quebec experience in language policy should be of interest to other countries — especially at a time when concern about the fate of regional languages throughout the world has become so widespread (Mackey, 1982).

For the presentation of Quebec's language problems to the international public it seems particularly appropriate that the task should be undertaken by a *Québécois* specializing in issues related to language, ethnicity and intergroup relations, who has spent part of his career in Europe and part of it in both Quebec and English Canada. Yet, since no question concerning man in society is unaffected by language, the wide-ranging research on the language problems of Quebec has to be distributed among several different disciplines. So must it be with this timely volume on Quebec's language policy.

In the following chapters, Professor Bourhis has succeeded in enlisting the collaboration of scholars from such disciplines as social psychology,

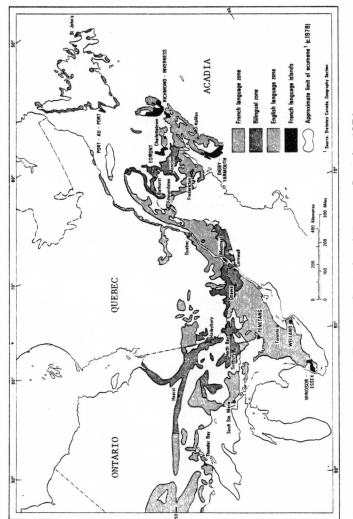

FIGURE 1 *Language Zones in Central and Eastern Canada, 1976*

Source: Cartwright, D. G. 1980, *Official Language Populations in Canada: Patterns and Contacts.* Montreal: The Institute for Research on Public Policy, p. 53.
Note: The designation of each of the above language zones were based on the language-related data from the 1971 and 1976 Canadian census (e.g. mother tongue and home language).

sociolinguistics, political science, sociology, education and public administration. Each contribution focuses around the central theme of the Charter
of the French Language (Bill 101) whereby Quebec, after almost two
centuries of bilingualism, has become an officially unilingual state, with
French as its official language. As Professor Bourhis points out in the
Introduction to his volume, after five years of implementation, the time has
come for an interim appraisal of how well the Charter has achieved its
objectives and how the implementation of the new laws and regulations has
affected the social and economic fabric of one of the most important non-
English speaking areas in North America.

Although we may be limited to a five-year period, no understanding of
Quebec's language policy is possible outside its historical context. That is
why it is so important to begin as we do here with an historical overview: this
task has been put in the competent hands of Alison d'Anglejan, the bilingual
Montreal scholar and well-known specialist on psychological and educational aspects of second language learning.

Secondly, in dealing with language policy, it has become the practice to
distinguish between status and corpus. Although the distinction, first developed at the International Centre for Research on Bilingualism by Heinz
Kloss in 1969, has become current, the terms and categories have not always
been uniformly applied. Some scholars have distinguished between policy
(status) and planning (treatment) (Mackey, 1979). Others (like Haugen,
Rubin, Fishman, Ferguson) make further distinctions within and beyond
these categories (Cobarrubias & Fishman, 1982). Whatever the terminology,
however, the basic distinction between *how* the language is to be used
(corpus planning) and what the language is to be used *for* (status planning) is
a valid one. In this volume each of these two aspects is treated by a specialist
in these respective areas. Pierre E. Laporte has devoted his career to the
study of status language planning; Denise Daoust has long been associated
with the implementation of the normative aspect of language policy (corpus
planning). Both are full-time professionals working at l'Office de la langue
française (OLF) in their respective fields. As practitioners of language
planning, each contributes important insights on how language policies are
being implemented and evaluated in various domains of Quebec society
including the ever-important corporate and business sectors. Complement-
ing these two chapters is a contribution by Roger Miller who discusses key
findings from a series of his own studies dealing with the response of large
business firms to the Francization process legislated through Bill 101.

Thirdly, there is the effect of each of these policies on the relationships
between different social groups and forces within Quebec society. The

chapter contributed by William Coleman presents a timely political analysis of the class bases of Quebec's recent language policies. These policies also have an impact on the relationship between the two main language groups in Quebec: the Francophones and the Anglophones. Both Don Taylor and Lise Simard are prominent social psychologists who have long been interested in French/English relations in Quebec. In their contribution they examine French/English relations by monitoring the attitudes of Francophones and Anglophones towards Bill 101 and towards those labelled as being for or against Bill 101. Also using a social psychological perspective, Richard Y. Bourhis not only presents a series of insightful studies investigating the impact of Bill 101 on self-reports of French/English language usage by Francophones and Anglophones but also monitors their actual language choices during real life French/English encounters in downtown Montreal.

Finally, and also revealing, is the potential of the Charter to modify the demographic and political behaviour of the new official minority — the English of Quebec. Gary Caldwell has made several searching studies of this population and has long been recognized as a specialist in this area. Yet, since the treatment of this Anglophone population had developed into a sort of do-unto-others sort of policy, it can now only be understood in the context of what had been meted out to comparable Francophone minorities outside Quebec. This comparative perspective is here ably handled by John Mallea, who brings to the task both his studies of educational policy in Canada and his year of work at our Centre in Quebec where he worked on the only book in English devoted to the Official Language Act (Bill 22), the language law preceding the current Charter of the French Language (Mallea, 1977).

In sum, this book assures the reader a balanced treatment of a complex problem, the solutions to which are not without significance for those many nations faced with the great dilemma of our century — the conflict between the right of the individual to cultural freedom and the right of the group to ethnic survival.

References

COBARRUBIAS, J. & FISHMAN, J. S. (eds) 1982, *Progress in Language Planning: International Perspective*. The Hague: Mouton.

KLOSS, H. 1969, *Research Possibilities on Group Bilingualism*. Quebec: International Centre for Research on Bilingualism.

MACKEY, W. F. 1973, *Three Concepts for Geolinguistics*. Quebec: International Centre for Research on Bilingualism.

— 1978, *Le Bilinguisme Canadien: Bigliographie analytique et guide du chercheur*. Quebec: International Centre for Research on Bilingualism.

— 1979, Language Policy and Language Planning. *Journal of Communication*, 47–53.

— 1982, *International Bibliography on Bilingualism*. Quebec: Presses de l'Université Laval.

MALLEA, J. R. (ed.) 1977, *Quebec's Language Policies: Background and Response*. Quebec: International Centre for Research on Bilingualism.

VALLEE, F. & DUFOUR, A. 1974, The Bilingual Belt: A Garotte for the French? *Laurentian University Review*, 6, 19–44.

1 Introduction: Language policies in multilingual settings

Richard Y. Bourhis
McMaster University

The Charter of the French Language (Bill 101) making French the only official language of Quebec has received much criticism in the anglophone popular press of both Quebec and Canada. Public charges that the Quebec Government was unfairly treating the English of Quebec through Bill 101 have been widely aired in the mass media across Canada. To many anglophones in Quebec and Canada, Bill 101 remains the most controversial and most negatively perceived legislative act ever promulgated by a Quebec Government in recent years. In contrast, for most Québécois francophones, Bill 101 remains one of the most popular and most favourably perceived legislative measures ever adopted by the Parti Québécois since it came to power in November 1976. More than anything else in recent years these contrasting perceptions of a single act of Parliament attest to the linguistic conflict that has so long characterized relations between francophones and anglophones in both Quebec and Canada.

Five years have passed since the passage of Bill 101, and its effects in Quebec have already been felt. At this juncture it seemed appropriate to plan a first assessment of the impact of Bill 101 on the fabric of Quebec society. To achieve this goal within the confines of a single volume the present editor recruited key scholars and professionals already involved in monitoring and assessing the effect of the Charter of the French Language on different sectors of Quebec society. The wide-ranging background of the scholars and professionals who collaborated to achieve this task is evident from a perusal of the *Notes on Contributors* while the range of topics they contributed can be gleaned from a reading of the *Foreword* provided by William F. Mackey.

Before briefly discussing some of the main points raised by each chapter contributor it seems important in this Introductory chapter to situate Quebec language planning within the broader context of language planning activities in the world. Necessarily, a discussion of world language planning issues must remain relatively selective and brief within the confines of this Introductory chapter. Readers wishing to acquaint themselves with the full range of language planning issues as they apply to different linguistic situations across the world should consult classic and current contributions by Fishman, Ferguson & Das Gupta (1968), Rubin & Jernudd (1971), Fishman (1972; 1974; 1978), Cobarrubias & Fishman (1983) and Weinstein (1983). In addition, interested readers should consult three journals which regularly deal with language planning issues: *Language Problems and Language Planning*, the *International Journal of the Sociology of Language* and the *Language Planning Newsletter* (published by the East-West Culture Learning Institute based in Honolulu, Hawaii).

The first part of this chapter is devoted to an overview of some of the major types of language planning activities in the world. Through a summary presentation of each chapter contribution to this volume, the second part of the chapter discusses language planning issues as they specifically relate to the Quebec setting.

Notes on language planning in the world

Many now take for granted state intervention in various aspects of public affairs including the economy, social welfare, education, environmental protection and national security. The premise of much state intervention is that "natural" market forces are not sufficient to address or solve perceived needs and problems prevalent in society. Thus, Government leaders often resort to planning as a rational and co-ordinated state action to solve problems and reach goals perceived to be in the best interest of the collectivity. As the privileged tool of human communication, the vehicle of culture, and often the distinctive symbol of "peoplehood", it is not surprising that language too has become the target of state planning by Government leaders and policy makers.

Most simply language planning has been defined as "decision making about language" (Rubin & Jernudd, 1971). A more comprehensive definition was recently formulated by Weinstein (1980) who describes language planning as:

"a government authorized long term sustained and conscious effort to alter a language itself or to change a language's functions in a society for the purpose of solving communication problem" (p. 37)

The first important point in this definition is that language planning is not the result of state intervention for its own sake but is state intervention that must be formulated to address real and concrete communication problems within the society. In developing countries the communication problem may be illiteracy which thwarts economic development and modernization. In the developed states the problem may be one of accommodating linguistic minorities within the main stream mode of production and culture. In either case language planning can be seen as a rational problem-solving measure designed to address serious communication breakdown in society.

Secondly, as is suggested from the above definition, two major areas of language planning can be identified: the first is what is known as corpus language planning, while the second is known as status language planning (Kloss, 1969). Corpus language planning has to do with decisions about the structure of language in terms of its orthography, lexicon, spelling and grammar. Status language planning has to do with decisions about what functions each language(s) should have in a region, territory or nation state. Language planning may be designed to achieve very limited and specific linguistic goals such as the introduction of minority language teaching in the educational system of a city, province or state. Alternatively, as in the case of Quebec (this volume), language planning can be designed to achieve goals which will affect language usage not only in education but in all domains of activity whether these be public administration, the business world, culture, recreation etc. A coherent co-ordination of corpus and status language planning is vital for the success of both limited and broad language planning goals. For instance, there is no point in introducing a minority language teaching program in a school system (status planning) if orthographies and grammars (corpus planning) in the minority language are as yet unavailable. Thus, what must often be done to a language to achieve the goals of status planning can be understood to be what we mean by corpus language planning.

At least four goals of language planning can be identified (Nahir, 1977). Language planning programs may be designed for the purpose of language purification, language reform, language revival or language standardization. Most language planning programs combine more than one of the above goals. For instance, language standardization programs usually also involve some language purification and some language reform. In turn each of these goals can only be reached through corpus and status language planning decisions. Thus a plan to standardize a language will involve status planning decisions when it comes time to decide which variety of the language should be the target of standardization while corpus planning will involve the actual procedures used to codify the language such as the creation of dictionaries and guides to grammar.

Each of the above four types of language planning activities will be discussed using examples from language planning programs undertaken in various parts of the world. In most cases both the status and corpus aspects of these language planning goals will also be discussed. It is hoped that this presentation of language planning activity in different parts of the world will help readers situate the current language planning efforts of Quebec in a broader world perspective.

Language purification

Studies in numerous parts of the world have shown that people who use the "correct" prestige style of a language are often perceived more favourably in terms of competence and social attractiveness than speakers who use nonstandard "incorrect" speech styles (Ryan & Giles, 1982). Studies have also shown that what is considered "correct" usage is more often the product of socio-historical forces reflecting the success of dominant elites in imposing their own style of speech as the prestige "correct" variety, than a reflection of the inherent linguistic aesthetic "superiority" of the standard form (Giles, Bourhis, Trudgill & Lewis, 1974). Thus, contemporary norms favouring "correct" usage often reflect earlier concerns based on the notion that the "elite" or "state" must promote and defend the "purity" of its national language (Bourhis, 1982).

The best-known example of a language planning institution involved with the purification of its language is the "Académie Française" founded in 1637. L'Académie Française had the task of purifying and perpetuating correct French usage as rendered by the Court and esteemed authors of the day. Claude Favre de Vaugelas, an influential member of "Les Immortels", fully expected that the succession of the 40-member elite constituting "Les Immortels" would guarantee the harmonious development of correct French through the ages. Today, linguists, terminologists and members of l'Académie Française are involved in corpus planning through the creation of French words designed to replace English loan words which filter into the French language as a result of the popularity of Anglo-American culture and technology in France.

France was not alone in creating its language Academy. Language Academies involved in language purification were founded in Italy (1582), Spain (1713), Sweden (1786) and Hungary (1830). Vigorous language purification programs were also undertaken at the turn of the century in the United States in favour of American English and in Germany in favour of "hoch Deutsch" or high German (St. Clair, 1982). Language purification programs still go on today. For instance in the United States the "Back to Basics" and "Competency Based" movements promote "correct" General American syntax while dissuading non-standard varieties of English such as Black English, Chicano English and Indian English (St. Clair, 1982).

Today the spread of English (Fishman, Cooper & Conrad, 1977) seems to have sparked a renewed concern for language purism in France, Spain, Quebec and Hispanic America (Nahir, 1977). For instance in Quebec during the 1960s, the Office de la language française adopted a normative approach to language purity through its concern with maintaining Quebec French usage in line with "correct" standard French as spoken in France. However, by the early 1970s Quebec language planners shifted the target of their corpus planning efforts. In this case they sought to maintain language purity by creating French terminology designed to replace English loan words commonly used in Quebec industries, business and public administration (McConnell, Daoust & Martin, 1979). Likewise, Mexico recently created a Commission for the Defense of the Spanish language which has as one of its goals the elimination of English loan words known as "pochismos" (rottenisms!) which have invaded Spanish usage in Mexico. The Commission is in charge of creating and diffusing Spanish words designed to replace English loan words. Interestingly enough, a booklet produced by the Mexican Commission salutes Quebec's current Charter of the French Language (Bill 101) as an admirable attempt in defence of its language (Globe & Mail, 3/8/83). Language purification is a language planning activity that will remain important so long as relatively weaker languages are in contact with relatively stronger languages throughout the world.

Language reform

Language reform usually entails the simplification or modernization of a language system to suit present day communicative needs. Language reform is often the domain of corpus planning since it involves the modification of all or some aspects of language including lexicon, spelling, grammar and orthography. Since the 19th century, planned reform of one or more of the above aspects of language has been undertaken for languages spoken in Spain, Greece, Germany, Norway, Poland, Hungary, Russia, Israel, Turkey, etc.

The best-known case of successful and speedy language reform was undertaken for the Turkish language from 1922 onwards under the leadership of Kemal Ataturk. Following World War I, Turkey was involved in redefining its national identity. This redefinition of national identity included a government-sponsored language reform aimed at transforming the ancestral Ottoman language to a modern language known as Turkish. The language reform was quite extensive and not only involved the replacement of Arabic and Persian loan words by European ones but went as far as replacing the entire writing system from the Arabic script to the Roman alphabet. According to Gallagher (1971) the radical switch from Arabic to Roman script was facilitated by the fact that in 1927 as little as 10% of the population was literate and very few people were concerned with maintaining their Perso-Arabic literary heritage. By 1929 Arabic writing was abolished and from then on the world of education and most cultural and scientific activities were pursued using the Roman script. In addition, the language reform program also involved the simplification of the grammar, vocabulary and phraseology to better suit everyday modern conversational needs. The continuing efforts of Turkish language planners were still quite evident in the Turkish dictionaries and guides to orthography published in the 1950s and 1960s. On the whole Gallagher (1971) concludes that carefully-planned language reform can be quite successful and this was shown to be true in the case of the modernization of the Turkish language.

Other examples of language reform can go back centuries. There is the case of script modernization which occurred in China in 213BC when the Chinese leader of the day commissioned a revision of the writing system to eliminate competing script forms and provide a common set of Chinese characters for scholars and Government officials across China. A more recent instance of script modernization involves the 1977 Japanese Language Council decision to simplify written Japanese to bring it more in line with modern middle class Japanese usage. To achieve this goal the Council dropped 33 traditional characters and adopted 83 new ones considered better suited to the needs of a more democratic post-industrial Japan (Weinstein, 1983).

Finally, language reform also involves the coining of new words and terminology needed to keep apace with techological innovation. This may be needed even for well-established languages such as French as is evident in France where linguists and terminology committees are busily involved in coining new words to describe advances in computer technology, aeronautics and space exploration. The new French terminology is passed on to the Haut Comité de la langue française which is itself linked to the Prime

Minister's office, which sees to it that proposed new teminology is ratified by state laws and decrees (Weinstein, 1983).

In Quebec, today's Office de la language française (OLF) is not only involved in the creation of new French terminology through its Terminology Commission but also offers extensive consulting services for individuals and firms needing assistance in dealing with terminology issues (see Daoust, this volume, chapter 4). In addition, the *Banque de Terminologie du Québec* consists of an extensive computer data bank of new and existing French terminology relevant to all domains of French language use in business, industry and administration. As will become evident from a careful reading of the chapter contribution by Denise Daoust (this volume, chapter 4) Quebec language planners today are at the forefront of language reform and language modernization in the world.

Language revival

Language planning efforts have been made across the world to revive old ancestral languages to their former status and usefulness. A language can be revived through corpus planning activity such as codification which involves the production of modernized dictionaries for the old language, as well as new spelling, grammar and pronunciation guides. The status planning aspect of language revival will usually involve all the measures needed to popularize the chosen revived language. Such efforts may include the re-introduction of the ancestral language in the educational system, the provision of ancestral language services in government institutions and even the introduction of the ancestral language in the electronic media such as television and radio broadcasting.

The most successful instance of language revival is perhaps that of the Hebrew language in Israel. The Hebrew language was not only dead when it was revived, it was no longer anyone's mother tongue or dialect. The revival thus had to be based solely on literary and traditional sources (Blanc, 1968). In 1980 the Committee for the Hebrew Language was created with one of its aims being:

> "the development and codification of Hebrew for use as a language spoken in all matters of life, at home, in the schools, in public life, in commerce and business, in industry, art and science" (cited in Nahir 1977: 110–111).

In 1953 the committee was named the "Hebrew Language Academy" following the creation of the State of Israel. The success of Hebrew language planners was evident as early as 1961 when Israel's census figures showed that 75% of the Jewish population stated that Hebrew was their main or only language of daily communication (Blanc, 1968). The revival of the Hebrew language involved every aspect of corpus planning including extensive modifications of the Hebrew lexicon, grammar and pronunciation. Modern Hebrew is a revived language that seems to have succeeded for a number of reasons. It was introduced to a multilingual community that did not already speak in a common language and needed a shared language for daily communication. Hebrew also served as a unifying symbol of Israel's national identity and newly-gained statehood.

The successful revival of Hebrew in Israel inspired attempts to revive other ancestral languages, especially in Europe. Inspired by the notion of one language one nation (Smith, 1971) many European nations of the 19th century had imposed a single language as the national language of their newly-created nation states. The rise of officially unilingual nation states often had the consequence of forcing existing ancestral language groups into minority status within their own traditional enclaves (van der Plank, 1978). This was the case for language communities such as the Welsh, the Irish and the Scots Gaelic in the United Kingdom; the Bretons, Corsicans and the Flemish in France; the Catalan and Basques in Spain, and the Frisians in Holland.

Following decades of institutional neglect and/or suppression, many ancestral languages and cultures were close to extinction by the middle of this century. However, despite strong pressures to assimilate these national minorities, many of these in recent years have re-asserted their linguistic and cultural distinctiveness in the context of struggles for more political power and varying degrees of autonomy (Williams, 1982). Pressures from these ethnic revival movements (Smith, 1981) have forced the central governments of numerous European states to introduce language revival programs for their minorities. So far Nahir (1977) has noted that the language revival attempts involving the Welsh, the Catalan, the Provencals, the Bretons, and the Irish have been on the whole much less successful than the revival of the Hebrew language in Israel.

The lack of success obtained in the language revival programs of Western Europe seem due in part to the piecemeal nature of the status and corpus language programs implemented in these settings. Such programs compare unfavourably with the thoroughly integrated Hebrew language revival program established in Israel since its creation. In Europe, while a minority ancestral language may be revived as an available language for obtaining government services in the region, measures to introduce the language throughout the educational system of the region may be too limited or be hampered by a lack of adequate textbooks and qualified teachers. In each European case the language revival plans can only involve the introduction of the ancestral language as a *second language* in only a *few* domains of language use, thus maintaining the drawing power of the nation-state's official dominant language (Nahir, 1977).

Another reason for the relative lack of success of language revival programs is that by the time such plans are implemented, the number of native speakers of the ancestral language has usually dwindled to a very small percentage of the population. This is the case today for Welsh speakers in Wales, Breton speakers in Brittany, and Gaelic speakers in Scotland. This is also the case even in independent Ireland. There, following decades of British rule before independence, the English language has become the mother tongue of 98% of the population. English is seen to be the appropriate language for most domains of language use including the home, church, work and school settings. Government efforts to revive the ancestral language of the Irish people must compete with the predominance of English not only in the work and school setting but also in the cultural domains. Thus, even in independent Ireland, language planning efforts to revive a rich ancestral language such as Irish has not yet been successful (Macnamara, 1971; Domhnalian, 1977). Though language revival programs can help slow down the tide of linguistic assimilation, they often come too late to promote a real demographic resurgence of ancestral language users.

Turning to Canada, one could characterize the Federal Government Official Languages Act of 1969 and minority languages education rights enshrined in the 1982 Canadian constitution as language policies designed to promote the revival of the French language in Anglo-Canada. Though French has maintained its prestige as a major language of culture and technology internationally, it remains that in Anglo Canada, French was historically relegated to a low status position not unlike that of ancestral languages in Europe. Francophone minorities in Anglo-Canada have long been the target of discriminatory practices which have in turn contributed to the anglicization of French Canadians across the whole of the country (Breton, Reitz & Valentine, 1980; FFHQ, 1978; Mallea, this volume, chapter 10). For instance, when French was banned from both the Manitoba school sytem and from the provincial legislature in the 1890s, francophones still numbered a significant minority of the population in this province. Close to a century later, when in 1979 the Canadian Supreme Court declared unconstitutional the banning of French in Manitoba, French was finally reintroduced in the Manitoba legislature. However, by then the population of French origin of this province had dwindled to no more than 8% (approximately 80,000) of whom only 39% still used French at home (approximately

31,000; Canada, 1983). Plans to revive official English/French bilingualism in Manitoba announced in 1983 may slow the rate of Anglicization amongst francophones; but as in European language revival programs, such overdue measures will not likely contribute to a substantial demographic revival of the francophone presence in this province. It is ironic that the same 1979 Canadian Supreme Court ruling that officially declared unconstitutional the banning of French in the Manitoba legislature — 90 years after the fact — also declared unconstitutional — only 2 years after the fact — the Bill 101 clauses making French the only official language of the Quebec legislature and Courts.

As the Province containing the largest francophone population outside Quebec (653 thousand; Canada, 1983), the Ontario Government still refuses to implement a French language revival program which would guarantee Franco-Ontarians their own separate schools and schoolboards as has long been the case for the anglophone minority in Quebec even under Bill 101 (Arnopoulos, 1983). In addition, the Ontario government still refuses to adopt sections 16–22 of the new Canadian Charter of Rights and Freedom regarding the use of English and French as official languages. This is the case despite the fact that both the Federal Government and New Brunswick have already adopted these sections of the 1982 Charter of Rights and Freedoms. For those Franco-Ontarians seeking to regain control of their own linguistic destiny, a language revival program in favour of guaranteeing separate French schools and schoolboards would go a long way in healing the wounds of Regulation 17 which in 1912 banned all traces of French from the Ontario school system and whose spirit still lingers in many anglophone majority schoolboards of Ontario today (Arnopoulos, 1983).

More language revival programs will continue to be designed across the world in this century. In Europe alone van der Plank (1978) has estimated that as many as 20 million Europeans are still in a linguistic minority position within existing European nation-states. Many of these states have signed the European Convention of the Rights of Man which states that minorities have the right to receive adequate instruction in their own language. Demands for greater linguistic rights by these groups have grown so persistent that numerous central government must implement language revival programs to avoid the growth of more radical separatist movements (Williams, 1982).

Language standardization

Language standardization can be considered the backbone of language planning activity. Nahir (1977) defined language standardization as "a process whereby one language or dialect spoken in a region becomes accepted as the major language of the region for general usage" (p. 14). Decision-making about which local dialect, local language or foreign language is to become the prestige standard language of a region, province or nation state is closest to what Kloss (1969) meant by status language planning.

Status planning for language standardization becomes most evident when one considers that any choice in favour of one variety of speech as the prestige standard often implies the exclusion of all other varieties as contending alternatives. Thus, decision-making in favour of the promotion of one language or variety of language involves explicit or implicit decisions concerning the tolerance or suppression of all other contending language varieties. As such, the types of choice made to bring about language standardization can become a revealing barometer of the different forces at play in multilingual societies and ultimately come to reflect society's views towards its weaker minorities. The familiar saying that a society can be judged by the way it treats its minorities is particularly relevant in the case of choices made in language standardization. An example of language standardization that successfully imposed state unilingualism through a policy that suppressed all contending local languages and dialects is that of France (Bourhis, 1982).

After the French Revolution of 1793, the Ile de France variety of French spoken by the Parisian bourgeoisie was seen as the potentially unifying symbol to inspire the nationalism of the New Republic. The victorious bourgeoisie felt it needed to suppress existing regional, commercial and language barriers to establish its own economic control across multilingual France. During this period and some time thereafter French patriotism was associated with the speaking of French while non-French speakers were viewed as potential traitors to the revolution and a threat to the political unity of the emerging French Republic. During this period a series of laws was passed by the National Convention which made the teaching of French compulsory in primary school and proclaimed French unilingualism in all parts of France, including non-French speaking regions such as Brittany, the Basque country, Alsace/Lorraine, Corsica and the whole of southern France known as l'Occitanie. Though this first attempt at status language planning in favour of French resulted in a complete failure for linguistic unity in France, subsequent laws such as those of Jules Ferry passed in the early 1880s successfully entrenched French unilingualism in the Republic. During this later period the contempt for non-French languages in France was epitomized in Brittany, Occitanie, Alsace and Corsica, where pupils caught speaking their non-French mother tongue on school premises were punished by being forced to wear the infamous Signum or Token. Pupils still wearing the Token at the end of the school day were punished by the teacher. A student could only dispose of the Token by catching another pupil using the non-French language and reporting him to the teacher before the end of the school day. Such practices fostered distrust between non-French speakers and often made school children ashamed of using their parents' language both at school and at home. As a result of these and other restrictive measures, non-French languages in France after the First World War declined while the linguistic unification of France was well under way. By the late 1960s Pottier (1968) noted that apart from the German/French bilingualism in Alsace/Lorraine and migrant workers thoughout France, 95% of the 53 million inhabitants of France identified French as their mother tongue.

Language standardization in favour of the Ile de France variety of French to the exclusion of all other varieties of French was also pursued with great vigour since it too was viewed as a way of promoting linguistic unity in France. Education decrees banning non-standard accent and dialect usage in the schools contributed greatly to the demise of regional French speech styles in France. In addition, with the almost exclusive use of the Ile de France variety of French in the mass media, it is not surprising to find that this variety, now better known as "standard French" or "international French" is the prestige form against which all other varieties of spoken French are assessed in "le monde de la francophonie" (Bourhis, 1982).

French language planners were not alone in Europe in adopting firm policies towards language standardization. Throughout the 19th and 20th centuries in Europe restrictive language policies favouring unilingualism to the detriment of weaker or competing language groups were promulgated in settings such as Austria/Hungary, Spain, Belgium (Inglehart & Woodward, 1972). In the United Kingdom the promulgation of the 1870 Education Act favouring English as the sole medium of education eliminated Welsh medium schooling in Wales and Gaelic schooling in Scotland for close to a century. In Wales, as in France, the equivalent of the Token known as the "Welsh Not" was successfully used as a stigma and penance to dissuade Welsh pupils from using their mother tongue in class or in the schoolyard.

The choice of one standard language as the unifying symbol of national identity and communication need not involve the suppression of all other language varieties as was seen to be the case in France (Bourhis, 1982). Many young post-war African and Asian states opted for official bilingualism and multilingualism rather than unilingualism. Following the post-World War II decolonization period many African and Asian states were made up of complex configurations of linguistic minorities and majorities, none of which on their own could successfully impose their own language on the others. However, the varied linguistic groups making up these new states often shared a common colonial experience which included contact with metropolitan languages such as French, English, Dutch, Portuguese or German. Upon independence these new states were faced with difficult language standardization choices which needed to take into consideration the role of language as a symbol of national authenticity and mobilization, the use of language as a tool of modernization and the use of language as a vehicle of widest possible communication for all the inhabitants of the land. The ingenuity and range of solutions achieved by many of these states in solving their language standardization problem is impressive and can only be alluded to here (see Fishman *et al*, 1968; Fishman, 1978). One thing is clear and this is that solutions to language problems of developing nations have often been found in the promulgation of official bilingualism or multilingualism rather than in official unilingualism.

Though not without its problems (das Gupta, 1975), perhaps the best example of planned official state multilingualism is India, which has both Hindi and English as official languages and whose constitution recognizes 14 additional national languages (Pandit, 1979). Even if 16 recognized languages seem a lot, there are over 1,652 languages and dialects spoken in India with Hindi, however, being spoken by 38% of its 684 million inhabitants. Though the founders of independent India in 1948 felt that Hindi might one day unite all its citizens, many leaders of the other linguistic minorities felt that standardization in favour of a single indigenous language such as Hindi might threaten the freedom and survival of the other major linguistic groups in the country. An official policy of state multilingualism was a realistic response which greatly contributed to the relative linguistic peace in India (Krishnamurti, 1979).

Official state bilingualism which endorsed a former colonial language as one of its official languages is especially common in developing nations that are part of today's francophonie (Gordon, 1978; Weinstein, 1980; Bourhis, 1982) or today's Commonwealth (Whiteley, 1974; Fishman *et al*, 1977). In *le monde de la francophonie*, French is an official language in the multilingual states of Chad, Gabon, Mali, Madagascar, Senegal, Togo, etc. (Gordon, 1978). Likewise, multilingual Commonwealth countries have often chosen English as one of their official languages. This is the case for Kenya, Tanzania, Uganda, Nigeria, Sierra Leone, Malawi, Ghana, etc. Even newly-independent states such as Mozambique, Angola, and Guinea-Bissau have chosen Portuguese as their official state language even though Portuguese is the language of the former colonial rulers.

Language standardization in favour of official bilingualism or multilingualism has also emerged as a partial solution to language problems in older developed nation-states such as Switzerland and Canada. The solutions to language problems adopted by these states illustrates two types of approaches to language standardization which can be applied to language policies in many parts of the world. The case of Canada illustrates the "personality" approach to language standardization while the case of Switzerland illustrates the "territorial" approach to standardization (Mackey, 1979).

In Canada, where both French and English are official languages, the Official Language Act of 1969 adopted a personality approach in which federal government .public services were to accommodate the linguistic preferences of individuals whose mother tongue was either French or English across the country. Thus, theoretically at least, francophones or anglophones whose group concentration exceeded 10% of the regional population could expect federal government services in their mother tongue. However, this per cent provision proved somewhat difficult for French Canadians since this group was thinly distributed as a minority across the nine anglophone majority provinces. This was not a problem for the Quebec anglophone minority, concentrated as they are in Montreal and Quebec's eastern townships. More specifically, however, Mackey (1979) showed that a language policy based on the "personality" principles for its *citizens* can clash with the right of *public servants* to work in the official language of their choice. Such a clash can undermine the policy considerably. At the cost of millions of dollars the Canadian policy for promoting bilingual public services is seen by many as a costly failure (Mackey, 1979; 1983).

The territorial approach to language standardization is based on the notion that it is individuals who accommodate to the language of the region, district or province in which they reside (Mackey, 1979). Through the 1848 Constitution which established the Swiss Confederation, Switzerland adopted a 'territorial' approach to language standardization. The autonomy granted to the Cantons over a wide range of state functions including schooling is evident in Article 1 of the Constitution which states: "The peoples of the twenty-two sovereign cantons of Switzerland form together the Swiss Confederation". In turn, the relative autonomy of the Canton reflects the checker board geography of the Swiss Alps where pockets of population have evolved in their separate ways, isolated as they were from each other by mountain ranges and deep gorges. With a population of 6.3 million, Switzerland has four official languages which are German (spoken by 65% of the population), French (spoken by 18% of the population), Italian (spoken by 12% of the population) and Romansch (spoken by 1% of the population). In today's 26 Swiss Cantons the territorial approach applies since individuals must adapt to the language of their Canton or district. In the officially French Cantons of Geneva, Vaud, and Neuchatel *all* Canton services including public schooling are offered only in French. In the Cantons and districts that are German, services are only offered in that language. While Switzerland's official languages are taught as second languages in the school system, knowledge of the nation's official languages is not necessary except for federal civil service jobs while language skills in foreign languages such as English are particularly valued.

Recently in Switzerland, the territorial solution was again applied to settle a longstanding linguistic conflict in the largely German-speaking Canton of Bern. Over the years French speakers had grown increasingly frustrated with their minority position within the Canton of Bern. In 1974 a plebiscite within the French-speaking Jura districts of the Canton voted in favour of a separate Canton. By 1979 a country-wide referendum ratified the creation of the 26th Swiss Canton known as "le Canton du Jura" which was declared officially unilingual French.

The territorial approach to language standardization is often adopted as a solution to language conflict since it stabilizes the demographic position of linguistic groups on the language map. As adopted in Switzerland and Belgium (Lorwin, 1972; Rudolph, 1982) the territorial approach of giving complete control of a linguistic territory to a single language group helped allay fears that changes in immigration or emigration patterns might eventually change the linguistic balance to the disadvantage of the group. After centuries of language imbalance between French and English in Quebec and Canada it is interesting to note that Quebec moved from a personality to a territorial approach within this last decade (Bill 22, 1974; Bill 101, 1977) while in contrast the Canadian Federal Government since 1969 has been moving towards a personality approach. It is ironic that this crossing of the paths through the adoption of divergent language policies seems inspired by similar historical circumstances. Both levels of Government and the two official language groups have taken stock of the dramatic anglicization of francophone minorities outside Quebec (see Mallea, this volume, chapter 10).

Short of turning back to the *de facto* unilingual English territorial approach of pre-1969 Anglo Canada, could a federally sponsored "bilingual" territorial approach offer a solution to the linguistic problem in Canada? Cartwright (1980) has argued that a territorial approach to providing such services would also be highly problematic as a solution to Canada's language problems. In 1973, suggestions for the implementation of integrated bilingual services including municipal and educational ones in federally-appointed "bilingual districts" of Ontario met with resistance from many ethnic groups including francophones. Franco-Ontarian minorities feared such measures would split the communities further along French/English lines, create an anti-French backlash and further exacerbate French/English tensions. Though a policy of "bilingual districts" in Ontario could hardly be discussed without similar provisions for anglophone minorities in Quebec, Cartwright (1980) concluded that such a federal policy applied in Quebec would simply reinforce already existing trends favouring the English language in Quebec as the lingua-Franca of North American culture. In addition to pointing out that the Quebec Anglophone minority already enjoys all the linguistic rights for which so many francophones outside Quebec are still fighting, it is doubtful that such a federally-sponsored policy could ever be acceptable for any Quebec Government elected since the passage of Bill 101. Commenting on the fading concept of "bilingual districts" for Canada, Cartwright (1980) agreed with McRae (1975) that "despite efforts to find a plurilingual model elsewhere that would suit Canada's requirements, it may be stated that no such model exists" (p. 141). Cartwright (1980) points out that if Canada was ever to solve its linguistic problem it would have to do like Quebec and invent its own solutions. He concludes:

> "We must possibly develop our own model, and structure a policy that is relevant to the Canadian situation alone. There is no evidence to suggest that the government of Quebec looked elsewhere before its own language policy and programmes were formulated. These were designed to suit the perceived needs of that particular society" (p. 147).

Cartwright (1980) was of course referring to Bill 101, a language policy which merits not just the attention of Canadians and which is the focus of each of the chapters presented in this volume.

Overview of the Volume

The logic which underlies the sequence of chapters presented in this volume has already been made evident thanks to the comments made by Professor Mackey in his *Foreword*. Perhaps the most convenient way of introducing a few additional comments concerning each chapter is to briefly outline the basic steps involved in designing language planning programs (Karam, 1974). As can be seen from figure 1, four basic activities are involved in the language planning process: planning, policy decision, implementation and evaluation.

The other elements in figure 1 reflect the fact that language planning activity and the creation of a language planning agency is usually a response to a perceived communication problem within the language communities

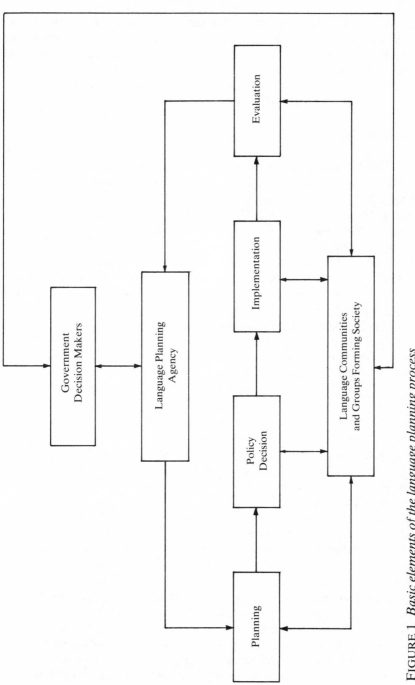

FIGURE 1 *Basic elements of the language planning process*

and groups forming the society. In response to community pressures or on their own initiative, it is politicians forming the ruling Government who usually appoint the language planning agency in charge of solving the language problems within society. Each step in the language planning process can now be discussed in terms of its relationship to the chapter contributions dealing with Bill 101 in Quebec.

Planning

This activity includes the socio-historical analyses, the sociolinguistic surveys and all the data collection which are needed to fully describe language problems and identify possible solutions. Both the contributions by d'Anglejan (chapter 2) and Laporte (chapter 3) make it clear that Quebec policy makers had at their disposal an unparalleled data base upon which policy decisions regarding language planning in Quebec could be taken. Voluminous studies such as those sponsored by the Royal Commission on Bilingualism and Biculturalism (Canada, 1969) and by the Gendron Commission (Quebec, 1972) were conducted to examine the bases of the bitter linguistic conflicts opposing the anglophone and francophone communities of both Canada and Quebec. Results from these extensive studies converged to show that the vitality of the French language was seriously threatened by the predominance of the English language not only in Canada as a whole but within Quebec itself. D'Anglegan (chapter 2) and Laporte (chapter 3) agree that four factors threatening the survival of the French language led Quebec language planners to decide in favour of a language law such as the Charter of the French Language. On the demographic front, Quebec francophones were confronted with the reality of a dramatic decline of the francophone population in Anglo-Canada. This decline left Quebec as the last territorial enclave in North America where French could hope to be maintained as the language of the majority and as a symbol of the distinctive Québécois culture. Secondly, demographic changes within Quebec showed a dramatic drop in the birth rate of francophone Québécois indicating that the "revanche des berceaux" could no longer be counted on to counterbalance the growth of the Quebec English-speaking community. A third factor which gave cause for alarm to Quebec francophones was the freedom accorded Quebec immigrants to choose either French or English as the language of instruction for their children. As it happens, the vast majority of immigrants to Quebec chose English rather than French as the language of schooling for their children. This choice had the effect of increasing the size of the anglophone community to the point that demographic projections predicted the eventual decline of francophones relative to anglophones in bilingual Montreal. Finally, Québécois francophones felt that the dominance of English as the language of business and economic advancement in Quebec was unfair and should be changed. The public debate concerning the negative impact of these factors on the survival of francophone Quebec had quite an impact not only on the formulation of Bill 101 but in bringing to power the government which designed and promulgated the Bill.

Policy decision

Significantly, the first legislative act of the pro-Quebec independence Parti Québécois was the adoption of the Charter of the French Language in August 1977. A careful reading of the official English version of the Charter of the French Language (provided in Appendix 1 of this volume) shows that the Charter was specifically designed to counteract each of the afore-mentioned threats to the vitality of the French language in Quebec. Both d'Anglejan (chapter 2) and Laporte (chapter 3) concur that indeed the Charter was a policy decision specifically designed to counteract these threats mainly through language standardization in favour of French and through language purification involving the creation of French terminology. While Laporte feels that the provisions enshrined in Bill 101 are probably sufficient to achieve these goals, d'Anglejan considers that Bill 101 has gone too far in protecting the French language and that in doing so Québécois francophones are not given the opportunity to come face to face with the issue of cultural pluralism as it is experienced by other host communities of North America. D'Anglejan's concerns raise basic issues regarding language standardization policies which we have already touched upon in this chapter and to which we will return in discussing other chapters of this volume.

As in decision-making elsewhere in the state and private sector, the issue of financial cost of the policy decision must be considered. There is no point in creating a language planning program which at some point in its implementation stage will run out of funds. Laporte (chapter 3) discusses the issue of cost and benefit of Quebec language planning and concludes that the social benefits gained by the Québécois francophone majority are worth the financial costs of carrying out the policy.

Implementation

Policy decisions concerning language are reduced to pious wishes if they are not backed up by the institutional means needed to implement them. Within the text of the Charter, the architects of the law have built terms of reference for three state bureaucracies created to implement the law. The most important of these is the "Office de la Langue française" whose job it is to:

> "define and conduct Quebec policy on linguistic research and terminology and to see that the French language becomes as soon as possible the language of communication and work in the civil administration and business firms" (see Bill 101, articles 99 to 156, this volume, Appendix 1).

Through the contribution by Denise Daoust (chapter 4) we are fortunate to obtain a first hand account of the francization and terminology work carried out by the Office de la Langue française (OLF) since 1977. In this chapter Daoust presents a step-by-step account of the means and procedures undertaken by the OLF to achieve the francization of Quebec business firms. Daoust also describes the substantial terminology consulting services offered by the OLF to support the business firms' efforts in the francization of their terminology. The scope of the francization process and the range of services offered by the OLF to help firms francize their organization again begs the question of financial costs. Table 1 presents the annual budget of the OLF from its creation in late 1977 up to the 1982 fiscal year. At a total cost of $53 million in its first five years of operation, this expenditure compares very favourably with the $500 million spent by the Language

TABLE 1 *Size of Personnel and Expenditures of the Office de la Langue française (OLF) per year of operation from August 1977*[1]

Year of Operation ending on the:	Size of OLF personnel[2]	Expenditures Salaries	Total Expenditures[3]
1/4/1978	239	$ 3,492,500	$ 5,160,800
1/4/1979	385	$ 6,041,400	$ 8,758,700
1/4/1980	398	$ 8,516,366	$11,480,478
1/4/1981	413	$10,499,344	$13,544,918
1/4/1982	399	$11,550,425	$14,035,809

1. All figures are taken from the Annual Reports of the OLF: Office de la langue française (1978, 1979, 1980, 1981, 1982) *Rapport d'activité*. Québec: Editeur Officiel du Québec.
2. Personnel includes permanent staff, contractual positions and part time employees.
3. In addition to salaries total expenditures include costs associated with computer services to the OLF and the public, communications, OLF research and publications, research grants, library acquisitions, francization and terminology, public relations, supplies, rents and transport.

Branch of the Canadian Secretary of State in its first five years (1970–75) of support for bilingual education and bilingual programs for business and public administration across Canada (Mackey, 1983).

The Commission de Surveillance de la Langue française (CSLF) is the agency responsible for receiving and investigating complaints concerning business firms and organizations that do not conform to the stipulations of the Charter (see articles 157–184, Bill 101, Appendix 1). Once a complaint is received by the CSLF, one of a team of eight investigation commissioners and six inspectors determines if the complaint is a valid one. If the firm or organization is indeed not proceeding according to the law a dossier is opened and the CSLF informs the firm by letter or in person that it is contravening the Charter. At this point, through a consultation process, a deadline is agreed upon to allow the firm to rectify its linguistic situation. In the majority of cases firms contravene the law simply because they are not aware of its specific application to their organization. Also in the majority of cases, firms carry out the language modifications within the mutually-agreed deadlines.

In 1981–82 the CSLF opened 4,182 new dossiers, an 85% increase over the previous year coinciding with the passage of the September 1981 deadline for the francization of Quebec billboards and commercial signs (article 58, Bill 101, Appendix 1). Taking into consideration the open and shut dossiers processed in 1982, there remained in April 1982 a total of 3,889 active dossiers out of the 11,975 dossiers opened at the CSLF since the promulgation of Bill 101 in 1977 (Quebec, 1983).

In instances of non-compliance the CSLF may forward the record of the case to the Quebec Attorney General for his consideration. The CSLF may also recommend to the OLF the withdrawal of the firm's provisional or permanent francization certificate which, following court action procedure, can result in firms paying fines of up to $2,000 a day (see Bill 101, sections 205–208, Appendix 1). In 1981–82, the CSLF brought a total of eight cases to the attention of the Attorney General while one court proceeding was undertaken and one other led to a $100 fine (Quebec, 1983). Though much of the CSLF work is indeed routine, some highly publicized cases of non-compliance have become symbolic for the Anglophone community and have earned the CSLF some derisive appellations especially in the Anglophone media.

The third organization created by the Charter is the "Conseil de la Langue française" (CLF) (see Bill 101, sections 195–204, Appendix 1). The CLF plays an advisory role to Government Ministers concerning the application and evaluation of the Charter. The CLF regularly publishes Research

Reports and Documents concerning aspects of the language situation in Quebec, many of which are cited in this volume.

Evaluation

This activity involves monitoring and assessing the results of the planning, policy decision and implementation activities of the language program. A major aim of this volume is to evaluate the impact of Bill 101 on Quebec society and as such this volume is itself a contribution to the evaluation of this particular language planning program. Numerous studies sponsored by the OLF and CLF are designed to specifically assess the impact of various parts of the law on specific sectors of Quebec society. Each of these contributions provides feedback to language planners and government policy makers, who can use the information to refine policy decisions and improve implementation procedures. Such feedback may show that specific language planning goals have been achieved and that it is time to either "close shop" (sunset clause) or define new language planning goals. For instance, following the relative success of Quebec's language status policies in favour of French in these last years, Quebec language planners are turning their attention to corpus planning especially as regards the improvement of the "quality" of the French language.

Indeed, as regards status planning in favour of French, d'Anglejan (chapter 2), Laporte (chapter 3) and Daoust (chapter 4) have each cited evidence that the use of French is increasing in Quebec. However, Laporte raises the point that it is difficult to establish a direct causal link between language planning activity and the rise in status of the French language in Quebec. Daoust on the other hand observes that the francization of business firms can only lead to greater French usage and therefore more status for French if the French terminology needed for everyday functioning is not only readily available but is also deemed acceptable by its potential users. Daoust then discusses very recent OLF studies which investigated the factors facilitating or hindering the acceptance of French terminology in business firms.

Still on the important topic of the francization of business firms, Miller (chapter 5) presents his own findings which show that, on the whole, large business firms established in Quebec have had no great difficulty in adapting to the linguistic requirements of Bill 101. Miller notes that while French usage has increased at the operational level of business firms, English remains predominant at the higher echelons of large business firms, including Head Offices. Miller's most important finding is that while unilingual francophone recruits are advantaged at entry point in business firms since

Bill 101, anglophone recruits who have become bilingual to better compete at entry point, end up with better career opportunities than their unilingual francophone counterparts at the higher echelons of business firms. Notwithstanding the business firms that may have left Quebec because of the climate surrounding the adoption of Bill 101, Miller makes the interesting point that Bill 101 formalized a change process in favour of francization which was already underway in large business firms. To account for these findings Miller proposes a model of the impact of social regulation on the market place which seems to readily accommodate the case of Quebec as regards the francization of business firms.

Coleman's (chapter 6) contribution is distinctive for the language planning literature both because it provides a class analysis of Quebec language policies and because it examines important policy changes made between the first (Bill 1) and final version of the Charter (Bill 101). Contrary to popular belief, Coleman demonstrates that the Parti Québécois was extremely sensitive to the needs of the Quebec business community in formulating its final version of the Charter (Bill 101). By stopping short of francizing Head Offices and Research centres, Coleman notes that Bill 101 can not be looked upon as a tool for shifting the basic ownership structure of the Quebec economy from anglophone to francophone control. In this light, Miller's findings (chapter 5) that French usage has not increased in the high echelons of Quebec business firms are not surprising. Through a class analysis of the organized interest groups which supported or opposed various sections of the first version of the Charter (Bill 1), Coleman concludes that francophone support for the Bill was not unanimous nor uniform. Finally Coleman presents some stimulating thoughts concerning the effects of Bill 101 in advancing or thwarting the goals of the Quebec Independence movement.

Both the contributions by Taylor & Dubé-Simard (chapter 7) and Bourhis (chapter 8) attest to the longstanding linguistic cleavage in Quebec society. Both contributions present findings which have been obtained using social psychological methodologies. A premise of this approach is that much can be learned by investigating experimentally a focused problem or issue using a limited sample of individuals which are acknowledged not to be necessarily representative of a full cross-section of the population. So what may be lost by the use of limited numbers and narrow sampling can be regained at a different level by the experimental and focused nature of social psychological methodologies. Nevertheless the number of individuals who participated in the studies described in chapters 7 and 8 were not insubstantial. While Taylor & Dubé-Simard focused their attention on the attitudes of francophones and anglophones totalling close to 200 respondents, the total number of francophones and anglophones who participated in the three studies presented by Bourhis amounted to more than 1,200 individuals each of which was recruited within the boundaries of the city of Montreal.

The contribution by Taylor and Dubé-Simard provides a complex though fascinating analysis of how both Bill 101 and the 1980 referendum on Quebec independence seem to have accentuated the linguistic cleavage between francophones and anglophones in Quebec society. Predictably enough, anglophones were found to feel particularly threatened by Bill 101 while they also perceived the law as unfair. However, for a pro-French law that was partly designed to provide a sense of cultural security amongst francophones, it was particularly surprising to find that even after Bill 101, the francophones in this study still felt culturally insecure. Finally, it is worth noting that the necessary psychological conditions (categorization, threat and perceived injustice) postulated by Taylor & Dubé-Simard for the mobilization of anglophone individuals into collective action (e.g. Alliance Quebec) were perhaps also those that spurred Quebec francophones into collective actions in the early 1970s and which culminated not only in the election of the Parti Québécois but which also led to the promulgation of Bill 101.

The main findings to emerge from the studies presented by Bourhis (chapter 8) indicate that while anglophones report using French more frequently since Bill 101 than before it, the experimental studies show that English not only retains much of its traditional prestige for both anglophones and francophones but that both linguistic groups are more likely to use English than French in their actual face-to-face cross-cultural encounters in downtown Montreal. However, trends obtained in the more recent language use experiments suggested that anglophones were on the road to using more French when interacting face-to-face with their francophone Québécois compatriots. Bourhis concludes by pointing out that language planners could gain by broadening the range of their monitoring tools to include not only traditional survey techniques but to also use more field experimental procedures which can more accurately reflect the real life language changes that may result from language planning efforts.

Caldwell (chapter 9) offers a lucid and stimulating contribution to the debate concerning the future of the anglophone population within Quebec society since Bill 101. From his review of the current demographic situation Caldwell concludes that anglophones are faced with a much smaller though much more stable population in Quebec. Following a searching inquiry of what constitutes the cultural identity of anglophone Quebec, Caldwell identifies two alternative ideological banners around which anglophones could mobilize to insure their survival within Quebec society. The first of these he labels the "linguistic community" option which he feels has been adopted by Alliance Quebec and which triggers the traditional opposition betwen francophone Quebec and the federalist forces of the anglophone majority of Canada. Though this option offers the path of least resistance for Quebec anglophones, Caldwell argues that in the long run it may well prove a dead end for the survival of Anglo-Quebec. In its stead, Caldwell proposes a "cultural minorities" option which he presents as the cultural strategy which may, with sufficient vision, insure the survival of Québécois anglophones as a distinctive collective entity not only within Quebec but within North America as well.

We end this volume with the contribution by Mallea (chapter 10) on "Minority language education in Quebec and Anglophone Canada" because so often in the history of linguistic minorities we have seen that "une langue qu'on n'enseigne pas est une langue qu'on tue." Indeed, the considerations raised in Mallea's chapter raise fundamental issues regarding the treatment of linguistic minorities in majority settings. In the first parts of his chapter Mallea traces a broad though bleak panorama of minority language education in anglophone Canada. For so long across Canada, francophone minorities, faced as they were with the threat of linguistic assimilation, have fought both for the repeal of laws banning their language and for the adoption of laws enshrining their rights as linguistic minorities. For these minorities even laws assuming or proclaiming freedom of expression in the language of one's choice simply meant that the stronger language became more powerful at the expense of the weaker ones (Mackey, 1983). Mallea's discussion of minority language education in Quebec along with his overview of current federal-provincial issues should convince linguistic minorities everywhere in Canada that they do share much in common. For both the francophone minorities in anglophone Canada and the anglophone minorities in Quebec the motto has become Lacordaire's famous statement: "Entre le fort et le faible, c'est la liberté qui opprime et la loi qui affranchit". Indeed, even Québécois Anglophones have come to realize that sometime in the future of a *de facto* unilingual French Quebec, the *absence of language laws* as much as the *presence of language laws* could jeopardize their chances of survival as a linguistic minority. However at the moment it is the *presence of language laws* which enshrines English schooling to all "Québécois Anglophone" individuals and which provides the vital guarantees needed to safeguard the demographic presence of the anglophone minority in Quebec. Finally, another reason for ending this volume with a comparison of Quebec and Canada is that until further notice Quebec remains a Province of Canada, and as such its fate is delicately tied to that of nine anglophone majority provinces and one "bilingual" Federal Government.

26   CONFLICT AND LANGUAGE PLANNING IN QUEBEC

Acknowledgements

I wish to thank William Coleman and Ellen Bouchard-Ryan for their useful comments on an earlier draft of this chapter.

References

ARNOPOULOS, M. S. 1983, *Voices from French Ontario*. Montreal: McGill-Queen's University Press.
BLANC, H. 1968, The Israeli Koine as an emergent National Standard. In: J. A. FISHMAN, C. A. FERGUSON & J. DAS GUPTA (eds), *Language Problems of Developing Nations*. New York: Wiley.
BOURHIS, R. Y. 1982, Language policies and Language Attitudes: Le monde de la francophonie. In: E. B. RYAN and H. GILES (eds), *Attitudes towards Language Variations*. London: Edward Arnold.
BRETON, R., REITZ, J. G., & VALENTINE, V. 1980, *Cultural Boundaries and the Cohesion of Canada*. Montreal: The Institute for Research on Public Policy.
CANADA, GOVERNMENT OF, 1969, *Royal Commission on Bilingualism and Biculturalism*, Vol. 3: The Work World. Ottawa: Queen's Printer.
CANADA 1983, *Highlight Information on the 1981 Census of Canada*. Ottawa: Statistics Canada.
CARTWRIGHT, D. G. 1980, *Official Language Populations in Canada: Patterns and Contacts*. Montreal: The Institute for Research on Public Policy.
COBARRUBIAS, J., & FISHMAN, J. A. (eds) 1983, *Progress in Language Planning*. Berlin and New York: Mouton Publishers.
DAS GUPTA, J. 1975, Ethnicity, Language Demands, and National Development in India. In: N. GLAZER & D. P. MOYNIHAN (eds), *Ethnicity Theory and Experience*. Cambridge, Mass.: Harvard University Press.
DOMHNALIAN, T. O. 1977, Ireland: The Irish Language in Education. *Language Problems and Language Planning*, 1, 83–96.
FFHQ 1978, *The Heirs of Lord Durham: Manifesto of a Vanishing People*. Ottawa: Fédération des francophones hors Québec.
FISHMAN, J. A. 1972, *Language and Nationalism*. Rowley, Mass.: Newbury House.
—(ed.) 1974, *Advances in Language Planning*. The Hague: Mouton.
—(ed.) 1978, *Advances in the Study of Multilingualism*. The Hague: Mouton.
FISHMAN, J. A., COOPER, R. L., & CONRAD, A. W. 1977, *The Spread of English*. Rowley, Mass.: Newbury House.
FISHMAN, J. A., FERGUSON, C. A., & DAS GUPTA, J. (eds) 1968, *Language Problems of Developing Nations*. New York: Wiley.
GALLAGHER, C. F. 1971, Language Reform and Social Modernization in Turkey. In: J. RUBIN & B. H. JERNUDD (eds), *Can Language be Planned?* Hawaii: University Press of Hawaii.

GILES, H., BOURHIS, R., TRUDGILL, P., & LEWIS, A. 1974, The Imposed Norm Hypothesis: a Validation. *Quarterly Journal of Speech*, 60, 405–410.

GORDON, D. C. 1978, *The French Language and National Identity*. The Hague: Mouton.

INGLEHART, R., & WOODWARD, M. 1972, Language Conflicts and the Political Community. In: P. P. GIGLIOLI (ed.), *Language and Social Context*. Harmondsworth: Penguin.

KARAM, F. X. 1974, Toward a Definition of Language Planning. In: J. A. FISHMAN (ed.), *Advances in Language Planning*. The Hague: Mouton.

KLOSS, H. 1969, *Research Possibilities on Group Bilingualism*. Quebec: International Center for Research on Bilingualism.

KRISHNAMURTI, Bh. 1979, Problems of Language Standardization in India. In; W. C. McCORMACK & S. A. WURM (eds), *Language and Society*. The Hague: Mouton.

LORWIN, V. R. 1972, Linguistic Pluralism and Political Tension in Modern Belgium. In: J. A. FISHMAN (ed.), *Advances in the Sociology of Language*. The Hague: Mouton.

MACKEY, W. F. 1979, Proligomena to Language Policy Analysis. *Word*, 30, 5–14.

— 1983, U.S. Language Status Policy and the Canadian Experience. In: J. COBARRUBIAS & J. A. FISHMAN (eds), *Progress in Language Planning*, Berlin and New York: Mouton.

MACNAMARA, J. 1971, Successes and Failures in the Movement for the Restoration of Irish. In: J. RUBIN & B. H. JERNUDD (eds), *Can Language be Planned?* Hawaii: University Press of Hawaii.

McCONNELL, G. D., DAOUST, D., & MARTIN, A. 1979, Language Planning and Language Treatment in Québec. *Word*, 30, 87–104.

McRAE, K. D. 1975, The Principles of Territoriality and the Principle of Personality in Multilingual States. *International Journal of the Sociology of Language*, 4, 33–54.

NAHIR, M. 1977, The Five Aspects of Language Planning: A Classification. *Language Problems and Language Planning*, 1, 107–23.

PANDIT, P. B. 1979, Perspectives on Sociolinguistics in India. In: W. C. McCORMACK & S. A. WURM (eds), *Language and Society*. The Hague: Mouton.

VAN DER PLANK 1978, The Assimilation and Non-Assimilation of European Linguistic Minorities. In: J. A. FISHMAN (ed.), *Advances in the Study of Multilingualism*. The Hague: Mouton.

POTTIER, B. 1968, La Situation Linguistique en France. In: A. MARTINET (ed.), *Le Langage*, Bruges: Gallimard.

QUEBEC, GOVERNMENT OF, 1972, *Report of the Commission of Inquiry on the Position of the French Language and on Language Rights in Quebec* (Gendron Commission). Quebec: Editeur Officiel du Quebec.

QUEBEC 1983, *Rapport Annuel 1981–2*, Commission de Surveillance de la langue française. Quebec: Editeur Officiel du Québec.

RUBIN, J. & JERNUDD, B. H. (eds) 1971, *Can Language be Planned?* Hawaii, University of Hawaii Press.

RUDOLPH, J. R. 1982, Belgium: Controlling Separatist Tendencies in a Multinational State. In: C. WILLIAMS (ed.), *National Separatism*. Vancouver: University of British Columbia Press.

RYAN, E. B., & GILES, H. (eds) 1982, *Attitudes Towards Language Variation*. London: Edward Arnold.

SMITH, A. D. 1971, *Theories of Nationalism*. London: Duckworth.

— 1981, *The Ethnic Revival*. Cambridge: Cambridge University press.

ST CLAIR, R. N. 1982, From Social History to Language Attitudes. In: E. B. RYAN & H. GILES (eds), *Attitudes Towards Language Variation*. London: Edward Arnold.

WEINSTEIN, B. 1980, Language Planning in Francophone Africa. *Language Problems and Language Planning*, 4, 55–77.

— 1983, *The Civic Tongue*. New York: Longman.

WHITELEY, W. H. 1974, Language Policies of Independent African States. In: J. A. FISHMAN (ed.), *Advances in Language Planning*. The Hague: Mouton.

WILLIAMS, C. H. 1982, *National Separatism*. Vancouver: University of British Columbia Press.

2 Language planning in Quebec: An historical overview and future trends

Alison d'Anglejan
Université de Montréal

Language legislation enacted over the course of the past decade by successive Quebec governments has paved the way for profound changes in the relative status and use of French and English in the province. More has been done to enhance the status of French in Quebec during this period than at any other time in history. This chapter will trace the evolution of Quebec's language policy and the impact which it has had on Quebec society. Finally, it will consider the possible impact of emerging socio-political trends on future language policy decisions.

Background to Quebec's Recourse to Language Legislation

In the late 1950s it became apparent that "traditional" French Canadian social patterns were rapidly breaking down. Industrialization brought about the decline of the rural community, and contacts between French and English were becoming more numerous as French Canadians attempted to compete in an urban industrial setting long dominated by the English and for which they had been ill-prepared by their schools and institutions.

It was against this background that the Quiet Revolution of the 1960s took place, an attempt to accelerate the socio-economic development of French Canadian society to bring it into line with that of the rest of Canada. Concurrently the Quiet Revolution accelerated the growth of nationalism and heightened the feelings of resentment of many Quebec Francophones with respect to their subordinate linguistic and economic status, not only within Canada, but even within their own province (Royal Commission on Bilingualism, Canada, 1969; Quebec, 1972a; Porter, 1965). The "new" nationalism of the period differed in important ways from the earlier, traditional nationalism which had so greatly influenced the evolution of French Canadian society (Cook, 1972). According to Léger (1972) the early forms of nationalism displayed five main characteristics: "(1) defensive, it emphasized the preservation of the traditions and position of the French-Canadian community; (2) it became directed essentially toward the defence of language and culture, being interested in politics only when the autonomy of Quebec seemed at stake; (3) apostolic and formalistic, it tended to act more by means of propaganda and campaigns to influence public opinion than by the modification of political structures; (4) traditionalist, it stood aloof from the industrial revolution without complaint, it willingly abandoned the world of big business to the Anglo-American element, even in Quebec; (5) conservative and *bourgeois* it became an adjunct of the middle classes, and was impervious to economic and social transformations." This nationalism had another important characteristic: ". . . the close association of cultural and religious values, seen as mutually interdependent and destined to survive or die together." In contrast, the neo-nationalism which emerged in the 1960s is described by Léger as ". . . a universal awakening of awareness to the national fact, the concrete recognition of the reciprocal interaction of political, economic, cultural and social factors, the admission of the need for State intervention, the search for a growth that would provide at one and the same time for the internal progress of the French-Canadian society and for the emancipation of this society." Emphasis was placed on the forging of modern social institutions capable of attaining the social objectives of Quebec's francophone population.

The modernization of Quebec society which took place in the 1960s and 70s was both rapid and radical. The educational system, health care and other social institutions previously controlled by the clergy or by the English-speaking élite were restructured. The traditional religious or social values of these groups were displaced by an ideology of egalitarism and a "Québécois" linguistic and cultural nationalism promoted by the state bureaucracy. Provincial government intervention became ubiquitous in all domains of public life.

Whereas the original architects of the Quiet Revolution worked to promote pro-Quebec policies within the framework of the Canadian federation, by 1970 the Parti Québécois, a provincial party committed to negotiating the political separation of Quebec, had become a political force to be reckoned with. In 1976 it was elected to office with a plurality of over 40 per cent of the popular vote and an imposing majority in the National Assembly.

Although the referendum on "sovereignty-association" sponsored by the party was defeated in May 1980, the Parti Québécois was easily re-elected in 1981.

Although the question of its survival as a distinct French-speaking society has always been a major concern of Quebec's francophone population, it is interesting to note the absence of significant government initiatives in this domain prior to the 1960s. One indication of the government's awakening interest in language planning was the establishment in 1961 of an "Office de la langue française". This agency was given a mandate in the area that Kloss (1969) has categorized as "language corpus planning". It was to revitalize the low prestige variety of French spoken in Quebec by bringing it closer to a more standard European or International variety of French through the development and dissemination of French terminology to replace Canadianisms or Anglicisms in common use (d'Anglejan & Tucker, 1973; Daoust, 1982). This move on the part of the government served a number of purposes: it drew attention to the threat posed to the French language by its co-existence with English and heightened public awareness of the role of the French language as the manifestation and symbol of Quebecers' distinctive identity. Furthermore, it identified the provincial government as the custodian and protector of this important domain of public life. All subsequent provincial government language policy initiatives have included provisions for corpus planning.

At least four social factors can be shown to have prompted the Quebec government's decision to intervene in the area of "language status planning" (Kloss, 1969). These are 1) the decline of the French Canadian population outside Quebec; 2) demographic changes in Quebec brought about by a sudden decline in the province's birth rate in relation to that of English Canada; 3) the increasing tendency of immigrants to integrate into Quebec's minority English-speaking community via the educational system; and finally 4) the control of the important decision-making power in Quebec's business and industrial sectors by English-speaking interests.

1. The decline of francophones outside Quebec

The term "stability" was used by Lieberson (1970) to describe the relative position of the French and English languages in Canada between 1901 and 1961. During this period, the population able to speak French either monolingually or along with English remained stable at 32%. However, the 1971 census data showed some new trends. Between 1961 and 1971, the percentage of francophones in the Canadian population declined from 30.4 to 28.7. Demographic projections (Henripin, 1976) indicated that by the year 2000 this figure would further decrease to 23% and that 95% of Canada's francophones would reside in Quebec. Joy (1972) predicted that although the relative strength of the two major language groups might remain unchanged, a much more pronounced linguistic separation would take place. French would be spoken in Quebec and English elsewhere. Moreover, Arès (1975) showed that only 85.4% of the 6,160,120 Canadians of French origin still used French in the home, evidence of language transfer in favour of English. Henripin (1973) showed that the adoption of English as a mother tongue by francophones outside Quebec was quite substantial, ranging from 85% in Newfoundland to 65% in British Columbia and to 38% in Ontario. Thus, not only was there a decline in the relative proportion of French-Canadians in the Canadian population, but a concurrent tendency for French Canadians to adopt English as the language of use in the home, particularly in those provinces where they were in the minority. The report of the Federal Government Royal Commission on Bilingualism and Biculturalism tabled in 1969 (Canada 1969) provided additional evidence of the assimilation of francophones outside Quebec. It stressed the lack of services and education in French for French minorities. The report recommended that the Federal government institute a programme of systematic language planning in order to equalize the status of both languages and to make it possible for persons of either official language to educate their children, as well as to communicate with and to receive services from the Federal government in the official language of their choice. In response to the report of the Royal Commission and to pressures from Quebec, the Canadian parliament passed the 1969 Official Languages Act which proclaimed the equal status of French and English as the country's two official languages. (For more details concerning the language situation in anglophone Canada see Mallea, this volume, chapter 10.)

2. Demographic changes in Quebec

The remarkably high birth rate which characterized the first settlements until the 1960s sustained the growth of the francophone community and served as a bulwark against assimilation. However, child-bearing practices in Quebec changed rapidly in the 1950s–60s. Demographers' projections indicated that Quebec's high fertility rate, known as "The Revenge of the Cradle", which the clergy had encouraged as a reaction to the British conquest, could no longer be counted upon to counterbalance the growth of the English-speaking community through the integration of both English and non-English immigrants (Ministère des Affaires Sociales, Québec,

1976; Charbonneau, Henripin & Légaré, 1970; Arès, 1972; Lieberson, 1970). By 1971, the birth rate had declined from the highest in the country to the lowest of the ten provinces (Canada: 2.20, Quebec: 1.99). Furthermore, as demographers such as Henripin (1976) have pointed out, Quebec's high birth rate viewed from a broader perspective, was not an entirely desirable phenomenon since it appeared to have had a negative impact on the economic development of the province. In comparison with Ontario, which experienced a moderate birth rate during the same period, Quebec was consistently behind in terms of levels of schooling, quality of the labour force and productivity. While these problems cannot be entirely attributed to Quebec's high fertility rate, according to Henripin they reflect at least in part the economic cost of the province's demographic characteristics.

3. Freedom of language choice in Quebec schools

Yet another aspect of Quebec's demographic situation gave cause for alarm to the francophones. Immigrants to Quebec tended to concentrate in the Montreal area where the attraction of English was most powerful. With the implicit right to send their children to either the French or English school system enshrined in the British North America Act of 1867, many immigrants chose to enroll their children in English schools rather than French ones. It must be noted that section 93 of the British North America Act established the right to denominational schooling (Catholic and Protestant) which, for the next hundred years, tended to follow linguistic lines. The language of instruction in most Catholic schools was French; while that in the Protestant sector was almost exclusively English (Royal Commission on Bilingualism and Biculturalism, Book 1: Canada, 1967). Immigrant preferences for English schooling became most evident following the publication of Quebec Government enquiries during the 1960s and 1970s. For instance, the Gendron Commission (Quebec, 1972a) showed that whereas in 1943, 52% of the Italian children under the jurisdiction of the Montreal Catholic School Commission (MCSC) were enrolled in French schools, by 1972 this percentage had dropped to nine. In 1972, 89.3% of the MCSC's total enrolment of non-French and non-English background (known as allophones) were attending English classes while no more than 10.7% of the allophone children were receiving their education in French.

A variety of reasons were put forth to explain the lack of attraction of French schools for immigrants to the province. The Parent Report (Quebec, 1966) identified three reasons which were the relatively poor quality of French language education in comparison with that offered in English, the importance of English in North America and the less than adequate teaching of English as a second language in the French schools. In addition to these, the Gendron Commission (Quebec, 1972a) cited the attitude of non-acceptance and dissuasion conveyed to parents of immigrant children attending French Catholic schools in a number of school commissions. An additional factor detrimental to the enrolment of immigrants in French schools was the definition of the school system along denominational lines. Since Jews were classified by law to be included among Protestants, they and others of non-Catholic persuasion were urged to send their children to English schools. The Protestant sector thus evolved into a heterogeneous system in which children of a variety of linguistic and religious backgrounds received their schooling in English.

In addition to the above-mentioned deterrents to the choice of French schooling, both Commissions stressed the economic supremacy of English in Quebec as the key motivation for the choice of English schooling by immigrant parents (Quebec, 1972a; Canada, 1967).

4. The economic domination of English

The English establishment's domination of the Quebec economy has been documented by many authors. As can be seen in Table 1, the Report of the Royal Commission on Bilingualism and Biculturalism (vol. 3, Canada, 1969) noted the concentration of francophones in the low salaried occupations and the domination of higher management positions by anglophones.

From its findings, the Royal Commission concluded that French-Canadians were relatively more "disadvantaged" in Montreal than any-

TABLE 1 *Salaried personnel of 36 large manufacturing companies in greater Montreal according to the level of salary and language*

Salary level	Francophone	Anglophone
$ 5,000 – 6,499	49	51
$ 6,500 – 7,999	41	59
$ 8,000 – 9,999	27	73
$10,000 – 11,999	23	77
$12,000 – 14,999	17	83
$15,000 and over	17	83

Source: Report of the Royal Commission of Inquiry on Bilingualism and Biculturalism. Vol. 3: *The Work World* (Canada, 1969).

where else in Canada. Lieberson's (1970) detailed analysis of the relationship between ethnic origin, language and income in Montreal showed a persistent pattern: a relative absence of strong economic pressure among the British to learn French, but the presence of a distinct gain for French-Canadians who acquired English. The Gendron Commission's report (Quebec, 1972a) confirmed the above patterns. It showed that while French was widely used by francophones in the workplace to communicate with fellow workers and employers (97.4% of the time for workers in the primary sector and 83.2% of the time for management personnel) a sound knowledge of English was necessary for career advancement. On the basis of detailed studies the Gendron Commission established the overall model of the socio-linguistic structure of the Quebec work world shown in Table 2. Thus, while French was shown by the report to be alive and well and not in any immediate danger of extinction, the economic supremacy of English in the workplace was clear (Laporte, 1975). The Gendron report recommended that the Quebec government intervene to establish the primacy of French in the critical domain of the work world.

This linguistic cleavage, which coincided with social inequalities, did not augur well for the future socio-political climate of the province. Clearly the status of English resulting from the control of the Quebec economy by English-speaking North American business interests, and the predominance of anglophones in management, presented an obstacle to the upward mobility of Quebec francophones. Immigrants to the province were quick to

TABLE 2 *Sociolinguistic Structure of the Quebec Work World: 1970*

Language Use	Occupation	Categories	Income	Education
French domination	laborer in secondary sector; service employee	construction primary industry public admin. commerce	$ 4,000 $ 6,000 $13,000	2 – 5 years 6 – 8 years 12 – 14 years
English domination	administrators office employees	finance public utility	$17,000 $20,000	B.A. B.Sc.
Bilingual	transport & communications foreman, salesman	manufacturing	$ 8,000 $ 9,000 $10,000	9 – 10 years

Source: Gendron Commission, Vol. 1, p. 70 (Quebec, 1972a).

perceive this situation, and they responded to it by choosing English schooling for their children.

Language Legislation in Quebec

Predictably, the first overt conflicts over the right to English language
schooling broke out in 1968 in St. Léonard, a suburb of Montreal heavily
populated by Italian immigrants. It centred on the local Catholic school
board's desire to phase out bilingual classes and to resist the setting up of
additional classes in English. Immigrant parents objected strenuously to
what they perceived to be an obvious attempt to deprive them of English
instruction for their children. The francophone-dominated school board
dismissed their protests and stood its ground. The anglophone minority,
while not immediately involved, eventually sided with the immigrant parents
(Cappon, 1974; Macdonald, 1977). The introduction of Bill 85 in 1968, at the
height of the St. Léonard crisis, marks the first of a series of steps taken by
successive governments of Quebec to legislate in the area of language. The
bill, presented as an amendment to three existing education acts, was
designed to define the importance of the French language in the field of
education in Quebec. It advocated the creation of a Linguistic Committee
within the Superior Council of Education which would establish regulations
governing the language of education. School boards would be obliged to
provide instruction in either language if requested. However, a working
knowledge of French would be required of all pupils. The bill thus provided
protection for the right of parents to choose the language of instruction for
their children, while proposing provisions to ensure that persons settling in
the province would acquire a working knowledge of French and send their
children to French schools. It generated considerable controversy within the
French community and was condemned as unacceptable by militant uni-
lingualist groups, opposed to the principle of freedom of choice of language
of instruction which it embodied. The bill was sent to committee for study
and ultimately withdrawn.

Bill 63: An Act to Promote the French Language in Quebec

Bill 63 (tabled in 1969) entrusted the Minister of Education with new
responsibilities to ensure that immigrants to Quebec, and their children, as
well as persons attending English language schools would have a working
knowledge of French. However, it also confirmed the right of parents to
choose French or English schools for their children. The bill spelled out a
new mandate for the Office de la Langue Française: to foster the correction

and enrichment of the spoken and written language; to advise the government on any legislative or administrative measures deemed necessary to ensure that French would be the working language in the public and private sectors in Quebec; to ensure the priority of French in public posting and to hear complaints by employees to the effect that their right to use French in the workplace was not respected.

Thus, while maintaining the status quo in the province with respect to bilingualism and the right of parents to choose the language of instruction for their children, the bill established the principle of the priority of the French language in the public and private sectors and opened the door for future legislation in this domain. It also established the fundamental right to work in French for francophones.

Quebec's immigrant and English-speaking communities were generally satisfied with the bill in that, while promoting the use of French, it guaranteed English schools and the principle of free choice. On the other hand, it was vehemently opposed by francophone pressure groups and members of the National Assembly who claimed that it consecrated what heretofore had been a privilege — freedom of choice in the language of instruction — and did nothing to guarantee the survival of the French language and culture. The bill's failure to legislate the language of work was particularly criticised (Cappon, 1974; Daoust, 1982; Macdonald, 1977). Groups such as La Centrale des Enseignants du Québec, a powerful Quebec teachers union, demanded that the bill be withdrawn and replaced by legislation proclaiming French unilingualism and obliging immigrants to attend French schools. In spite of widespread demonstrations by highly organized and articulate opponents of the bill, and a parliamentary filibuster by members of the National Assembly opposed to its passage, it became law in November, 1969.

As will be shown below, the principle of the primacy of French in the public and private sectors which was set out in Bill 63 served as the point of departure for subsequent legislation. However, the means to achieve the language policy goals shifted from persuasion to the adoption of more forceful measures.

Bill 22: The Official Language Act

The Gendron report (Quebec, 1972a) contained recommendations regarding the formulation of a new language policy: 1) French should be the official language, but both French and English should be given the status of national languages; 2) persuasion and incentives should be used, with coercion as a last resort, to promote the use of French in the workplace; 3) with respect to education, Bill 63 should not be repealed until its long-term effects could be assessed; finally 4) incentives should be used to encourage immigrant parents to send their children to French schools. Bill 22, enacted by the legislature in 1974, diverged in important respects from the recommendations of the Gendron Commission.

Under the terms of Bill 22, French became the sole official language of the province. This initiative, marking another in a series of steps in language status planning, represents an organized attempt to shift the economic powerbase of the province away from the English language and the English-speaking community by establishing the primacy of French in the public administration (sections 6–17), the public utilities and professions (sections 18–23), labour (sections 24–35), business (sections 36–47) and education (sections 48–52). The bill established a special nine-member board, "La Régie de la langue française", to oversee the implantation of these provisions.

The law prescribed specific measures to assure the *de facto* as well as *de jure* pre-eminence of French and to promote its vigour and quality. A working knowledge of French was declared a prerequisite for employment and advancement in the public service; all professionals — doctors, lawyers, social workers, nurses — would henceforth have to demonstrate a working knowledge of French in order to be granted work permits; contracts with the government would have to be drawn up in French; French must be used in business activities at every level, in firm names, on product labels, public signs, etc. However, it is important to note that while stipulating the primacy of French in this domain, the law did not prohibit the concurrent use of English or another language, thus maintaining the legitimacy of bilingualism.

Incentives were laid down to encourage the business establishment to convert their operations to French and to promote career opportunities for francophones. In order to be eligible to receive contracts, subsidies, concessions or benefits from the public administration, the law required that business firms apply for "francization certificates". These certificates were to be issued on the basis of several criteria related to the language of work. Among these were the required knowledge and use of French by management personnel, as well as the presence of francophones in management. In addition, all manuals, catalogues, written instructions and other documents distributed to personnel had to be drawn up in French. Provisions must be made to ensure that personnel could communicate in French in their work, among themselves and with superior officers (article 29).

Other articles of the law dealt with the language of contracts, warranty certificates and directions supplied with products, as well as labels on consumer goods. Article 34 spelled out fines to be imposed on persons who failed to comply with the law.

The "Régie de la langue française" was mandated to assist firms in the setting up and implementation of francization programmes, to issue the francization certificates and generally to enforce the law. In addition, the Régie was to pursue the activities initiated by the "Office de la langue française" in the area of French terminology.

By far the most controversial chapter of the law (chapter V) dealt with the language of instruction in the schools. Whereas previously all Quebecers had been free to choose French or English instruction for their children — a privilege which became a right under Bill 63 — the Official Language Act restricted access to English schools to children already in possession of "a sufficient knowledge of the language of instruction to receive their instruction in that language" (article 41). All other pupils, whatever their mother tongue, were required to attend French schools. Language tests were to be used by school boards to ascertain which children would be admitted to English schools. In addition, the size of the English school system could be expanded only at the discretion of the Minister of Education and only to accommodate the English-speaking community. In practice this meant that English schooling would not be available to the children of immigrants from non English-speaking countries nor to the children of French Canadians unless they could demonstrate a prior knowledge of English. These measures were designed to curb the flow of immigrant children into the English school system, thus reducing the likelihood of their assimilation by the English-speaking community. They were also designed to prevent francophone parents from enrolling their children in English schools in order to learn English.

The law pleased no one. It was vigorously opposed by militant nationalist groups advocating the compulsory integration of all immigrants to the French school system and more coercive pressures on the business community. Even the more moderate francophones were concerned that the law contained too many loopholes and could be easily circumvented. At the opposite extreme, it was condemned by the immigrant communities and the English-speaking minority who deplored its potential effect on the economy, viewed it as discriminatory, and saw it as a denial of the principle of freedom of choice of the language of instruction for all Quebecers (Stein, 1977). For many, it was a shock to realize that since education is under provincial jurisdiction, the Canadian government could offer no protection for minority education rights. The law contained many ambiguities; it afforded considerable discretionary powers to the Minister of Education, school boards and the Régie de la langue française. Furthermore, the use of language tests to determine the English competence of pre-school children was denounced by educators and by society in general. The application of chapter V of the law became increasingly difficult owing to the reluctance of English school authorities at various levels to collaborate in the testing of the children.

In summary, Bill 22 spelled out the primacy of French in the public sector, in business and in education. While aspects of the law called for penalties for the violation of specific articles dealing with the use of French in business, incentives were still relied on to promote the francization process. In the realm of education, persuasion was abandoned in favour of legislation. However, the law continued to recognize the legitimacy, albeit subordinate, of English in the province. In the midst of the brouhaha surrounding the law, and the steps taken by the government to implement it, an election was called and in 1976 the official separatist party (Parti Québécois) came to power, bringing with it yet more radical plans to modify language policy.

Bill 101. The Charter of the French Language

Whereas Bill 22 was designed to assure the use of French in the courts, the public administration, business and industry, as well as to curb the flow of immigrants into the English-speaking community, it did recognize the legitimacy of the presence of the English language in the province. Bill 101, the language legislation enacted in 1977 by the Parti Québécois less than a year after it entered office, was designed to make Quebec both institutionally and socially a unilingual French state. It contains measures to curb the growth of the English-speaking community and to diminish its status. Thus the main thrust of the bill is in the domain of language status planning, with a lesser focus on corpus planning. The full English text of Bill 101 can be found in Appendix 1 of this volume.

The Bill declares that French is the official language of Quebec. Chapter II recognizes certain fundamental language rights, namely:
— The right of every person to have the civil administration, semi-public agencies and business firms communicate with him/her in French;
— The right of workers to carry on their activities in French;
— The right of consumers to be informed and served in French;
— The right of persons eligible for instruction to receive that instruction in French.

In her detailed analysis of the legislation, Daoust (1982) identified several points on which the Charter of the French Language differs from Bill

22. First, while French is maintained as the language of the legislature and the courts, the language of civil administration, public utilities and professional corporations, only the French version of laws, regulations or documents are official. The dispositions regarding the use of French in business and commerce, outlined in Bill 22, are intensified. Instructions on products, catalogues, brochures, toys and games, contracts, application forms and firm names must be in French. French only is to be used on public signs and posters, although a few exceptions are allowed in specific circumstances.

In its provisions regarding the use of French in public utilities and private enterprise, (chapters II & III) Bill 101 is more explicit and more rigorous in imposing the use of French at all levels. Whereas Bill 22 relied mainly on good will and incentives to motivate Quebec industry to increase the use of French, Bill 101 spells out specific deadlines and sanctions. By 1983, all business establishments having more than 50 employees must have obtained their "francization certificates". In the interim, "francization committees" including employees or representatives of labour unions must be set up and a plan for conversion to French must be worked out in collaboration with the Office de la langue française (OLF). Companies which fail to obtain their francization certificates by the deadline set by the OLF will be liable to three types of sanctions: ineligibility to receive government contracts or subsidies, substantial fines, and finally, moral sanctions and public denunciation likely to result in a loss of clientele and revenue (Laurin, 1977).

Chapter VI of the law stipulates that an employer is prohibited from dismissing, demoting or transferring an employee for the sole reason that he/she is exclusively French-speaking or has insufficient knowledge of a particular language other than the official language. Furthermore, an employer is prohibited from making the obtaining of employment contingent upon the knowledge of a language other than French unless it can be clearly demonstrated that the nature of the duties requires the knowledge of that other language.

With respect to the language of instruction, Bill 101 (chapter VIII, articles 72 and 73) prescribes that instruction given in kindergarten must be in French. However, upon request, eligibility for English instruction may be granted to a) a child whose father or mother received his/her elementary instruction in English in Quebec; b) a child whose father or mother, domiciled in Quebec on the date the law came into force received his/her elementary instruction in English outside Quebec; c) children already legally enrolled in the English school system; and d) the younger siblings of those designated in c. The law makes no provisions for English education for English-speaking migrants from other parts of Canada. Thus, while placing even greater constraints on the growth of the English school system by restricting access to members of the existing English speaking community and their descendants, Bill 101 eliminates some of the more arbitrary features of Bill 22 — the language tests for children and the discretionary powers of the Minister of Education.

To deal with the application and supervision of the law, Bill 101 establishes three different boards to carry out the functions formerly assigned to the Régie de la langue française:

1. The Office de la langue française (OLF) was given the mandate "to define and conduct Quebec policy and research in linguistics and terminology (chapter II, article 100). It was also mandated to direct and approve the francization certificates and to etablish and administer French proficiency tests. In addition it was given responsibility for setting up terminology committees and supervising the introduction and use of approved French terminology in all government organizations.

2. The Conseil de la langue française was designated to monitor the progress of language planning and its implemention with respect to the status, use and quality of the French language. Further, it was to pinpoint difficulties and weaknesses in the implementation process and to approve regulations set out by the Office (chapter IV, sections 188 & 189).

3. The Commission de Surveillance et des Enquêtes was set up to deal with failure to comply with the law (chapter III, section 158). The Commission is composed of investigators and inspectors who must carry out inquiries to see if the law is being respected, report infractions of the law to the Attorney general for his consideration and if necessary, institute legal proceedings.

With respect to the place of English in the province, the law has nothing to say. Whereas Bill 22 (chapter V) ensured instruction in English as a second language to pupils receiving their instruction in French, Bill 101 is silent on this point. Moreover, as mentioned earlier, it is significant that no special educational provisions are made in chapter VIII for English-speaking migrants from other parts of Canada. However, this aspect of the law, which conflicts with the right to minority education set forth in Canada's Constitution Act of 1982, was declared unconstitutional by the Quebec Superior Court in September, 1982 (see Mallea, this volume, chapter 10). Nevertheless, the omission was seen to serve two purposes: to discourage migration from the other provinces of Canada (over which the Quebec government has no control) and to convey, implicitly, the message that the relationship between Quebec and Canada is not important. Likewise, references made throughout the text to "languages other than French", without naming

English specifically, emphasize the non-official status of English by placing it on the same level as Italian, Greek or Portuguese, languages spoken by important minority groups in Montreal. Laporte (1977) draws attention to the fact that in allowing for the use of "other languages" by private enterprise for purposes of international relations, the law never singles out communications with the rest of Canada; the implication here is that Quebecers are to recognize that these communications have no special status. According to Laporte, "the phrasing of the legislation and its many dispositions about the new status of French and of Quebec, gives it a completely new political significance: Bill 101 is more than a language legislation; it is an attempt by the new government to move political consciousness away from its previous content to a Québécois content. Language legislation in Quebec, as it is in many 'new nations' of Africa and Asia, is now a nation-building mechanism."

The impact of Bill 101

Not unexpectedly, the shift in language policy resulted in mixed reactions. In general, francophones were pleased with the legislation in that it appeared to provide a secure future for the French language and culture in Quebec (d'Anglejan, 1979). Indeed, labour leaders, including La Centrale des Enseignants du Québec which had vehemently opposed Bill 63, and shown reservations with respect to Bill 22, expressed satisfaction with Bill 101 (see Laporte, this volume, chapter 3). While expressing full support for the law's objectives, Claude Ryan, editor of Quebec's influential newspaper *Le Devoir*, attacked the "rigid, dogmatic, jealous and authoritarian manner" in which the use of French was to be imposed in numerous domains where more flexible and realistic solutions might have been adopted. In a series of editorials he pointed out the unnecessarily negative impact the policy would have on the business community and condemned its denial of the legitimate status of the English-speaking community (Ryan, 1977). Since the newspaper had come out in favour of the Parti Québécois during the previous election campaign these comments could not be dismissed as political posturing.

In a statement made public on the occasion of a meeting with Camille Laurin, the architect of Bill 101 and Minister of Cultural Affairs (May 22, 1977), the president of the Federation of Ethnic Groups of Quebec warned that the ethnic minority groups would not allow their presence and interests to be ignored. While referring obliquely to the fact that the ethnic groups had not been consulted, the statement did not take a stand on Bill 101, perhaps reflecting a desire on the part of the Federation to differentiate its position from that of the anglophone community.

Reactions from anglophone groups were understandably critical. While there was a consensus of support for the basic principles of the legislation, the business community and educators expressed dismay at the probable impact of the law on the sectors with which they were concerned. The Positive Action Committee, an anglophone pressure group, took exception to the philosophy underlying the government's White Paper introducing Bill 101 (Laurin, 1977). It noted that the French language and culture were stronger than ever in Quebec, in spite of the attraction exercised by the rest of anglophone Canada and the United States. The committee criticized the government's White Paper for encouraging the myth that in order for the francophone community to flourish, the anglophone community must be diminished. It pointed out the paradox between the solicitude expressed in the White Paper (Laurin, 1977) with respect to the survival of the anglophone minority, and the message conveyed to that community in the rest of the document: "The anglophone collectivity has a place in Quebec on the condition that it is invisible and silent and progressively diminishes in number."

Predictably, the shift in language policy resulted initially in considerable resentment and some hostility on the part of private enterprise (Le Conseil du patronat, 1977; la Chambre de Commerce de la province de Quebec, 1977). Nonetheless, most firms have gone along with the government's francization policy and worked closely with the Office de la langue française to develop programmes for the conversion to French (Heller, Bartholomot, Levy, Ostiguy, 1982; Daoust, this volume, chapter 4; Miller, this volume, chapter 5). A notable exception to the pattern of compliance with regulations of Bill 101 is the behaviour of Crown corporations owned and operated by the Canadian government (e.g. Air Canada and Via Rail) which employ forty to fifty thousand Quebecers. These companies, as well as federal government agencies, continue to comply with federal language policy which calls for bilingual operations. Another pattern of response has been for firms to covertly or overtly shift their base of operation out of Quebec. It is difficult to know to what extent these departures are a reaction to the language legislation *per se*, or to Quebec's high taxation rates and a more general shift of economic interests toward the Western provinces. Whatever the reasons, demographers are attempting to interpret figures published by Statistics Canada in July 1982 which indicated a decline of 11.8% in Quebec's English-speaking population between 1976 and 1981. During the same period the number of French mother-tongue Quebecers increased by 6.4%.

At the individual level the majority of English-speaking Quebecers tend to feel threatened and to view the law as unjust (see Taylor & Simard, this volume, chapter 6). The fact that this view is not restricted to those who lack a sound knowledge of French, but is shared by *bilingual* anglophones suggests that their concerns extend beyond the fear of being unable to cope with language requirements brought about by Bill 101.

Five years after the enactment of Bill 101, most French-speaking Quebecers can now live and work entirely in French and French is gaining strength in the upper levels of the business world (see Laporte, this volume, chapter 3). A new, moderate anglophone pressure group known as Alliance Quebec has emerged to promote the interests of the English-speaking population. While supporting the objectives of Bill 101 it is committed to restoring the legitimacy of the English language and the anglophone community. One of the issues which the group is challenging is the elimination of English from public signs. In his 1977 White Paper the Minister of Cultural Affairs (Laurin, 1977) referred to "the francization of the Quebec landscape": the removal of virtually all visible evidence of languages other than French in public settings. This is proving to be one of the most psychologically provocative aspects of the law. It is seen by non-francophones to serve no useful purpose in terms of protecting the French language or the rights of francophones to live and work in their own language, for which there is widespread sympathy. Rather, it is viewed as a denial of the reality of Quebec's cultural and linguistic diversity (Alliance Quebec, 1982).

An additional problem which Alliance Quebec has set out to redress relates to the language testing of non-francophone professionals. The use of inappropriate tests has resulted in the improper denial of certificates to practice in Quebec, particularly among nurses and nurses aids whose professional training does not involve university studies (Gagnon, 1981). There are indications that the government may be considering the possibility of amending these aspects of the law, the first sign of any softening of its position since the legislation was enacted.

Language planning and pluralism in Quebec

Quebec's language planning initiatives are having a possibly unanticipated impact on the francophone population which is being called upon to adjust, virtually overnight, to the presence of minority groups within its social institutions. As Arnopoulos & Clift (1980) point out, until recently, French Quebec had not experienced the process of cultural accommodation which is now an accepted dimension of life in cosmopolitan cities such as San

Francisco, New York and Boston. As noted earlier, the school population to be found in Quebec's French schools was almost homogeneously French-Canadian and Catholic. Although the provincial government's own immigration department developed an aggressive policy to serve Quebec's cultural priorities, during the period of intense nationalism of the 1960s and 70s, French society remained inward-looking and showed little interest in outsiders. Immigrants were expected to assimilate; public institutions remained aloof and unresponsive to requests for special services.

The social pressures brought on by nationalism, by language planning, and by the resurgence of ethnicity (Novak, 1972) have caused Quebec minorities to demand changes in the province's French institutions. The inadequate teaching of English-as-a-second-language in French schools has been a long-standing obstacle to the acceptance of French schooling by ethnic minority groups. Furthermore, minorities want the French school system to reflect the ethnic and religious diversity in the province, particularly in the composition of the teaching staff, materials and programmes (Arnopoulos & Clift, 1980). The inadequate representation of minority groups in the public sector is also being challenged. It is evident that the government is not insensitive to these pressures. A recently published Plan of Action for Cultural Communities (Quebec, 1981) spells out the contribution of the province's minority groups and outlines measures to assure their civil rights and cultural well-being. These policies are placing new and challenging demands on the francophone community, coming as they do on the heels of historical indifference or even hostility towards outsiders; ethnocentric attitudes which have been shaped in turn by the struggle for Québécois cultural survival and ethnic nationalism. As in other parts of the world, Quebec's majority is now having to come to terms with pluralism.

One problematic aspect of the new language policy which remains unresolved is the link which it establishes between language, culture and nationhood. The preamble to the original version of the Charter of the French Language (*Le Devoir*, 1977) declared that ". . . The French Language has always been the language of the Québécois people . . . the instrument by which that people has articulated its identity." As Knopf (1978–79) and Williams (1980) have noted, this indicates that the government does not consider the official language to be simply a culturally neutral tool of communication which allows those of different cultures to engage in a common life, but insists that it is the vehicle of a particular culture. Although the final version of the Charter referred to French as "the distinctive language of a people that is in the majority French speaking," the notion of an official culture still prevails. The recent Plan of Action for Cultural Communities (Quebec, 1981) reiterates this position: "Having chosen

French as its official language, Quebec has made it understood that its culture ought to be firstly of French tradition." These statements, plus the fact that the present language policy goes well beyond the measures required to assure the welfare of the French language, have been interpreted by some* as indications that what began as a legitimate language reform has indeed become, with Bill 101, a blueprint for a French nation state in which the concept of what constitutes the well-being of the citizenry is not culturally neutral. The objectives of the state may thus not necessarily be ones which are consonant with improving the well-being of all citizens, but of advancing the cause of the group whose culture coincides with that of the state (cf. the situation in France, Bourhis, 1982). According to Knopf (1978–79), the contrast is between a "nationalist democracy" in which the majority rules, not so much because it is a majority, but because there is a natural right to rule which is independent of the majority-minority distinction, and a "liberal democracy" which is above all a limited democracy, in that the state limits itself to securing the rights of all without decreeing a particular mode of exercising these rights." Statements by the Positive Action Committee (1977) and Alliance Quebec (1982), as well as attitudes of the bilingual and monolingual anglophones toward Bill 101 reported by Taylor & Simard (this volume, chapter 7) point to a fundamental uneasiness on the part of minority groups which will not necessarily be allayed by changes in language testing procedures or minimal changes in the law regarding commercial signs. The problem was succinctly put by Christos Sirros (1982), a member of the Quebec National Assembly: "Does Quebec belong to all its citizens and, therefore, must respond to the needs of the population as a whole, or does it belong to its French majority first, and only owe tolerance to its minorities?"[1]

Future trends

In a recent analysis of the Quebec socio-political scene, Clift (1982) suggests that nationalist ideology is giving way to a more individualistic perspective in Quebec. As a result of the economic crisis of the 1980s the government is having to make dramatic cutbacks in its civil service bureaucracy and over-developed public services. It no longer has the financial means to mobilize public opinion for nationalist causes. On the other hand, the business sector, which was much maligned by the Parti Québécois for its identification with the English-speaking community and for its value system, is emerging as an important source of jobs and upward mobility for francophones. According to Clift: "Already it is apparent that private enterprise and business will emerge as the most dynamic sector of French society in Quebec, the one whose achievements will determine future prospects. It will have an impact as great as the establishment of a large bureaucratic apparatus has had on the period which is now coming to a close. Public servants and politicians will necessarily have to establish a close relationship with those who are pursuing careers in private business and they will have to provide social and political support by means of new policies adapted to the needs of French businessmen and to the competitive situation they will be facing." (Clift, 1982, p. 126).

Similar views are expressed in a recent article in the French language news magazine, *L'Actualité*, by Benoit Aubin (1982). He notes that anglophones in the business world are increasingly bilingual whereas francophones are losing their former advantage in this domain. He advocates the relaxing of the harsh attitudes toward English which may put French businessmen at a disadvantage. In this respect it is useful to recall the findings of a study which was carried out in 1972 by the Office de la langue française (Quebec, 1972b) on the use of various languages in the head offices of multinational corporations in several European countries. The agency concluded that if a linguistic group wishes to see its language used at the highest levels of management in large corporations it must make it possible for citizens to acquire a working knowledge of English. This can best be achieved, according to the report, "in a climate of open-mindedness which the state itself must help to create."

Despite the protection afforded the French language by Quebec's language policy, the English language and English language institutions are still viewed with anxiety in many sectors, a view encouraged by some nationalist policymakers. Underlying this defensive posture, according to Clift (1982) and Aubin (1982), is not so much any real linguistic or demographic threat posed by the English presence in Quebec. It is the English community's direct identification with North American society and its liberal institutions. This is worrisome because many Quebecers are now eager to join that society and accept its ideological foundations (Clift, 1982).

These tensions in contemporary Quebec may lead to socio-political changes which call for a reformulation of the province's language policy. One should not expect to see any reduction in the protective measures adopted to guarantee the primacy of French. However, in the light of the relative success of the francization process, what may be open to reexamination is the role of English and the English-speaking community (see Caldwell, this volume, chapter 9). Within the framework of a language policy less constrained by nationalist ideology, and in the perspective suggested by Jernudd & Das Gupta (1975), the English language would be viewed as a societal resource amenable to rational development and planning.

Acknowledgements

I wish to thank numerous colleagues, friends and the editor, for critical comments on earlier drafts of this paper. My own understanding of the issues benefited greatly from these friendly discussions. Special thanks to Louise Valois.

Notes

1. In October 1983, the Quebec Government held a 3-week Parliamentary Commission in which individuals and organizations from all sectors of Quebec society were invited to propose their amendments to Bill 101. Following these representations a bill to amend the Charter of the French language was tabled in the Quebec legislature by the Parti Quebecois. Among the minor changes proposed in Bill 57 are the following:
   — English education would be available for children whose parents were educated in English in a province (of Canada) which Quebec feels offers French-language educational services comparable to English-language services offered in Quebec.
   — Municipal governments with an anglophone majority which were only allowed to use French under Bill 101 would be able to use English as well as French in their communications.
   — Anglophone institutions would be allowed to communicate among themselves in English rather than in French only.
   — After June 1986 graduates from anglophone high schools seeking professional certification in Quebec would be exempt from French language tests.
   — Francization committees would become a permanent fixture in businesses employing 100 persons or more and would continue to meet at regular intervals.
   — Bilingual signs and posters will be allowed for establishments specializing in foreign national specialties or the specialties of a particular ethnic group. However, the definition of what constitutes a foreign specialty remains unclear and most likely excludes products and specialties of anglophone origin since these are deemed to be commonly consumed in Quebec.

   As this volume goes to press, the Quebec National Assembly has yet to vote on Bill 57. For anglophone groups, Bill 57 has still not addressed the issue of the status of the English-speaking community in Quebec. Meanwhile, there is speculation that other minor changes to the Charter of the French language may be forthcoming.

References

ALLIANCE QUEBEC, 1982, A policy for the English-speaking community of Quebec. Montreal, 16 March 1982.

D'ANGLEJAN, A. 1979, French in Quebec. *Journal of Communications*, 29, 2, 54–63.

D'ANGLEJAN, A., & TUCKER, G. R. 1973, Sociolinguistic correlates of speech style in Quebec. In R. SHUY & R. FASOLD (eds), *Language attitudes: Current trends and prospects*. Washington, D.C.: Georgetown Universty Press.

ARÈS, R. 1972, La montée des autres: 149%: La composition linguistique des cités et villes de l'ile de Montréal. *Relations*, 375, 282–283.

— 1975, *Les positions — ethniques, linguistiques et religieuses — des canadians française à la suite de recensement de 1971*. Montreal: Bellarmin.

ARNOPOULOS, S. M., & CLIFT, D. 1980, *The English fact in Quebec*. Montreal: McGill-Queen's University Press.

AUBIN, B. 1982, La loi 101 cinq ans après. *L'Actualité*, August.

BOURHIS, R. Y. 1982, Language policies and language attitudes: Le monde de la Francophonie. In E. BOUCHARD RYAN & H. GILES (eds), *Attitudes towards language variation*. London: Edward Arnold.

CANADA, GOVERNMENT OF. 1967, Royal Commission on Bilingualism and Biculturalism. Vol. 1: *The Official Languages*. Ottawa: Queen's Printer.

— 1969, Royal Commission on Bilingualism and Biculturalism. Vol. 3: *The Work World*. Ottawa: Queen's Printer.

CAPPON, Paul, 1974, *Conflit entre les néo-canadiens et les francophones de Montréal*. Quebec: International Center for Research on Bilingualism, 1974.

CHAMBRE DE COMMERCE DE LA PROVINCE DE QUEBEC. 1977, Statement, April 15, 1977. In: *Les dossiers du Devoir*, No. 3.

CHARBONNEAU, H., HENRIPIN, J., & LÉGARÉ, J. 1970, L'avenir démographiques des francophones au Québec et à Montréal en l'absence de politiques adéquates. *Revue de Géographie de Montréal*, 24, 2, 199–202.

CLIFT, D. 1982, *Quebec Nationalism in crisis*. Montreal: McGill-Queen's University Press.

COOK, R. (ed.) 1972, *French-Canadian nationalism*. Toronto: Macmillan.

DAOUST, D. 1982, Corpus and status planning in Quebec: A look at linguistic legislation. In J. COBARRUBIAS & J. FISHMAN (eds), *Progress in language planning: International perspective*. The Hague: Mouton.

GAGNON, L. 1981, *Les tests*. La Presse, 16, 19, 21 May.

HELLER, M., BARTHOLOMOT, J.-P., LEVY, L., & OSTIGUY, L. 1982, *Les processus de francisation dans une enterprise Montréalaise: une analyse sociolinguistique*. Montreal: Office de la langue française, Editeur officiel.

HENRIPIN, J. 1973, Quebec and the demographic dilemma of French Canadian Society. In D. C. THOMSON (ed.), *Quebec society and politics*. Toronto: McClelland & Stewart.

— 1976, La population du Canada en l'an 2000. *Les dossiers du Devoir*, No. 1, 7–8.

JERNUDD, B. H. & DAS GUPTA, J. 1975, Towards a theory of language planning. In J. RUBIN & B. JERNUDD (eds), *Can language be planned?* Honolulu: University Press of Hawaii.

JOY, Richard. 1972, *Languages in conflict.* Toronto: McClelland & Stewart.

KLOSS, H. 1969, *Research possibilities on group bilingualism: A report.* Quebec: International Center for Research on Bilingualism.

KNOPF, R. 1978–79, Democracy vs liberal democracy: The nationalist conundrum. *The Dalhousie Review*, 58: 4, 638–46.

LAPORTE, P. E. 1975, *Structure sociale, concurrence linguistique et législation linguistique au Québec.* Paper presented at a meeting on the relations between the English and French languages organized by the Conseil international de la langue française. Paris.

— 1977, *Ideological conflict and language policy schism in Canada.* Paper read at the colloquium on language planning practice. Summer Linguistics Institute. East-West Center Institute, University of Hawaii, Honolulu.

LAURIN, C. 1977, La politique québécoise de la langue française. White Paper presented to the Assemblée nationale du Quebec. April 1, 1977. *Les dossiers du Devoir*, No. 3.

LE DEVOIR. 1977, Le projet de loi no. 1: chartre de la langue française. *Les dossiers du Devoir*, No. 3.

LÉGER, J.-M. 1972, Where does neo-nationalism lead? In R. COOK (ed.), *French Canadian nationalism.* Toronto: Macmillan.

LIEBERSON, S. 1970, *Language and ethnic relations in Canada.* Toronto: Wiley.

MACDONALD, R. J. 1977, In search of a language policy: Francophone reactions to Bill 85 and 63. In J. R. MALLEA (ed.), *Quebec's language policies: Background and response.* Quebec: International Center for Research on Bilingualism.

NOVAK, M. 1972, *The rise of the unmeltable ethnics: Politics and culture in the seventies.* New York: Macmillan.

PORTER, J. 1965, *The vertical mosaic.* Toronto: University of Toronto Press.

POSITIVE ACTION COMMITTEE. 1977, Public Statement, 23 April, 1977. *Les dossiers du Devoir*, No. 3.

QUEBEC, 1966, *Report of the Royal Commission of Inquiry on Education in the Province of Quebec* (Parent Commission). Quebec.

—, GOVERNMENT OF. 1972a, *Report of the Commission of Inquiry on the Position of the French Language and on Language Rights in Quebec* (Gendron Commission). Editeur Officiel du Québec.

— 1972b, Office de la langue française. *Rapport de la mission d'étude sur le fonctionnement linguistique des sièges sociaux d'entreprises multinationales.* Quebec.

— 1976, Ministre des affaires sociales. Les données démographiques de l'année 1972. Une nouvelle baisse des naissances et de l'accroissement naturel au Québec. *Les dossiers du Devoir*, No. 1, 25–27.

— 1981, Ministère des Communautés culturelles et de l'Immigration. *Autant de façons d'être Québécois.* Quebec: Gouvernement du Québec.

RYAN, C. 1977, Un dangereux carcan. *Les dossiers du Devoir*, No. 3.

SIRROS, C. 1982, Government cold to minorities. Letter to the editor, *The Gazette*, September 20, 1982.

STEIN, M. 1977, Bill 22 and the non-francophone population in Quebec: A case study of minority group attitudes on language legislation. In: J. R. MALLEA (ed.),

Quebec's language policy: Background and response. Quebec: International Center for Research on Bilingualism.

WILLIAMS, C. H. 1980, The desire of nations: Quebecois ethnic separatism in comparative perspective. *Cahiers de géographie du Québec*, 24, No. 61, 47–68.

3 Status language planning in Quebec: An evaluation

Pierre E. Laporte
Office de la langue française

The past twenty years have witnessed a considerable expansion of the activities of language planning. These activities, encompassing a wide range of interventions concerning the status and the internal structure of languages are now conducted on a broad world scale (Fishman, 1974). Thus, a recent inventory of organizations devoted to language planning throughout the world brought to light the existence of over fifty such institutions including government, semi-private and private bodies (Rubin, 1979). Three factors seem to have influenced this expansion: decolonization, the rise of national-isms, and the astounding spread of English. These factors in turn gave birth, at least among the traditionally great tongues, to movements of self-assertion with language planning often as the tributary. We can thus state that lan-guage planning has become a worldwide phenomenon: it is carried on in the so-called developed countries and in those on the road to development. Even if language planning frequently coincides with problems resulting from great linguistic diversity, certain countries more linguistically homogeneous, such as France (Bourhis, 1982) have had recourse to language planning.

Far from having escaped these movements, Quebec has become during the past fifteen years the theatre of intensive activity in the area of language planning (see d'Anglejan, this volume, chapter 2; Daoust, 1982; Mallea, 1977). Indeed in Quebec, the number of public and private organizations dealing with language planning has, in fifteen years, multiplied fivefold, as have their personnel and budget. The reasons behind this growth are, moreover, very similar to those which gave rise to the expansion of language

53

planning elsewhere: the rise of nationalism, which some have linked to the phenomenon of decolonization, and the defence of a traditionally great tongue from the penetration of English. Even more, Quebec wanted, especially during the past ten years, to play the role of avant-garde in matters of language planning. Quebec has become a fertile ground for language planning through international symposia in terminology and sociolinguistics, through a vast program of linguistic and sociolinguistic research and through the creation and development of terminology banks. The aim of this chapter is to analyse language planning in Quebec from a double point of view: that of the relationships between planning and the language situation, and that of the impact of language planning on the economy and the language situation.

As understood in this chapter, language planning consists in decision-making concerning language problems, problems related either to the position of language in society or their structures. Thus, I recognize the distinction made by Kloss (1969) between status planning and corpus planning. I also believe it useful to keep in mind the suggestion made by Das Gupta (1977) that language planning means decision-making in conformity with State policy. Although the state is not the only actor, it is nonetheless the central figure from whom the initiative tends to come in most cases of language planning. Finally, I intend to limit my discussion to the status planning of French in Quebec. The question of corpus planning would require an entirely different discussion (see Daoust, this volume, chapter 4).

Relationships between the language situation and language planning in Quebec

Prior to the early sixties, state intervention on language problems in Quebec had been limited in scope and sporadic in occurrence. Rather than to the State, the responsibility of language promotion and purification were left to various patriotic and religious organizations. State intervention proper coincided with what became known as the "Quiet Revolution" and the politicization of language problems parallel to that of many other spheres of social and economic activities (Rioux, 1974).

The Lavergne Law of 1910 aimed at requiring public utility companies to place the French version alongside the English one in printed matters sent to their customers, whereas previously the script appeared in English only. As for the Duplessis Law of 1937, it aimed at granting priority to the French text in the interpretation of certain laws. The first law was enforced only gradually while the second gave rise to such an outcry among anglophones that it was rescinded a year after its passage (Bouthillier, 1981; Bouthillier &

Meynaud, 1972). Indeed, it is only with the creation of the Office de la langue française in 1961, that State intervention on matters of language began its fuller institutionalization. Notably, the initial mandate of the Office was almost exclusively centred on corpus planning: namely, the issue of French language purification. Preoccupations with questions of status, especially legal and economic, had yet to arise, but they were soon to appear when, in 1965, the Government tabled a white paper that proposed the first Quebec policy on language. In this white paper emerged, for the first time, some of the key ideas which have inspired language planning to this day. The subsequent development, especially after Bill 63, proceeded at a rapid pace. Following the Gendron Commission (Quebec, 1972) the sphere of state action in language matters greatly expanded to include: the Official Language Law in 1974 (Bill 22), the White Paper on Language Policy in 1977, and finally the Charter of the French Language in August 1977 (Bill 101). Thus, a veritable system of language planning has arisen in Quebec in which the state plays a central but not exclusive role. The system has in fact a pluralistic character: it allows for interventions by private and semi-private organizations as well as by the state which keeps, nevertheless, a major role in the initiation and the monitoring of change.

The aims of language planning are comprehensive. They touch not only the legal status of French as Quebec's Official Language, but all major domains of public life, including politics, governmental administration, education, the working world, the mass media, advertising and labelling (see Bill 101, this volume, Appendix 1). In all these domains the goal is to make French a language of universal use consistent with the concept of Quebec as an "essentially francophone society". The Quebec language policy, then, is one of resolute francization with broad implications for the linguistic organization of institutional life, especially economic life, for the demography of languages and, more generally, the linguistic identity of Quebec in Canada and in North America.

In order to understand the reasons for the developments which have occurred during the past twenty years, one must be familiar with the language situation in Canada and in Quebec. The late fifties and early sixties were times of fundamental change in Canadian linguistic demography. It is in fact during this period that the proportion of francophones among the Canadian population was to decrease for the first time since the mid-nineteenth century. While the proportion of francophones in Canada had hovered around 30% since 1871, date of the first Canadian census, it declined to 28% during the 1951–61 period, down to 25.9% in 1971 and to 25.6% in 1976 (Henripin, 1976). These changes, which have recently been described as "a rupture of the demographic equilibrium", are attributed to the drastic decline in francophone fertility since the second world war. Added to this first major transformation of Canadian language demography was the rapid linguistic assimilation of French Canadians everywhere in Canada except for Quebec, the Acadian part of New Brunswick and the regions of Ontario adjacent to Quebec (Joy, 1972; Castonguay & Marion, 1974; see Mallea, this volume, chapter 10).

The impact of these changes on the collective consciousness of francophones cannot be neglected. Historically, their sense of strength as a national minority rested upon their hopes for a stable and even growing demographic position as a language group (Siegfried, 1907). Signs of decline of the francophone demographic position exacerbated the francophone sense of vulnerability. Among francophone Quebecers this factor was certainly a crucial element in the movement which in the late sixties gave birth to state intervention on the status of the French language. Made more vulnerable than ever in Canada, francophone Quebecers opted for maximum linguistic protection within Quebec where they could expect to remain the majority. Language planning was the response to this feeling of threat on the demographic front.

Other dynamic factors had to do with the Quebec sociolinguistic situation which could be characterized by the fact that while English was the dominant language spoken by the minority, French was the subordinate language spoken by the vast majority of the population. Language situations where dominance is not based on demographic supremacy can produce social tensions (Ferguson, 1962). This has certainly been the case in Quebec. The dominance of English in Quebec was partly demographic since its status as a majority language in Canada and North America gave the local anglophone minority a sense of strength, which they would not have otherwise. But, much more important, given that Quebec is 80% French, is the economic basis of language dominance. In much of Quebec history, English has been the language of the economically powerful (Canada, 1969; Quebec, 1972). Today, the domains and functions of English dominance have been reduced in span and strategic significance but have not disappeared altogether. The great centers of commercial, financial, industrial and technological power in Quebec still function in English even today (Inagaki, 1980; Jannard, 1981). The concrete manifestations of English dominance are numerous and I will limit myself to those three that have had the most important effect on the development of language planning activities over the last fifteen years.

First, there are manifestations having to do with the status of English and French as languages of communication in the public domain: advertising, labelling of products, official names of corporations and generally speaking, what is known as "le visage linguistique du Québec" the linguistic ambiance of Quebec (Corbeil, 1980). English dominance has long been masked by the practice of institutional bilingualism which nevertheless helped to increase the status of French in Quebec. However, Montreal remained for many years a metropolis whose linguistic ambiance was heavily English. A sign of the prominence of English as a public language in Montreal is the fact that it is only since 1978 that large Quebec-based commercial firms began to spend more on translations from French to English rather than from English to French in their commercial advertising (Taneau, 1980). One should add that francophone complaints against English prominence in Montreal have been a constant feature of the Quebec language situation over many years. Complaints voiced by numerous categories of francophone "defenseurs de la langue" have been made both against the strength of English as a public language and against the lack of status conferred to French in the public domain. These were important factors leading to state intervention in favour of French in Quebec.

Second, on the economic front, English tended to dominate as the language of economic advancement. While French was used widely in the lower echelons of economic life, English usage dominated in the upper strata of the corporate world. Table 1 is based on 1971 data and shows how the use of English by francophones increases as they rise in positions of power in the corporate world. In contrast, the table shows that for anglophones, French usage increases the lower they are in the job hierarchy. This illustrates how the social structure of bilingualism in Quebec was quite a different reality for anglophones and francophones. The social pressures for using french as a language of communication at work are more strongly felt by lower status anglophones, while the pressures to use English increase as francophones rise in status in the corporate world.

The economic dominance of English in Quebec was more than a matter of the social stratification of languages as a means of communication. The social evaluation of languages as resources for economic advancement was also involved. This is to be expected in a society where a language dominates over another since, as Bourdieu (1979) would put it, one kind of 'cultural capital' — in this case knowledge of English — is of greater strategic value for advancement than other kinds of 'cultural capital'. An interesting illustration of the superior position of English as a language of economic advancement in Quebec in the early seventies was provided by the answer of salaried professionals to the following question: "In the business where you work, is knowledge of English more essential for advancement than knowledge of French?" Table 2 shows that the bigger the size and range of

TABLE 1 *Language use at work by anglophones and francophones — Quebec 1971*

Occupation	Anglophones using French	Francophones using English
Administrators	28%	45%
Office Staff	28%	48%
Salespeople	31%	37%
Workers in secondary industry	39%	25%
Workers in primary industry	31%	5%

Source: Laporte (1974).
Note: We have used only the occupational categories that refer to the corporate world where language groups are most likely to meet and the pressures for bilingualism likely to be felt.

TABLE 2 *Perceived importance of English relative to French in Quebec business firms in 1971*

Type of work milieu	Percent seeing English as more essential than French
Businesses controlled by:	
Quebec francophones	13%
Quebec anglophones	46%
Canadians	80%
Americans	82%
Where they do business:	
Quebec	12%
Canada	65%
Canada/US	68%
International	59%
Kind of business:	
Government	22%
Professional	30%
Commercial	45%
Industrial	71%
Number of employees:	
1–49	43%
50–1449	46%
1500 and over	60%

Source: Laporte (1974).

operations undertaken by the business firms in which respondents are located the more the English language was perceived as essential for advancement compared to French.

The third factor which prompted language planning in favour of French is related to the status of English and French as languages of adoption by non-English and non-French language groups. As a language of adoption for immigrants coming to North America, English was much stronger than French. This was the case especially in Montreal where the bulk of the Quebec anglophone population is concentrated. The strong drawing power of English for neo-Quebecers settling in Montreal was documented in a study by Kralt (1976) who used 1971 Census figures. Kralt showed that whereas only 8.2% of neo-Quebecers chose French as their language of adoption in Montreal, as many as 23.1% preferred English. It is on the basis of such trends that some demographers predicted the eventual decline of francophones in Montreal. Though English surpassed French in 1971 as the language of adoption by Quebecers of other tongues, such was not always the case. There was a time when the opposite trend prevailed. The turn of events took place towards the end of the 1951–61 period: in 1931, 52% of Quebecers whose origin was other than British or French had adopted French, while their number had fallen to 29% in 1961 (Charbonneau & Maheu, 1973).

A corollary to this movement of anglicization of language minorities deserves mention. Added to the preference of parents for the use of English in everyday life was the growing anglicization of minority language children through English schooling. Since the 19th century, freedom of choice granted to immigrant parents meant that these groups could send their children to state supported schools in either French or English. From the 1950s onwards the majority of immigrants of non-French/non-English mother tongue chose English as the schooling language for their children. It was anticipated at the time that these anglophone gains could result in a slow but gradual erosion of the demographic dominance of the French language in Quebec, especially in the Montreal area where most non-francophone Quebecers were concentrated. Indeed, by the early seventies, about a quarter of the student population of anglophone schools was made of pupils whose mother tongue was other than English. These included a small percentage of francophone pupils and a much greater proportion of students from language minorities. For the year 1970–71, 8.3% of the student population of Montreal English schools was of French mother tongue while 22.5% was from various language minorities. The comparison with French schools is revealing: in 1970–72, 1.9% of students in these schools were English mother tongue and

0.9% came from language minorities. These trends were revealing indicators of English language strength relative to French (Vanasse, 1981).

State intervention through language planning was designed to address each of these sociolinguistic and demographic issues from the point of view of the francophone majority. Language planning in Quebec can be viewed as a response to dissatisfactions expressed with the language situation by the francophone majority. Situations where the dominant language is not that of the majority can pose a real problem of social equality: in Quebec, anglophones and francophones cannot have the same chances of social success as long as English remains the main language of communication at work and the essential means of access even to middle levels of the economic hierarchy. Studies have brought to light the economic inequalities between anglophones and francophones in Quebec, inequalities which existed between individuals of equivalent education and job experience (Canada, 1969; Quebec 1972).

These inequalities were related to the phenomenon of English language domination and indeed were seen by the francophone majority as resulting from it. One of the main objectives of linguistic planning was to eliminate these inequalities and their consequences by making French the language of work in Quebec. The priority set by the state, on the use of French in the workplace is undoubtedly aimed at the resolution of social inequality for the francophone majority.

Another attempt to address the sociolinguistic issue has been to make French a language of widespread use in every domain of social activity in Quebec. The aim has been to create a "French ambiance" for Quebec through the francization of bill-boards, labelling, firm names, place names and other eye-catching elements (Corbeil, 1980). The aim has also been to spread French administrative, scientific and technical terms through corpus language planning. Quebec's interventions in this area are highly ambitious, both from the viewpoint of the goal of generalized French use and the means set out to accomplish it (see Daoust, this volume, chapter 4).

On the demographic front, francophones have remained strong by virtue of their group size and demographic concentration within the Quebec territory. Group numbers also contribute to political strength, since in a democracy the size of a community determines its political weight. Group size also contributes to language strength since the preservation of a language and its influence undoubtedly require an adequate demographic base. As we have seen, by the mid-sixties there were signs that the demographic base of francophones in Montreal was being eroded by the low francophone birth rate and the anglicization of neo-Quebecers through English schooling. Consequently, language legislation in both 1974 and 1977 included clauses limiting neo-Quebecer access to English schooling.

Finally, the state has intervened to change the legal status of the languages by making French the only official language of Quebec. This is highly symbolic for it granted French a prestige it formerly did not have. This move was also aimed at changing the *de facto* situation since the state committed itself to promote the use of French in its day-to-day legal, administrative and commercial practices throughout society.

Now that the language situation and the broad goals of language planning have been described, we will take up the question of the impact of this language planning in two important domains: the Quebec language situation and the economy.

The impact of language planning on the language situation

To what extent has the language situation developed in the direction of the broad goals set by Quebec's policy of francization? The question is difficult to answer for at least two reasons. First, there is lack of data permitting a comparison over time of the language situation. However, some data exist which indicate that the situation has changed. These data will be examined even if one must recognize their limitations.

Second, there is the problem of "effect lag" which complicates all attempts at evaluating change. As has been found in other cases of institutional interventions, the effect of such interventions are often felt only after a certain lapse of time (Weiss, 1972). In the case of language planning in Quebec, the "effect lag" is due in part to the fact that, in spite of sustained efforts made over a fifteen-year period, the major interventionist push has really only come about in the last few years. Thus, the 1977 Charter of the French Language has only been implemented in the past five years and we can surmise that its results will be more evident in the future than they are today.

A first set of indicators of change in the status of French is provided by mass perceptions of the evolving language situation. One set of indicators concerns the status of French as a public language: that which is used in commercial transactions with strangers, to obtain public services of all kinds and finally the language of commercial posters and public signs generally. At stake are not only linguistic opportunities but also what has already been identified as Quebec's linguistic imbalance. The data seem to show that French is making gains in this domain.

A survey conducted in 1979 about language use for commercial and public services shows that 71.2% of all Quebecers perceived that French is more widely used than it was five years ago (Bouchard & Beauchamp-Achim, 1980). The same survey reports on what are perceived to be the opportunities to obtain services in one's own language in 1979 compared to 1971. The results are revealing: among francophones the percentage of respondents reporting that they experienced difficulties obtaining services in French decreased from 13% in 1971 to 8.8% in 1979. Among anglophones, however, the percentage of respondents who reported they experienced difficulties in obtaining services in English increased to 34% in 1979 from 26% in 1971. At least on the basis of such survey results we have evidence that francization is gaining ground (cf. Bourhis, this volume, chapter 8). Perhaps as convincing are the results of a survey conducted by Bourgeois & Girard (1980) among tourists in Quebec during the summer of 1980. First 51.2% of respondents were of the opinion that "today" commercial posters were more likely to be presented in French than they were the last time they came to Quebec. Second, the more respondents' last visit dated back in time, the more they perceived changes in favour of francization of commercial posters. Thirdly, when tourists were asked if, judging by the use of languages in commercial posters and public signs generally, Montreal looked more like a French than a bilingual or an English city, 59% answered a French city. 39.0% reported a bilingual city, while only 1.7% felt Montreal looked like an English city (Bourgeois & Girard, 1982). A more recent survey (Crop, 1981) shows that whereas more than 75% of francophones feel quite positively about the francization of commercial posters and billboards in Quebec, a majority of anglophones felt quite negatively about these trends. These results suggest that the linguistic ambiance of Quebec is quickly changing in favour of French.

Other indicators concern mass perceptions about the changing status of French as a language of work. Breton & Grant (1981) summarized the results of surveys conducted during the seventies in the following way: "a solid majority of francophones and anglophones perceive that French is making gains, whether as a language of employment, as a language of communication with the employers or as the administrative and business language of firms". This observation is confirmed by recent surveys of mass perceptions and by studies of the changing roles of languages on the labor market. A recent survey by Crop (1980) not only showed that francophones (66%) and non-francophones (75%) perceive greater French language usage in the work setting "today" than was the case two years ago, but also showed that a third of the respondents from both groups reported using more French at work, especially since the promulgation of Bill 101.

However, the Crop (1980) survey needs a note of caution: data also showed that over the last two years, English maintained some of its status as a language of advancement on the labor market. This seems to be particularly true as regards job promotion, since 35% of francophones and 22% of non-francophones saw English as more useful for promotion today than two years ago. Group differences also emerged in these perceptions since more non-francophones (37%) saw English as *less* useful for job promotion today than did francophones (16%). Results from the 1981 Crop survey confirmed the distinction made by Breton & Grant (1981) between the functions of language as a means of communication and language as a means of economic advancement.[1] Results from the Crop (1981) survey suggest that gains made by French as a language of communication are more important than its gains as a language of occupational mobility.

One final piece of evidence concerning the changing status of French as a language of work comes from a study by Sécor (1980). Using records of ten large Quebec business firms, the Sécor study measured the representation of language groups at the managerial level, language knowledge and language requirements, first in 1964 and again in 1979. These provided a unique basis for comparison of language conditions studied at a fifteen year interval. We must note that the use of French was measured indirectly. The authors presumed that if both the presence of francophones at the executive and managerial levels and the French language requirements at these levels had increased during the past fifteen years, then effectively the use of French throughout these business firms would have increased in comparable proportions. This seems a valid and even ingenious assumption, considering the difficulty involved in both accurately measuring language usage and of monitoring such patterns over long periods of time. These indicators were used to assess changes in the status of French as the language of work during the last fifteen years in Quebec firms.

The study first noted that the presence of francophones among managerial staff in Quebec's large corporations had increased from 50% in 1964 to 63% in 1979. Note that the changes remain below the ideal of having francophones represented in the business hierarchy in proportion to their demographic presence in Quebec where they represent more than 80% of the population. It is nonetheless true that among managers of local branches, a 75% representation was achieved by 1979 relative to a 69% figure in 1964. However, francophone managerial presence remained low in Quebec head offices in both 1964 (32%) and 1979 (40%).

Table 3 deals with an important aspect of francophone presence in Quebec businesses of anglophone origin: francophones are better repre-

TABLE 3 *Change in francophone presence among managerial staff according to hierarchical level in anglophone business firms: 1964 – 1979*

	Francophone Presence	
	1964	*1979*
Head Offices		
— All executive and managerial staff	18%	30%
— Lower-level management	22%	45%
Local Branch Offices		
— All management staff	71%	78%
— Lower-level management	73%	84%

Source: Société d'études et de changement organisationnel (Sécor, 1980).

sented among lower-level management than among management as a whole, including higher-level executives. Moreover, it is in the lower level positions that francophone progress is most rapid. Finally, francophones remain the minority in head offices, where the strategic decisions are made.

Table 4 brings us closer to the phenomenon of French use in large Quebec corporations. It deals with language requirements in the exercise of a function and with language competence. There are three points to be noted. Firstly, there is an obvious increase in the French language requirements for anglophones. Secondly, we note that bilingualism is less often required of francophones at the lower branch level in 1979 than it was in 1964. This latter trend allows us to suppose that one of the results of state intervention was the elimination of the bilingual requirement often artificially imposed on francophones by English-speaking employers. Thirdly, knowledge of French among managerial anglophone personnel has increased between 1964 and 1979, which allows us to suppose that many anglophone employees have become bilinguals over the last fifteen years. This is especially noteworthy in head offices where knowledge of French on the part of anglophones in 1964 was very rare.

One must emphasize once again that the present data do not bear directly on the use of French as such, but on corporate requirement and job-performance. The results are consistent, however, with those of other studies on these issues. There seems to be no question, for instance, that knowing French is becoming more and more a condition of employment for anglophones in many great business firms operating in Quebec (Bourbonnais, 1979; see Miller, this volume, chapter 5; Vaillancourt & Daneau, 1980).

TABLE 4 *Change in language requirements and knowledge, 1964 and 1979*

| | Percentages in: | |
	1964	1979
Second language requirement:		
in Head Offices for		
Anglophones	10%	39%
Francophones	72%	71%
in Local Branches for		
Anglophones	46%	63%
Francophones	91%	23%
Language familiarity:		
of French by Anglophones in		
Head Offices	36%	62%
Local Branches	73%	92%
of English by Francophones in		
Head Offices	82%	88%
Local Branches	91%	53%

Source: Société d'études et de changement organisationnel (Sécor, 1980).

One last piece of evidence on the changing status of French concerns patterns of language usage in the work setting. In two labor market surveys, one in 1970 and the other in 1979, Vaillancourt (1981) asked respondents to report on the percentage of time they use French at work. Table 5 shows self-reports of language use for several occupational categories. The results indicate that from 1973 to 1979 the percentage of time where French was used as the language of work increased for both men and women of all occupational categories.

Thus, it appears that the status of French as a language of work has improved over the last decade. Not only is this systematically shown by mass perceptions but the change is also indicated by data on corporate linguistic representation, corporate language practices and corporate language usage patterns.

On the demographic and education front, gains made by English as a language of adoption by immigrant parents and their children coming to Quebec during the late 1950s and early 1960s was perceived as threatening by francophones. This anglicization trend contributed to the emergence of state intervention in the language domain limiting access to English lan-

TABLE 5 *Percentage of time at work where French is used: 1970 and 1979 for five occupations*

	Managers	Teachers, Health Workers	Office Workers	Sales People	Production Workers
1970					
— Men	63%	75%	70%	72%	83%
— Women	68%	82%	63%	82%	85%
1979					
— Men	75%	89%	81%	83%	90%
— Women	80%	88%	82%	86%	92%

Source: Vaillancourt (1981).

guage instruction for immigrant children in the primary and secondary school levels (e.g. Bill 22 and Bill 101). Studies of the evaluation of school attendance by language groups over the last ten years show that as a consequence of state intervention, French is making gains as a language of instruction. Though these gains still look small, their cumulative effects could be substantial in the long run. Indeed the weight of the francophone primary and secondary school sector has increased in the period from 1976 to 1981 (St-Germain, 1980). The change has resulted in part from the increasing birth rate since 1973 and from language policy in favour of French especially since 1977. Most impressive perhaps is the growing number of non-francophone children attending francophone schools. At the nursery school level, the change has been rapid, moving from 17% of such children in French nurseries in 1977–78 to 30% in 1979. The change is even more visible if only children of non-French/non-English mother tongue are taken into account. In 1971–72, 23.9% of these children were attending French nursery schools while in 1978–79, the attendance was up at 57.9%. Though the present changes are most dramatic amongst nursery school children they have not yet reached higher school levels where English instruction remains predominant for children whose mother tongue is neither English nor French. Finally, there are indications that changes in favour of French as a language of instruction may not be due entirely to the coercive elements built into Bill 101. An encouraging sign that attests to this trend is the increase since 1977 of the number of children eligible for English school instruction who prefer attending francophone schools: their number went from 3,690 in 1977 to 7,956 in 1979. This is probably as good an indicator as any that the status of French is changing in Quebec and that people are perceiving the pay-off of adjusting to that change (St-Germain, 1980; Vanasse, 1981; Proulx, 1980).

The impact of language planning on the economic situation

First, let us review what we now know about the economic impact of Bill 101. In the immediate period prior to and following the adoption of Bill 101, the Charter was viewed with great apprehension by businessmen and by important sectors of anglophone *and* francophone public opinion. An indication of this was a public opinion poll conducted by Multi-Réso (1978) among Quebec businessmen just a few months after the Charter was promulgated. Results showed that the economic consequences of the law came third in businessmen's scale of concerns after inflation and political uncertainty. However, a poll conducted at the end of 1980 again among businessmen showed that the Charter this time came in eleventh place in their concerns (Secor, 1980). The change of opinion of the general public was even more striking. A survey published in March of 1981 by *Finance*, a Montreal business weekly, showed that a majority of francophone Quebecers — namely 60.6% — thought that the Charter of the French Language has had either positive effects (31.1%) or no effect at all (29.5%) on the Quebec economy. Nevertheless 22.8% of francophones felt Bill 101 had a negative effect on the Quebec economy while 16.6% had no opinion. This, it must be emphasized, is the climate of opinion among francophone Quebecers; other Quebecers might have responded differently (see Taylor & Simard, this volume, chapter 7).

The point to make is that social evaluations of the economic impact of the Charter of the French Language are changing. The Charter is not seen any more, if it ever was, by francophones, as an economic threat. These changing evaluations of the Charter have much to do with the flexibility with which it is being implemented. Indeed, when the Charter is looked at from the viewpoint of its implementation, its economic costs look quite reasonable, well within the limits of business firms to cope with and, to some extent, offset by its economic benefits. What are the economic costs of Bill 101? We will be primarily concerned with its cost to business firms since, to our knowledge, there are no other measures available. This is unfortunate, but remains a limitation that we need to accept for the time being.

What is wrong with the Charter according to its critics (Boucher, 1977; Migué, 1979) is that it is protectionist legislation; meaning not that it aims to protect the French language in Quebec, but that it does so by creating undue barriers of communication and trade between the Quebec economy and the rest of the national, continental and international economy. These barriers, it is argued, are economically wasteful and will generate unfavorable economic consequences for Quebec: losses of jobs, major shortages of highly skilled manpower and excessive costs for business firms.

In my opinion, this pessimism is groundless for two major reasons. First, the predictions of the critics are nowhere empirically substantiated. Consequently, they look more like a moral condemnation of the Charter from the point of view of free trade economics than criticism based on an empirical evaluation of its economic impact. Indeed, we will show later that when such empirical evaluation is made, the results contradict pessimistic predictions. Second, the critics have based their argument on what is a truncated perception of the Charter. Two examples should suffice, which will be discussed before examining the question of costs proper. The first example has to do with the measures contained in the Charter with its regulations about the linguistic functioning of the head offices of business firms and that of industrial research and development units located in Quebec. The second one concerns the realm of education. They both show that when the economic impact of the Charter is evaluated from the point of view of how it is actually implemented, pessimistic predictions of its costs appear unjustified.

When the Charter was first designed by the government and later implemented by the Office de la langue française, a great deal of attention was given to the question of how to promote the use of French in business firms without at the same time cutting them off from the larger economic world where English is the main language of international communication for administrative, scientific and technological purposes. Two problems were central in this respect: the status of English as a language of communication for head offices of large national and multinational companies established in Quebec; and English usage within the research and development units established in Quebec by national business firms. The government not only wished to prevent the flight from Quebec of these strategic centers of administration and research but it was deeply concerned with creating a linguistic environment where they could grow. The decision was taken to grant a special status to these corporate entities within the legal framework of the Charter. In practice, English was to remain the primary language of business of these entities. What was asked of head offices of large corporations operating mainly outside Quebec and of research and development units, was to keep extending the use of French in their official relations with the Quebec government, in their administrative dealings with their francophone employees and, particularly, as far as head offices were concerned, with the local units which they are co-ordinating in Quebec. No legal constraint was imposed on their use of English or any other language as a medium of broader communication and a language of day-to-day internal functioning. Basically the working language of these corporate centers has remained English.

The impact of this adjustment on the ecnomic costs of the Charter for business firms is extremely significant since the law, as implemented, removes from their agenda the need to change in a basic way their customary pattern of linguistic functioning. The adjustment took the form of a particular regulation which was prepared in consultation with head offices and research personnel themselves. This regulation was well received and has posed as yet very few if any problems of application. A recent study of industrial research units (ADRIQ, 1981) concluded that among the 38 units where the survey was conducted only three reported having problems with the language Charter. These problems, it should be pointed out, have to do with the recruitment of highly skilled manpower. The source of this problem is reported to be not the Charter itself but current Quebec government fiscal policy. In all the other cases, the survey indicates that there are no difficulties with the law and that the use of French as a language of day-to-day communication is indeed making progress. This is a first example of how implementation has led to mutually satisfactory arrangements between business firms and the government (cf. Coleman, this volume, chapter 6).

Another example of the way implementation influences costs concerns the part of the Charter having to do with education. The accessibility of English language education at the primary and secondary levels for the children of people coming to Quebec from outside was a topic of heated controversy when the Charter of the French Language was publicly debated in late 1976 and early 1977. Because the Charter makes it mandatory for children of all people moving to Quebec, including Canadians from other provinces, to attend French-language schools at the primary and secondary levels, it was feared, especially among business people, that a major supply of highly skilled manpower would be lost. Anglophone managers, professionals and technicians would refuse to come to work in Quebec if their children were not allowed to receive their primary and secondary education in English public schools. At the post-secondary levels, the problem was absent since anglophone college and university education was not affected by the Charter. The government responded to these pressures by introducing in the final version of the Charter, section 85 which creates an exemption for children of people coming to Quebec on a temporary basis (see Bill 101, appendix 1). The exemption period is three years with a possible extension of three more years if necessary. These include members of the Armed Forces, diplomats and international officials, graduate students and employees of all categories brought to Quebec by their employers for short periods of time. These people have access to state-run English instruction for their children during the full length of their stay in Quebec. This legal arrangement is being implemented in ways that have direct bearings on the question of the economic impact of the Charter of the French Language. First, it is quite clear that the adjustment had led to a significant drop in the number of people whose children are not eligible for English-language instruction. Of all categories of Quebecers (whether residents or immigrants), the number who were refused access to English schools for their children went from 2,762 in 1978 when the Charter began to be applied to 337 in 1980. In percentage points, this represents a diminution from 11.5% to 2.6%. The drop cannot be explained by the provisions of section 85 alone but they must have seriously contributed to it. Second, the use of temporary resident status as a means of access to English-language instruction is increasing on the part of business firm personnel who move to Quebec for a short length of time. In 1978, 54.4% of people classified as temporary residents were employees of such firms while the percentage was 65.2% in 1980.

These adjustments which were arrived at during implementation have contributed to preventing friction between the requirements of the Charter and the needs of the Quebec economy. The adjustments which have been mentioned are probably the most crucial ones in terms of their economic implications since they remove the risk of Quebec losing important sources of jobs and economic growth. When they are taken into consideration, they make the most pessimistic predictions about Bill 101 debatable. Possibly other adjustments can be expected. For instance, proposals have been made recently by Quebec business leaders regarding the creation in Montreal of special schools for children of highly mobile parents. These schools would be organized on the pattern of those found in capitals throughout the world: international schools where the choice of the language of instruction takes account of the special needs of highly mobile children. If such proposals were to be co-operatively implemented by business and government, possible economic costs from the Charter would be further removed.

At the same time, one should not exaggerate the importance which barriers of admission to English-language schools have for people moving to Quebec. Indeed, these barriers are opportunities to enter French language schools and we know from consultations with personnel placement agencies in Montreal that executives and specialists of all kinds coming to work in Quebec respond positively to this opportunity for their children. In the same way, they see the need to work in French and live in a French milieu as an opportunity for self-development. Unfortunately, these attitudes are reported to be more frequently found among American and European than among Canadian managers and professionals. But this may change with time as the Charter of the French Language becomes accepted in Canada as a basic feature of the Quebec environment (Econosult, 1981).

We can now examine the results of two studies designed to assess the actual costs of implementing Bill 101. The findings of these preliminary studies do not support the pessimistic predictions made by critics of the Charter. The major findings of the studies are the following. The first set of findings concerns the total costs of implementing what is called "a francization program". These costs were computed from case studies of francization in individual firms. A first study by Allaire & Miller (1980) estimated that, in firms with 500 employees or more, implementing the Charter would cost about $60.00 per employee during the three years required by the law to design a francization program, getting it approved by the Office de la langue française and implementing it. For smaller firms, the cost would be about $50.00. The authors of the study have estimated that, for all firms employing 50 or more people, the annual cost of implementation would be around $96,000,000, or about 1/5 of 1% of Quebec's gross national product. This, as they mention, is not a negligible sum of money but it compares quite favorably with the costs of other government programs such as metrification, consumer's protection and environmental protection (see Miller, this volume, chapter 5).

Results from a second study by Econosult (1981) showed that in large firms interviewed at the time when francization programs were in their most active phase (that is in the first three years of implementation), costs incurred amounted to 0.1% to 0.5% of the firm's business turnover in Quebec. In one case, the cost of francization rose to 5.9% because the firm, a financial institution, had to acquire facilities to translate into French its monthly periodical published for the Quebec market. It must be added that these costs are before taxes. Considering that firms pay 36% and 13% of their profits respectively to the Canadian and Quebec governments, it follows that they pay in practice only half of the cost of francization, the rest being defrayed by the taxpayers. Furthermore, part of the remaining costs, one can assume, will be paid by the firms' trading partners: its suppliers and its customers.

For small and medium-sized firms, however, the above studies showed that expenses involved in implementing a francization program were somewhat lower. Francization programs in such firms are usually smaller in scale due to a less complex system of communication. It must also be mentioned that many of the small and medium-sized firms were owned by French-speaking businessmen who already operated in French and faced few problems in meeting the requirements of the law.

A second set of findings has to do with the types of costs involved in implementing a francization program. Both studies mentioned above arrived at the conclusion that four types of costs were most important: 1) translation, 2) language training, 3) administrative costs and 4) consultation costs. The Econosult (1981) study showed that translation costs are by far the most important, accounting for as much as 50% to 75% of the total cost of francization. Language training costs are much lower. They apply mainly to the teaching of French to unilingual anglophones and entail up to 36% of the total cost of implementation. Administrative costs and consultation costs are much lower, seldom reaching 15% of total expenses. It must be noted that these costs are temporary. Once a technical document has been translated, it may have to be kept up-to-date, but the major expense of putting it into French has been incurred. The same is true for language training costs: an employee begins a French course and finishes it at one point in time. Administrative and consultation costs are even more temporary since, after a francization program has been designed and is applied, the cost should decline.

One can conclude by saying that the economic costs of Bill 101, at least the costs which the law entails for business firms, have been overestimated, if not simply exaggerated by its critics. When the Charter is examined, not in the abstract, but from the point of view of how it is *implemented*, its economic costs appear to be low and entirely within the limits acceptable to business firms. But, costs are one thing. What about economic benefits? We shall now turn to this question.

There is an economic rationale in Bill 101, an "unstated premise", suggesting that the affirmation of the French language, of its status, of its opportunites for use, of its social usefulness and its numerical strength will bring economic benefits to *francophone* Quebecers. This has not always been apparent for the opponents of the Charter, and for obvious reasons, but if the economic rationale was not there in the first place, why would the priority of the law be the francization of the workplace? The economic gamble behind the Charter would seem to be that francization will make Quebec francophones more satisfied and probably more productive. This assumption makes sense when one considers the close link that exists between language and identity in French Quebec (Taylor, Bassili & Aboud, 1973). Indeed, since this link is close, it should be expected that improving the status of the French language will contribute to the social identity of francophone Quebecers, making it more positive, more secure, more satis-

TABLE 6 *The benefits of francization for francophone employees as reported by francophone managers in 15 Quebec firms*

Type of benefit	Number of firms where favourable changes were reported
Better management-labour relations (fewer greivances)	5/15
Better employee morale and increased job satisfaction	7/15
Fewer work accidents	0/15
Better corporate identification	3/15
More efficient communications	6/15
Better productivity and job motivation	8/15
More creativity, participation and initiative, especially among managers	9/15
Fewer problems of recruitment, especially at the managerial level	7/15

Source: Econosult (1981).

fying and consequently produce beneficial results, both economically and otherwise (Fishman, 1972; Giles, Bourhis & Taylor, 1977; Ross, 1979).

Let us examine the findings of an Econosult (1981) study which have to do with the impact of francization on various aspects of the performance of business firms. Two words of caution seem necessary before we present these findings. First, the study reports on the benefits of francization as they are perceived by managers who are personally involved in francization programs. The findings are not direct measures of economic performance, such as the ones found in usual productivity and job satisfaction studies. Second, the findings concern business firms where francization has been relatively intense. Consequently, the results can certainly not be generalized to apply to all firms and it would seem that, as an attempt to evaluate the benefits of francization programs, the findings must be taken as approximations.

Table 6 summarizes the findings of the Econosult (1981) survey for 15 firms where data on the impact of francization were collected extensively. Note that the data concern the effects of francization on *francophone* employees only.

Table 6 suggests that francization is beneficial for business firms but not in an overwhelming way. However, there are some interesting changes occurring, since francophone managers report that morale and job satisfaction, as well as productivity and job motivation, have improved. Respondents also report more creativity, participation and initiative, especially among managers. There are also fewer problems of managerial recruitment. These last two changes seem important. Business firms where English predominates as a language of work often report difficulties recruiting young francophone university graduates and keeping them once they have been recruited. By removing this problem, francization creates at least two important benefits for such firms: that of increasing their opportunities to profit from the wealth of human francophone resources now available in Quebec; and that of facilitating their own francization since we know that having a stable French-speaking managerial staff greatly helps a firm to function in French. Finally, reports that francization can increase creativity, productivity and job satisfaction particularly among francophone managers is perhaps not too surprising. Francophone managers in Quebec have traditionally had to use a great deal of English on the job. It should not be surprising to learn that increasing their opportunities to use their mother tongue at work could have positive effects not only on their participation and initiative but also on their productivity, morale and job satisfaction (Lamy, 1978).

Though "francization" seems beneficial for francophone employees, the responses of anglophone employees are, generally speaking, more negative than positive. Among the firms interviewed by Econosult (1981), many have reported various manifestations of opposition and resistance to francization by anglophones: complaints, requests for transfer and reluctance to learn French and use it. These reactions were to be anticipated since francization is seen as a cost by many anglophones: lost opportunity to use their mother tongue as the language of work and loss of status for their language group. These constitute identity threats for anglophones that result from language planning in favour of French in Quebec. A number of studies have investigated anglophone minority group reactions to both Bill 22 (Stein, 1977; Smith, Tucker & Taylor, 1977) and Bill 101 (Heller, 1982; Taylor & Simard, this volume, chapter 7; Bourhis, this volume, chapter 8). It can be argued, however, that francization of business firms need not be achieved at such great costs for anglophone employees. First, the Charter, which does not set a terminal point for the implementation of French as a language of communication and production in business firms, leaves ample room for people to adapt to change. Francization is assumed to be a developmental process which can evolve indefinitely while being self-sustaining. Second, it is necessary to realize that French is already a widely-used language in Quebec business firms. The Charter extends French usage rather than introducing it from scratch. We have seen that both knowledge and usage of French is increasing in numerous domains of language use including the

Quebec business world. The trends observed in business firms suggest that opportunities to learn and use French on the part of anglophone employees are abundant and that the Charter, rather than being seen as a threat, could be viewed as a realistic challenge.

Finally, Putzel (1980) suggested that *how* francization programs are implemented in business firms can make all the difference. Putzel (1980) concluded that if more time was given for discussion, experimentation and adaptation during the implementation of francization programs as suggested in the literature on organizational development, there would be less distress and the benefits would be more readily perceived by all the participants. If this suggestion was taken more seriously, there is little doubt that much of what is left of the threatening image of the Charter would disappear.

Our analysis of the economic impact of the Charter of the French language remains inevitably incomplete. Many would argue that other measures of economic performance, especially more macro-economic ones, are needed before we can arrive at a convincing evaluation. Incomplete as it is, our analysis has shown that, as far as business firms are concerned, the costs of the Charter are well within the limits of their ability to adjust to the new linguistic environment without undue stress on their performance. In addition, some of these economic costs are offset by benefits for franco-phone managers employed in firms that have been prompt to implement the francization programs.

Conclusion

Our purpose was to analyze the emergence and the impact of language planning in Quebec over the last fifteen years. We have shown that the status of French relative to that of English has been improved: French is more extensively used in several domains of social life and its place in Quebec society has been strengthened. However, it is much more difficult to con-clude about the magnitude of change: mass perceptions would seem to indicate that it has been substantial while the evolution of actual language usage patterns seem to suggest that change has been slow even if self-sustained. The question of the magnitude of change, then, poses many problems of evaluation which remain unsolved for the time being.

One intriguing finding concerns the status of English as a language of economic advancement in Quebec. Mass perceptions suggest that English has maintained much of its status relative to French as the language of business. This finding is unexpected given the many recent studies showing that the socio-economic status of francophones has improved over the last ten years (Bernard & Renaud, 1980; Vaillancourt, 1979, 1981). More specifically, since these studies indicate that the share of managerial jobs held by francophones is increasing, we expected that the salience of English as a language of economic advancement should have declined. However, survey results showed a slow decline and in some cases an increase in the perceived importance of English. As the socio-economic status of francophones improved in the business world, francophones may have become even more aware of the importance of English in the international business community.

Also important is what we have seen regarding the economic impact of language planning and especially its costs for business firms. Our review of available research suggests that these costs are less than one might have expected. We have seen that such costs might even be compensated by financial benefits having to do with the ways francophone employees are responding to their improved opportunities to use their own language at work. We have argued that the actual costs of change have much to do with how language planning is being implemented through consultation, negotiation and accommodation. More than the question of economic costs and benefits there is the issue of legitimizing the aims and means of language planning to the general public. If language planning was seen as a threat to the material well-being of Quebec society, its future prospects would be greatly compromised. Indeed, we have seen that while language planning in favour of French has received strong support from the francophone majority, much less support for these measures has come forth from Quebec anglophone and allophone minorities (d'Anglejan, this volume, chapter 2; Taylor & Simard, this volume, chapter 7; Bourhis, this volume, chapter 8; Caldwell, this volume, chapter 9).

We have assumed throughout this chapter that favourable changes in the status of French was the consequence of language planning. But, how do we know that this is so? How do we establish the causal link between the growth of language planning activities and the improvement of the status of French? Indeed, one could argue that such linkage does not exist and that the changing status of French is the product of much broader social trends which span a longer period than the ones we have envisaged. For instance, Laponce (1980) argued that language groups have a natural tendency to concentrate demographically within a given territory. In the case of Quebec, such concentration, which was supported by industrialization and urbanization, created strong social demands for the use of French in an increasing number of social domains which had the effect of increasing the status of French and francophones quite independently of conscious interventions by the State. Another argument could simply be that the increase in French language status was the result of improved educational facilities for francophones, who consequently played a more active role in the business and corporate world. In this case, the supply of qualified francophones and the anticipatory adjustments of business firms could have been more important than language planning *per se* (Vaillancourt, 1981). One can mention, finally, the growing more sophisticated Québécois francophone commercial market as a powerful source of social pressures for francization.

The assumption that the rising status of French is the result of language planning is difficult to prove. However, mass perceptions leave no doubt that such a link is seen to exist: when people are asked about what accounts for the changing status of the French language, State intervention is spontaneously and systematically seen as an important factor. Such results were especially clear in survey studies conducted since the promulgation of Bill 101 (Multi-Réso, 1978; Crop, 1979; Crop, 1980; Crop, 1981). Another factor which reinforces the link between language planning and the changing status of French is the institutionalization of language planning activity itself. As state-run language planning activities become more "professionalized" and more important in terms of budgets and staff, it becomes more difficult to deny that this type of activity has had an impact on the status of French in Quebec (Breton & Grant, 1981). Finally, it would seem that by raising the cost for non-francophones to move to Quebec and by lowering the benefits for unilingual anglophones to stay in Quebec, successive language legislations (especially Bill 22 and Bill 101) have increased French linguistic homogeneity, thus raising the status of French in Quebec. At best, however, these are rough ways of assessing the link between language planning and the changing status of French in Quebec, consequently our evaluation must remain tentative.

Acknowledgements

I would like to thank Richard Y. Bourhis for his very useful comments on earlier drafts of this chapter.

Notes

1. This useful analytical distinction was first made by Breton & Grant in their recent book on the language of work in Quebec (Breton & Grant, 1980). The distinction points to two functions of language in work organizations: as instruments for transmitting information and as skills that one is expected to possess to be eligible for advancement and promotion in work organizations. Breton & Grant argue that the two functions need not be strongly correlated. For instance, French can become generalized as a language of communication while English remains essential as a language of advancement.

References

ALLAIRE, Y., & MILLER, R. 1980, *Les entreprises canadiennes et la loi sur la francisation des milieux de travail.* Montréal: Institut C. D. Howe.

ADRIQ, 1981, Association des Directeurs de Recherche Industrielles du Québec. *Rapport du president.* Montréal.

BERNARD, P. & RENAUD, J. 1980, *L'évolution de la situation socio-économique des francophones et des non-francophones au Québec (1971–1978).* Montréal: Office de la langue française.

BOUCHARD, P., & BEAUCHAMP-ACHIM, S. 1980, *Le français, langue des commerces et des services publics.* Québec: Dossier du Conseul de la langue française, Etudes et recherches, No. 5, Gouvernement du Québec, Editeur officiel du Québec.

BOUCHER, M. 1977, *La loi 101: Une approche économique.* Québec: Ecole Nationale d'Administration.

BOURBONNAIS, J. P. 1979, L'Evolution de la demande de cadres bilingues dans l'enterprise privée anglophone au Québec de 1974 à 1978. *Gestion*, 4, 60–67.

BOURDIEU, P. 1979, Les trois états du capital culturel. Paris: *Actes de la recherche en sciences sociales*, 30.

BOURGEOIS, M., & GIRARD, B. 1982, *Réactions des touristes à la francisation de l'affichage et de la publicité commerciale au Québec.* Montréal: Studax Inc.

BOURHIS, R. Y. 1982, Language policies and language attitudes: "le monde de la francophonie". In: E. BOUCHARD-RYAN & H. GILES (eds), *Attitudes towards language variation: social and applied context.* London: Edward Arnold.

BOUTHILLIER, G. 1981, *Aux origines de la planification linguistique Québécoise: L'Etat et la planification linguistique.* Montreal: Office de la langue française, Montréal: Editeur officiel du Québec.

BOUTHILLIER, G., & MEYNAUD, J. 1972, *Le choc des langues au Québec 1760–1970.* Montreal: Presses de l'Université du Québec.

BRETON, R., & GRANT, G. 1981, *La langue de travail au Québec.* Montréal: L'Institut de recherches politiques.

CANADA. 1969, Royal Commission on Bilingualism and Biculturalism, Vol. 3: *The Work World.* Ottawa: Queen's Printer.

CASTONGUAY, C., & MARION, J. 1974, L'anglicisation du Canada. *Bulletin de l'Association des démographes du Québec*, 3, 19–40.

CHARBONNEAU, H., & MAHEU, R. 1973, *Les aspects démographiques de la question linguistique.* Québec: Editeur officiel du Québec.

CORBEIL, J. C. 1980, *L'Aménagement linguistique du Québec.* Montréal: Guérin.

CROP. 1979, *Le bulletin Crop*, Montréal: November.

— 1980, *Le bulletin Crop*, Montréal, November.

— 1981, *Le bulletin Crop*, Montréal, December.

DAOUST, D. 1982, Corpus and status language planning in Quebec: In: J. L. COBARRUBIAS (ed.), *Progress in Language Planning: International Perspective.* Paris & New York: Mouton Publishers.

DAS GUPTA, J. 1977, Language Planning in India. In: Joan RUBIN *et al.* (eds), *Language Planning Processes*, Paris & New York: Mouton Publishers.

ECONOSULT. 1981, *Etude sur les advantages et les couts de la francisation*. Montréal: Office de la langue française, Editeur officiel du Québec.

FERGUSON, C. A. 1962, The Language Factor in National Development. In F. A. RICI (ed.), *Study of the Role of Second Languages*, Washington, D.C.: Center for Applied Linguistics.

FISHMAN, J. A. 1972, *Language and Nationalism*. Rowley, Massachusetts: Newbury House.

— 1974, Language Planning and Language Planning Research: The State of the Art. In J. A. FISHMAN (ed.), *Advances in Language Planning*. Paris & New York: Mouton Publishers.

GILES, H., BOURHIS, R. Y., & TAYLOR, D. 1977, Towards a theory of language in ethnic group relations. In H. GILES (ed.), *Language, ethnicity and intergroup relations*. London & New York: Academic Press.

HELLER, M. 1982, *Le processus de francisation dans une entreprise Montréalaise: une analyse sociolinguistique*. Montreal: Office de la langue française, Editeur officiel du Québec.

HENRIPIN, J. 1976, Quebec and the Demographic Dilemma of French Canadian Society. In P. LAMY (ed.), *Bilingualism in Montreal: Linguistic Interference and Communicational Effectiveness*. Papers in Linguistics, REDNA DARNELL (ed.), Fall–Winter.

INAGAKI, M. 1980, *La situation linguistique dans les CRDI au Québec. Vol. 2.* Montreal: Office de la langue française, Editeur officiel du Québec.

JANNARD, M. 1981, Les cadres supérieurs francophones: Très lente percée dans les grande entreprises. *La Presse*, Samedi, 20 juin 1981.

JOY, R. J. 1972, *Language in conflict*. Toronto: McClelland & Stewart.

KRALT, J. 1976, *Profile Studies: Languages in Canada*, Vol. 5, Part 1 (Bulletin 5, 1–7) Ottawa: Statistics Canada.

KLOSS, H. 1969, *Research Possibilities on Group Bilingualism: A Report*. Quebec: Centre internationale de recherche sur le bilinguisme. Les Presses de l'Université Laval.

LAMY, P. 1978, *Bilingualism and Work Satisfaction. The Canadian Case*. Paper presented at the 9th World Congress of Sociology. Uppsala, Sweden.

LAPONCE, J. 1980, Le comportement spatial des groupes linguistiques: solutions personnelles et territoriales aux problemes des minorités. *International Political Science Review*, 1, 478–495.

LAPORTE, P. E. 1974, *L'usage des langues dans la vie économique au Québec*. Québec: Synthese 7, Commission sur la situation du français et les droits linguistiques, Editeur officiel du Québec.

MALLEA, J. R. 1977, Introduction. In J. R. MALLEA (ed.), *Quebec's Language Policies: Background and Response*. Quebec: Centre internationale de recherche sur le bilinguisme. Les Presses de l'Université Laval.

MIGUÉ, J. L. 1979, *L'économiste et la chose publique*. Montréal: Les Presses de l'Université du Québec.

MULTI-RÉSO. 1978, *Survey of Business Opinions*. Montréal: Quebec Chamber of Commerce.

PROULX, J. P. 1980, *L'accesibilité aux écoles anglophones et la Charte de la langue française*. Quebec: Ministere de l'Education du Québec.

PUTZEL, R. 1980, *Le haut patronat et la francisation des entreprises*. Montréal: Office de la langue française, Editeur Officiel du Québec.

QUEBEC, GOVERNMENT OF, 1972, *Report of the Commission of Inquiry on the Position of the French Language and on Language Rights in Quebec* (Gendron Commission). Québec: Editeur Officiel du Quebec.

RIOUX, M. 1974, *Les Québécois*. Paris: Editions du Seuil.

ROSS, J. A. 1979, Language and the mobilization of ethnic identity. In H. GILES & B. SAINT-JACQUES (eds), *Language and Ethnic Relations*. Oxford & New York: Pergamon Press.

RUBIN, J. 1979, *Directory of Language Planning Organizations*. Honolulu, Hawaii: East-West Culture Learning Institute, East-West Center.

SÉCOR. 1980, *Le processus de francisation dans 10 grandes entreprises établies au Québec*. Montréal: Office de la langue française.

SMITH, P. M., TUCKER, G. R., & TAYLOR, D. M. 1977, Language, Ethnic Identity and Intergroup Relations: One Immigrant Group's Reaction to Language Planning in Quebec. In H. GILES (ed.), *Language, Ethnicity and Intergroup Relations*. London & New York: Academic Press.

STEIN, M. B. 1977, Bill 22 and the Non-Francophone Population in Quebec: A Case Study of Minority Group Attitudes on Language Legislation. In J. R. MALLEA (ed.), *Quebec Language Policies: Background and Response*. Québec: Centre Internationale de recherche sur le bilinguisme, Les Presses de l'Université Laval.

SIEGFRIED, A. 1907, *The Race Question in Canada*. London: Eveleigh Nash.

ST-GERMAIN, C. 1980, *Provisions de la clientele scolaire selon le réseau d'enseignement: 1976–77 à 1981–82*. Québec: Editeur officiel du Québec.

TANEAU, V. 1980, *French is Money*. Montreal: Opération Solidarité Economique, Editeur officiel du Québec.

TAYLOR, D., BASSILI, J., & ABOUD, F. 1973, Dimensions of ethnic identity: an example from Quebec. *Journal of Social Psychology*, 89, 185–192.

VAILLANCOURT, F. 1979, *Les cadres québécois et la présence des francophones: L'évolution récente et la situation en 1971*. Montreal: Secor Inc.

— 1981, *The Economics of Language Planning: An Application to the Case of Quebec (1960–1980)*. Paper read at the Sixth International Congress of Applied Linguistics, Lund, Sweden.

VAILLANCOURT, F., & DANEAU, A. 1980, *L'évolution des exigences linguistiques pour les postes de cadres et d'ingénieurs au Québec — 1970 à 1979*. Montréal: Département des sciences économiques, Université de Montréal, Cahier 8035.

VANASSE, D. 1981, *L'évolution de la population scolaire du Québec*. Montréal: Institut de recherches politiques.

WEISS, C. H. 1972, *Evaluation Research*. Englewood Cliffs, N.J.: Prentice Hall.

4 Francization and terminology change in Quebec business firms

Denise Daoust
Office de la langue française

The Charter of the French language (Bill 101), adopted in August 1977 by the Parti Québécois government, institutes French as the official language of Quebec in all public domains of Quebec's society. French is declared the language of legislature and the courts, of the civil administration, of the public utility firms, of the professional corporations, of labour relations, of instruction and of commerce and business. Whereas "natural persons", that is, individuals, are not directly touched by these measures, Bill 101 sees to it that all "artificial" or public persons deal in French in all public activities. Bill 101 provides ample measures to ensure that French is used in all public domains in order that it acquire, through these measures, the prestige once held by English. Thus, linguistic change is but a step toward the more fundamental aim of changing the socio-economic and sociolinguistic environment of Quebec. Although Bill 101 may be seen as status language planning in favour of French, it can also be viewed as corpus language planning aimed at promoting French usage in both everyday and technical domains of language use. Thus, following Kloss's definition, as discussed in Fishman (1974) and the current literature on language planning, the Charter of the French language can be analyzed from both a status and a corpus language planning point of view.

In this chapter, we shall focus our attention on the corpus language planning measures explicitly or implicitly contained in Bill 101 regarding the francization of Quebec business firms. First, after having examined the measures imposed by the law for the francization of business firms we shall discuss the specific measures prescribed for the francization of terminology. We shall see how this aspect of corpus language planning is complementary to the more extensively developed and more specifically described measures regarding the status language planning component of the francization of business firms and which make up the bulk of the francization programs. To do so, we shall describe the aims and working of both the francization programs in general and the terminology programs as well as the services offered to the business firms by the Office de la langue française (OLF), the language board responsible for the application of the law. This will enable us to measure the importance of the francization of terminology with respect to a general francization program as well as the specific problems linked to the implementation and adoption of a new terminology. Having paid attention to some major factors influencing terminological change in Quebec business firms, the chapter will close with a discussion of the language planning strategies most likely to increase the use of French terminology in Quebec firms.

1. Cultivation and elaboration approaches to language planning in Quebec

Historically, Quebec has always been aware of the necessity of preserving its French language not only from the influence of English, but also from the danger of developing a variety of French which would be substantially different from the variety spoken in France (Daoust, 1982). Thus, in 1961, in its earliest official attempt at language planning, the Quebec government initiated, with the creation of its first language board, language planning which could be best described, following Neustupny's typology (1970), as a *cultivation* approach to language planning. In fact, the main task of the 1961 language board was one of determining matters of *correctness* regarding the French variety spoken in Quebec and, more generally, of defining which variety of French should be used in Quebec. However, another type of language planning was initiated by the 1961 language board which could be described, following Neustupny (1970), as an *elaboration* approach. This approach aimed at expanding the use of French in a broader range of domains including the technological and scientific fields.

In order to do so and thus add a new broader sociolinguistic function to French in Quebec, extensive terminological work was undertaken to either translate English or American terms in French or adapt the technical terms used in France to the Quebec reality. A few French-Canadian local terms were promoted and, when necessary, new French terms were proposed. At first, there was no policy as to what type of terminological work was to be undertaken. Since French terminology was needed in every industrial and economic sector, the first language board concentrated its efforts on those sectors where the largest number of workers were involved, namely the mining industries and other primary industrial sectors.

After 1972, however, the language board oriented its terminological research towards those vocabularies which were common to most industrial sectors: that is, the general technical vocabulary as well as the vocabulary relating to general management and administration. This general policy was adopted following the conclusions of the Gendron Commission (Quebec, 1972). Thus, in 1976, the Régie de la langue française, the language board created by Bill 22 (the linguistic law preceding the Charter of the French language), published a policy paper (Régie de la langue française, 1976) where it stated its goals regarding terminological work. The language board took on the responsibility of general terminology work in all public domains while it stated that all terminological work related to specific work domains were to be undertaken by the business firms concerned. This second language board prefigured the present orientation in language planning in that it favored a status-oriented language planning approach to the detriment of a corpus-oriented one.

Actually, the cultivation type of corpus planning approach was abandoned, officially at least, after 1974, when Bill 22 became operative under the Liberal government. Whereas the first language board had proclaimed in 1965 that variation between standard European French and Quebec French should be reduced to a minimum in everyday language, the second language board now proclaimed that French-speaking Quebecers were equal partners with France regarding the evolution of the French language. A distinction was made between everyday language, technical language and official language (Corbeil, 1975a). As regards everyday language, the official policy was that, from a language planning perspective, individuals should be provided with the opportunity to become aware of the existence of different speech styles in order to adapt their own speech style to different social and cultural circumstances. As for the technical vocabulary, the objective was to reduce, as much as possible, the differences between the Quebec and French usage, this being justified by the fact that scientific and technical domains do not admit linguistic divergences. The main target of this language planning strategy, was the "Official Language", that is, the oral and written language of the state and the media. This form of French was to be "as close as possible to the French spoken in France", every single difference having to be justified.

2. Francization and the Charter of the French language

As we have already mentioned, the coming into force of the Charter of the French language in 1977 resulted in an intensification of the Quebec government's linguistic planning efforts toward the promotion of French in all public domains. Even though the previous law, Bill 22, had marked a spectacular shift toward status language planning, the Charter of the French language was to initiate an even more systematic approach to language planning. The measures provided by the Charter of the French language reflect a "conscious, predictive approach to changes in language and language use" (Rubin & Jernudd, 1971). Bill 101 can really be viewed as the source of both "a political and administrative activity for solving language problems" (Jernudd & Das Gupta, 1971) and thus can be examined as an official approach to language planning. In fact, what characterizes the Charter of the French language is that it provides ample measures and guidelines for the implementation of the language decisions it puts forth as well as, in accordance with Das Gupta's (1972) definition, "an ordered schedule of time" for the implementation process.

Francization programs and the business firms

The language planning approach of the Charter is reflected in the administrative measures designed by the law to implement the Francization of Quebec business firms. First of all, the law prescribes general francization measures aiming at the francization of the commerce and business world as well as the francization of the language of work. Thus, as far as business firms are concerned, firm names, signs, posters, as well as job-application forms, order forms, contracts, catalogues, brochures, instructions on products, toys and games have to be in French. As for firm names, public signs and posters, only French can be used. These measures have the effect of putting an end to the bilingual image of Quebec. As regards the language of work, the Charter decrees that all written communications to employees shall be in French and that offers of employment or promotion shall also be in French (see Bill 101, section 41, this volume, Appendix 1). Exclusive knowledge of French or insufficient knowledge of a language other than French cannot be a reason for dismissing, laying off, demoting or transferring a staff member (section 43). Finally, the obtaining of an employment dependent upon the knowledge of a language other than French is prohibited: the burden of proof that the knowledge of such a language is needed falls upon the employer, and the Office de la langue française (OLF) has the power to rule on any dispute (section 46). Actually, of the 10 admissible cases examined by the OLF between August 26, 1977 and May 18, 1983, 5 firms were authorized to declare certain jobs as specifically requiring the knowledge of English.

Moreover, failure to respect these provisions may result in a fine. For example, a first offence may bring a fine of $25 to $500 plus costs for a "natural" person while fines of $50 to $1,000 plus costs apply to "artificial" persons. The fines are more important for any subsequent offense (section 205).

Between April 1981 and April 1983, the OLF received 14,500 complaints regarding infringements of the law. Out of these, 23 cases were brought to court, 11 of which were settled by Quebec's Attorney General. Of these latter cases, nine firms were condemned to fines, one firm was acquitted and one firm complied with the law before having been tried. All of the other complaints brought to the attention of OLF were settled out of court.

In addition, the Charter decrees that every public utility and business firm employing fifty or more employees is required to obtain a "francization certificate" attesting that the firm is applying a "francization program" or that French already enjoys a high enough status in the firm so that no such program is needed (sections 135–138). Furthermore, all of the above firms must hold such a francization certificate by December 31, 1983 at the latest although, of course, the implementation process of the francization program may last much longer. It is to be noted that every business firm which will not have obtained its certificate by this date will be "liable, in addition to costs, to a fine of $100 to $2,000 for each day during which it carries on its business without a certificate" (section 206).

For firms employing less than fifty employees, the Charter declares that the Office "may, with the approval of the Minister and on condition of a notice in the *Gazette officielle du Québec*, require a business firm employing less than fifty persons to analyze its language situation and to prepare and implement a francization program" (section 151).

The new language board, the "Office de la langue française" (OLF), which replaces the last two language boards, is given the mandate to ensure that French becomes "the language of communication, work, commerce and business in the civil administration and business firms" (section 100). The OLF has the authority to direct and approve the francization operation of business firms, as well as to issue or suspend francization certificates. It is also responsible for setting up terminology committees, standardizing and publicizing the terms and expressions it approves (sections 113–114).

The Charter also provides more general guidelines concerning the objectives of francization programs which are intended to generalize the use of French in all Quebec business firms. As is evident in section 141 of Bill 101 (see Appendix 1, this volume) the francization program has the following goals:

a) knowledge of French by the management, the members of the professional corporations and other staff members;
b) an increase, at all levels, in the number of persons having a good knowledge of French;
c) the use of French as the language of work and as the language of internal communications as well as of the working documents of the business firms and in communications with clients, suppliers and the public;
d) the use of French terminology;
e) the use of French in advertising; and
f) appropriate policies for hiring, promotion and transfer.

Let us now examine how the above francization guidelines are actually applied to large and medium sized business firms in Quebec.

Business firms employing more than 100 persons

There are four stages in the francization procedure for business firms employing more than 100 persons. To facilitate its administrative procedure, the OLF established 12 classes of business firms distributed in 10 sectors representing 37 types of economic activities and taking into account the number of employees in each firm. Each class of business firms was then assigned a date of eligibility for assistance from the OLF, which constitutes the first stage of the legal francization procedure. Each firm is also issued with requirement dates for each of the three subsequent legal procedures involved in the francization process (see Table 1 & 2 for details). Thus, each business firm may, by a specific date, ask the OLF for its help in undertaking its francization procedures. The OLF then sends a specialist, called a "program negotiator" in order to help the firm undertake the necessary official steps of the francization procedures.

From this date, the firms have three months in which to ask officially for what is known as a "temporary francization certificate". This will be granted if the firm completes a questionnaire form requesting general information on the firm's internal structure and business activities. Firms must also provide the names of the persons making up the firm's francization committee. This committee becomes responsible for the application of all franciza-

TABLE 1 *Francization schedule for firms employing 500 persons or more in Quebec*

Economic Sector	Category	Eligibility date for help from the OLF	Eligibility date for the certificate	Requirement date for the approval of the francization certificate	Deliverance of the Permanent francization certificate
1a Retail Trade	A	7–1–78	7–5–78	7–5–79	7–5–81
1b Public Works and Construction Industry	↓	↓	↓	↓	↓
2a Transportation and Storage					
2b Accommodation and Food Services					
2c Communications					
2d Paper Industries					
3a Wholesale Trade	B	7–5–78	7–9–78	7–9–79	7–9–81
3b Food and Beverage Industries	↓	↓	↓	↓	↓
4a Financial Institutions					
4b Personnel Services					
4c Miscellaneous Services					
4d Insurance					
5a Insurance Agencies and Real Estate Industry					
5b Agriculture					
5c Mine, Quarries & Oil Wells					
6 Clothing Industries					
7a Metal Fabricating Industries					
7b Primary Metal Industries					
7c Forestry					
7d Services to Business Management					
8a Wood Industries					
8b Public Utilities					
8c Amusements and Recreation Services					
8d Printing and Publishing					
8e Electrical Product Industries					
9a Miscellaneous Manufacturing Industries					
9b Chemical Industries					
9c Machinery & Transportation Equipment Industries					
9d Furniture & Fixture Industries					
10a Non Metallic Product Industries					
10b Fishing & Hunting					
10c Rubber & Plastic Product Industries					
10d Petroleum & Coal Product Industries					
10e Leather Industries					
10f Knitting Mills					
10g Tobacco Product Industries					

TABLE 2 *Francization schedule for firms employing between 100 and 499 persons in Quebec*

Economic Sector	Category	Eligibility date for help from the OLF	Eligibility date for the francization certificate	Requirement date for the approval of the francization certificate	Deliverance of the Permanent francization certificate
1a Retail Trade 1b Public Works and Construction Industry	C	7–6–78	7–10–78	7–10–79	7–10–81
2a Transportation and Storage 2b Accommodation and Food Services 2c Communications 2d Paper Industries	D	7–12–78	7–4–79	7–4–80	7–4–82
3a Wholesale Trade 3b Food and Beverage Industries	E	7–4–79	7–8–79	7–8–80	7–8–82
4a Financial Institutions 4b Personnel Services 4c Miscellaneous Services 4d Insurance	F	7–6–79	7–10–79	7–10–80	7–10–82
5a Insurance Agencies and Real Estate Industry 5b Agriculture 5c Mine, Quarries & Oil Wells	G	7–8–79	7–12–79	7–12–80	7–12–82
6 Clothing Industries	H	7–10–79	7–2–80	7–2–81	7–2–83
7a Metal Fabricating Industries 7b Primary Metal Industries 7c Forestry 7d Services to Business Management	I	7–1–80	7–5–80	7–5–81	7–5–83
8a Wood Industries 8b Public Utilities 8c Amusements and Recreation Services 8d Printing and Publishing 8e Electrical Product Industries	J	7–5–80	7–9–80	7–9–81	7–9–83
9a Miscellaneous Manufacturing Industries 9b Chemical Industries 9c Machinery & Transportation Equipment Industries 9d Furniture & Fixture Industries	K	7–7–80	7–11–80	7–11–81	7–11–83

10a Non Metallic Product Industries	7–8–80	7–12–80	7–12–81	.7–12–83
10b Fishing & Hunting				
10c Rubber & Plastic Product Industries				
10d Petroleum & Coal Product Industries L				
10e Leather Industries				
10f Knitting Mills				
10g Tobacco Product Industries				

tion measures inside the firm and is given the mandate to negotiate with the OLF regarding the francization measures needed by the firm. The francization committee of firms employing 100 and more persons were to be formed by November 30th, 1977. These committees were made up of at least six persons, a third of whom had to officially represent salaried employees.

The granting of the temporary francization certificate, which is valid for three years, initiates the second official francization stage. During this second phase each firm must analyze its linguistic situation and present its analysis to the OLF's certification committee within the year following the requirement date of its provisional francization certificate. This linguistic analysis is done with the help of the program negotiator using special forms designed by the OLF (Office de la langue française, 1978a, b).

After examining the firm's linguistic situation, the OLF then determines whether the use of French is generalized enough so that the firm does not have to elaborate and apply a francization program. If this is so, a permanent francization certificate is delivered. If not, the firm is asked to elaborate and present a francization program.

All francization programs have to be examined and approved within the year following the eligibility date for the provisional certificate. The francization program is elaborated by the firm's francization committee, with the help of the OLF program negotiator. Its main objective is the generalization of the use of French at all levels and in all activities of the firm. It must take into account the conclusions of the preceding linguistic analysis as well as each provision included in section 141 of the law.

Note that the OLF deals directly with each business firm concerned and all francization programs are negotiated on an individual basis. The elaboration of the francization program is done in constant collaboration with the OLF staff members who see to it that all relevant elements are included in the francization program presented by the firm. In order to help the firms in the elaboration of their francization program, the OLF has devised a standard model program in which it defines the objectives of such a program, the domains that it must cover and suggested timetables for the different stages involved (Office de la langue française, 1978c).

Actually, as we have already mentioned, staff members of the OLF act as technical advisors throughout the whole administrative process. Thus, they help the business firm with the analysis of its linguistic situation and they also help elaborate the francization program. They are the ones who negotiate with the firm until they reach an agreement for a francization program that can be presented to the OLF certification committee. Two types of specialists supply help to the business firms: a person knowledgeable in business working and administration: the "program negotiator", and a terminology specialist: the "consulting linguist". The crucial role of these specialists in implementing the francization of Quebec business firms is evident when one considers that the number of program negotiators has increased from about 30 in 1978 to nearly 50 in 1983. As for the consulting linguists the OLF started with four specialists in 1978 and now has seven.

After the francization program has been elaborated, it is presented to the OLF certification committee who either approves it or asks the firm to make the necessary modifications or even, in some cases, to elaborate an entirely new program.

The approbation of the francization program thus marks the beginning of the third official stage of the francization procedures. This stage, for which a two-years period is allowed, consists mainly in the application of the francization program. During the first 24 months after the program has been approved by the OLF, the firms have to report on their progress every six months. Finally, after this 24 months period is over, a permanent francization certificate is delivered attesting that French has attained the desired status in that firm or that the firm is applying a francization program approved by the OLF. This is the fourth and final stage of the procedure. Of course, the fact that the firm has a permanent francization certificate does not necessarily mean that the francization process is completed. It may mean that the firm concerned is applying a francization program whose date of expiration may well go beyond the official December 31st, 1983 deadline stipulated in the law to mark the limit when all firms employing fifty or more employees must hold a francization certificate.

It is also important to note, however, that certain types of business firms do not have to comply with the francization requirements of Bill 101. Sections 143 and 144 of Bill 101 recognize the special linguistic needs of head offices, scientific laboratories and research centres. These establishments may negotiate with the OLF a special agreement in which English may be recognized as the main language of work and communication and where the hiring, promotion and transfer policies may be adapted to their particular personnel needs (see Laporte, this volume, chapter 3; Coleman, this volume, chapter 6). Usually though, these establishments are asked to francize their communications with other groups or branches of the same company in Quebec who are not eligible to these special provisions. Moreover, great care is taken to ensure that all English speaking personnel in these establishments are able to communicate in French and that French is used on inside signs and posters in areas where head office personnel work.

What progress has been achieved in the francization of large Quebec business firms since 1977? To answer this question I will refer to statistics taken from two sources: an unpublished September 1982 report entitled "Les orientations de l'Office de la langue française pour les cinq prochaines années" and the April 1983 internal monthly reports from the different OLF departments. When the OLF began its mandate in 1977, the business firms employing 100 and more employees totalled 1,571, those employing between 50 and 99 totalled 2,053, while the public and semi-public agencies totalled 3,264. A proportion of these agencies had already attained the level of francization aimed at by Bill 101 which explains why, for example, 84% of the public or semi-public agencies now hold their certificate. The main task thus consisted in helping the business firms in the private sector attain the level of francization prescribed by the law.

The administrative procedure of the francization of the business firms was officially initiated on January 7, 1978 when the 117 business firms in class A, all of them employing 500 or more persons, became eligible for assistance from the OLF. These firms were distributed mainly in the following economic sectors: wholesale and retail businesses, the building trade, public works, transportation and warehousing, the hotel and restaurant trade, communications, the paper industry and the food industry. Actually, between January 7, 1978 and August 7, 1980 all the large business firms, employing 100 and more persons, had become eligible for assistance from the OLF. By the end of April 1983, 99.7% of these had returned their general information forms and had obtained their temporary francization certificate. Moreover, 353 out of the 1,571 firms concerned had obtained a permanent francization certificate without having had to elaborate a francization program and thus, officially at least, approximately 113,000 persons were able to work in French. These firms can be found in all 10 economic sectors. Furthermore, 1,058 of the 1,218 remaining firms had had their francization program approved and were thus in the process of implementing their francization program. Of these, 65 had already obtained their permanent francization certificate and thus had already attained the desired francization level. Thus, by April 1983, out of the 1,571 business firms concerned, only 160 (13%) had yet to present their francization program or to have it examined by the OLF.

It is hoped that the whole process of francization will be completed by April 1984. Actually what might appear at first glance a delay can easily be explained by a number of factors. First, on the OLF's part, one must take into account the fact that there was an administrative backlog due to the impressive number of cases which had to be treated simultaneously. Also there was slow progress at the onset of francization due to the issue of specially designed regulations regarding the special status of head offices and research centres. On the business firms' part, some delays can be accounted for simply since newly formed companies are still being brought into the process. Of course, the difficult Quebec economic situation can also account for some delays since francization costs are paid out of firm's coffers. Generally speaking, the firms do not show ill will regarding the francization measures, thus bad faith cannot be viewed as a delaying factor.

Business firms employing between 50 and 99 persons

The francization procedure for business firms employing between 50 and 99 persons is slightly different from that of large business firms (Office de la langue française, 1978d). Though these medium size firms must meet the same francization goals, the administrative process to which they must comply is slightly simplified due mostly to the fact that such firms do not have to form francization committees. First, the business firms must, follow-ing the calendar set up by the OLF, ask formally to be registered in order to obtain their francization certificate. Moreover, they have to present, in addition to general information, an evaluation of their linguistic situation regarding: a) the knowledge of French by their personnel at different levels of employment; b) the use of French in written and oral communications inside the firm as well as with clients, suppliers, the public and in advertising; c) the use of French terminology; and d) the policies for hiring, promotion and transfer. Finally, these firms must also elaborate the plans and schedule needed to generalize the use of French in all domains covered by section 141 of Bill 101.

Following this procedure, the OLF can deliver a formal attestation that the firm has now entered the francization process. Then, a francization certificate is delivered if, following the analysis of the firm's linguistic situation, the OLF recognizes that the use of French in that firm is sufficient-ly generalized to satisfy the requirements of the law. If this is not the case, the firm must negotiate a francization program with the OLF which must be devised and approved within a twelve months period. Afterwards, and all through the period during which the firm applies its francization program, it has to present yearly reports.

The administrative process for these medium size business firms was initiated in January 1980. By April 1983, 99.5% of the firms concerned, that is 2,042 out of 2,053 firms, had received their formal attestation from the OLF. More precisely, 1,109 firms (54%) were already implementing a program, while 115 (5.6%) had already obtained their permanent francization certificate after having applied their program. Finally 593 firms (29%) had obtained their permanent certificate without having to elaborate a francization program.

Actually, 236 firms (11.5%) have presented their program and have yet to negotiate with the OLF. It is hoped that this process will be completed by January 1st, 1984. The implementation of these francization programs should be completed by April 1988.

Here again, as for the larger firms, the delays can be accounted for by the administrative backlog resulting from the important number of cases to be treated. In addition there is no doubt that medium size firms have been hard hit by the difficult economic situation in Quebec.

Business firms employing less than 50 persons

As far as the 150,000 to 200,000 Quebec firms employing less than 50 persons are concerned, no specific procedures have yet been laid down concerning their francization process. Up to now, they are of course subject to the executory dispositions of the law but the OLF has not proceeded to any verifications in this matter. It is possible that a decision concerning these firms will be taken by the Quebec Government, since the issue was raised by National Assembly deputies during a meeting of Parliament on April 26, 1983.

3. The OLF as a terminology consulting service

Although the general francization process is well on its way, and most of the business firms comply with the law and regulations, it has been found that terminology problems can delay the general francization of the firms. For some, the goal of general francization is nearly met except for terminology. And, since terminology is used throughout the whole communication system, be it written or oral, no thorough francization can be achieved without the francization of terminology. Actually, the analysis of a sample of francization programs reveals that in about 95% of the francization programs where action has to be undertaken for the francization of written documents and communications, it can be said that one of the most important problems at stake is a *terminological* one, since the lack of French terminology is the main factor retarding the whole francization process. Furthermore, it seems that the fact that French terminology is available is no way a guarantee that it will be used. Although no formal data has been gathered on this subject, it is common knowledge that the OLF has been producing lexicons for nearly two decades without having succeeded in implementing them on a large scale. Moreover, most of the terminologists or translators working for business firms and whom I have interviewed agree with this fact. This has also been pointed out in a Sorecom (1981) study on the terminological situation within 12 Quebec business firms.

Thus, although the emphasis had been put on the *status* aspect of language planning throughout the legal and administrative procedures put forth either in Bill 101 or by the OLF in the interpretation of its mandate, it became necessary to develop the *corpus* aspect of language planning mostly through the terminology programs and their implementation. Here again, the implementation of terminology programs created a great deal of problems since the adoption of new French terminology by Quebec business firms did not follow automatically the fact that it was made available. Thus the OLF was brought to develop or reinforce different types of services related to terminology in order to help the business firms in their francization efforts. This aspect of language planning measures was born out of necessity and developed quite intuitively with the passing of years. No specific provisions were made for this type of implementation in Bill 101 so that the terminological francization measures are the result of the OLF's day to day experience with the general francization process. To this day, this whole process is not yet rationalized and is in constant evolution.

Terminological work

As we have already mentioned, since the middle of the 1970s, terminological work had been oriented mainly in those domains which were common to most economic and industrial sectors: that is, general management and administration as well as basic technical concepts. It also pursued goals of the previous language board in that it encouraged business firms to undertake their own terminological work. To spur this endeavour, the OLF reissued a methodological guide for terminological work which had been published by the previous language board (Auger & Rousseau, 1977). In addition, the new OLF intensified measures aimed at supporting business firms in their francization enterprise. Thus, in order to help the business firms meet the December 31, 1980 deadline regarding the francization of firms' names, the OLF published a methodological and linguistic guide on firm names and distributed more than 40,000 copies of this brochure to Quebec's business firms (Office de la langue française, 1980b).

This new orientation was intensified during the 1981–82 fiscal year when the OLF established new priorities in matters of terminological work in order to provide more direct help to business firms as well as to the individuals and public and semi-public agencies touched by the legislation. It was decided that before any terminological work would be undertaken, all existing terminological data already stocked in the OLF terminological data bank would be revised and put in a more economical and more directly accessible format for its users. Following a survey of user needs on this bank, terminological work was concentrated on those lexicons which were identi- fied as priorities by the bank. Thus, the OLF now pursues terminology work mainly in the fields of industrial equipment, food and food-products as well as accountancy. By May 1983, of the 33 specialists working in the terminol- ogical department, 6 of them were refining the terminological data of the computerized data bank while only 6 were doing terminological work proper either in neological terminology, that is, in domains necessitating new words altogether, or in the priority fields of legislature and court terminology.

The Banque de Terminologie du Québec (BTQ)

As we have just seen, the OLF has given priority to its terminological data bank whose mandate consists in making documentation and terminol- ogical data available to individuals, business firms and other public or semi-public organizations concerned. The bank aims to help two types of publics: the specialists concerned by terminological work, be they translators or terminologists, and the users of these terminologies, that is, the business firms and different types of organizations.

Since its creation in 1974, the B.T.Q. has succeeded in drawing up an inventory of all national and international organizations involved either in terminological work or in terminological documentation. It also collected a vast inventory of terminological lexicons or related documents so that, by the end of April 1983, this inventory consisted of more than 32,000 titles in all types of terminological works. Furthermore, as we have already seen, by the end of 1981, work was undertaken to filter and refine all the data available. Starting with the priority fields, the Bank aims at completing the data available, eliminating redundancy and controlling the quality of the stocked data.

As regards new data stocks, the B.T.Q. focused on priority fields such as public works, health, computer sciences, electronics, transport, energy, textile, metallurgy and general administration as well as general technical data. In order to facilitate the interrogation of the data, a network of some forty terminals was set up and made available to all firms and organizations concerned. By May 1983, the B.T.Q. had 50 subscribers, most of whom were business firms, but also different public or semi-public organizations, and one of them a terminological centre in France thus making directly available the French data bank of that organization. Also, in order to reach the smaller business firms and organizations who cannot afford to buy computer time, the data bank publishes terminological bibliographies as well as all types of terminological data in book form. Up to April 1983 it has published 12 terminological publications.

Furthermore, the data bank set up a type of answering service in order to fulfil the specific needs of the business firms and different organizations who are now in the process of elaborating or applying a francization program. Thus, the data bank undertakes to provide, usually within a five-day period, the documentation or terminology needed by firms. This is called the "Data bank differed information service".

Altogether, the data bank's professional and technical personnel involved in either stocking the data or making it available in a published form totals about 90. As for the differed information service, it employs four specialists.

The OLF terminology committee

The OLF instituted a terminology committee whose mandate is to make an inventory of new technical words and expressions of different technical and economic sectors and to submit its recommendations to the OLF for approval (see sections 113–118 of Bill 101). These terms and expressions are presented to the OLF terminology committee either by committees established in other departments and agencies of the Quebec civil administration or by groups or organizations outside the civil administration, or even by individuals. Once terms or expressions are approved by the committee, the OLF either decides to recommend their use without any legal obligation, or else it officially "standardizes" these terms so that, upon their publication in the *Gazette officielle du Québec*, the use of these terms and expressions "becomes obligatory in texts and documents emanating from the civil administration, in contracts to which it is a party, in teaching manuals and educational and research works published in French in Québec and approved by the Ministre de l'éducation, and in signs and posters" (sections 118).

The OLF terminology committee is made up of seven members, four of whom are terminology specialists from the OLF, while three others are linguists or translators from the educational and industrial world. The committee meets at least 10 times a year. Since its creation in April 1978, the OLF's terminology committee has normalized or standardized 474 lexical items and has recommended the use of 450 more. It also recommended the use of 6 lexicons, each of them covering a complete technical field. Lexical items and whole lexicons cover the fields of food industry, social development, transportation, education and geography. It is to be noted that about half of the lexical items studied were submitted by the terminological committees of different government agencies.

The interbusiness firms terminological workshops

Since 1976, in order to provide even more direct help to the business firms, the OLF inaugurated a new type of terminological workshop where the different firms concerned by the same technical field could meet and elaborate the terminology they needed with the help of the OLF terminologists. Between 1976 and 1983, about 12 workshops were set up. However, although the idea appealed to quite a number of firms, the results of this venture were not as positive as one might have expected. One reason for these poor results is that terminology tends to be considered the exclusive property of the firm which developed it. One must add that such terminology is closely linked to specific technology developed by firms which competitively market their product. It thus sometimes proved difficult to develop a workshop climate appropriate to open and free terminological exchange. Of course, other technical factors account for the poor results such as lack of personnel at the OLF and the difficulty of developing a research methodology which would satisfy both the firms and the OLF. In addition, members of these workshops did not necessarily have the same technical and terminological background. Perhaps the most important reason for the poor results was that the committee was entirely responsible for the whole terminological research process. This proved quite unrealistic since some of the committee members were not terminologists while all of them lacked the time needed to pursue the research. All these reasons help account for the fact that only six of these workshops were still operational by 1983.

In an attempt to rationalize these workshops, the OLF has split up this activity in order to fulfill the business firms' expectations. First, it has reinforced its technical support in order to help provide the business firms concerned with the technical terms they need. Whereas, before May 1982, the workshops were conducted by the consulting linguists, they are now assigned to terminologists specialized in terminology research who act not only as technical advisors and co-ordinators but who are also responsible for the actual terminological research. They are the ones who gather all pertinent bibliographical and technical information either through the data bank or their own research in order to provide the firms with the lexicon they need. Three terminology specialists are now in charge of the six active workshops who deal with the terminology of transportation, printing, tobacco and knitted wear.

However, these workshops, if they provide a much needed terminology, do not attempt to resolve the problem of diffusing and implementing this new terminology. That is why the OLF now offers a new service taken up both by the consulting linguists and the terminology specialists who now act as consultants in the actualization of the terminological aspects of the francization programs within the business firms. The main task of the seven consulting linguists who are now responsible for this sector consists in providing the business firms with the documentary and technical sources they need. In order to maximize their impact, they have developed a sectorial approach so that they can reach most of the business firms concerned by the same terminology. From a strategic point of view, however, we can see that the OLF, through these means, helps diffuse terminological information; it does not, in a strict sense, implement it.

The terminological assistance telephone service

In addition to the above, the OLF expanded a service instituted in 1962 by the first language board: a terminological consultation telephone service. This service was created in order to provide, as quickly as possible, an answer to the most urgent terminological needs, although it also has the mandate to provide general linguistic assistance. This service is offered to the general public although it privileges the business firms and the public and semi-public agencies. Actually, the clients of this service are of different backgrounds and range from the technical specialist or the language specialist to the white collar worker in the secretarial or clerical fields. The general public accounts for 20% of the requests while the business firms account for 48% and the public and semi-public agencies, for 33%.

Actually, nearly 55,000 questions are answered annually, although it is believed that if the technical answering facilities were more important, the information treated would be much greater. Before 1977, nearly half of the questions posed were related to general grammatical or orthographical points while the rest dealt with terminological information. Now, if these statistics still hold for the whole of the province of Quebec, it is interesting to note that there has been a shift in the type of information requested by the Montreal clientele. Originating mostly from Montreal business firms, as much as 75% of the information requested has dealt with terminological issues. These patterns reflect the emphasis given by the OLF to the business world.

By April 1983, twelve terminology specialists were working either in Montreal or in Quebec city for this terminological answering service. To this number though, one must add the ten linguists or terminologists in the regional offices throughout the province of Quebec, whose work consists partly in helping the business firms and other clients with their terminological problems.

The regional offices

Furthermore, in order to make itself more easily available to the population it aims to francize, the OLF has pursued a regionalization policy. Before 1977, the OLF already had five regional offices besides the main offices in Montreal and Quebec: four others were added so that now the network covers all of the province of Quebec. Each one of these regional offices is responsible for most of the general francization work in its geographical area. With the exception of the francization programs of the large business firms, the regional offices are responsible for the administration of the francization programs of all other firms. Furthermore, most of these offices are active within intermedia committees which they have set up in order to sensitize the media to the francization objectives of Bill 101 as well as to the OLF's mandate and different activities.

Actually, each of these offices recreates, at a microscopic level, and with minimal means, the whole structure of the OLF's Montreal main branch since it offers most of the major services. Thus, with usually only two specialists in each regional office, more than 23,000 linguistic consultations were given during 1982. Moreover, in the last two years, an average of 7,000 requests for information concerning the Charter of the French language were treated. Interestingly enough, it is through these regional offices that the OLF puts forth most of its policies regarding the general enrichment of the French language of Quebec. In this sense, the present OLF also pursues the cultivation mandate of the first language board.

As we can see, the OLF has devoted a lot of energy toward the francization of business firms. Furthermore, while trying to fulfil the needs expressed by the business world, it has been brought to take into account the specific problems related to the francization of terminology. This explains why we can note a change in the interpretation of its mandate. From a beginning which focused on the status aspect of language planning, the OLF subsequently adopted a more global point of view which gives more importance to corpus language planning measures from an elaboration point of view. This preoccupation thus marks a return to corpus planning policies. But, although the structures of terminology programs are more clearly defined, and in spite of all the efforts the OLF displays in matters related to terminology, problems remain as to the diffusion, implementation and adoption of French terminology in Quebec business firms.

4. Factors influencing the diffusion of French terminology in Quebec business firms

What are the factors which influence, positively or negatively, the adoption of French terminology in Quebec business firms? Only a few empirical studies have directly addressed this issue in Quebec so far. On the basis of results obtained in these preliminary studies it is possible to identify some factors which seem important in promoting the adoption of and spread of French terminology in Quebec business firms.

First, a study carried out by Sorecom (1981) found that the attitude of high management regarding the francization of terminology was perhaps the most important factor influencing the implementation and diffusion of French terminology within Quebec business firms. Of the 12 large business firms examined in this study, the seven firms which had reached the highest level of francization each had high management personnel which held positive attitudes toward francization. The five firms which lagged behind were those whose high management expressed negative opinions regarding the francization process and the Charter of the French language.

Other results from the Sorecom (1981) study showed that favourable attitudes held by high management toward the francization of terminology seemed to facilitate the emergence of "language spread agents" working in favour of francization within the firm. What were the characteristics of individuals identified as "language change agents"? Sorecom (1981) found that the age, sex, mother tongue and political opinions of these individuals were *not* the major factors that contributed to the special motivations of these individuals as "language change agents". However, Sorecom (1981) found that such individuals had a vast linguistic repertoire not only in French and in English but also in the different speech styles used in both of these languages. It was also found that such individuals not only had privileged access to personnel in most levels of the firm's hierarchy but also had a very good knowledge of the attitudes and opinions of both the management and the employees concerning terminology change and francization in general. The "language change agents" identified in the Sorecom (1981) study were also found to identify strongly with their firm's objectives and as such were endowed with special status and trust from the management as well as amongst their peers. Finally it was found that these individuals were in positions where they could directly or indirectly bestow rewards (psychological or otherwise) to those in the firm who joined their efforts in the francization process.

Another factor found to affect the implementation process in the firms studied by Sorecom (1981) was the favourable or unfavourable attitudes of firm members towards the usefulness of adopting French terminology. When asked to choose between a number of disadvantages in adopting French terminology, 21% of the 120 francophone respondents replied that the use of French terminology constituted a barrier to communication with the outside world while 16% replied that French terminology would slow down work. In addition, 12% replied that French terminology was not explicit or clear enough while 8% replied that French terminology lacked efficiency. When asked to compare French and English terminology, English terminology was judged to be more rapid, more functional and clearer than French. Conversely, French terminology was perceived to be more awkward and clumsy than English. There is little doubt that such unfavourable attitudes toward the usefulness of French terminology held even amongst francophone firm members must have a negative influence on the diffusion of French terminology in Quebec business firms.

Nevertheless results from the Sorecom (1981) research showed that French terminology was used more often than English terminology at all levels of the business firms sampled by the study. Sorecom (1981) surveyed self reports of terminology use in conversations between francophone superiors and subordinates in each of the 12 business firms they investigated. During conversations held in French, superiors reported they used French terminology 67% of the time with subordinates while they used English terminology 28% of the time. Subordinates in similar conversations reported they used French terminology 74% of the time when addressing their superior while they reported making use of English terminology 24% of the time. In interactions between peers, self-reports of language use showed that French terminology was used 70% of the time, while English terminology was used 26.5% of the time. In spite of francization and efforts to implement French terminology these results show that English terminology remains important even in business firms where francophones constitute the majority of the working force.

Language attitudes can play a more subtle role in the diffusion of French terminology than is evident from the above study. Heller (1978) found that within a given language, a new terminological item seems more readily accepted if it does not compete with other items of usage already existing within the language. More specifically, if a Quebec French technical term is used, it is very difficult to implement a standard or international French term in replacement. But if only the English term is known, it becomes relatively more easy to implement and diffuse a standard French item. Thus, it seems more difficult to implement a change when two linguistic varieties of a same language are competing than when two different languages are competing and the proposed change results in replacing one language by a term from a different language. In fact, Heller (1978) found that the substitution of one linguistic variety of a language by another variety of the same language gives rise to negative attitudes which are unfavourable to the implementation of change.

It is worth noting that the attitudes of French terminology users in Quebec seem to differ from those of French terminology users in Belgium (Daoust & Martin, 1982). For the Belgian users, French terminology is seen to be as clear and explicit as English terminology. French terminology is also considered to be adequate, linguistically speaking, in expressing scientific and technical realities. However, when asked to evaluate the sociolinguistic appropriateness of French terminology, both Quebec and Belgian users agree: French terminology does slow down work and proves less efficient. Thus, while for Belgian users, English terminology is preferred mainly for practical reasons, for Quebec users English terminology is often preferred because it is seen as intrinsically better suited for technology than is French.

Other results from both the Sorecom (1981) and Heller, Bartholomot, Levy & Ostiguy (1982) studies showed that females, who usually hold clerical positions within the firms were more likely to adopt French terminology than males in all positions of the firm. The Sorecom (1981) study also showed a tendency for the younger age group (18–30 years old) to use more French terminology than most others. This study also suggests that role position within the firm's hierarchy combined with the "functional network" of firm members seemed to have some impact on the adoption of

French terminology. Other studies suggest a correlation between the language of terminology used in the firm and the language of terminology used in the technical and professional training provided for by the firms (Daoust & Martin, 1982). Results of research in progress (Daoust, 1983b; Daoust & Martin, 1983) suggest that the type of business firm may also be a factor regulating the implementation and diffusion of new French terminology in Quebec business firms.

Finally, it is interesting to note that many of the above factors shown to have had some impact on the diffusion of French terminology in Quebec business firms are also those proposed by Cooper (1979) in his general model of the diffusion of linguistic innovation and language spread in organizations and speech communities (Daoust, 1984).

5. Strategic approaches to the francization of terminology in Quebec

In the final section it is worthwhile examining the strategies used by the OLF to implement the francization of terminology in Quebec business firms. A discussion of these strategies will help in clarifying some basic issues regarding status and corpus language planning in Quebec.

Production and dissemination strategies

We have seen how much Quebec's language board has tried to support the business firms' efforts in the francization of their terminology. We have enumerated the different types of services offered by the OLF regarding terminological work and documentation. However, each type of service offered is characterized by the fact that it aims at producing or diffusing either terminology or terminological documentation. Thus, we can say that the main strategies used by the OLF are of the production or dissemination type. In this respect, the present language board uses the same strategic approach as the first Quebec language board created twenty years ago.

In fact, one can say that such a production and dissemination strategy is characteristic of all *elaboration* types of language planning whose aim is to add a new function to a language. In Quebec, the objective is to promote the use of French in the technical and scientific domains where, traditionally, English has nearly always been used, even by the French-speaking population. It is to be noted that, even in the most francized business firms, it is not uncommon to find that the language of work is French throughout except for the technical and scientific terms.

Actually, such an elaboration type of language planning has always been seen, in Quebec at least, as an integral part of a more global type of language planning: corpus planning which focuses on language change within the language itself, as opposed to status planning designed to regulate the relative status of competing languages such as French and English. Furthermore, all terminological planning in Quebec has always been characterized by a *cultivation* type of approach, which aims mainly at determining matters of correctness in a language and thus can be seen as an integrated aspect of corpus planning measures.

These two facts explain, in part at least, why the present language board has put the emphasis on the production and dissemination of terminology in its effort to promote the francization of Quebec business firms. On the other hand, these same facts may also explain why, in spite of the OLF's efforts in promoting a status-oriented policy, it is still sometimes perceived as carrying out a mainly cultivation type of approach within a corpus-oriented policy.

Terminology and status language planning

I would like to argue that an elaboration-type language planning approach for terminology should be integrated within a *status* language planning framework rather than within a corpus language planning one. This would help to minimize the pitfalls inherent to the social acceptance of any corpus planning measures within complex post-industrial societies such as Quebec.

First, let us examine the objectives pursued by Quebec's language planners with respect to terminology as well as the part played by terminology within the general francization program of Quebec business firms. As far as terminology is concerned, we have already mentioned that, even for the French-speaking population, the use of English terminology, either in its written or oral form, remains quite popular. This is so even when French terminology is available. This situation, which has its origin in historical, socio-economic and socio-cultural phenomena, reflects the traditional dominant position of Quebec Anglophones in the industrial and business domains of Quebec society. Consequently, English has spread as the language of work and of socio-economic power and has thus become a language of prestige for both the English and the French-speaking population. In making French the official language of Quebec and the language of work, the Quebec government hopes to promote French in both the socio-cultural and socio-economic domains. By doing so, it also goes along with the wishes of Quebec's French-speaking population who, during the 1960s and the 1970s became more and more discontented with their situation and who exerted pressure on their government for remedial action on both the economic and linguistic fronts (see d'Anglejan, this volume, chapter 2; Laporte, this volume, chapter 3; Coleman, this volume, chapter 6).

In declaring French the language of work, the Government of Quebec thus materializes the French-speaking population's dream and, ideally speaking, makes it possible for all French-speaking workers, at all levels of work, to use their mother tongue at work.

But, the francization of terminology poses quite a different problem since, for a number of French-speaking workers, English may be the only language they know for the use of technical and scientific terms. Thus, when the Charter decrees that French terminology shall be used at work, it imposes as important a change on the French-speaking population as it does on the English-speaking population. Furthermore, for those technical domains where some French terminology is used, the terms and expressions used may not be in conformity with the terminology used in France and other French-speaking communities in the world. Thus, following the OLF policy in this matter, some Quebec French terms must also be changed in favour of an international type of terminology.

One can easily visualize the sociolinguistic consequences of implementing such a change within the French-speaking community. In industry and business for example a study by Heller, Bartholomot, Levy & Ostiguy (1982) has shown that different synonyms are used by different occupational groups to refer to a single reality. These synonyms, which often are Quebec French terms or English loan words can serve as linguistic symbols of group solidarity within the firm's different occupational sectors. Any imposed change in terminology usage may threaten the group since it may destroy an important means of intragroup identification and intergroup differentiation (cf. Bourhis, 1979). Add to this the fact that the English language itself, even apart from its terminology, is felt to be prestigious and we can see how menacing terminology change may be, even for francophones.

Thus, we can see that any change in terminology affects the status of both languages concerned: English because it loses a function or domain, and French because on one hand it gains a function while on the other hand it has to align itself to the international French norm. As for the user of both languages in Quebec, a change in terminology usage presupposes a modification of attitudes toward English as the language of socio-economic advancement and sociocultural prestige.

From another point of view, francization of terminology can be viewed, if not as a prerequisite to the francization of business firms, at least as a priority item in any francization of such domains as written documents, reports, forms, production and sales literature, etc. In this respect, the francization of terminology has a direct influence on Quebec's status-oriented language planning policy regarding the business world.

To sum up, the francization of terminology implies more than a change of technical terms from English to French or from Quebec French to standard or international French: it implies a deep sociolinguistic change in the attitudes of both linguistic communities toward French as the language of socio-economic power in Quebec and as the language of technological and scientific domains. This helps account for why a corpus-oriented policy which focuses on an elaboration-type of planning from a cultivation point of view will meet with some problems at the implementation stage.

Standardization within a cultivation-type corpus planning framework

Let us now turn back to the strategies used by the OLF in the promotion of a French terminology within Quebec business firms. We have seen that the main strategy has been one of production of terminological items as well as dissemination of terminology and terminological documentation. To illustrate this fact I would like to point out that, between 1977 and 1983, the OLF has published 204 lexicons in such diverse fields as food industry, brass-founding and finishing, automobile industry, garment industry, management, mechanics, pulp and paper industry, banking, etc. Furthermore, we have also seen that the OLF has been active in another domain: the normalization of technical lexical items through its terminology committee. Of course, the main objective of this committee is to make sure that the lexical items used are "correct" and that the general "quality" of the technical language used is of a high enough standard to be judged acceptable. Thus, through this committee, the OLF pursues the "cultivation" objective of the 1961 language board: that of "correctness" and "improvement" of the French language spoken in Quebec. As we can see, even though the OLF officially carries on an "elaboration" policy regarding technical terms, it does so through a cultivation-type of corpus language planning. Besides, through its terminology committee, the OLF pronounces itself regarding the "correctness" of general language usage since some of the technical terms it studies are borderline cases between terminology and everyday lexical items.

Moreover, the OLF has even published, in 1980, a policy paper on the orientation of this terminology committee which constitutes the only official position with respect to the OLF corpus planning policy (Office de la langue française, 1980a). This policy paper declares that the OLF aims to take into account the sociolinguistic characteristics of Quebec French within the American continent. It dwells on general considerations with respect to the particular situation of Quebec in North America, the fact that it is a francophone province as well as the fact that it is isolated from the rest of the French-speaking communities of the world. It also recalls the fact that Quebec's economy has traditionally been controlled by Quebec anglophones and it reasserts the wishes expressed by the 1961 language board that Quebec should play a more prominent role in the francophone worldwide community since it occupies a very special position in Northern America (cf. Bourhis, 1982). It also takes upon itself a distinction put forward by the 1974 language board regarding the difference between general language and technical languages as well as between the official usage of a language and the personal usage (Corbeil, 1975a,b). To sum up, the new OLF corpus planning policy document recognizes the existence of different linguistic levels or varieties and states that all users of French in Quebec should be made aware of these levels in order to adapt their speech styles to the different sociolinguistic situations by which they are confronted. The policy document asserts that technical vocabulary should be as standardized as possible and, in order to facilitate communication with the outside world, it should be as close as possible to the international usage. As far as usage is concerned, the OLF document declares that, although personal language usage should not fall under its jurisdiction, technical language usage and official language usage should be standardized and should be subject to a language planning policy.

Within this general framework, the OLF elaborates on its policy regarding linguistic borrowings of technical items. First, it states that the OLF aims at normalizing or standardizing technical language usage in order that the French language "maintain its autonomy and rigour" (Office de la langue française, 1980a). To do so, the OLF declares that it will accept a Quebec French technical language item if:

a) it is used throughout the community, the Quebec community and preferably the international francophone community;
b) it fills an international communication need;
c) it constitutes a mainly lexical type of borrowing, that is, it does not contain a non-French grammatical or morphological structure;
d) it is productive morphologically speaking;
e) it does not compete with already existing international or standard French terms;

f) it designates a reality which has no denomination in international or standard French.

As we can see, these criterions are very strict and mean that practically no Quebec French terms will be accepted unless they designate a technique either developed in Quebec or typical of a Quebec reality. All in all, we can see that this political position is not far from the one adopted 20 years ago by the first language board. Furthermore, these criterions, even though they officially apply only to the technical language, are also used in borderline cases for semi-technical terms used in everyday life. Indeed, as far as the general language is concerned, the OLF has now officially announced its intention to elaborate a policy regarding a Quebec French norm. It is against this background that terminological services are offered by the OLF to the business firms for their francization enterprise. With the legal aspects of francization well on their way, there seems to be a change of emphasis now toward the "bettering" of the Quebec French language. Through terminology, the OLF reaches a vast population made up of a majority of francophones for whom francization means the use of a "purer" French. Phase II of Quebec's language planning policy could well mean a return to a cultivation type of language planning through terminology change, though as yet there is no hard evidence supporting this change of approach.

Social animation strategy within a status planning framework

Even though the OLF has used a mainly production and dissemination policy in the past, it has also made great efforts to fulfil the business firms' needs. In the past two years, the OLF has tried to reorient its terminological services in order to be more effective in reaching the business firms. Thus, the data bank now distributes terminological documentation without it being officially screened by the OLF. It also tolerates some linguistic variation within the technical domains although it promises to sort out the lexical production of those technical domains. Thus, in terms of strategy, we can see a shift from what we could call "qualitative dissemination" to "quantitative dissemination".

Furthermore, through the present work of the linguistic consultants who now offer technical help to the firms in francizing their terminology, a new strategy is taking form which could be called a "social animation strategy". Even if this approach still consists mainly in diffusing documentation and technical information regarding terminology, one can feel that the OLF is more sensitive now to the sociolinguistic consequences of terminological dissemination. It is now more aware of the importance of attitudes in the implementation process of French terminology as well as the social implications of such a policy. In fact, we could say that the OLF is now conscious of the fact that the francization of terminology affects the socio-economic and socio-cultural status of French. At this point in its history, I feel that the OLF is reaching a crucial stage which could determine the type of language planning policy it will put forth in the future. On one hand, its renewed preoccupation with the "quality" of Quebec French could lead to the adoption of a cultivation type of approach to corpus planning as we have just mentioned. On the other hand, the fact that it is now more aware of the sociolinguistic repercussions of language planning policies and more pre-occupied by the human and social aspects of such a policy may well initiate a new era in language planning policy in Quebec: a status-oriented elabora-tion type of language planning where a more social oriented approach would be used rather than a cultivation and corpus-oriented approach. In my opinion, the course that the OLF will adopt will depend largely on the approach it will privilege as regards terminology change.

Finally, an analysis of the different strategies adopted by Quebec language planners suggest that, implicitly at least, the following hypotheses regarding the implementation of their policy have been formulated.

First, it is assumed that, by francizing Quebec's "visage linguistique" or linguistic environment, a deeper francization will follow throughout Quebec society. Secondly, it is also assumed that by presenting the measures of Bill 101 as means taken to safeguard the rights and needs of the francophone majority, the Charter of the French language will give rise to more positive attitudes towards the French language. It is hoped that, by creating such a context, the French-speaking population will support and promote the linguistic change and see to it that such a change is implemented within Quebec's institutions and organizations.

These two hypotheses constitute, in my opinion, the most important ones, but we can extract a few others which are directly related to the francization of terminology. These are:

a) the belief that oral terminology change, as well as general language change, can be brought about by francizing the written form first. That is why Bill 101 makes sure that all written texts, posting, documentation, etc. are in French;

b) the belief that the language used in professional and technical train-ing can influence the language of work;

c) the belief that the diffusion of the French language and French terminology can affect language change.

Although these hypotheses have not been tested formally, they should prove useful in future studies of language change and terminological spread not only in Quebec but in other cultural settings as well.

Summary Notes

Throughout this chapter, we have tried to give a global picture of the francization of Quebec business firms brought about by the promulgation of the Charter of the French language.

We have described in some detail the procedures implemented by the OLF to francize Quebec's public agencies and business firms. Following an overview of the progress achieved in the francization of business firms we concluded that the lack of French terminology was the major stumbling block retarding the francization process. To address this problem we have seen that the OLF created an impressive array of terminology consulting services to help Quebec business firms find and adopt French terminology. The full range of these services were described in part 3 of this chapter. Despite all these efforts, problems remain in the adoption and diffusion of French terminology in Quebec business firms. To illustrate some of the factors which seem determinant in the adoption and diffusion of French terminology, we have also examined results from the first sociolinguistic studies done in Quebec on this subject. The review of existing studies has brought us to stress the importance of a phenomenon which we have called the "language spread agents". We have seen that high management's positive attitude toward francization seems to facilitate the emergence of "language spread agents" within Quebec business firms. We have seen that individuals identified as "language change agents" can have a major positive impact on the adoption and diffusion of French terminology within Quebec business firms. We have also stressed the importance of language attitudes in a terminological change policy.

In trying to sum up the role and importance of all these different factors, we have been brought to question some of the strategies used by Quebec language planners in the implementation of terminology change. We have focused our attention on the different types of language planning strategies adopted by Quebec's government. Within the classical model of status and corpus planning, we have tried to analyze Quebec's position toward the francization of terminology. In order to do this, we have examined two types of approaches that emerge from the strategies used by the OLF: the elaboration and cultivation-types of approaches. Throughout this analysis, we have tried to define the role played by terminology in the general francization process. This has brought us to propose that terminology change be treated within a *status-oriented* policy instead of a *corpus-oriented* one.

We wish to stress here that Quebec's language policy has reached a critical point as is exemplified by its ambivalent terminology change policy which partakes now from the two main streams of language planning policies: the corpus-oriented approach and the status-oriented approach. The choice between these two types of approaches will have, in our opinion, a determining effect on the success or failure of the implementing process of French terminology in Quebec. Failure to take into account the social context and social implications of a terminological change would surely compromise the success of such an enterprise.

Acknowledgement

I wish to thank the editor of this volume, Richard Y. Bourhis, for the valuable comments, support and encouragement provided during the completion of this chapter.

References

AUGER, P., & ROUSSEAU, L. J. 1977, Méthodologie de la recherche terminologique. In: *Etudes, recherches et documentation*, No. 9. Régie de la langue française, Québec: Editeur officiel du Québec.

BOURHIS, R. Y. 1979, Language in ethnic interaction: a Social Psychological Approach. In: H. GILES & B. SAINT-JACQUES (eds), *Language and Ethnic Relations*, Oxford, Pergamon Press.

— 1982, Language policies and language attitudes: Le Monde de la Francophonie. In: E. BOUCHARD-RYAN & H. GILES (eds), *Attitudes Towards Language Variation*, London: Edward Arnold.

COOPER, R. L. 1979, Language planning, language spread, and language change. In: J. E. ALATIS & G. R. TUCKER (eds), *Language in Public Life*. Georgetown University Round Table on Language and Linguistics, Washington, D.C.: Georgetown University Press.

CORBEIL, J. C. 1975a, Notes sur les rapports entre le français québécois et le français de France. In: *Etudes, recherches et documentation*, No. 1. Régie de la langue française, Québec: Editeur officiel du Québec.

— 1975b, Description des options linguistiques de L'Office de la langue française. In: *Etudes, recherches et documentation*, No. 2. Régie de la langue française, Québec: Editeur officiel du Québec.

DAOUST, D. 1982, La planification linguistique au Québec: un aperçu des lois sur la langue. *Revue québécoise de linguistique*, 12, 9–76.

— 1983a, Corpus and status language planning in Quebec: a look at linguistic legislation. In: J. COBARRUBIAS & J. FISHMAN (eds), *Progress in Language Planning*. The Hague: Mouton.

— 1983b, Stratégie d'implantation terminologique dans une entreprise de transport: étude de cas. Montréal: Office de la langue française (forthcoming.)

— 1984, Terminological change within a linguistic communication diffusion model. Montreal: Office de la langue française (forthcoming.)

DAOUST, D., & MARTIN, A. 1982, Facteurs organisationnels et sociolinguistiques qui soustendent la diffusion et l'utilisation des terminologies techniques de langue française dans l'entreprise: un premier bilan. *Revue de l'Association Québécoise de linguistique*, 2, 31–45.

— & MARTIN, A. 1983, *Les facteurs sociolinguistiques et organisationnels qui soustendent l'utilisation et la diffusion des termes techniques dans l'entreprise*. Montréal: Office de la langue française (forthcoming).

DAS GUPTA, J. 1972, Language planning and public policy: analytical outline of the policy process related to language planning in India. In: R. W. SHUY (ed.), *Sociolinguistics: Current trends and Prospects. Monograph Series on Language and Linguistics*, 23rd Annual Round Table. Washington, D.C.: Georgetown University Press.

FISHMAN, A. 1974, Language planning and language planning research: the state of the art. In: J. A. FISHMAN (ed.), *Advances in Language Planning*, The Hague: Mouton.

HELLER, M. 1978, *L'usage et la connaissance de la terminologie de l'automobile à Montréal: variation et distribution sociale*. Montréal: Office de la langue française (unpublished report).

HELLER, M., BARTHOLOMOT, J. P., LEVY, L., & OSTIGUY, L. 1982, *Le processus de francisation dans une entreprise Montréalaise: une analyse sociolinguistique*. Québec: Editeur officiel du Québec.

JERNUDD, B. H., & DAS GUPTA, J. 1971, Towards a theory of language planning. In: J. RUBIN & H. JERNUDD (eds), *Can language be planned?* Hawaii: University of Hawaii Press.

NEUSTUPNY, J. 1970, "Basic types of treatment of language problems". *Linguistic communications*. Monash University, 1, 77–98.

OFFICE DE LA LANGUE FRANÇAISE 1965, *Norme du français écrit et parlé au Québec*. "Cahiers de l'Office de la langue française", No. 4. Ministère des Affaires culturelles, Quebec: Gouvernement du Québec.

— 1978a, *Analyse linguistique de l'entreprise*. Montreal: Gouvernement du Québec.

— 1978b, *Guide d'utilisation du document Analyse linguistique de l'entreprise*. Montreal: Gouvernement du Québec.

— 1978c, *Programme-type de francisation des entreprises comptant plus de 100 employés*. Montréal: Gouvernement du Québec.

— 1978d, *Le processus de francisation des PME employant de 50 à 99 personnes au Québec*. Montréal: Gouvernement du Québec.

— 1980a, *Enoncé d'une politique relative à l'emprunt de formes linguistiques étrangères*. Montreal: Gouvernement du Québec.
— 1980b, *Les maisons sociales*. Montréal: Gouvernement du Québec.
QUEBEC GOVERNMENT OF, 1972, *Report of the Commission of Inquiry on the Position of the French Language and on Language Rights in Quebec* (Gendron Commission). Quebec: Editeur Officiel du Québec.
RÉGIE DE LA LANGUE FRANÇAISE 1976, *Partage des taches en matière de travaux terminologiques*. Québec: Editeur Officiel du Québec.
ROGERS, M., & SHOEMAKER, F. F. 1971, *Communication of Innovations. A Cross-Cultural Approach*. New York: The Free Press.
RUBIN, J. & JERNUDD, B. H. 1971, Language planning as an element in modernization: Introduction. In: J. RUBIN & B. H. JERNUDD (eds), *Can Language be Planned?* Hawaii: University of Hawaii Press.
SORECOM 1981, *Diffusion et utilisation de la terminologie technique de langue française dans douze entreprises québécoises*. Montreal: Office de la langue française (unpublished report).

5 The response of business firms to the francization process

Roger Miller
Université du Québec à Montréal

The aim of the Charter of the French Language is to extend the use of French to all levels of business in Quebec in order that a company's internal operations be consistent with the virtual right to work in French and with the right to be informed and served in French. The goal of this chapter is to sketch the structural and manpower adaptations which large business firms are making in response to this provincial legislation within the Canadian federal framework.

This chapter is divided into five sections. The first section outlines the mechanisms by which social pressures are brought to bear on business firms. In the second section, a summary is given of the key characteristics of the Charter of the French Language with respect to business firms. A conceptual framework for understanding francization as a process of organizational change is sketched in the third section. Then, the impact of the francization process on firms, management and jobs is briefly analyzed. The final section provides a summary and conclusions.

1. Mechanisms of social change: private and public solutions

Pressures from customers or interest groups from within the socio-political sphere can induce firms to take voluntary actions to correct situations viewed as problematic. The ability of firms to correct a perceived problem on a voluntary basis will depend not only on the initiatives of senior executives but also on the firms' profitability and on the context in which they operate. Some firms will change rapidly, others will proceed at a slower pace in harmony with management expectations. Should pressure groups not be satisfied with private solutions they may require the executive arm of government to propose social regulations.

Linguistic legislations are only a special case of social regulation of business in areas such as consumer protection, labour relations, worker safety, public safety and air and water quality (Miller & Lapointe, 1980). Social regulation means direct interventions in the operation and management of private economic activities. Its effect is to substitute directives and rules of conduct for executive decisions and for the signals and impersonal incentives of the marketplace. Its aims are to alter internal and market decisions in order to attain specific socio-political objectives. Public intervention on the market through the use of these social regulations is portrayed in Figure 1.

FIGURE 1 *A Simplified Model of Social Regulation*

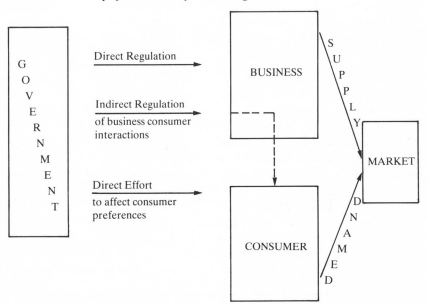

Regulation of business activities by governments can occur in three distinct fashions. First, direct intervention through legislative actions which specify the content or methods of decision-making: standards with respect to air or water pollution are examples of this mode of action. Second, indirect regulations which determine the conditions under which interactions of management with employees or customers occur. Finally, regulation may occur through direct pressures by government to influence the preferences of customers: advertising to reduce cigarette or gasoline consumption is a case in point. The issue then becomes to what degree do these government interventions affect the targeted business firms, consumer demands and the market place as a whole. We shall explore this question as it applies to the francization of Canadian business firms in Quebec.

2. Public intervention with respect to francization of business firms

Pressures for the francization of the business firm in Quebec are the result of changes in attitudes and expectations within the socio-political framework. In turn, these pressures lead to organizational changes either through voluntary actions by management or through public regulation or work organizations. Insofar as linguistic matters are concerned, many firms in Quebec had decided in the early sixties and even before, to modify corporate practices in manufacturing and sales operations in order to cope with changing internal and socio-political expectations (Morisson, 1970). Many senior executives had voluntarily decided, well before discussions took place about the desirability of government intervention, to change linguistic policies within their firms. Sécor (1980) and Allaire & Miller (1980) reported detailed examples of such actions.

However, a number of Quebec pressure groups and political leaders believed that reliance solely upon private actions was insufficient. First, only those companies that attract public attention or whose management is socially responsible will establish voluntary programs, resulting in considerable variations between firms. Without compulsory regulations, private actions are often limited to the most easily applicable measures short of fundamental changes. Fundamentally, modifications brought about through private actions were felt to be inadequate in meeting the evolving expectations of the French-speaking population in Quebec. Thus, a case was built for introducing social and organizational changes through public regulation (see d'Anglejan, this volume, chapter 2; Laporte, this volume, chapter 3).

The government of Quebec concluded, after the Gendron Commission (Quebec, 1972) and the Royal Commission on Bilingualism and Biculturalism reports (Canada, 1969), that public action was not only possible but necessary. In 1974, the Quebec National Assembly adopted the Official Language Act (Bill 22) which included universal measures as well as a process of change based on voluntary compliance (see d'Anglejan, this volume, chapter 2).

Pursuant to the election of the Parti Québécois in November 1976, it was obvious to observers that the Official Language Act, insofar as language of work was concerned, would be modified given it only emphasized *voluntary* compliance. In a first proposal called "Bill 1", the Government of Quebec not only undertook to promote the use of French, but also set out to make French the common language of all Quebecers — in other words, the language that "everyone must know" in order to be able to communicate (Quebec, 1977; Laurin, 1977). *The pursuit of this objective implied a policy of official institutional unilingualism of work organizations that did not exclude individual bilingualism.*

Following the hearings of the Parliamentary Commission on Education, Cultural Affairs and Communications, in the spring of 1977, a substantially modified bill was introduced. Bill 101 was ratified on August 26, 1977, by the Quebec National Assembly under the title of the Charter of the French Language. Voluntary adaptation by companies was replaced by the *obligation* to comply with statutory measures and to obtain a permanent certificate of francization. The Charter, however, acknowledged that not all sectors of economic activity offer the same opportunities to work in French, specifically that certain positions in head offices or in research divisions require the use of English. Arrangements could thus be negotiated with the Office de la langue française, the regulatory body, when sales outside Quebec represented more than 50% of the revenues or whenever particular competitive situations existed.

The Charter's objectives are strictly linguistic, without direct reference to the promotion of social mobility. Individual knowledge of French became a general target, and pursuit of that target was viewed as a means of ensuring the use of French at work. The Charter provided for two types of measures:

— *The language of business:* universal measures dealing with public signs and posters, labor relations, contracts, invoices, and personnel notices (see Bill 101, this volume, Appendix 1, sections 51–71).

— *The language of work:* universal provisions with respect to the francization of business by means of specific action programs are proposed and implemented by the firm in order to obtain a francization certificate (see Bill 101, this volume, Appendix 1, sections 135–156).

The premises underlying Quebec's public intervention with respect to linguistic matters are the following:

— Francization of the workplace is a critical lever for reaching a new linguistic equilibrium in Quebec. The objective was the omnipresence of French in business in Quebec and not simply the co-existence of English and French.

— Companies, as legal persons created by law, do not have a language but are instruments which must be operated in such a way as to respect the virtual rights of employees and customers. Consequently, operating regulations, working documents, and linguistic policies and practices of firms must be adapted to accommodate French usage.

— A greater francophone participation in business is a means of spreading the use of French over the long run. Raising francophone presence will be achieved by linguistic means. Francophone participation is defined as the presence of persons who know French. Individuals whose native tongue, or whose most commonly used language, is not French but who can and want to work in French, contribute to the francophone presence.

3. A conceptual framework for understanding francization as a process of change

The language change process intended by the Charter of the French Language hinges on modern organization theory as basically stated in texts by March & Simon (1958), Thompson (1967) and Quinn (1980). The change process was based on organization theory from which effective means of action could be inferred. The long-term objective of making the use of French general at all levels within firms meant that many firms had to modify their internal organizational practices. Firms were not asked to meet immediate norms but rather to design programs based on explicit conceptual scheme which will be briefly discussed in this section (for full details see Daoust, this volume, chapter 4).

The architects of Bill 101 did not directly use organizational change theories in the process of designing the legislation. However, change theories *were* used to design ways and means of *application* of the legislation. It is precisely at the stage of designing regulations that organizational change theories were used by consultants and governmental officials. The application of the legislation was conceived as a planned organizational change process. Here are the key elements of this change framework.

Francization as the trigger of organizational change. Francization and francophonization of the business firm are two action dimensions which are related but, as indicated in Figure 2, not in a directly linear fashion. *Francization* is defined as the use of the French language in management documents, official documents, forms, meetings and formal superior-subordinate relations. *Francophonization* is defined as the presence of *persons* whose knowledge of the French language is such that they can function in a working environment where French is the language of work.

Two fundamental change options can be inferred in Figure 2. Policy I insists on francophonization as the main trigger variable promoting francization. Firms using such a policy would stress a *manpower* approach through the recruitment of persons with a strong command of French to attain their targets. The second policy approach implies that firms will francize most of their management *documents* and will eventually need to raise the degree of knowledge of French of their manpower resources. The extensive use of French in the workplace will make it possible for persons with an unsatisfactory knowledge to learn on the job. Policy II is the change theory which underlay the design of regulations with respect to the language of the workplace within Bill 101.

FIGURE 2 *Two Dimensions of the Francization Process*

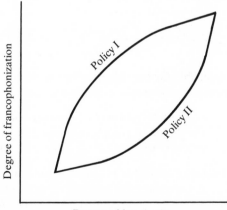

Degree of francization

Firms are composed of distinct organizational spaces. An enterprise does not constitute a monolithic unit integrated by managerial authority but, on the contrary, is divided into distinct organizational spaces having different linguistic requirements. The notion of internal differentiation has been prevalent in the socio-technical approach to organization best described in Miller & Trist (1967). An organizational space is a sub-system within the firm which is differentiated from others by: its managerial, commercial and technical relationships; its tasks, whether management, research or production; and the linguistic capabilities of its employees. Contingent changes, objectives and program are formulated for the particular situation of each organization group. There are four types of organizational groups: head offices, research centres, operations, and high technology groups.

Individual customers may be served in the language of their choice. However, French is to become the language of work at the operational level. The general use of French is the ultimate objective for factories, workshops, retail stores, and branch offices of financial institutions such as banks and trust companies. In certain cases, owing to an unusual combination of requirements, the use of English is permitted. French will also be the language of written communications and of technical or administrative documents, particularly at the foreman and subordinate levels.

Head offices and research laboratories as distinct organizational spaces may be exempted upon request. Furthermore, highly specialized technological companies can negotiate specific agreements with the regulatory body. These agreements may provide for exceptions to take account of a company's particular character and its North American business relationships (see Laporte, this volume, chapter 3). To qualify, organizational spaces must be:

— national or international head offices of businesses with more than 50% of gross revenue generated outside Quebec;

— centres responsible for managing and carrying out a firm's research and development activities;

— companies with frequent national or international communications and in which the technical complexity of operations and the highly specialized manpower require the use of English.

Long lasting changes focus on key strategic variables and program. The Charter of the French Language seeks to influence a company's management to modify the organizational situations that are the probable causes of the low use of French among its managerial staff. Consequently, the approach is to induce management to modify key variables by means of programs. The key decisional variables on which these programs focus their concern deal primarily with the linguistic policies and practices governing a firm's operations.

Establishing a language policy is certainly the most important elements of a firm's posture with respect to its employees, clients, and suppliers. Such a policy enables the firm to define its responsibilities with respect to its employees and to lay down the specific conditions of language use in each of its organizational groups. A language policy may deal with the following elements: human resources, communication with clients and suppliers, internal communication, signs and posters, and official and management documents.

Changes will be achieved through coherent programs. Francization programs are not uniform across firms and pursue distinct objectives. Programs for changing the use of languages within business firms will shape key variables into an articulated framework to achieve selected targets. Examples of key strategic variables are:

— Official policies and practices concerning:
   the firm's general language policy for head office and operations;
   languages used in official documents, management documents and forms;
   rules with respect to language use in meetings.

— Internal structures:
   the location of the head office, research laboratories, and central services;
   decision with respect to the location of jobs requiring the use of English.

— The composition and attributes of human resources, particularly policies and practices with respect to:
   recruitment selection, and training;
   promotion, and linguistic requirements;
   career development.

Certain decisional variables such as organizational climate, social norms, and informal relations cannot be influenced in the short run. However, in the medium term, management can change the climate by deliberate and constant actions with respect to language used, systems and incentives.

Programs emphasize the francization of management documents as well as communication with suppliers and terminology. Therefore, the implicit hypothesis is that the francization of written communications is the driving force that will lead to the effective use of French in wider domains of language use and the gradual increase of the managerial staff's proficiency in French (see Daoust, this volume, chapter 4).

4. The impact of the francization process

A number of research ventures have attempted to measure the impact of the Charter of the French Language on Canadian business and manpower recruitment. A brief account will be given of the key research findings contained in the three studies which were used as information sources. The first study conducted in 1979 by Yvan Allaire and Roger Miller was based on a survey of 50 firms amongst the 300 or so firms in Quebec with 500 or more employees. The purpose of the study was to assess the economic impact of Bill 101 on the business firm. Furthermore, an attempt was made to arrive at a synthesis of all available published studies pertaining to the francophone presence within large Canadian business firms (Allaire & Miller, 1980).

The second study by Roger Miller and Ian McKinnon was conducted in 1980 through interviews with thirty-two presidents of large Canadian firms employing more than 500 employees. The purpose of the study was to assess the impact of Bill 101 on the recruitment practices as well as on internal policies. Particular stress was put on the recruitment of bilingual university graduates (Miller & McKinnon, 1982).

The third study was a major research project involving an in depth analysis of the change strategies in 10 large Canadian firms. Fifty senior executives were interviewed for the purpose of understanding the change strategies which were pursued. The careers of more than 200 managers were studied in detail through a formal survey approach (Sécor, 1980).

An interpretation of the key findings will be presented so as to highlight the most critical elements stemming from these studies. As one would expect from an analysis of existing large business firms established in Quebec, the business firms surveyed in these three studies were of predominantly anglophone tradition though a few large firms of predominantly francophone tradition were also surveyed in the original studies. The key findings presented in this chapter apply to firms of both linguistic traditions unless stated otherwise.

The legislation formalized a change process already underway. A dominant finding is that the Charter of the French Language did not have major effects on the conduct of business in Quebec (Miller & McKinnon, 1982). The linguistic requirements for doing business successfully in Quebec had changed quite markedly in the last few years, prior to Bill 101. Yet a linguistic legislation was introduced.

The resolution of this paradox lies in the belief that the changed linguistic demands of the market and the passage of linguistic legislations have a common genesis in the changed times and opinions in Quebec.

Corporations respond to perceived market and socio-political forces and those forces had already made conducting a major business in Quebec solely in English an anachronism. Business responds to consumers and as a consequence, there is a strong consumer preference for service in his/her primary language (see Figure 1). Similarly, individual bilingualism is viewed by business executives in economic terms, namely as a valuable asset and as a pre-requisite for many jobs. Consumer demands for French, whether individual or corporate, is viewed as exogenous to such specific government actions as the implementation of the Charter of the French Language. Changed patterns of consumer demands and preferences were not ascribed to government actions in our studies since it was felt that market and socio-political forces had already had their effect in favour of greater French usage.

French and English are used as languages of business (Sécor, 1980). Serving customers in the language of their choice has been easy to achieve. However, the necessity to install bilingual interfaces between firms and their customers or suppliers did not lead to the extension of bilingualism within the operational core of most firms, except for business which render services requiring extensive contact with clients.

In addition to a mass market in Quebec which is predominantly French-speaking, there is general agreement that the linguistic composition of the management group had changed. In commercial relations there is a tendency to deal in the customer firm's language of choice, particularly for the firms which are providers of services or highly substitutable products. Firms which produce homogeneous and substitutable products are in no position to impose their language of business especially when customers wish to use their economic bargaining power to spur the use of their own language. As French-speaking Canadians increasingly become involved in management functions, the demand for French service and communications increases correspondingly, even between firms.

Operational units function largely in French (Allaire & Miller, 1980). Voluntary adaptations as well as regulations have succeeded in making French the language of internal communications of most workplaces except in head offices. In essence, there are substantial economies perceived in running internal operations unilingually. Therefore, the result has been to create significant incentives for moving to French as the language of work at the operational level. This has been particularly noticeable in firms which provide standardized goods or services. Manufacturing, service and sales operations of large firms in Quebec are using French as a language of work and both French and English as languages of business. Employees who are in contact with customers have to be bilingual. In many cases, supervisory employees in Quebec operations need to be bilingual, but in many firms, knowledge of English is not even required.

Canadian head offices in Montreal make extensive use of English (Miller & McKinnon, 1982). Most head offices of large Canadian firms have special agreements with the Office de la langue française. As a consequence, much of the general management work is still conducted in English even in centralized common services which are not general management activities. Thus, in a large number of head office departments such as finance, computer services or engineering, unilingual anglophone employees are still being recruited. However, the number of persons recruited directly at the head office is small as employees begin their careers at the operational level.

The main effect of the Charter of the French Language at the head office has been to introduce some form of bilingualism. Written communications at the head offices are still in English. However, the possibility to function without at least a passive ability to work in French is gone. Promotion to the head office is usually from operations where French has become the language of work, thus bringing French usage to management levels which in the past operated mostly in English.

There is some tendency for head offices and research units to be used as a place to locate unilingual anglophone employees whom firms do not wish to or cannot train in French. This expedient is viewed as a temporary stage because there would, as time went on, be fewer and fewer senior, unilingual anglophone employees.

High technology firms have chosen new organization designs. High technology firms do not function strictly in French at the operational level. Specialized departments and organizational units still function in English, given the importance of interacting with the customers in the production of the goods or the service which to this day remain predominantly anglo-continental rather than based in francophone Quebec. The structural adaptation which high technology usually makes is the creation of task forces or project units, each of which works in the client's preferred language.

The linguistic requirements of jobs and recruitment. Most firms have only broad linguistic requirements for entry or promotion. In our study of recruitment practices (Miller & McKinnon, 1982) our survey results showed that large firms formally use a linguistic definition of francophone and not an ethnic one. What happens informally is difficult to measure. In only two firms out of 32 did the senior personnel officer distinguish between a cultural/ethnic definition of francophone. Small firms on the other hand, especially insofar as customer relationships are concerned, tend to choose an ethnic definition so as to minimize the risk of having difficulties with clients.

Our survey results (Miller & McKinnon, 1982) showed that for the vast majority of job-seekers, at least a passive ability to understand written and oral French is a minimum requirement. For clerical or managerial jobs, an active ability to work in French is required. There are highly specialized niches in which employees of large or specialized companies can be employed and work without understanding French. Table 1 presents a summary of formal hiring policies of a sample of 32 large Canadian firms with head offices in Montreal. It must be emphasized that these are minimum standards and that the case of the "no linguistic requirements" reflects an absence of formal requirements and not a willingness to hire someone with no ability in French.

Results described in Table 1 show that while French unilingualism is possible in the lower echelons of business firms, French-English bilingualism becomes a necessity at the upper echelons of business firms (Miller & McKinnon, 1982).

Individual bilingualism for career advancement. As a consequence of the francization process, the vast majority of jobs require a knowledge of French. Yet, we have found (Miller & McKinnon, 1982) that to advance one's career, bilingualism is extremely important. This creates a paradox: at entry level, the pressure is on anglophones to demonstrate that they can function in French; at higher levels, there is a pressure on francophones to demonstrate their ability in English.

Language skills are akin to any other marketable skill. That is, jobs usually carried language requirements depending on the demands of the task. Thus, prospective employees have to offer the skills which are sought by firms. Bilingualism is almost always viewed as an advantage even when the immediate job requirements do not call for it. For anglophone applicants, the requirement of bilingualism is explicit, while for the francophone candidates, the requirement is implicit.

Economic effects on firms and jobs. The costs and benefits of implementing francization programs show wide inter-firm variations. Many firms, as a result of previous voluntary actions, incurred minimal costs while other firms had to pay substantial translation costs (see Laporte, this volume, chapter 3).

In firms employing more than 500 employees, linguistic analyses and the implementation of francization programs on average represent costs

TABLE 1 *Summary of minimum linguistic requirement for recruitment into selected jobs in large Canadian firms with head offices in Montreal*

Linguistic requirements for recruitment at head office for management and staff positions

— Intermediate bilingualism (oral and reading)	21/32
— No linguistic requirements (but preference for bilingualism)	11/32
— Requirements waived for selected skills	15/32

Linguistic requirements for management and technical recruits in Quebec operations

— Intermediate bilingualism (oral and reading)	22/32
— Intermediate bilingualism (oral and reading) with *temporary* preference for bilingual francophones	5/32
— No linguistic requirements at entry*	5/32

Linguistic requirements for employees in contact with customers

— Full bilingualism (oral, reading, writing)	16/32
— Full bilingualism (oral, reading, writing)	8/32
— No linguistic requirements (customers are often outside Quebec)*	8/32

Linguistic requirements for technicians

— Knowledge of French (oral and reading)	22/32
— Knowledge of French (oral and reading) with temporary preference for bilingual francophone	5/32
— No formal linguistic requirements*	5/32

Linguistic requirements for foremen and blue collar workers

— Knowledge of oral and reading French	24/32
— No formal linguistic requirements*	8/32

Linguistic requirements for secretaries in manufacturing and sales

— Full knowledge of French (oral, reading and writing level)	28/32
— No formal linguistic requirements	4/32

Linguistic requirements for secretaries at head office

— Full bilingualism (oral, reading, writing)	28/32
— No formal linguistic requirements	4/32

---

*Absence of formal requirements, but an implicit expectation of some bilingualism.

Source: Miller, R. & McKinnon, I. 1982, *Corporate recruitment practices*. Montreal: Alliance Quebec.

equivalent to $60 per employee per year for the five year duration of the program (Allaire & Miller, 1980). In aggregate terms, for all firms employing 50 or more employees, the cost of francization represents an estimated annual cost of $96 million or approximately 0.2% of the annual gross national product of Quebec. Such costs cannot be ignored, but are in line with other public interventions in domains such as consumer protection, anti-pollution controls and conversion programs from imperial weights and measures to the metric system (Allaire & Miller, 1980).

Losses of jobs over five years as a result of the moves of head offices out of Montreal, though important, seem to be in line with the estimates of 14,000 jobs made by Sécor in 1977 (Allaire & Miller, 1980). Such a price seemed acceptable in 1977 but less so in the period of economic decline which Quebec is experiencing along with Canada in the 1980s. The transfer of head office jobs to Toronto probably had the effect of partly reducing the role of Montreal as a major economic center. However, the rise of a dynamic francophone managerial and entrepreneur class is slowly replacing the gap that was created by the departure of anglophone firms and personnel from Quebec.

In the absence of a federal legislation establishing a minimal form of institutional bilingualism within the private national enterprises it regulates such as banks and transportation companies or without constant persuasion to encourage Canadian firms to promote linguistic duality in their head offices regardless of their location, it is natural that managements would prefer to withdraw activities away from Quebec and escape costs imposed by a provincial legislation.

The actions of the Quebec government with respect to language matters has had effects that are at the same time beneficial and prejudicial. Bill 101 helped satisfy the expectations of the majority of the population but at the same time led to a loss of jobs resulting from the transfer of activities outside Quebec, slow investment growth and uncertainty. However, various polls conducted since the Charter came into effect in 1977 indicate that, with the exception of certain provisions, the francophone population welcomes linguistic interventions (see Laporte, this volume, chapter 3). The same is not true for the anglophone population (see Taylor & Simard, this volume, chapter 7; Caldwell, this volume, chapter 9; d'Anglejan, this volume, chapter 2).

5. Summary and conclusions

The key targets of the Charter of the French Language were, first, to make French the language of work at the operational level; second, to spur the use of French as a language of business between corporate bodies in Quebec; and third, to ensure that individual customers are served in the language of their choice.

Except in high technology industries with North American or world-wide sales, the implementation of means to achieve those targets has modified substantially the linguistic requirements for entrants into the Quebec market. More precisely:

— French has become, at least officially, the language of work for the operational level units, such as manufacturing and sales. Most new employees recruited into these units face new linguistic requirements with respect to minimum knowledge of French.

— Head offices continue to use English as the language of work, even though they are spurred into actions aimed at increasing the language abilities of employees and the use of French in official documents.

— Employees in contact with customers are expected to have a degree of bilingualism compatible with the requirements of the tasks. In some cases only an oral ability is required; in others full reading, writing and speaking skills are required.

One of the key changes observed has been that economic and legal incentives exist for many anglophones in Quebec to become bilingual while the Charter of the French Language has removed the prerequisite of knowledge of English for many jobs in Quebec. Thus, firms do not expect, at least officially, young francophones in sales and manufacturing to be bilingual while they expect anglophones to have reading and oral abilities in French. Fluently bilingual anglophones in Quebec are in a particularly enviable position, especially those with administrative or technical skills who are indeed in high demand. Fluently bilingual anglophones have more career opportunities than any other group in Quebec. The hypothesis that this group might be discriminated against because they do not have a French background was not confirmed in our research (Miller & McKinnon, 1982).

Given the fact that large Canadian firms serve the Quebec market whatever the location of their head offices, the most dysfunctional effect of the Charter of the French Language has been to impose extra costs on head offices located in Montreal. Other provinces do not impose such costs. A possible response to some of these dysfunctional effects could be to improve bilingualism in Canadian business firms serving the Quebec market. More bilingualism within such firms would reduce extra costs on head offices located in Montreal and obviate the need to transfer head offices. To stimulate bilingualism within Canadian business firms, the Canadian Government could persuade publicly regulated industries such as transportation, telecommunication and banking to become more bilingual. Enforced bilingualism in head offices of Canadian Crown Corporations could also be an appropriate action to serve such goals. Though such government measures could produce their intended effect, there is as yet little indication that the Canadian Federal Government is moving in this direction.

References

ALLAIRE, Y. & MILLER, R. 1980, *The Canadian Business Response to Legislation of the Workplace*. Montreal: C. D. Howe Research Institute.

CANADA 1969, *Report of the Royal Commission on Bilingualism and Biculturalism*. Ottawa: Queen's Printer.

LAURIN, C. 1977, *Quebec's Policy on the French Language*. Quebec: Editeur officiel du Québec.

MARCH, E. J. & SIMON, H. A. 1958, *Organizations*. New York: Wiley.

MILLER, E. J. & TRIST, E. 1967, *Systems of Organizations*. London: Tavistock.

MILLER, R. & LAPOINTE, A. 1980, *La reglementation sociale de l'entreprise*. Montreal: Chambre de Commerce de Montréal.

MILLER, R. & MCKINNON, I. 1982, *Corporate recruitment practices*. Montreal: Alliance Québec.

MORRISON, R. 1970, *Corporate Adaptability to Bilingualism and Biculturalism*. Ottawa: Queen's Printer.

QUEBEC GOVERNMENT OF, 1972, *Report of the Commission of Inquiry on the Position of the French Language and on Language Rights in Quebec*. (Gendron Commission). Québec: Editeur officiel du Québec.

— 1977, *Quebec National Assembly, Bill 1: Charter of the French Language in Quebec*. Québec: Editeur officiel du Québec.

QUINN, J. B. 1980, *Strategies for Change*. Homewood, Illinois: Irwin.

SÉCOR, 1980, *L'adaptation linguistique des entreprises canadiennes*. Ottawa: Department of Supply and Services.

THOMPSON, J. D. 1967, *Organizations in Action*. New York: McGraw-Hill.

6 Social class and language policies in Quebec

William D. Coleman
McMaster University

More than five years have now passed since the introduction of the Charter of the French Language (Bill 101) and nine years have gone by since the passage of the Official Language Act of 1974 (Bill 22). The province of Quebec has thus experienced a comprehensive language policy for close to a decade. As the years slowly edge by, public recollection of the debates surrounding the introduction of these two laws and how various social groups reacted to them begin to fade. Certain facts become submerged under dominant impressions, impressions that assume more and more almost mythical forms. As these myths become fixed in the public perception of the Charter in particular, political debates become coloured by them. They enter into arguments as unquestioned assumptions and the debates become potentially misleading.

Four myths in particular seem to be in the process of developing around Bill 101, both in Quebec and in English Canada.

1. The Parti Québécois government was insensitive and hostile to business and introduced Bill 101 in the face of the uniform and hostile opposition of the business community.
2. As a result of Bill 101, the world of business in Quebec is moving rapidly toward becoming monolithically French.
3. Francophones in Quebec were collectively supportive of the government when it introduced Bill 101 and remain united as a community today behind the legislation.
4. Bill 101 was perhaps the most positive step since the heyday of the

"Quiet Revolution" in the early 1960s in moving Quebec toward the political status of an independent nation-state.

Like all myths, the four statements above are deviations from reality and only partly based on what in fact has actually occurred with Bill 101. Questioning these myths requires a careful examination of Quebec politics. This examination must include three components. A set of social concepts must be developed for describing the social and political divisions within Quebec's francophone, anglophone and allophone communities. Secondly, the overall policy context within which both Bill 22 and Bill 101 were passed must be established. Finally, a careful analysis of the political process spanning the introduction of the White Paper on language in April 1977 to the passage of the final version of Bill 101 in August 1977 must be made. We shall begin here with a definition of the social groups that participated in the debates on the Charter. Part two of the chapter will sketch out the overall policy context. Parts three, four, and five will then be devoted to an analysis of the politics surrounding the passage of Bill 101 into law.

1. The definition of social groups

The organized interest groups that involved themselves in the political debates over language planning in Quebec were divided along two lines of cleavage, social class and language. By social class, we shall follow Poulantzas (1978) and define it as a grouping which shares first of all a common place in the production process. However such a common place is not sufficient for identifying social classes because they are formed in political and ideological struggles (Przeworski, 1977). Below we shall identify the class-based and language-based groupings that took an active part in the discussions of Bill 101. These groupings will be presented in their order of importance within the Quebec economy.

a) English-Canadian and American employer class. This class dominates the resource and manufacturing industries in Quebec. According to Sales (1979:183), it controlled 78.7% of the manufacturing industries in Quebec in 1974. The political interests of this class tend to be represented by the large corporations themselves and in the Bill 101 debate by the following interest groups: the *Conseil du Patronat du Québec* (CPQ), the Quebec Division of the Canadian Manufacturers' Association, the Positive Action Committee, and the Montreal Board of Trade.[1]

b) The francophone employer class. This group owns a little over 20% of the manufacturing industry in Quebec. It is strongest in the food and beverage industries, wood manufacturing, and transportation materials. However, even in these sectors, this class owns less than 50% of the production. The following interest groups tended to represent the views of this class in the language debates: the *Chambre de Commerce de la Province du Québec* (CCPQ), the *Chambre de Commerce du District de Montréal* (CCDM) and the *Centre des dirigeants d'entreprise* (CDE).[2]

c) The francophone *petite* bourgeoisie. This class includes primarily those individuals who neither own nor possess means of production and do not engage in the production of goods. Often, a distinction is drawn between the "new" and the "traditional" members of this class. The "new" category includes those who perform services whose products and activities are consumed directly as use values. Examples would be public service professionals (engineers and accountants), teachers, journalists, professors and other *travailleurs de la langue*. The "traditional" group embraces primarily independent commodity producers such as farmers, small shopkeepers, and self-employed professionals such as doctors and lawyers. Some of the groups participating in the language debate tended to draw from both components of this class: the *Mouvement Québec français* (MQF) and the *Société Saint-Jean-Baptiste de Montréal* (SSJBM) for example.[3] Other groups participating were more clearly in one component than the other — the *Union des producteurs agricoles* (UPA) and the *Centrale de l'enseignement du Québec* (CEQ) being prominent examples.

d) The anglophone *petite* bourgeoisie. The most vocal representatives of this class were drawn from those who worked in the various educational and health bureaucracies or who taught in the English-speaking schools and universities. The Protestant School Board of Greater Montreal and the Provincial Association of Catholic Teachers were participants in the debate who were drawn from this class.

e) Organized labour. Primarily francophone but also with small anglophone and allophone segments, this class took part in the debate through the representatives of the Confederation of National Trade Unions (CNTU), a Quebec-based and almost exclusively French organization, and the Quebec Federation of Labour (QFL). The latter was the home of the American-based unions active in Quebec and also was the labour organization most clearly identified with the *Parti Québécois*. The CNTU tended to be strongest among public sector workers while the QFL was more concentrated in private sector industries. The majority of workers in Quebec are not unionized and were not represented directly in the language planning debates.

f) The allophone *petite* bourgeoisie. Various groups tended to speak for the smaller cultural communities in Quebec with the *Fédération des groupes ethniques du Québec* and the *Congrès national des Italo-Canadiens* being prominent examples.

In conclusion, it should be noted that these six groups are not exhaustive of Quebec's class structure. However, in the context of the specific debates over language planning, these were the groups that dominated the public discussions that occurred.

2. The policy context

Perhaps the dominant goal of the "Quiet Revolution" in Quebec that began late in 1959 and ended sometime in 1965 was economic *rattrapage* ("catching-up"). Led ostensibly by the francophone employer class working with the provincial government, the francophone collectivity set its course for catching up economically with the rest of North America. The goal of *rattrapage* therefore entailed an acceptance of the advanced industrial society found elsewhere in North America and a desire to participate fully in that society. Implicitly, then, there was an assumption that French-speaking Quebecers shared important values and cultural norms with the rest of North America.

Economically, this goal was pursued in the early sixties with the active support of the Quebec provincial government. Hydro-electric power companies were nationalized in 1963, an investment corporation (the *Société générale de financement*) was created in the same year, and crown corporations for steel-making and mineral exploration (Sidbec and Soquem respectively) were set up in 1964 and 1965 respectively. Services supporting industry were expanded and modernized. In the early seventies, the government shifted its policy direction slightly by giving more emphasis to the private sector and to co-operation rather than competition with multinational corporations controlled by the Anglo-Canadian and American employer class. The emphasis therefore became explicitly one of integration into the corporate structure of North America.

The commitment to economic *rattrapage* was complemented by changes in educational and social welfare institutions as well. The education system was secularized and put under the authority of a Ministry of Education rather than the bishops in 1964. The classical colleges were abolished and replaced by a system of high schools (*polyvalentes*) and general and vocational colleges (CEGEPs) which emphasized strongly the development of skills appropriate to advanced industry in 1967. Similarly, hospitals and other health and welfare institutions were transferred from Church control to the provincial government in the late sixties. Capital expansion took place and new structures were built to accommodate the growing needs of urban Quebec.

These economic, educational and social changes helped pave the way for francophone Quebecers to aim for positions at middle and senior levels of management in Quebec's economy. The growth of the francophone employer class occurred at the same time that the working class was increasing its organizations' strength and radicalizing. The very institutions of advanced capitalism that the francophone business class was seeking to penetrate with the support of the state were coming under an intensive critique by labour. This critique was even more powerful in emotional force because it could be expressed simultaneously in ethnic terms. We have already indicated that Quebec's economy was dominated by English Canadian and American corporations. These corporations tended to present themselves with an English face not only to their own workers but to the public at large in the province. The normal class cleavages then between workers and employers were *reinforced* by the cleavage between French and English-speaking groups. Hence as the labour organizations such as the CNTU, the QFL and the CEQ intensified their critique of capitalism in Quebec, they were politically very effective because the normal class antagonisms in labour struggles were supplemented by the historical ethnic antagonism long present in Quebec society. Nonetheless by the early seventies, the pursuit of the objective of economic *rattrapage* had come to mean working with the English-speaking corporations. If this objective was to be successfully pursued, somehow this increasingly devastating critique of capitalism by the labour organizations had to be defused.

The global policies on language that came in the form of the Official Language Act of 1974 (Bill 22) and the *Charter of the French Language* of 1977 (Bill 101) had two objectives relevant to this defusion process when it came to the world of business. First, they were to open doors for francophones aspiring to management positions in the private sector without, it should be added, changing the basic ownership structure of the economy. Industry continued to remain in the control of the English Canadian and American employer class. Secondly, they were designed to integrate the dominant overwhelmingly English-speaking corporations more solidly into the fabric of Quebec's social life. They were expected to remove the lightning rod of ethnicity that added so much fervour to the critique of capitalism in Quebec. These arguments will be developed by looking at language policy as it affected three aspects of the world of business in Quebec: the linguistic image of business, the language used on the shop floor, and the language used by management. For the purposes of this chapter, the analysis will be focussed primarily on the *Charter of the French Language* with relatively little attention paid to the Official Language Act of 1974.[4]

3. The situation prior to Bill 22 and Bill 101

The traditional francophone *petite* bourgeoisie in Quebec had been a critic of the way English Canadian and American business presented itself to consumers. A series of organizations such as the *Société du bon parler français* and the *Comité permanent de la survivance française* (later the *Conseil de la vie française*) had been erected by this class to lead the attack on the language practices of business. Campaigns were conducted to pressure businesses to adopt at a minimum bilingual names, to label their products and write their notices and signs in French as well as English. Typical of these campaigns was the struggle over the naming of the new Canadian National Railways hotel being built in Montreal in the fifties. The corporation had proposed the name "The Queen Elizabeth" after the recently-crowned British monarch. Nationalist groups countered with the name "Le Château Maisonneuve", a name rooted in the city's history and parallel to the names of the corporation's hotels in Quebec City and Ottawa (the Château Frontenac and the Château Laurier respectively). An intense media blitz was carried out and a petition with over 200,000 signatures was sent to Ottawa, but all to no avail. The CNR prevailed as did the similar language practices of the other large corporations in the province.

The situation was no more encouraging when it came to the language practices of workers on the shop floor. Surveys carried out by one of Quebec's major trade union centrals, the CNTU, and the Quebec Division of the Canadian Manufacturers' Association in the mid-sixties showed that workers often could not communicate with their superiors in French. Collective agreements were drawn up in English as often as they were drawn up in French. Not infrequently, they were unable to bargain collectively in French. These early rather limited surveys were later substantiated by studies carried out by the Commission of Inquiry on the Position of the French Language and on Language Rights in Quebec (Gendron Commission) which was created in 1968. The Commission wrote: "We have defined a socio-linguistic structure which proves beyond question that the domain of the French language is particularly characterized by inferior duties, small enterprises, low incomes and low levels of education" (Quebec, 1972:77). Gradually then during the sixties and into the early seventies, organized labour with the support of the francophone *petite* bourgeoisie began to press the demand that they had the *right* to work in French. Organizations representing the francophone employer class agreed in principle with this demand. However, organizations representing the English Canadian and American employers such as the Montreal Board of Trade and the Quebec Division of the Canadian Manufacturers' Association along with such firms as Imperial Oil Ltd. and Dominion Glass opposed the recognition of such a right (Coleman, 1980:100).

The extensive control of business by English Canadian and American firms (Sales, 1979; Raynauld, 1974) meant as well that the language used at the level of management was overwhelmingly English. The Gendron Commission through the studies it commissioned confirmed this practice (Quebec, 1972). It demonstrated that movement up the management ladder where reading and writing activities become more important in conducting the business of the firm also entailed movement away from French to English. These findings supported francophone employers who demanded that steps should be taken to "encourage" or "persuade" firms operating in Quebec to incorporate more francophones into management positions and to increase the use of French at these levels. Even the *Conseil du Patronat* (1973:46) which tended to represent English Canadian and American corporations conceded that such proposals were not unreasonable and perhaps needed.

In summary, by the mid-seventies, a series of critiques had been mounted against language practices within business firms. The stage was set for the government to move to change some of these practices. The examination of the steps taken by the *Parti Québécois* government in the spring of 1977 to address these problems will now allow us to reflect systematically on the myths we presented at the outset of this chapter.

4. The introduction of Bill 1

On April 1, 1977, Dr Camille Laurin, the Minister of State for Cultural Development published a White Paper entitled *La politique québécoise de la langue française* which set out the general principles of the *Parti Québécois* policy on language (Laurin, 1977). Four weeks later on April 27, he introduced to the National Assembly Bill 1, the first version of the *Charter of the French Language*. The proposed law was then sent to the Permanent Parliamentary Committee on Education, Cultural Affairs and Communications for public study. Briefs were invited by the Committee and publicly televised hearings were held. In the end, it received 270 submissions and invited 62 individuals and groups to appear before the cameras (Coleman, 1981:464). At the beginning of July, the bill was withdrawn, changed, and resubmitted as a new bill, Bill 101, to speed its passage through the legislature.

Bill 1, the first version of the law, is important for two reasons. First, *it* was the piece of legislation discussed extensively by the citizens of Quebec and provides us with a barometer of the distribution of opinion on Quebec language policies. Secondly, the bill was developed in relative isolation from the business community in particular and reflected the ideal language policy as it would have been drafted by the francophone *petite* bourgeoisie. In this respect, it incurred some opposition from the business community *and was eventually changed to meet some of that community's concerns.*

We shall return to these changes below. Before doing so, however, it is useful to note that an examination of the briefs presented to the parliamentary committee shows two things related to the myths with which we began this chapter. First, the briefs fell into four categories when it came to assessing the legislation (Coleman, 1981:474).

1. Unqualified supporters. Typical of this category is the following statement by the QFL: "La Fédération des travailleurs du Québec appuie profondément le projet de la Charte de la langue française, et nous lançons un appel aux travailleurs québécois pour qu'ils ne se laissent pas prendre au jeu des sondages alarmistes, des déclarations catastrophiques. Notre appui au projet de loi est inconditionnel" (QFL, 1977:1–2).[5]

2. Supporters with limited criticisms. This category contains groups who did not question the overall goals of the legislation but offered specialized criticisms of particular, limited aspects of the law.

3. Qualified supporters. Individuals and groups falling in this category accepted the overall goals of the legislation but were very critical of selected, important parts of the bill. Typically, these groups and individuals chided the government for ignoring economic reality. The Positive Action Committee wrote: "We are absolutely convinced that language and culture can only flourish to their full potential in a climate of economic growth and prosperity. Thus the aims of the legislation should be accomplished in a way that does not unwittingly or unnecessarily penalize Quebec's economic development" (PAC, 1977:5).

4. Unqualified opponents. An admittedly extreme sample of the opinion in this category comes from the St Andrew's Society of Montreal. "Je suis bouche bée devant une telle loi, cela ouvre la porte sur le retour de l'Inquisition, ou plus récemment le régime hitlérien alors que les enfants pouvaient dénoncer leurs voisins ou même leurs parents! Pour un pays comme le Canada qui a des traditions de liberté ancrées dans la Magna Carta de 1215, et dont le Canada français a profité depuis 200 ans, cette loi n'est pas en conformité avec l'histoire de notre pays" (St Andrew's Society, 1977:1).[6]

TABLE 1 *Classification of Responses to Bill 1 on the basis of briefs submitted to the Parliamentary Committee: May–June, 1977*

Language community	Virtually unqualified supporters	Accept overall goal with limited and specialized criticisms	Accept overall goal with numerous criticisims	Virtually unqualified opponents
Francophone	— Francophone petite bourgeoisie (UPA, CEQ, SSJBM, MQF, les Fils du Québec, Mouvement national des Québécois) — Organized labour (CNTU, QFL)	— Francophone petite bourgeoisie (traditional) (Le Barreau du Québec)	— Francophone employer class (CCPQ, CCDM, CDE) — Francophone petite bourgeoisie (new) (Ordre des ingénieurs du Québec)	
Allophone and Aboriginal Peoples		— Grand Council of Crees Les Indiens Naskapi Northern Quebec Inuit Association	— Allophone petite bourgeoisie (Congrès national des Italo-Canadiens; Fédération des groupes ethniques du Québec)	
Anglophone	— Anglophone petite bourgeoisie (Comité anglophone pour un Québec unifié)	— International Air Transport Association; Comité des directeurs des centres de recherches industriels	— English Canadian and American employer class (CMA, CPQ, MBT, PAC, Alcan, Bell Canada, Royal Bank of Canada) — Anglophone petite bourgeoisie (Provincial Association of Protestant Teachers)	— Anglophone petite bourgeoisie (McGill University, Protestant School Board of Greater Montreal, Provincial Association of Catholic Teachers)

The individuals and groups falling into these four categories are summarized in a fashion in Table 1. Several points emerge from this table. First, it is clear that the francophone community in Quebec was not at all united in its evaluation of Bill 1. The most pronounced difference was between the *petite* bourgeoisie and organized labour on the one hand and the employer class on the other. Secondly, where the employer class was quite united on its evaluation of the law, the *petite* bourgeoisie could not have been more divided. The differences between francophones and anglophones in this class derive as much from the educational provisions of the bill as from the economic provisions discussed in this article (Coleman, 1981). Thirdly, although the francophone and anglophone components of the employer class appear to be more united on language policy than the *petite* bourgeoisie, anglophone-based companies have manifested more discontent with the law since its passage than francophone employers. The departure of head office operations from Montreal that began in the late sixties has continued and perhaps accelerated. Furthermore, the laggards in francization reported by the *Office de la langue française* (OLF) in its most recent reports have been anglophone-based companies virtually without exception (OLF, 1983). Finally, although the business community was critical of parts of the bill there was generally speaking a willingness to accept the overall policy objectives of the government. The criticisms that were offered were constructive, usually carefully thought-out, and well-argued. There was no real evidence of a destructive approach to the bill as was found in submissions from the anglophone *petite* bougeoisie. We turn now to examine what these criticisms were and how the government responded to them.

5. From Bill 1 to Bill 101: Accommodation

In section 3 we noted three aspects of language legislation affecting the private sector: those affecting the linguistic image of business firms, the language of work on the shop floor, and the language used at management levels. The treatment of these areas has been quite extensive in previous chapters of this volume. For the purposes of this chapter, it will be sufficient to briefly review what the Charter proposed for changing linguistic practices in business firms. This review will be followed by an analysis of the aspects of Bill 1 relating to francization of management levels that were opposed by business groups and later amended by the government.

Bill 101 contained a series of articles designed to ensure that the linguistic image of the private sector in Quebec became unilingual French. All notices and signs advertising products were to be in French only. Exemptions from this rule were given only to businesses employing less than four people, to certain cultural organizations, and in 1979 to firms advertising cultural and educational products. Firm names and product labels were to give priority to French but not to the exclusion of English (see articles 51–71, Bill 101, this volume, Appendix I).

Secondly, the Charter reinforced significantly legal protections for the use of French as the language of work. Workers were given the right to work in French. All written communications with superiors, collective agreements, grievance proceedings and the like were to take place in French. Employees could not be fired, laid-off, or displaced because they spoke only French. Employers were expected to prove to the *Office de la langue française* (OLF) that a position required knowledge of another language before they could demand knowledge of a language other than French for that position.

The francization process to increase the usage of French at the level of management has been described in the previous three chapters at some length. The process of francization as it has emerged out of Bill 101, however, is different from the process that would have emerged out of Bill 1. An examination of these changes is useful because it will allow us to address two of the myths with which we began this chapter, namely, that the Parti Québécois government was insensitive to business demands and that the legislation has had the effect of pushing the business world in Quebec to be monolithically French.

Bill 1 was significantly more coercive as regards the francization of business firms than both Bill 101 and Bill 22. Article 106 of Bill 1 stated that firms without a francization certificate would not have the right to receive subsidies, premiums or even permits from the government. Such permits might include a licence to operate a business or even to receive electricity from Hydro Quebec. Similarly, Bill 1 provided for the creation of a *Commission de surveillance* for enforcing the law. This commission had the power to investigate suspected violations of the law and to submit them to the Attorney General for prosecution. There was no appeal mechanism or even grace period for offenders to respond, making the supervision of the language policy considerably more strict than the previous Bill 22 enacted under the Liberal government (Coleman, 1983:29). Virtually all of the major francophone business groups (the *Chambres de Commerce*, the *Centre des dirigeants d'entreprise*) and those representing the English Canadian and American employers (CMA, Montreal Board of Trade, *Conseil du Patronat*) as well as such major corporations as the Bank of Montreal and the Royal Bank of Canada protested against both of these measures very strenuously. When Bill 101 was presented to the National Assembly at the beginning of

July 1977, the offending Article 106 had been dropped completely. An appeal procedure was set up for firms who had their francization certificates revoked and the procedures of the *Commission de surveillance* were made more flexible and open (Coleman, 1983:29).

Another aspect of Bill 1 that generated considerable resentment among business interest groups and firms was the mechanism to be used in the plant for implementing the francization programme. In each establishment, a francization committee was to be set up for this purpose and one third of the members of this committee were to be named by the workers in the plant. The business class argued that decisions on the processes governing franciza- tion were management decisions and that workers had no place in that realm of the firm. The *Conseil du Patronat* (1977:6) stated in its brief to the Parliamentary Committee for example that the government must define "the role and the composition of the 'francization committees' in industrial establishments in a way so as not to introduce artificially management principles contrary to the ones normally used in our milieu".

When Bill 101 was tabled for the first reading in early July 1977, no change had been made to the francization committee procedure. However, between the first and the third reading of the Bill when public attention was no longer focused upon it, an important change was quietly made in the legislation. The francization committee was no longer to report directly to the OLF but to the *management* of the firm which would, in turn, com- municate with the *Office*. With management now clearly responsible for francization, the workers on the committee saw their possible influence considerably diminished. This change shows clearly how the Parti Québécois government sought to accommodate business. Politically, it made little sense because the party was risking offending one of its electoral constitu- encies, labour, in order to respond to a group that was heavily *anti-péquiste*, business (Hamilton & Pinard, 1976; 1977; Fournier, 1975). Despite these negative arguments on a political plane, the government proceeded anyway.

Two other changes between Bill 1 and Bill 101 are important because they show that the government left considerable room for the use of English in the superior levels of the corporate sector in Quebec. Bill 1 had stated in Article 113 that francization programmes should be set up taking account of head office operations. Briefs by the Montreal *Chambre de Commerce* and the Positive Action Committee argued that the article was too restrictive and should include research centres and regional head offices as well as national head offices. Others argued for even more specialized treatment of head office operations.

Again, in this instance, the version of Bill 101 presented at first reading was unchanged from Bill 1. However, the final, less scrutinized version of the bill and its accompanying regulations exempted head offices and research centres from the normal francization procedures. Companies with these types of offices and centres were given the option of signing special agreements with the OLF to allow for their particular language needs.

A provision of the law very much related to the treatment of head offices and research centres was that concerned with the treatment of professionals. Under the terms of Bill 1, all individuals in occupation listed under the province's Professional Code were required to have a working knowledge of French in order to receive a licence to practice. The banks, the Positive Action Committee and the Canadian Jewish Congress among others argued that the provision was too restrictive. Professionals in job situations that did not bring them into direct contact with the public should have been exempted from this requirement in their view. These individuals would be those fulfilling specialized functions in head offices and research institutes among others. Again the government relented. In Bill 101, an exemption was introduced specifically for those professional persons whose jobs were isolated from the public. In making the change, the government was in effect returning to the situation as it had been established under the Official Language Act (Bill 22) of the previous Liberal government.

The Parti Québécois government complemented this treatment of professionals in the educational provisions of Bill 101. Professionals and business managers posted to Quebec for a "temporary" stay (up to six years) were also exempted from the articles of Bill 101 requiring parents to send their children to French schools if they were not native Anglo-Quebecers (see Articles 72, 73, 85, Bill 101, this volume, Appendix I). Both the Liberals and the Parti Québécois retained quite strict French language requirements for professions having regular contact with the public such as doctors, nurses and the like.

Finally, one apparently minor change in the law from Bill 1 to Bill 101 illustrated a shift in emphasis in the law from promoting French Canadians as a national group to promoting French as a language. Such a change had been stoutly demanded by business and by other class representatives as well. Bill 1 had defined as a goal of francization an increase in the numbers of *Québécois* at all levels of employment. Bill 101 in its Article 141 replaced the word *Québécois* with the phrase *personnes ayant une bonne connaissance de la langue française*. In doing so, it made the language spoken by the individual and not his or her national background the reference point of the law.

In reviewing these several changes in the legislation from Bill 1 to Bill 101, the pattern of accommodation and of flexibility toward business described by Pierre Laporte (this volume, chapter 3) and by Denise Daoust (this volume, chapter 4) is clearly presaged. The Parti Québécois government used the opportunity provided by the Parliamentary Committee hearings to listen intently to representatives of the anglophone and the francophone business class and to make a number of adjustments in the Charter to accommodate that class's concerns. In no way can it be said that the government was insensitive or uncaring when it came to the demands of business groups and firms.

Similarly, the government can hardly be accused of running roughshod over the business community imposing unreasonable language restrictions at will. In advanced industrial economies with their centralized and large corporate structures, the key power centres are the head offices and the centres for research and development where efforts at continuous technological innovation are made. Under the terms of the Charter these decision centres which had long been the private preserves of English Canadian and American capital, were treated very generously. They and the specialized professionals working in them were allowed to make special arrangements with the OLF for language use. To argue then, as many have, that the government inflexibly imposed French on all of business in Quebec is simply wrong. The process of francization extends primarily to middle management and only very selectively beyond that point. The Charter is unlikely to result in the placing of francophones at the pinnacles of economic power in Quebec (see Miller, this volume, chapter 5).

6. Conclusions

In order to bring this chapter to a close, we shall return to the four myths with which we began.

Myth 1: The Parti Québécois government was insensitive and hostile to business and introduced Bill 101 in the face of the uniform and hostile opposition of the business community.

The analysis of language planning in Quebec contained in the previous three chapters of this volume showed quite clearly that the application of the Charter and its regulations has been done with a certain degree of sensitivity to businesses. In only rare instances, one can point to a business firm complaining of being seriously wronged by the law. It should now be evident from this chapter that this spirit behind the application of the law was already present when the terms of the law were being finalized by the

National Assembly. The *Parti Québécois* government accommodated itself very well to the demands of business when it came to the provisions applying to the *modus operandi* of the private sector. In other areas of the law dealing with education and local public institutions, the government was far less accommodating (Coleman, 1981; 1983) and this resulted in some opposition by anglophone groups (see d'Anglejan, this volume, chapter 2). What is particularly striking about the law as it applies to the private sector is its strong continuity with Bill 22, the Official Language Act of 1974 (Coleman 1981).

Myth 2: As a result of Bill 101, the world of business in Quebec is moving rapidly toward becoming monolithically French.

Under the terms of the Charter, head offices and research centres are exempted from francization as a main objective. What is more, those professionals, whether in the areas of finance or science, who work on their own in isolation from the public, were exempted from even having to know French. Therefore, those areas of the economy most important in advanced industrial societies, head offices and research institutions, were considerably less pressed to francize. Bill 101 stopped short of tampering with the operations of the central power centres of the Quebec economy. The bill's authors were satisfied with seeking the insertion of francophones at middle levels of management. They were not seeking to expand the ranks of the francophone bourgeoisie. In choosing this approach, the Parti Québécois trod a careful political path by satisfying the *petite* bourgeoisie and organized labour without excessively offending the francophone employer class. The government also managed to keep political tempers low by introducing many of its changes when few had the time or the interest to notice, between the first and third readings of Bill 101.

Myth 3: Francophones in Quebec were collectively supportive of the government when it introduced Bill 101 and remain united as a community behind the legislation.

Table 1 illustrated well that there was a range of opinion among francophones on Bill 1. The francophone employer class was considerably less positive in its assessment than was the *petite* bourgeoisie and organized labour. These divisions continue to exist in the francophone community. For example, the employer class argues that the restrictions on English language schooling even with the possibility of temporary certificates of exemption are hampering the functioning of Montreal as a business centre. The francophone *petite* bourgeoisie and organized labour respond that without these restrictions, the relative proportion of francophones in Quebec will begin an unwelcome decline over the next half century. Another possible issue for

disagreement between the francophone *petite* bourgeoisie and the francophone employer class is the continued English language practices of head
offices and research centres. The employer class sees this aspect of the law as
essential if Montreal is to retain its status as a national financial centre. On
the other side, the *petite* bourgeoisie under Bill 101 will still need to know
English if it is to advance to the upper echelons of the private sector in
Quebec.

Myth 4: Bill 101 was perhaps the most positive step since the heyday of the
          "Quiet Revolution" in moving Quebec toward the political status
          of an independent nation-state.

It is first of all obvious that the policy on language was compatible with, if not
facilitative of, the other policies associated with the desire for *rattrapage*.
The attempt at language planning helped to increase access for francophones
to many previously forbidden areas of the corporate economy. In that sense,
it aided in the integration of francophone Quebecers into higher levels of
management in North American capitalism. On the other hand, the legislation also integrated previously foreign economic institutions into Quebec
society. Institutions which had presented an English image to Quebecers for
decades, which had functioned predominantly in English, and which had
few francophones above the level of foreman, were changed on all of these
fronts and were made to appear more a part of Quebec's francophone
community.

At the same time, Quebec's basic ownership structure was not at all
altered by Bill 101. Not one important corporation shifted from anglophone
to francophone control. No one could safely say that as a result of Bill 101
Quebec's francophone community had increased its control over the economic fortunes of the province. This is an important point to note because the
control of much of Quebec's economy by English Canadians and Americans
had long been a powerful force motivating people to work for the goal of
political independence. It was powerful because the English image and
practices of the large corporations were so obvious and in many cases so
immediately insulting. Ironically, Bill 101 may have robbed the anglophone
ownership of Quebec's economy of much of its emotional importance. The
law has taken those corporations and made them appear to be much more
legitimate members of Quebec society. By defusing one of the flash points
motivating francophones to opt for independence, the Parti Québécois may
have in fact undermined its own raison d'être. Other issues will need to be
developed by the party to show why independence is necessary but it is
questionable whether they will be as effective for mobilizing people as were
the language practices of foreign corporations in the past. If the party does

not succeed in finding those new issues, language policy may have moved Quebec further away from independence rather than closer to it. The natural alliance between the party and labour where labour could fight the bosses and the party could fight the English all in the same struggles has been dissolved. Labour may now need to fight more in strict class terms. The *petite* bourgeoisie base of the Parti Québécois will not feel as at home in class struggles as it was in language struggles. If labour and the *petite* bourgeoisie are unable to find an issue like the old one of language on which they can unite, the very existence of the Parti Québécois may come into question.

Acknowledgements

The author would like to thank Richard Bourhis for his comments on an earlier draft of this chapter.

Notes to Chapter Six

1. The *Conseil du Patronat* receives its heaviest financial backing from large, mainly non-francophone firms. The CMA is a member but the two largest francophone business organizations, the CCMD and the CCPQ, are not members. The Positive Action Committee also derived its support primarily from large corporations. It had representatives from Celanese Canada, CIL, the Royal Bank of Canada and Alcan. Its brief listed two lawyers and three academics on the committee with the remaining 17 members being corporate or bank executives.
2. The *Centre des dirigeants d'entreprise* (CDE) is an organization representing small and medium-sized francophone firms. It had been founded as the *Association professionnelle des industriels* under the auspices of the Church in the forties.
3. The MQF was the successor organization to the *Front du Québec français* which was a coalition of the nationalist societies, teachers unions, students and labour leaders formed to fight against Bill 63.
4. A comparison of the Charter with the Official Language Act can be found in Coleman (1981).
5. "The Quebec Federation of Labour profoundly supports the proposed Charter of the French Language and we are appealing to Quebec's workers that they not be taken in by alarmist surveys and catastrophic declarations. Our support for the proposed law is unconditional" (author's translation).
6. "I stand open-mouthed before such a law; it opens the door to the return of the Inquisition, or more recently to Hitler's regime when children are able to denounce their neighbours or even their parents! For a country like Canada which has traditions of liberty rooted in the Magna Carta of 1215 and from which French Canada has benefited for 200 years, this law does not conform with the history of our country" (author's translation).

References

COLEMAN, W. D., 1980, "The Class Bases of Language Policy in Quebec, 1949–1975". *Studies in Political Economy*, No. 3 (1980), 93–118.

— 1981, "From Bill 22 to Bill 101: *the Politics of Language under the Parti Québécois*". *Canadian Journal of Political Science*, XIV, 3, 459–485.

— 1983, "A Comparative Study of Language Policy in Quebec: A Political Economy Approach", in M. M. ATKINSON & M. A. CHANDLER (eds), *The Politics of Canadian Public Policy*. Toronto: University of Toronto Press, 21–42.

CONSEIL DU PATRONAT DU QUEBEC 1973, *Détruire le système actuel? C'est à y penser*. Montreal: Publication les Affaires.

— 1977, Brief to the Permanent Parliamentary Committee on Education, Cultural Affairs and Communications. Hearings on Bill 1.

FOURNIER, P. 1975, *The Quebec Establishment*. Montreal: Black Rose Books.

HAMILTON, R. & PINARD, M. 1976, "The Bases of Parti-Québécois Support in Recent Quebec Elections". *Canadian Journal of Political Science*, IX, 1, 3–26.

— 1977, "The Independence Issue and the Polarization of the Quebec Electorate: The 1973 Quebec Election". *Canadian Journal of Political Science*, X, 2, 215–260.

LAURIN, C. 1977, La Politique québécoise de la langue française. White Paper presented to the Assemblée nationale du Québec. April 1, 1977. Montréal: Les Dossiers du Devoir, No. 3, 1977.

OFFICE DE LA LANGUE FRANÇAISE (OLF) 1983, *Rapport d'Activités 1981–82*. Quebec: Editeur officiel du Québec.

POSITIVE ACTION COMMITTEE: LANGUAGE OF WORK COMMITTEE (PAC) 1977, Brief to the Permanent Parliamentary Committee on Education, Cultural Affairs and Communications. Hearings on Bill 1.

POULANTZAS, N. 1978, *Classes in Contemporary Capitalism*. Trans. David Fernbach. London: Verso.

PRZEWORSKI, A. 1977, "Proletariat into a Class: The Process of Class Formation from Karl Kautsky's *The Class Struggle* to Recent Controversies". *Politics and Society*, VII, 4, 343–401.

QUEBEC, GOVERNMENT OF, 1972, Commission of Inquiry on the Position of the French Language and on Language Rights in Quebec (Gendron Commission). Quebec: Editeur officiel du Québec.

QUEBEC FEDERATION OF LABOUR (QFL) 1977, Brief to the Permanent Parliamentary Committee on Education, Cultural Affairs and Communications. Hearings on Bill 1.

RAYNAULD, A. 1974, *La propriété des entreprises au Québec*. Montréal: Les Presses de l'Université de Montréal.

SALES, A. 1979, *La bourgeoisie industrielle au Québec*. Montréal: Les Presses de l'Université de Montréal.

ST ANDREW'S SOCIETY OF MONTREAL 1977, Brief to the Permanent Parliamentary Committee on Education, Cultural Affairs and Communications. Hearings on Bill 1.

7 Language planning and intergroup relations: anglophone and francophone attitudes toward the Charter of the French Language

Donald M. Taylor
McGill University

Lise Dubé-Simard
Université de Montréal

Language legislation aimed at changing the status relationship between language groups inevitably involves the categorization of people along ethno-linguistic lines. Such categorizations enhance the salience of ethnic group membership and can have a profound impact on the dynamics of intergroup relations.

The study of language legislation and its effects on intergroup relations would seem to be particularly suited to social psychology, a discipline whose major aim is bridging the gap between the social and psychological aspect of human behaviour. To date, however, the contribution from social psychology has been modest. The reasons for this lack of interest have been discussed in detail elsewhere (see Frazer & Scherer, 1982) but can be traced partially to the dominant role played by the United States in defining social psychology as a discipline. The American emphasis on an individualistic rather than collective ideology (see Taylor & Brown, 1979) and the fact that language rights for ethnolinguistic groups have only recently surfaced as an issue in the United States (see Fishman, 1981) partially explain the relative neglect of language issues in social psychology.

It is in this context of historical neglect that the present study addressed the question of the role of language legislation for intergroup relations from a social psychological perspective. The details of the events which led to the

Charter of the French Language (Bill 101) have been discussed elsewhere in this volume (d'Anglejan, chapter 2; Laporte, chapter 3). For the present study it is important to note that from an intergroup perspective the anglophone minority in Quebec has historically enjoyed a privileged position in a province 80% of whose population claims French as their mother tongue. Francophone Quebecers have traditionally faced not only economic disadvantages in Quebec but also an imminent threat to their language and culture arising out of their minority status in the context of English-dominated North America. Legislation designed to protect French language and culture was introduced in 1974 (Bill 22) and culminated in the passing of Bill 101 (in 1977) which declares French to be the only official language in Quebec.

With attention focused on the reactions of the English community to Bill 101 and given the paucity of theory the present study was guided by an initial framework which outlines the necessary conditions for a group to take collective action in the face of language legislation. Three conditions are posited: (a) the social environment must be perceived as clearly categorized along dimensions of language; (b) at least one of the groups must feel threatened by the legislation; and (c) the threat must be perceived as unjustly imposed.

Each of these conditions was the focus of our research. While the *categorization* condition might appear to have been met with respect to language legislation in Quebec, important empirical questions remain. Do the English and French speaking communities represent two clearly divided categories with opposing views on Bill 101? Are there popular group labels which define these opposing categories? What role are the groups of other than French or English heritage perceived to play with respect to the legislation? Each of these questions was addressed in order to determine the extent to which the most basic condition for intergroup conflict existed with respect to Bill 101.

The importance of the *threat* condition lies with how it is perceived. It is to be expected that English speaking Quebecers will feel threatened, but how precisely is the threat interpreted? If Bill 101 is judged to be a threat directed at the English speaking community only, the reaction would be different to if it is judged to be threatening for all Quebecers. If the threat is perceived by the English community to be related only to language then bilingual English speakers may not feel threatened and those who are unilingual may well see the learning of French as an immediate and obvious solution to the threat. If, however, the threat is perceived to be directed at English *people* then the consequences may be more pervasive from an intergroup perspective. Finally, it will be important to assess the extent to which members of the French speaking community feel threatened by the legislation.

The final *justice* condition is crucial. Language is never legislated in a social or historical vacuum. So, while the English community may not like Bill 101 they may appreciate its inherent justice from an historical perspective, in which case no collective action would be anticipated. Alternatively, they may well appreciate its need but feel its application to be unjust. For example, the English community has been most critical of three features of Bill 101: the restriction on children who can attend English schools, the insistence that all public signs in Quebec be in French only and the requirement that professionals pass a French proficiency test to become licensed. The extent to which the justice condition is met may well determine whether or not the response to Bill 101 is benign or conflictual.

The issues of social categorization, threat and justice were addressed from a social psychological perspective. The aim was not merely to sample current opinion but to understand the underpinnings of reactions to Quebec's legislation. Thus, large sample survey techniques and/or open ended interview techniques were not deemed appropriate. Rather, a relatively small sample of respondents was chosen to complete an in-depth set of questions requiring responses on a 9-point Likert type scale as well as the categorization of stimulus materials.

The anglophone population is concentrated in the major metropolis of Montreal and it is here that issues of language and culture become most salient. A sample of 196 francophone and anglophone adults were selected from Montreal to represent a cross-section of social class, age and sex. A detailed description of the final sample is presented in Table 1.

A respondent was defined as francophone if French was the mother tongue and major language used; an anglophone was defined as someone whose mother tongue was English and whose language in the home is English. Respondents were excluded from analyses if there was any evidence of language or ethnic background other than French or English. Unfortunately, and in spite of their importance in Quebec society, respondents from groups of other than French or English heritage could not be included in this study (Arnopoulos & Clift, 1980).

A final research instrument, prepared initially in English and translated in French by means of a "back translation" method, was administered in the home of the respondent. The investigator explained the various tasks and mode of responding and then waited while the respondent completed the tasks privately and anonymously.

TABLE 1 *Distribution of Sample according to mother tongue, social class, sex and age*

	Francophones	Anglophones
Middle class	52	37
Working class	62	45
Men	72	46
Women	42	36
20–29 years	31	19
30–39 years	34	12
40–49 years	26	21
50 plus years	23	30
Total	114	82

1. Social categorization

Legal decrees that increase the status of one language group over another imply well established group categories. However, ethnolinguistic group boundaries are rarely so clearly defined, with the result that anticipating a society's reactions to language legislation can be problematic. To date, emphasis in social research has been on the results or consequences of social categorization, not on its genesis. So, for example, processes of ingroup bias, intergroup stereotyping and ethnocentrism are all outgrowths of the categorization of people into groups. Little is known about the forces that determine which of a number of characteristics emerge as salient in the creation of social categories. The first question addressed in the present research was "What social categories are reinforced or created by language legislation?"

Ethnolinguistic groups may differ in their attitudes toward controversial language laws such as Bill 101. With the emphasis on potential intergroup conflict the concern here is with the extremes of this continuum. At one pole would be those who support Bill 101 and believe it to be a just piece of legislation. At the opposite pole would be those who are against Bill 101 and feel it to be unjust. The aim of the first part of this study was to explore the extent to which anglophone and francophone respondents categorize themselves and each other at opposite poles of this attitudinal continuum.

Beyond this the aim was to examine the clarity of these categories by obtaining reactions to popular group labels. Quebec society is comprised of a number of ethnolinguistic groups and a number of them can be referred to by more than one label. Quebec's majority group can be referred to as "francophone", "French-Canadian", or "Québécois". The historically significant minority is variously labelled as "anglophone", "English-Canadian", or "WASP". Other ethnolinguistic groups are referred to collectively as allophones, or by a more specific group label (e.g. Italian, Jewish, etc.; Arnopoulos & Clift, 1980).

Each respondent in this study was presented with a list of ethnolinguistic labels including the label "MYSELF", and asked to categorize them into one of the two major categories: "FOR Bill 101" or "AGAINST Bill 101".

In addition, respondents rated on a nine-point scale the extent to which the "FOR Bill 101" and "AGAINST Bill 101" category of people had gained or lost privileges, experienced positive or negative effects in their career, had become more or less exploited and had experienced more or less threat to their culture since the promulgation of Bill 101.

The first result confirmed the basic attitude of the two major language groups toward Bill 101. Eighty-seven per cent of the anglophone respondents placed "MYSELF" in the "AGAINST Bill 101" category, whereas 77% of the francophones placed themselves in the "FOR Bill 101" category.

The results presented in Table 2 describe the categorizations for the various labels referring to French and English speaking people. These results confirm the basic protagonist positions in the conflict over language

TABLE 2 *Percentage of anglophone and francophone respondents who categorized Group Labels as belonging in the For or Against Bill 101 categories*

Group labels	Categorization made by anglophone respondents		Categorization made by francophone respondents	
	"For Bill 101"	"Against Bill 101"	"For Bill 101"	"Against Bill 101"
Francophones	85%	12.5%[1]	94%	3.5%
French Canadians	74%	21%	89%	10%
Anglophones	1%	99%	5%	94%
English Canadians	0%	100%	5%	95%

1. Where percentages do not add to 100, some participants could not clearly categorize label in the For and Against categories.

legislation. Both francophone and anglophone respondents associate the French speaking labels (francophone, French-Canadian) as being in the "FOR Bill 101" category. Conversely, both francophone and anglophone respondents associate the English speaking labels (anglophone, English-Canadian) as being in the "AGAINST Bill 101" category. These results, along with the "MYSELF" categorization, confirm the basic social conflict in Quebec associated with Bill 101.

Table 3 presents the categorizations of labels which do not make explicit reference to language group but which are often associated with the English and French language communities.

The responses to the label "Québécois" point particularly to the fact that it is not merely language issues that are involved in the categorization process. The label "Québécois" is even more strongly associated with the "FOR Bill 101" category than those labels referring to language directly (e.g. francophone, French-Canadian). The importance of the label "Québécois" receives independent support from a study by Bourhis (1983) who found that 86% of francophone respondents chose this label as most appropriate for themselves. Similarly, "WASP" (White-Anglo-Saxon-Protestant) rather than anglophone or English-Canadian is the group label most clearly associated with the "AGAINST Bill 101" category. It is striking to note that whereas "Québécois" best defines the "FOR Bill 101" category, its English equivalent "Quebecer" does not. The fact that this perception is shared by both francophone and anglophone respondents indicates that the

TABLE 3 *Percentage of anglophone and francophone respondents who categorized Group Labels indirectly referring to language groups as belonging in the For or Against Bill 101 categories*

Group labels	Categorization made by anglophone respondents		Categorization made by francophone respondents	
	"For Bill 101"	*"Against Bill 101"*	*"For Bill 101"*	*"Against Bill 101"*
Québécois	87%[1]	8%[1]	92%	8%
Quebecer	62%	30%	38%	56%
Canadiens	56%	39%	24%	71%
Canadians	4%	87%	13%	83%
WASP	0%	98%	1%	88%

1. Where percentages do not add to 100, some participants could not clearly categorize label in the For and Against categories.

media and government documents may well be advised not to use the labels "Québécois" and "Quebecer" as equivalent in the respective languages; they certainly are not equivalent in the minds of citizens.

The categorizations for labels depicting groups of other than French and English heritage (usually referred to as allophones) are summarized in Table 4. Both francophone and anglophone respondents agree that most of these groups (the label France is one exception) should be placed in the "AGAINST Bill 101" category. Beyond this, however, there is evidence of a systematic bias in respondents' categorizations: anglophone respondents tend to bias their categorization of non-French/English heritage groups as being "AGAINST Bill 101" whereas francophone respondents tend to label these groups as being in the "FOR Bill 101" category. It would appear that the views of groups of other than French or English heritage regarding Bill 101 are not known with any certainty. Both francophones and anglophones claim that these groups are more likely to share their own attitudes toward Bill 101 than that of the outgroup.

Finally, the two major categories were each rated on four dimensions related to potential conflict; gain or loss of privileges, positive or negative effect on the work environment, feelings of exploitation and threat to culture. The ratings were analyzed by means of four separate analyses of

TABLE 4 *Percentage of anglophone and francophone respondents who categorized Group Labels other than English or French Canadian (allophones) in the For or Against Bill 101 categories*

Group labels	Categorization made by anglophone respondents		Categorization made by francophone respondents	
	"For Bill 101"	*"Against Bill 101"*	*"For Bill 101"*	*"Against Bill 101"*
Minority groups	4%[1]	91%[1]	16%	53%
Immigrants	10%	68%	23%	50%
Jews	11.5%	77%	13%	64%
Italians	9%	81%	9%	83%
France	55%	13%	90%	1%
Britain	1%	92%	16%	74%
Americans	3%	69%	19%	56%
India	5%	65%	8%	50%
West Indies	9%	65%	61%	14%
Native Peoples	2%	75%	5%	57%

1. Where percentages do not add to 100, some participants could not clearly categorize label in the For and Against categories.

variance where the independent variables included language group of respondent (francophone, anglophone), social class (working, middle), and category (FOR, AGAINST Bill 101).

For gain or loss of privileges two significant main effects emerged. All respondents agreed that persons in the "FOR Bill 101" category have gained privileges whereas those in the "AGAINST Bill 101" category have lost them. Similarly respondents agreed that in terms of the work environment, there has been a positive effect for those in the "FOR Bill 101" category but a negative one for those in the "AGAINST Bill 101" category. These results present a striking contrast to those focusing on exploitation and threat to culture. In both these latter cases a significant two-way interaction emerged and these are plotted in Figures 1 and 2.

Francophones feel that those in the "FOR Bill 101" category are relatively exploited and face a threat to their culture. The anglophones, by contrast, feel it is those in the "AGAINST Bill 101" category who are exploited and culturally threatened. These results have important implications for gauging future reactions to Quebec's language legislation. That those in the English speaking category (AGAINST Bill 101) perceive threat and exploitation is not surprising, given that the legislation is designed to promote the French language. However, this legislation, designed in part to provide a sense of security among francophones, has not, to date, had this effect. Even though it is clearly recognized that privileges in *language* and work have been gained by francophones, this has not generalized to a greater sense of *cultural* security. The overall result of the legislation then may be to have produced anxiety in one community without alleviating a previous anxiety in the other.

In summary, Quebec's language legislation is associated with important developments in social categorization. Consistent with the first precondition for collective action there exist two well defined opposing categories; one composed of French speaking people who support Bill 101 and an opposing category of English speakers who are against the Bill. And these opposing categories are not associated with one particular social class. No social class differences emerged in the analyses, clearly indicating that the key differences in categorization involve language and ethnic identity. The question of language, then, would seem to be sufficiently salient and important that it even over-rides a dimension as pervasive as social class.

Despite the clear categorization along ethnolinguistic dimensions the labels used to refer to various groups had subtle, but important, differences in their psychological meaning for the respondents. Groups of other than French or English heritage (allophones) appear to be used as social pawns

FIGURE 1 *Significant interaction involving effect of language group of respondent and category on perceptions of exploitation* $(F(1,192) = 58.90, p < 0.01)$

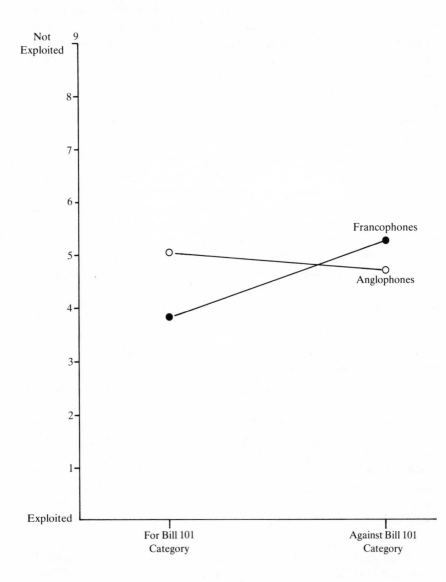

FIGURE 2 *Significant interaction involving effect of language group of respondent and category on perceptions of cultural threat* (F(1,192) = 11.14, p < 0.001)

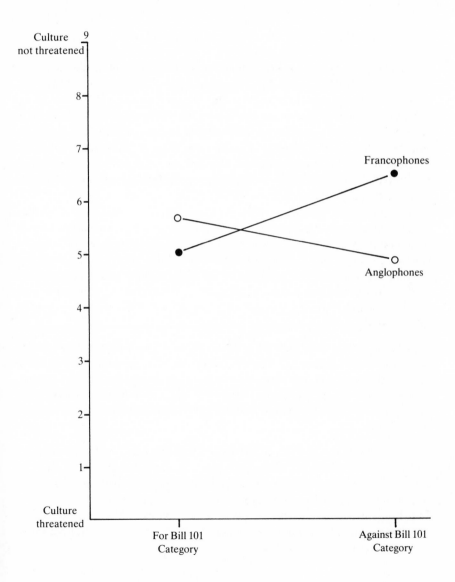

for the opposing categories, each claiming the support of this third force (see d'Anglejan, this volume, chapter 2; Caldwell, this volume, chapter 9). Finally members of both opposing categories feel exploited and culturally threatened.

2. Social threat

Respondents were asked a number of questions about the extent to which they felt threatened by Quebec's language legislation. Answers to these were made on a nine-point scale anchored at one end by "not at all threatened" and at the other by "extremely threatened". For each item respondents were asked first to answer with respect to their feelings at the time of testing, which was some six months prior to the crucial May 1980 referendum on Quebec separation. As well, respondents judged how they would feel *if* the referendum results supported political separation of Quebec from Canada, and how they would feel *if* the referendum vote indicated a desire to remain a province within the Canadian framework. The introduction of the speculative questions about the referendum on separation were designed to assess the extent to which feelings of threat were associated with specific social conditions and whether these feelings were related only to the language legislation itself or to significant social changes in other domains as well. The referendum on political separation represented a dramatic and threatening possibility for social change but one which did not reflect directly on language.

The first two questions about threat focused on a conceptual distinction between threats perceived to be directed at the self, personally, as opposed to threats directed at one's entire ethnolinguistic group. Both types of threat may produce similar levels of emotional response but the former suggests a personal coping strategy whereas the latter would more likely lead to collective action.

The initial question about *personal* threat was analyzed by means of an analysis of variance where the independent variables included language group of respondent (francophone, anglophone), response condition (current situation, vote for separation, vote against separation) and social class (working, middle). The major result was a highly significant interaction involving language group of respondent and response condition which is presented graphically in Figure 3.

From Figure 3 it is clear that anglophones feel very threatened and francophones quite secure about their respective situations. It must be noted, however, that the security experienced by francophones is with

FIGURE 3 *Significant interaction involving effect of language group of respondent and response conditions on feelings of threat since Bill 101* (F(1,192) = 45.50, p < 0.001)

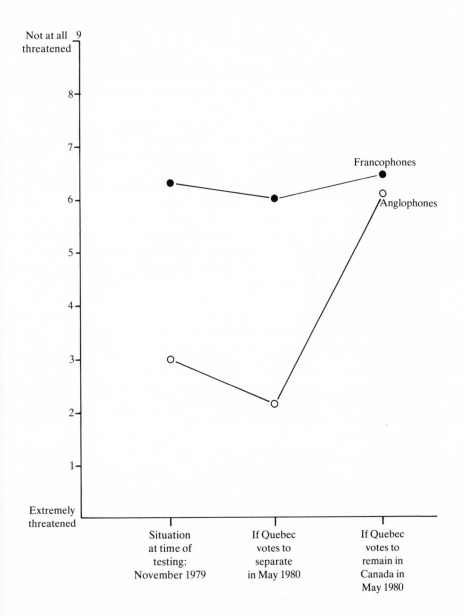

respect to language *per se*; as the earlier results point out there remain uncertainties about culture. The high level of threat reported by anglophones is a finding which confirms all informal and mass media impressions of sentiments expressed by the anglophone community. The reactions of the two groups of respondents to possible social political change are quite different. Francophones feel unthreatened by Bill 101 and these feelings would not be altered even by a dramatic social change such as a referendum vote either in favour of or opposed to Quebec separation.

By contrast, anglophone feelings are dramatically influenced by anticipated social change. In the event of an endorsement for Quebec separation, anglophone feelings of threat, which are strong to begin with, would become even more extreme. However, such threats would be removed completely if the majority of Quebecers chose to remain in Canada.

Respondents' reactions in terms of threat are striking for two reasons. First, it is surprising that francophone feelings of threat are so little affected by the referendum. It would suggest that these respondents perceive language legislation and political separation as two separate issues such that a change in one may not have any implications for the other. For anglophones the issues of language and politics appear completely interdependent; Bill 101 implies a particular political orientation, and conversely this political stance is reflected in the philosophy and application of language legislation.

A second striking feature of these results is the apparent lack of realism expressed by the anglophone sample. They feel threatened by the current legislation but feel that most causes for threat would be removed in the event of a NO vote in the referendum. Given that a NO vote would simply mean maintenance of the status quo, it is inconceivable that any substantial change in language legislation could be anticipated.

In order to more fully comprehend the nature of the threats experienced in relation to Bill 101, respondents were asked two additional questions. First, they were asked the extent to which Bill 101 threatened them, not personally, as in the initial question, but as a *group*. The results of an analysis of variance indicate that indeed anglophones feel that the legislation threatens anglophones as a group just as it had threatened them personally. This perception which makes a clear distinction between ethnolinguistic communities in Quebec is of particular interest because previous research has indicated a tendency among anglophones to interpret social events in Quebec as not revolving around ethnolinguistic groups (Taylor Wong-Rieger, McKirnan & Bercusson, 1982; Taylor, Simard & Papineau, 1978). Specifically, anglophones in these studies interpreted threat as directed at all of Quebec society, not just at anglophones. This interpretation seemed to provide anglophones with a mechanism for avoiding the perception of intergroup conflict. It would seem, however, that the present legislation makes the intergroup feature of the issue unavoidable to anglophone respondents.

The next question required respondents from one language group to rate how threatened the members of the other group felt about Bill 101 and the referendum. Results showed that while anglophones perceived francophones to feel secure regardless of the outcome of the referendum, francophones perceived that anglophones felt quite threatened by both Bill 101 and a vote in favour of Quebec separation. As with anglophone self rating, francophones perceived a dramatic rise in anglophone security in the event of a NO vote to separation. Not only, then, do francophones and anglophones have clear and different feelings about the implications of Bill 101 for their *own* group, but they are quite aware of the reaction of the *other* group towards the legislation. Consistent with the earlier findings on categorization, no social class differences in threat emerged. Again this suggests that the language issue in Quebec is so salient that within each ethnolinguistic group there is a shared set of perceptions and attitudes.

The final question relating to threatening aspects of Quebec's language legislation dealt with the language competence of the respondents themselves. If language by itself is the central issue it would be expected that anglophones who are bilingual would not experience the degree of threat experienced by those who speak only English. An analysis of variance was performed which compared bilingual and monolingual anglophone respondents. The results indicated that bilinguals felt as threatened as monolinguals. This finding reinforces those obtained in the results on categorization; that is, perceptions and feelings about Quebec's language legislation extend beyond language *per se* to include social and political factors as well.

In summary, four conclusions seem warranted on the basis of the present results focusing on threat. First, anglophones are highly threatened by Bill 101 whereas francophones feel no direct threat. Second, anglophone reactions seem quite unrealistic in the face of social change, feeling that a vote to have Quebec remain within Canada will reduce all political threats related to language. Third, whereas anglophones have had a tendency in the past to avoid viewing events in Quebec in terms of conflict between language groups, the present results indicate a recognition that the differential implications of Bill 101 for the two language communities cannot be avoided. Finally, the threat provoked by Bill 101 involves more than strict issues of language. That anglophone bilinguals are as threatened as monolinguals suggests that language, economic, cultural and political issues are perceived to be strongly inter-related.

3. Social justice

The third condition necessary for the instigation of collective action is that the legislation be perceived by at least one of the groups as not only threatening, but unjustly imposed. The importance of this third condition cannot be over-emphasized. Examples abound of situations where disadvantaged groups experience great inequalities and feel severely threatened and yet do not take collective action to redress the situation. To suggest that fear of reprisal from the dominant group explains the lack of action does not recognize social reality. Often it is the most disadvantaged, powerless and most threatened group which instigates collective action.

A number of social psychological theories including relative deprivation (e.g. Crosby, 1976), equity theory (Walster, Walster & Berscheid, 1978), and social identity theory (Tajfel & Turner, 1979), explicitly or implicitly refer to the perception of injustice as a precursor to collective action. In the present context, then, it will be argued that the threat experienced by anglophones must be associated with feelings of injustice for collective action to be initiated; admitting the justice of Bill 101 would lead anglophones to accept, albeit reluctantly, the implications of the legislation.

The questions presented to respondents addressed three facets of their perceptions of justice; 1) the justice of Bill 101 itself; 2) the justice of the Bill for the respondent him or herself personally; and 3) respondents' perception of the organization charged with the responsibility of directly implementing Bill 101.

Before examining the responses to these questions it was important to establish the extent to which respondents were actually familiar with the details of the legislation. The less that is known about the specific regulations the more room there is for bias in the interpretation of its fairness. Respondents were asked to rate their knowledge of the contents of Bill 101 on a nine-point scale ranging from no knowledge (1) to complete knowledge (9). An analysis of variance was performed on the ratings for the independent variables, language group of respondent (francophone, anglophone) and social class (working, middle).

Two significant main effects emerged from the analysis. First, anglophones reported that they were more aware of the contents of Bill 101 than their francophone counterparts. Second, middle class respondents claimed more knowledge of the Bill than those from the working class. These results are not surprising. It is probably the case that middle class Montrealers have a greater awareness of legislation details in any domain. Moreover, since it is anglophones who are most threatened and most directly implicated by the legislation, they would be expected to have a heightened awareness of the Bill's contents.

Of special interest is the fact that even the anglophone respondents claim only a modest knowledge of the Bill (a mean of 5.3 on a nine-point scale). The responses to the questions regarding the justice of Bill 101 must be understood in this context; the perceptions are based on little information for the most part, and modest information at best.

To what extent do respondents judge Bill 101 to be just? Respondents' judgements were made on a nine-point scale first in terms of the situation as it existed at the time of testing (November 1979, 6 months prior to the referendum) and then projecting a YES or NO vote in the referendum on political separation in May 1980. The major result to emerge from the analysis of variance was a significant interaction involving language group of respondent and response condition, and this result is presented in Figure 4.

Francophone ratings follow a familiar pattern; the Bill is judged to be relatively just and the outcome of the referendum will have little impact on their perception of justice. The anglophone profile is striking by contrast. First, anglophones judge Bill 101 at the time of testing to be quite unjust. In the event of a YES vote in the referendum, a condition which they earlier reported to be extremely threatening, anglophone respondents would judge the bill to be *more* just.

These results have important implications in light of the three necessary preconditions for collective action examined in this study. First, the anglophone pattern of results provides support for the conceptual distinction made between threat and justice. That is, it is not the case that perceived injustice follows automatically from feelings of threat. The anglophone ratings demonstrate that perceptions of justice can actually increase as feelings of threat become more severe. The anglophone feelings also reinforce earlier observations that language legislation is, for these respondents, inexorably interwoven with social conditions. Thus, the very same legislation can actually become more or less just as social conditions change.

Finally, and more directly related to an understanding of collective action, the results indicate that there are circumstances where, despite feelings of extreme threat, collective action may not be instigated. In the event of a political move in the direction of more autonomy for Quebec, anglophones view the language legislation as relatively more just, obviously feeling that to the extent Quebec becomes a separate entity, the more it would be reasonable to recognize the prominence of French spoken in Quebec. Under these circumstances feelings of threat, disappointment and

FIGURE 4 *Significant interaction involving effect of language group of respondent and response conditions on perceived justice of the Bill 101 legislation*
($F(1,192) = 7.43$, $p < 0.001$)

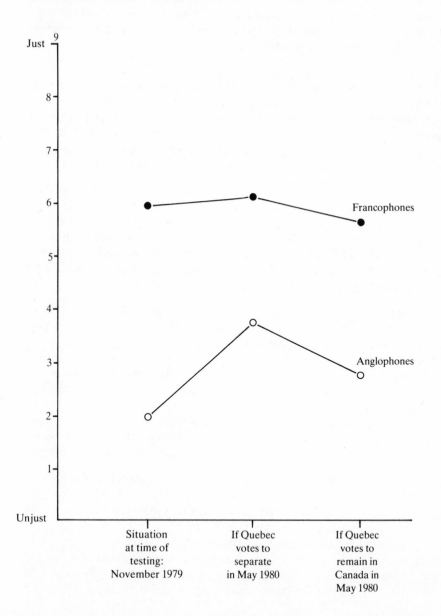

resignation may be predominant, but lacking would be the anger and outrage associated with the instigation of collective action.

For the second question, attention was directed to the fairness that individual respondents feel for themselves *personally* when considering Bill 101. The results of the analysis of variance for this question are summarized in Figure 5. Again francophone respondents judge their personal situation at the time of testing to be more just than the anglophone participants. As in the previous analysis, francophone perceptions are little affected by social changes that might arise from the referendum.

The anglophone respondents, however, change their judgements markedly in relation to possible social change. But the pattern is not the same as that for the responses to the justice of Bill 101 described in the previous analysis. The differences are noteworthy. First, whereas anglophones judged Bill 101, as a piece of legislation, to be highly unjust (see Figure 4), they feel the Bill has not been as unjust to them personally (see Figure 5). It would seem that Bill 101 carries an aura of injustice which is reinforced for anglophones perhaps by media accounts of those who have been directly affected by it, and through second-hand accounts about those who have received unfair treatment. However, the respondents themselves have not experienced this same degree of injustice directed at them personally.

What anglophones apparently fear is the implications of a vote in favour of independence, for it is in this response condition that anglophones perceive the most personal injustice. But when asked about the justice of the Bill itself these same respondents judged that Bill 101 would be more just in the event of a vote in favour of separation. So anglophones seem to distinguish at least two dimensions of justice; one which, on the one hand, considers language legislation in the broad social and historical context, where a move in the direction of political independence would render the Bill relatively just, but which, on the other hand, would, from a purely personal perspective, become more unjust.

The third question covers the perceived manner in which Quebec's language legislation is applied concretely. The Office de la langue française is charged with the responsibility of interpreting and enforcing Bill 101 and its respondents were first asked if they knew about the Office and its function. A large majority of working- and middle-class anglophone respondents (89%) were aware of this agency, middle-class francophones were slightly less aware (75%) and only a third of working-class francophone respondents (35.5%) had heard of the Office de la langue française. There

FIGURE 5 *Significant interaction involving effect of language group of respondent and response conditions on perceptions of personal justice* (F(1,192) = 27.29, p < 0.001)

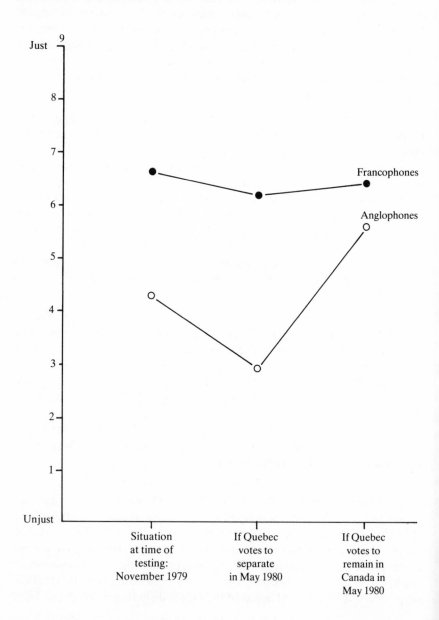

is, then, a general awareness of the Office and its function, especially among anglophones whose lives are potentially directly affected by its function.

In terms of how the Office functions, respondents were asked how severe or accommodating the agency is in its interpretation and enforcement of Bill 101. The results of the analysis of variance revealed a significant interaction involving language group of respondent and response condition. Francophone responses were concentrated toward the middle of the scale indicating that in their view the Office has not been especially strict or lenient in its interpretation of Bill 101. As well, these ratings are little affected by the response condition. Not surprisingly, anglophone respondents feel that a severe interpretation has been made by the Office. This perception of severity is altered dramatically in anticipation of social change; a vote for independence being associated with increased severity and more leniency in the event of an endorsement for remaining in Canada. This pattern of results for anglophone respondents may be more emotional than rational. If the purpose of the language legislation is to protect French language and culture there would presumably be less need for stringency in an independent Quebec. Continuing to remain in Canada would likely require greater vigilance in order to insure the preservation of French within Canada. Anglophones may well find that their expectations are not met when the results of the referendum become known.

In summary, anglophone respondents not only feel highly threatened by Bill 101 but feel a sense of injustice as well. This is not to suggest that perceptions of justice and threat are one and the same. While anglophones feel a *personal* sense of injustice and feel that the Bill itself is fundamentally unjust, they nevertheless recognize that under different social conditions the legislation could be viewed as relatively just. Anglophone reactions to the legislation, then, may well be modulated by the extent to which they judge its justice under specific social and cultural conditions. Again, anglophones seem to be somewhat unrealistic in their expectations of how Bill 101 will be implemented; viewing it as relatively severe under current conditions but imagining a much more lenient attitude in the event that Quebec remains within Canada.

Conclusion: Toward intergroup conflict?

We are now in a position to describe anglophone and francophone perceptions with regard to each of the three preconditions for collective action. The preconditions and a brief summary statement of the perceptions are contained in Figure 6.

FIGURE 6 *Schematic representation of necessary conditions for the instigation of collective action: summary of results for anglophone and francophone respondents*

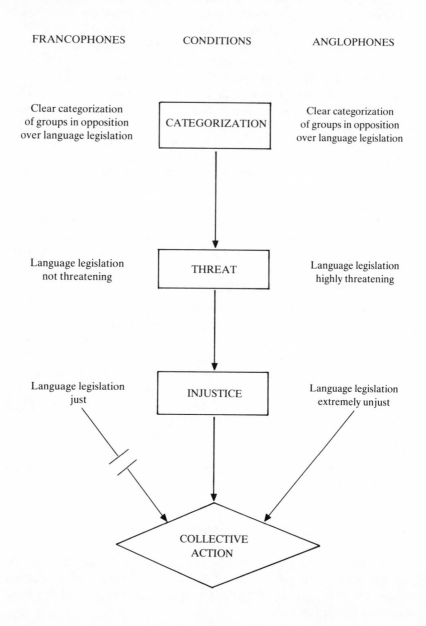

All three preconditions point to a delicate situation where collective action on the part of anglophones might be expected. Indeed, perhaps the most dramatic development within the anglophone community since the completion of this study has been the formation of a formal anglophone pressure group named "Alliance Quebec". A recent Montreal English newspaper editorial (Auf Der Maur, 1982) notes, "Until now, one of the major problems of the English-speaking community in Quebec has been the question: Who speaks for it?" In the same editorial "Alliance Quebec" is described as "a group which is rapidly being accepted as the principal voice of and lobby for English Quebec". However, drawing the conclusion that this development is the first step toward collective conflict may be premature for certain qualifications must be made about each of the three stages of the present model.

The first precondition for collective action is the clear categorization of society into distinct opposing groups, and it would appear that this condition is met with respect to Quebec's language legislation. English speakers are clearly opposed to Bill 101 and even French speakers, who support the Bill, nevertheless still feel culturally threatened and exploited. Two factors, however, may attenuate the likelihood of collective action on the part of anglophones. First, the anglophone community has not had a history of collective action in Quebec. Hence, there is not a clearly established social infrastructure to facilitate such action. Second, there is a popular and dramatic *individual* response to the legislation available to members of the anglophone community; leaving the province to settle in one of the nine anglophone provinces of Canada. Such action, of course, removes from the English speaking community important resources and the possibility for collective action will probably emerge only when the exodus has diminished and a stable English speaking community, committed to staying in Quebec, remains (for a discussion of Quebec anglophone options see Caldwell, this volume, chapter 9). Even here, however, caution in predicting collective action must be exercised. Anglophone feelings are highly unstable and there is actually the belief that if Quebec votes to remain in Canada all current feelings of threat will be removed. Under such conditions collective action would not be anticipated; however, it does raise a serious question. What if in the event of a NO vote in the referendum fundamental threats do not disappear? Is it possible that the potential unexpected threat might be even more explosive?

The justice component of the model is the most complex even though anglophones feel a basic sense of injustice regarding Bill 101. The complexity arises because the perception of justice seems dependent upon the particular perspective taken. From a personal perspective it is viewed as highly unjust, but when viewed from an historical or political perspective, Bill 101 is perceived to be more just. It is difficult at this stage to predict precisely what perspective will predominate among anglophones. Whichever perspective emerges it may well dictate the nature of anglophone reactions to the language legislation.

The present projections regarding the potential for intergroup conflict derived from the model can be compared with respondents' own attitudes toward the other group. Respondents from each group expressed their attitude toward the other group on a nine-point scale, ranging from negative (1) to positive (9), and the results of the analysis of variance appear in Figure 7.

At the time of testing francophone and anglophone respondents' attitudes toward each other were mutual. Both groups expressed a cautious and relatively neutral attitude toward each other. While the lack of positive attitudes may be disquieting, it is somewhat surprising that anglophone attitudes are not more negative given the threat they feel. It may be that whatever hostility is being felt by the anglophone community is not being directed at francophones as a group, but may instead centre on the provincial government *per se* (see Taylor *et al.*, 1982).

Francophone attitudes are little affected by social change resulting from the outcome of the referendum. Anglophone attitudes toward francophones, which were relatively benign at the time of testing, will change radically in the event of social change. So, in the event of a vote for Quebec separation anglophones anticipate becoming quite negative in their attitudes toward francophones. Anticipation of an endorsement of the status quo is associated with more positive intergroup attitudes. Beyond this it is middle-class anglophones who are the more volatile in their attitudes. Intergroup attitudes then are neutral at best, and anglophone middle-class respondents' attitudes are quite unstable; they may become quite negative under specific circumstances such as a YES vote for Quebec sovereignty.

The present research was conducted and analyzed prior to the crucial referendum on Quebec separation. That vote has now taken place and while the majority voted to remain within Canada (60%), the minority vote in favour of Quebec separation was significant (40%). This raises two fundamental questions regarding the present study of attitudes toward Bill 101. First, it is clear to all Quebecers, indeed to all Canadians, that political separation for Quebec is not an issue which has been laid to rest. The political climate remains unstable such that the issue of perceived threat and justice are likely to remain key factors leading to collective action which in turn may lead to intergroup conflict. Secondly, the anglophone community appears quite unrealistic in its expectations regarding the consequences of a

FIGURE 7 *Significant interaction involving effects of ethnic group of respondent, response condition and social class on intergroup attitudes* $(F(1,192) = 74.25, p < 0.001)$

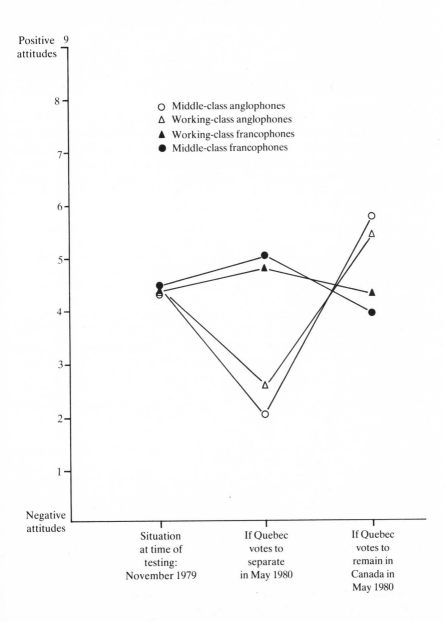

NO vote on the question of Quebec separation. Following a NO majority vote they expect all threats from Bill 101 to dissipate, all perceived injustices related to language to be removed, and intergroup relations in Quebec to be positive and constructive. How will the anglophone community react to the inevitable reality that, regardless of the vote, the language legislation and its implications will remain?

Acknowledgements

The research summarized in this chapter was supported by a grant from the Office de la langue française. A complete description of the research and statistical findings presented in this chapter is available in a book by D. M. Taylor and L. M. Simard entitled "Les relations intergroupes au Québec et la loi 101: les reactions des francophones et des anglophones" published by the Editeur Officiel du Québec, 1981. The authors are grateful to Louise Auger, Serge Guimond, Gillian Watson and Durhane Wong-Rieger for their collaboration in the research.

References

ARNOPOULOS, S. H., & CLIFT, D. T. 1980, *The English fact in Quebec.* Montreal: McGill-Queen's University Press.

AUF DER MAUR, N. 1982, Roots of Alliance go back to 1976. Montreal: *The Gazette,* Wednesday, June 2.

BOURHIS, R. Y. 1983, Language Attitudes and Self reports of French-English usage in Quebec. *Journal of Multilingual and Multicultural Development,* 4, 163–180.

CROSBY, F. 1976, A model of egoistical relative deprivation. *Psychological Review,* 83, 85–113.

FISHMAN, J. 1981, Language policy: Past, present and future. In: C. FERGUSON & S. B. HEATH (eds), *Language in the United States.* New York: Cambridge University Press.

FRASER, C., & SCHERER, K. R. 1982, *Advances in the social psychology of language.* New York: Cambridge University Press.

ROSCH, E. 1977, Human categorization. In: N. WARREN (ed.), *Advances in cross-cultural psychology,* Vol. 1. London: Academic Press.

TAJFEL, H., & TURNER, J. 1979, An integrative theory of intergroup conflict. In: W. AUSTIN & S. WORCHEL (eds), *The social psychology of intergroup relations.* Monterrey: Brooks Cole.

TAYLOR, D. M., & BROWN, R. J. 1979, Towards a more social social psychology? *British Journal of Social and Clinical Psychology,* 18, 173–180.

TAYLOR, D. M., SIMARD, L. M., & PAPINEAU, D. 1978, Perceptions of cultural differences and language use: a field study in a bilingual environment. *Canadian Journal of Behavioural Science,* 10, 181–191.

TAYLOR, D. M., WONG-RIEGER, D., MCKIRNAN, D. J., & BERCUSSON, T. 1982, Interpreting and coping with threat in the context of intergroup relations. *Journal of Social Psychology*, 117, 257–269.

WALSTER, E., WALSTER, G. W., & BERSCHEID, E. 1978, *Equity: Theory and research*. Boston: Allyn & Bacon.

8 The Charter of the French Language and cross-cultural communication in Montreal

Richard Y. Bourhis
McMaster University

Language planning can be quite a controversial enterprise when it involves the promulgation of a single language as the only official language of a society or nation state. Status language planning in favour of one language community which tends to exclude the recognition of other language communities has been found to foster intergroup tension and conflict in settings such as Belgium (Lorwin, 1972), France (Bourhis, 1982), Canada (Joy, 1972), and Quebec (this volume). Though the relationship between language planning and language conflict has often been examined at the societal level (e.g. Rubin & Jernudd, 1971; Weinstein, 1983), few studies have explicitly investigated the impact of status language planning on the language usage of *individual* speakers during everyday cross-cultural encounters. The controversy surrounding the promulgation and implementation of the Charter of the French language (Bill 101) in Quebec, provides an ideal occasion to explore possible links between status language planning and individual language usage in cross-cultural communication.

In multilingual settings, cross-cultural encounters inevitably involve decisions concerning which language to use in conversations with members of linguistic groups other than one's own. In some circumstances bilingual speakers may switch to the language of their interlocutor to insure communicative effectiveness and/or to foster better interpersonal relations. Alternatively speakers may decide not to switch to the language of their interlocutor either because they feel their skills in the second language are too weak, because they dislike their interlocutor or because they feel it is their interlocutor who should make the effort to switch language. Such language choices during cross-cultural encounters may not only reflect speakers' motives and beliefs but may also have important consequences for the development of favourable or unfavourable intergroup attitudes and behaviours. This is especially the case in settings such as Quebec where intergroup conflicts have often centred around language issues (Cappon, 1978) and where language has come to serve as an important badge of ethnic group identify for both Quebec francophones (Corbeil, 1980) and Quebec anglophones (Clift & Arnopoulos, 1979). Consequently status language planning in favour of French, as embodied in Bill 101, can be seen as having considerable relevance for cross-cultural communication in Quebec. This point is more evident when one considers that Bill 101 was the outcome of a great deal of pressure from the Quebec francophone nationalist movement striving to insure the survival of the French language in Quebec (d'Anglejan, this volume, chapter 2; Laporte, this volume, chapter 3). Conversely, this same legislation was seen by Quebec anglophones as a major threat to their survival as a distinctive linguistic minority in Quebec (Taylor & Simard, this volume, chapter 7; Caldwell, this volume, chapter 9). It was therefore no surprise that with the controversy surrounding the adoption of Bill 101 numerous francophones and anglophones may have come to view language choices in interpersonal encounters as being not only a matter of optimizing communication efficiency but also a matter of asserting one's ethnolinguistic group identity.

The aim of this chapter is to present and integrate the main findings from three recently published studies which were designed to investigate the possible impact of the Charter of the French Language on individual cross-cultural communications between Quebec francophones (QFs) and Quebec anglophones (QAs) in Montreal (Bourhis, 1983; 1984; Genesee & Bourhis, 1982). The city of Montreal provides an ideal setting for a study of the impact of Bill 101 on the dynamics of language usage in cross-cultural communication. Montreal is well known for the degree to which its two major ethnolinguistic groups (QFs and QAs) have settled in geographically distinct parts of the city (Lieberson, 1970). The traditional residential, social, cultural and economic segregation of QFs and QAs in Montreal has meant that contact between these two groups has been minimal. Simard & Taylor (1973) concluded that there was little more than superficial cross-cultural communication between the QF numerical majority and the QA numerical minority in Montreal. Opportunities for *casual* cross-cultural contact in Montreal appear most likely in the downtown areas of the city where QFs and QAs must interact in public settings such as large department stores, shopping promenades, restaurants and public transportation.

Given the complexity of language issues in settings such as Quebec one cannot expect language policies such as the Charter of the French Language to be the only determinants of language switching strategies in cross-cultural encounters. The determinants of language usage in cross-cultural encounters have been discussed in theoretical contributions by Bourhis (1979), Giles, Bourhis & Taylor (1977) and Simard (1981). At least four factors are likely to be especially important in determining the language switching strategies used by QF and QA interlocutors in Montreal. These factors are: 1) speakers' linguistic skills; 2) motivational basis of language switching behaviour; 3) situational norms dictating appropriate language usage in particular settings; and 4) the language status of French and English as affected by recent language legislation such as Bill 101. Each of these factors will be discussed in turn as they apply to the Montreal setting.

1. Linguistic competence

The poor quality of second language training provided in schools for QFs and QAs has often been proposed as the explanation for the lack of communication between QFs and QAs in Montreal. Taylor & Simard (1975) reviewed studies designed to test whether traditional second language education in Montreal was sufficient for basic cross-cultural communication. These authors found that both QFs and QAs were capable of communicating effectively in both the French and English language. Taylor & Simard (1975) concluded that QFs and QAs in Montreal often choose *not* to communicate even though they have sufficient linguistic skills to communicate with each other. These authors proposed that motivational factors could very well account for the lack of cross-cultural communication in Montreal.

2. Motivational variables

Recent social psychological studies investigating the role of motivational variables on language switching suggest that speakers often adapt or "accommodate" their speech towards that of their interlocutors (Giles, Taylor & Bourhis, 1973). Instances in which speakers tend to adopt the speech patterns of their interlocutor have been shown to occur at various linguistic levels including speech rate, vocal intensity, regional accents and language switches (Giles & Powesland, 1975). It appears that such switches known as speech *convergence*, not only allow for efficient communication but may also reflect speakers' conscious or unconscious need to be liked by their interlocutor. In multilingual settings, convergence to an outgroup language may be an effective strategy for promoting interpersonal liking and for improving the climate of cross-cultural encounters. This was demonstrated in a study carried out in Montreal by Giles, Taylor & Bourhis (1973). In this study it was found that male and female bilingual QA students perceived a male QF bilingual more favourably when he converged to English than when he maintained French. Moreover, the QA students were more likely to communicate in *French* with the QF interlocutor if the latter had previously converged to *English* than if he had maintained his communication only in French. Since both the QA and QF communicated in each other's weaker language (the QA used French while the QF used English), this study showed that mutual language convergence could be used as a strategy to promote both interpersonal and ethnic harmony even at the potential cost of communicative effectiveness.

Though speakers from different language groups may wish to converge linguistically towards each other, there may be circumstances where speakers wish to *maintain* their own language or *diverge* linguistically from their interlocutor (Bourhis, 1979). Speakers may use speech maintenance and speech divergence sometimes because they dislike their interlocutors as individuals or as outgroup members, or because speakers wish to assert their group identity vis-à-vis outgroup interlocutors. In Montreal, an example of language maintenance might involve a QA with some knowledge of French who refuses to use French with QF interlocutors. An example of language divergence could be a situation where a QF conversing in English with a QA interlocutor switches to French refusing to pursue the conversation in anything other than French. Instances of speech divergence and speech maintenance have been documented at both the accent and language levels in intergroup settings such as Wales (Bourhis & Giles, 1977) and Belgium (Bourhis, Giles, Leyens & Tajfel, 1979). The results of these studies indicate that speech maintenance and speech divergence can be used as strategies to express speakers' dislike of their interlocutor as an outgroup member or can be used as a symbolic tactic for asserting group identity and cultural distinctiveness in the presence of outgroup speakers.

Also related to motivational factors is the notion that group members in contact with outgroups strive to maintain a positive social identity (Tajfel, 1978). In addition to affecting speakers' language strategies as we have just seen, motivations for maintaining and asserting positive group identity can also lead speakers to display ingroup favouritism when evaluating representative speakers of their own group relative to outgroups (Giles *et al.*, 1977). Ingroup favouritism is evident when group members evaluate ingroup speakers more favourably than outgroup speakers. Ingroup favouritism responses can also be inferred when group members favour the use of their own language over that of outgroup languages. Thus, motivations for maintaining a positive social identity can help account for strategies of language maintenance and language divergence as well as choices and biased evaluations of ingroup/outgroup language use (Bourhis, 1979).

3. Situational norms

Sociolinguists have shown that speech behaviour including language switching can be determined by social norms that prevail in particular situations and settings. Hymes (1972) developed a taxonomy of situational determinants of speech behaviour including the topic of conversation, the social setting in which it occurs and the purpose of the verbal exchange. In Montreal, situational norms concerning the appropriate use of French and English may vary depending on the purpose and setting of such encounters. For instance, both QFs and QAs have long shared the view that French was appropriate as the language for the home environment of QFs but inappropriate for the work setting (Quebec, 1972). In public encounters such as business transactions, norms which hold that the "customer is always right" imply that salespersons should converge to the language of their client (Scotton & Ury, 1977). Indeed, an observational study by Domingue (1978) carried out in Montreal prior to Bill 101 in early 1977 indicated that both QFs *and* QAs expected to be served in their own language when being served by clerks in stores situated in downtown Montreal. However, this situational norm may be changing to the disadvantage of English usage as a result of Bill 101 which is designed to improve the status of French at most levels of business firms including the language of client/clerk relations (see Bill 101, clauses 5 and 141, this volume, Appendix 1). It seems quite plausible then that situational norms can be affected by changes in the relative status of languages brought on by language planning such as Bill 101 in Quebec.

4. Language status

Shared socio-cultural norms dictating appropriate language usage in cross-cultural encounters often do emerge in multilingual societies (Herman, 1961). In numerous multilingual settings, it is the high prestige of the dominant group that is deemed most appropriate for cross-cultural communication. In Quebec, QFs have long been the economically subordinate majority relative to the dominant QA minority (d'Anglejan, this volume, chapter 2; Laporte, this volume, chapter 3). Consequently, the English language has dominated over the French language in prestige value and as the language of business and economic advancement in Montreal (Lambert,

1967; Bourhis, 1982). As was shown in a number of studies (Quebec, 1972; Taylor, Simard & Papineau, 1978), the resulting language switching norms have been in favour of English usage. This has meant that whereas QAs have usually maintained English while interacting with QF interlocutors, the latter have usually had to switch to English while interacting with QA interlocutors.

However recent demands voiced by the QF nationalist movement have resulted not only in the election of the pro-independence Parti Québécois in 1976 and 1981 but also led to the passage of Bill 101 which seeks to increase the status of French by making Quebec both institutionally and socially unilingual French (Corbeil, 1980). Though Bill 101 has received overwhelming support amongst members of the QF majority (Laporte, this volume, chapter 3) this legislation remains a contentious issue for members of the QA minority. Numerous QAs view Bill 101 as threatening (Taylor & Simard, this volume, chapter 7; Locher, 1983) since it challenges the traditionally dominant position of the English language by: regulating the francization of Quebec business firms, instituting French tests for professionals trained in Quebec's English institutions, and stipulating that newcomers to Quebec can only benefit from free public schooling by registering their children in the francophone educational system. In spite of reservations voiced by the QA minority, indications are that Bill 101, as the embodiment of the changing power base in Quebec, is increasing the socio-cultural status of French relative to English (d'Anglejan, this volume, chapter 2).

What are the effects of Bill 101 on the language strategies used by individual QFs and QAs in cross-cultural encounters? Bill 101 may allow many QFs to feel less compelled to converge to English when interacting with QA interlocutors. Indeed, with Quebec now officially French numerous QFs may feel proud to assert their legislative right and ethnic identity by maintaining French when interacting with QA outgroup interlocutors (Bourhis, 1979). On the other hand, with Bill 101, QFs may feel completely reassured about the survival and prestige of French in Quebec and consider ethnic assertion through French maintenance unnecessary. In this case one may expect QFs to converge to English not because it is the prestige language of the formerly dominant minority but because QFs wish to communicate efficiently and pleasantly with QAs as individuals. Alternatively, QFs may now converge to English because they recognize English as the lingua-franca of the dominant Anglo-American culture in North America.

What are the effects of Bill 101 on the language strategies of QAs? On the one hand QAs may feel so threatened by recent events that they may be less willing than ever to accommodate to the "French fact" in Quebec. If this tendency prevails, QAs may be more likely to use strategies of English language maintenance and divergence with QFs than was ever the case before. Alternatively, QAs made more aware of the importance and prestige of French in Quebec may be more willing to converge to French when interacting with QFs than was the case in the past.

Linguistic competence, motivational factors, language status and situational norms must be taken into consideration when examining the impact of Bill 101 on the language usage of individuals during cross-cultural encounters. The three studies designed to address this issue from complimentary methodological perspectives consisted of a sociolinguistic survey (Bourhis, 1983), a laboratory experiment (Genesee & Bourhis, 1982), and field experiments (Bourhis, 1984). The main findings from each of the above studies will be discussed in terms of whether status planning in favour of French has had an impact on the language strategies of individual QF and QA speakers in Montreal.

Study 1: The sociolinguistic survey

The sociolinguistic survey (Bourhis, 1983) was conducted in November 1977, two and a half months after the promulgation of the Charter of the French Language by the Quebec National Assembly. The sociolinguistic questionnaire was completed by 65 QF undergraduates attending the Université de Montréal (38 females, 27 males) and by 65 QAs attending McGill University (42 females, 23 males). The two groups of respondents were equated for age (early twenties) and social class background (predominantly middle class). Though unilingualism was as likely in the QF sample (35%) as it was in the QA sample (40%), QFs were more likely to be bilingual in English (57%) than were QAs to be bilingual in French (37%). In addition to being asked about their attitudes toward various language issues in Quebec, respondents were asked to describe the type of language strategy they most frequently used in encounters with outgroup interlocutors. To verify the possible impact of Bill 101 on cross-cultural communication, QF and QA respondents were also asked to recall language choices they made in cross-cultural encounters before and since the promulgation of Bill 101. All the responses gathered in the survey were obtained using standard 7 point Likert scales. The survey questionnaire was written in French for QF respondents while QAs completed an English version of the survey. Since responses obtained from QFs and QAs are reported in detail in Bourhis (1983), only the main findings obtained in the survey will be discussed in this chapter.

The first important pattern of results that emerged in the survey was that QF and QA university students differed dramatically in their attitudes concerning language issues in Quebec. Whereas QF university students overwhelmingly agreed with the clauses and principles included in Bill 101, QA university students were in total disagreement with these provisions and were opposed to making French the only official language of Quebec. While QF respondents felt very strongy about the importance of speaking French in Quebec and about sending their children to French unilingual schools, QA respondents felt it was important to speak *both* French and English and favoured sending their children to bilingual schools rather than to either French or English unilingual schools. As in other recent studies (Locher, 1983), interest in the outgroup culture was minimal and personal contacts with outgroup members was only moderate for both QF and QA university students in Montreal.

As regards self reports of language usage in Montreal, results showed that while both QAs and QFs reported they used their own language more frequently than the outgroup language, QAs reported using French more frequently than QFs reported using English. Respondents were also asked to report on the language strategies they used when as *clients* they communicated with *outgroup clerks* in public settings such as shops and restaurants in downtown Montreal. These questions yielded very systematic patterns of results. In support of the situational norm in favour of the notion that "the client is always right" both QFs and QAs reported using their own language quite frequently when beginning a conversation with clerks in shops and restaurants. However, QAs reported being more likely to converge to French with QF clerks "today" than they had been "in the past" prior to the implementation of Bill 101. QAs also reported that today QF clerks were less likely to converge to English with them than they had been in the past prior to Bill 101. Very different patterns of results emerged for QF respondents. Though QFs reported being as likely to maintain French with QA clerks today as they were in the past, results showed that today QFs were more likely to maintain French with QA clerks than were QAs likely to maintain English with QF clerks.

Thus it is the QA respondents rather than the QFs who reported having changed their pattern of language usage recently. The pattern of change for QA respondents is in the direction of using less English but more French, even in situations such as client/clerk encounters where clients, by virtue of their buying power and the situational norm could demand service in their own language. The trends in favour of the use of more French by QAs may reflect willingness to accommodate to the French fact in Quebec, now that the legislative measures have established that French is the official language.

Interestingly this trend seemed confirmed by QF respondents' own experience who reported that QA clerks were more likely to converge to French today than in the past. Conversely QAs reported that QF clerks were less likely to converge to English today than they had been in the past. Whether or not this effect could have been achieved without language legislation is open to question (Laporte, this volume, chapter 3). The results obtained with the QF respondents suggest that for this group language usage in favour of French in client/clerk encounters has remained stable over the last few years. QF self reports of French language maintenance before and since the promulgation of Bill 101 supports the notion that legislation in favour of French did address the demands made by QFs to improve the status of French in Quebec. Indeed, for numerous QFs, the promise of vigorous legislation in favour of the French language and culture in Quebec was one of the important factors that brought the Parti Québécois government to power in 1976.

That a combination of the above factors working in favour of more French usage in Quebec could have had an effect on respondents' feelings when using French is apparent when one considers that QAs reported being more at ease using French in Montreal today than they had been in the past. A similar pattern of results emerged for QF respondents who also reported feeling more at ease using French today than they did in the past. In addition, it does appear that QAs felt more positively about the idea of switching to French when not understood in English than was the case for QFs switching to English. Indeed QAs reported that when not understood in English they "enjoyed" switching to French, whereas QFs did not enjoy switching to English when not understood in French by QA interlocutors. These results are a good indication that measures for promoting French usage in Quebec are producing their desired effect not only for QFs but for QAs as well. This may be the case even though our QA respondents do not overtly agree with the promulgation of Bill 101.

Finally, it is noteworthy that the patterns of results in favour of French obtained in this 1977 Sociolinguistic Survey were on the whole corroborated in a major telephone survey carried out in 1979 by the Quebec Government's Conseil de la Langue Française. In this detailed Quebec-wide survey it was found that 70% of the QF sample and 87% of the QA sample felt that French was more frequently used in commercial and public service transactions in 1979 than five years earlier prior to the promulgation of Bill 101 (Bouchard & Beauchamp, 1980).

Study 2: Evaluations of French/English usage in Montreal client/clerk encounters

Results from our Sociolinguistic Survey (Bourhis, 1983) suggest that status language planning in favour of French did have an impact on QF and QA self reports of language use in Montreal. In public settings such as stores and restaurants QAs did report using more French today than they did in the past prior to the passage of Bill 101. Conversely, QFs reported that QAs were indeed more likely to speak French to them since Bill 101 than they had been in the past. However, obtaining self reports of language use in Sociolinguistic Surveys is not sufficient for a thorough assessment of the impact of language planning on the language attitudes of individual speakers. More subtle techniques than surveys are needed to monitor respondents' truly candid attitudes towards controversial issues such as language planning in Quebec.

The present study employed the segmented dialogue technique developed by Bourhis, Giles & Lambert (1975). In this procedure listeners must rate the personality of two speakers engaged in a dialogue heard on a tape recording. This experimental procedure is very much akin to the real life situation in which we overhear a conversation between two speakers in a store or restaurant and cannot help but form an impression of these speakers based on what they say, how they speak, and which language they use. The conversational setting chosen for this study was that of a client/clerk encounter in a downtown Montreal retail shop.

As mentioned earlier, client/clerk encounters in downtown Montreal are perhaps the most likely casual setting in which QFs and QAs have a chance to interact in everyday life. Client/clerk encounters are also interesting because both clause 5 and 141 of Bill 101 stipulate that all Quebec consumers of goods and services have a right to be informed and served in the French language. Consequently client/clerk encounters in downtown Montreal were chosen as the best cross-cultural setting in which to further investigate individual attitudes concerning French/English usage since the promulgation of Bill 101.

In the present study QF, QA and QA bilingual listeners (QAb) were asked to form their impressions of a QF and QA speaker heard on tape in the role of a client or clerk in a Montreal retail store. In study 2A a QF salesman was portrayed serving a QA customer while in study 2B a QA salesman was portrayed serving a QF customer. The verbal content of the dialogues in the two studies was always the same. Each dialogue sequence consisted of three speaker turns: Turn 1 = salesman speaks; Turn 2 = customer speaks; Turn 3

= salesman speaks. In each dialogue the salesman began the conversation in his native language, but subsequent replies by the customer and salesman were systematically varied in different combinations of French and English language switches reflecting common patterns of language choices heard in downtown Montreal stores.

It was expected that the listeners' reactions to the French/English language choices in the client/clerk encounters portrayed in our scenarios would depend on a complex interaction of the factors described in the introduction of this chapter. The following are competing expectations based on each of our previously discussed factors.

In line with the situational norm implying that "the customer is always right", it was expected that the customer would be evaluated similarly whether he used English or French. Also in accordance with this situational norm, it was expected that the salesman would be downgraded if he maintained use of his native language when replying to the customer. However it was expected that the salesman would not necessarily be upgraded for complying with the situational norm by replying in the customer's native language (Scotton & Ury, 1977).

As regards the language status factor, it could be expected that all three listener groups would evaluate the use of English more favourably than the use of French. This follows from the preferential status that English has traditionally enjoyed as the language of business and advancement in Quebec. However the popularity of Bill 101 amongst QFs leads to the expectation that this group would favour the use of French over English in our scenarios. Furthermore, self reports of increased French usage by QAs obtained in Study 1 suggest that QAs may also favour French usage in our scenarios.

Motivations in favour of interpersonal accommodation suggest that language convergence between the clerk and the client would be evaluated positively relative to maintenance or divergence regardless of whether the convergence was in favour of French or English. Alternatively, language maintenance by ingroup speakers may be evaluated positively as an assertion of group pride and loyalty by both QF and QA listeners given that language issues have become so controversial in Quebec recently. Relatedly, on the basis of the notion of ingroup favouritism, one could expect both QF and QA monolinguals to favour the use of their respective ingroup language over that of the outgroup language in the scenarios. Previous research with bilingual QAb students indicate that this group expresses more positive attitudes towards learning and using French than do monolingual QAs (Genesee, 1981). Consequently, it was expected that bilingual

QAb listeners' evaluations of French usage would be more favourable than those of QA monolinguals but not perhaps as favourable as those of QF listeners.

Additional details concerning the procedures used in Study 2A and Study 2B can now be provided. The QA listener group was made up of grade 11 students (16–17 year olds) attending English language secondary schools in Montreal. These QA students had followed a regular program of English instruction with one second language course in French taken each year from grade 1 to grade 11. A total of 91 QAs participated in Study 2A while 107 QAs participated in Study 2B. The Quebec anglophone bilingual group (QAb) was made up of Grade 11 students who had successfully completed a late French immersion program begun in grade 7 in the Protestant School Board of Greater Montreal. A total of 88 QAb students participated in Study 2A while 123 QAbs participated in Study 2B. The QF group consisted of francophone grade 11 students attending French language secondary school with a regular French curriculum including one course of English-as-a-second-language per year from grade 5 to 11. A total of 154 QF students participated in Study 2A while 107 QFs participated in Study 2B. All listener groups were equated for sex composition, age and socio-economic background.

Study 2A consisted of four separate tape recorded dialogues between the QF salesman and the QA client. The four language switching combinations used in study 2A were: (1) F-E-F, (2) F-E-E, (3) F-F-F and (4) F-F-E. These four dialogues allowed one to investigate listeners' perceptions of a QA client who *maintained* English in response to a QF salesman (dialogues 1 and 2) in contrast to their perceptions of a QA client who *converged* to French with a QF salesman (dialogues 3 and 4). These dialogues also allowed an examination of listeners' perceptions of a QF salesman who either *maintained* French in turn 3 (dialogues 1 and 3) or *converged* to English (dialogues 2 and 4) in response to a QA client who earlier had either maintained English or converged to French.

Four subgroups of QA listeners, QAb listeners and QF listeners each heard *one* of the four dialogues tape recording. Using a 9 point rating scale listeners rated their impressions of the client and clerk after they heard each actor speak in their turn. To control for voice quality the same two actors played the client/clerk roles in both studies. A native French-speaking Canadian male played the QF in both roles and spoke French with a middle class Montreal accent. A native English speaking Canadian male played the QA in both roles and spoke English with a middle class Canadian English accent. The QF was always recognizable as a French speaking Canadian even when he spoke English (E) because he had a noticeable French accent when speaking English. Likewise the QA was always recognizable as an English speaking Canadian even when he spoke French (F) because he had a noticeable English accent when speaking French. The two actors were competent in both languages and were chosen for their ability to play their roles realistically and comfortably, thus producing plausible dialogues that were rendered in an amiable and calm tone of voice. The questionnaire and procedures were carried out in the respondents' native language by experimenters of the listeners' own ethnic background. Since results from both studies are reported in detail in Genesee & Bourhis (1982), only the major findings obtained in each study will be discussed in this chapter.

How did the three groups of listeners rate the QF salesmen when they first heard him in turn 1 of Study 2A? Results showed that QF listeners rated the QF salesman to be more considerate, kind and honest than did both groups of anglophone listeners. Conversely results showed that both groups of anglophones rated the QA customer in turn 2 to be more friendly, considerate and honest than did the QF listeners. Thus the QF listeners and both groups of anglophones displayed ingroup favouritism by rating speakers of their own group more favourably than speakers of the outgroup. These results are especially important in the case of QFs who in the past had been found to favour QA speakers while denigrating speakers of their own group (Lambert, 1967). These findings provide the first experimental evidence that QF self perceptions are becoming more positive, suggesting that status language planning in favour of French may be having its desired effect on QF social identity. Indeed, the first preamble to Bill 101 is based on the premise that status planning in favour of French can have a positive impact on the social identity of the Québécois francophone majority (see Bill 101, this volume, Appendix 1).

The results were also noteworthy in that the bilingual QAb students demonstrated as much favouritism towards their owngroup QA customer as did the QA unilingual students. These findings suggest that second language competence in French does not necessarily foster the adoption of more favourable attitudes towards Quebec francophone speakers.

Whether or not the QA customer maintained English or converged to French did make a difference for QF listeners but not to the two groups of anglophone listeners. The QF listeners felt that the QA client liked and respected the QF clerk more when the former converged to French than when he maintained English. These results suggest that QF listeners can be quite appreciative of a QA speaker who uses French in a situation where no normative pressure requires the use of French.

Was the QF salesman perceived differently depending on whether he maintained French or converged to English in his reply (turn 3) to the QA customer? The three groups of listeners including QFs did downgrade the QF salesman when he violated the situational norm by maintaining French in his reply to the QA client. Indeed, the QF salesman was rated to be less considerate, friendly, kind, honest, competent and intelligent when he failed to switch to English in his reply to the anglophone customer. These results were obtained regardless of the language used by the QA customer indicating, as the situational norm would imply, that "the client is always right" and can use the language of his choice in addressing the clerk.

In addition, important differences in the reactions of the three listener groups towards the violation of the situational norm did emerge in the results. Most noteworthy was the finding that bilingual QAb students were even less tolerant of French maintenance by the QF clerk than were either the QA or QF students. These findings suggest that compared to monolingual QA students, bilingual QAb students who have made a personal effort to learn French may expect nothing less than a reciprocal effort in favour of English learning on the part of QF speakers. This may be the case especially in Quebec where QAs as members of a once dominant minority feel they have made a considerable effort learning the language of a traditionally low status group. If such trends are further corroborated, then one could caution that QA bilingualism in French may not necessarily lead to ethnic harmony in Quebec French-English encounters.

However, perceptions of the QF salesman who converged to English in his reply to the QA client did improve somewhat since the salesman was rated to be more considerate and intelligent by both groups of anglophones but not by the QF students. Overall, the QF clerk was mildly rewarded evaluatively for conforming to the situational norm in favour of using the client's native language.

Finally, interpersonal accommodation played some part in the results since all three groups rated the QA client to feel more pleased and comfortable when his French or English language voice was matched by the clerk's language of reply.

To sum up, while both anglophone and francophone students downgraded the salesman who violated the situational norm, QA students and especially bilingual anglophone students (QAb) were more critical of this violation than were the QF students. In addition, both anglophone groups did upgrade the QF salesman when he converged to English, whereas QF listeners did not. The possibility remains that anglophone students (QA and QAb) may have been using the situational norm to promote the use of

English as a group serving biased response rather than in support of the situational norm *per se*. Study 2B was designed to explore this possibility by assigning the salesman role to the QA and the customer role to the QF. If ingroup favouritism was the basis of the QA and QAb students' reactions, then one could expect these two groups to continue favouring English usage even when the roles are reversed with the situational norm now working in favour of French usage.

The four dialogues used in Study 2B between the QA salesman and the QF client were made up of the following language switching combinations: (1) E-F-E, (2) E-F-F, (3) E-E-E and (4) E-E-F. The procedures used to obtain listeners' evaluations of the dialogues in Study 2B were exactly the same as those used in Study 2A.

Unlike results obtained in Study 2A, QF listeners and the two groups of anglophone listeners did not rate speakers of their own group more favourably than outgroup speakers. However, a strong preference in favour of the English language was evident from both anglophone groups who rated the QF client more favourably when he converged to English than when he maintained French. These results were obtained even though as a client the QF had the prerogative to use either French or English as had been the case for the QA client in Study 2A and for whom language choice had no such evaluative consequences. Furthermore, QFs did rate the client equally, regardless of his language choice in both studies, whether the client was depicted as a QF or as a QA. The above patterns of results suggest that both groups of anglophone listeners were biased in favour of the use of English rather than French in our scenarios. Also, in accord with the traditional prestige associated with speaking English in Montreal, the results showed that the three groups of listeners rated the QF client to be more pleased, more comfortable, less insulted and less annoyed when he *converged* to English than when he *maintained* French with the QA salesman. Again, these results in favour of English usage were obtained in spite of the situational norm and Bill 101 giving the QF client the freedom to use French in his replies.

As in Study 2A, violation of the situational norm was downgraded by listeners in Study 2B. The QA salesman was downgraded equally by the three groups of students when he failed to converge to the native language of the client. Relative to their rating of the salesman in turn 1, all three listener groups rated the QA salesman to be less considerate, kind, friendly, intelligent and competent when he maintained English in his reply to the QF client. Conversely the three groups of listeners did rate the QA salesman to be more considerate, honest and intelligent when he converged to French with the QF client. It seems that as a member of the traditionally high status group the QA salesman was rewarded for converging linguistically to the traditionally low status QF interlocutor. In Study 2A no such rewards accrued for the traditionally low status QF client converging to the language of the traditionally high status QA speaker. Finally, all three groups showed their awareness of the situational norm in favour of the QF client since they rated the QF client to be more pleased, more comfortable, less insulted and less annoyed when the QA clerk converged to French than when he maintained English.

In summary, as hypothesized, the listeners' evaluations of the dialogues did depend on a dynamic interaction of factors including situational norms, language status, interpersonal accommodation and ingroup favouritism. Listeners' evaluations of the dialogue speakers were most influenced by the situational norm. In both studies the salesman was downgraded for violating the situational norm. Despite Bill 101, French language maintenance by the QF salesman was downgraded not only by both anglophone groups but by QF listeners as well. Similarly, despite the traditional status ascribed to the English language in Quebec, the three listeners groups downgraded the QA salesman who violated the situational norm by maintaining English with the QF client. In a tense intergroup setting such as Montreal, closely adhering to the situational norm seemed the safest way of conducting a potentially conflictual cross-cultural encounter between a QF and a QA interlocutor.

However, the relative status of the French and English language in Quebec did have an impact on the listeners' evaluations of the client/clerk dialogues. Despite Parti Québécois status planning in favour of French, results from this study show that the English language still enjoys a great deal of prestige as the language of business in Montreal. The three groups of listeners including QFs accorded preferential evaluations of English usage by QA and QF speakers at numerous points in the dialogues. Though survey results such as those obtained in Study 1 indicated that French was gaining in status and use in Quebec, such results may have been a better reflection of how respondents thought things *ought to be* rather than how they felt things *really were*. Compared to conventional surveys, the dialogue technique used in this study was a more subtle and less transparent method of eliciting QF and QA attitudes towards French/English language usage in Montreal. For more than 200 years English dominated French as the prestige language in Quebec. To expect QFs to change their feelings regarding the status of French relative to English within only a few years of status language planning in favour of French would seem premature. To expect a similar radical change on the part of the traditionally dominant QAs would also seem unlikely.

While ingroup favouritism emerged as a significant factor in some of the reactions of all three listener groups, it was particularly evident amongst both groups of anglophone students. The clearest example of this pattern emerged in Study 2B where the two anglophone groups rated the QF client more positively when he used English than when he used French. So why were the two anglophone groups so keen to reward English rather than French language usage in our scenarios? The QA students may have been prone to endorse the use of English even at the expense of violating a basic social norm because they felt threatened by recent sociopolitical events in Quebec such as the promulgation of the Charter of the French Language (Taylor & Simard, this volume, chapter 7). More simply these patterns may reflect the traditional prestige of English as the dominant language of business in both Quebec and North America.

The present results show that interpersonal encounters between QAs and QFs may embody latent intergroup conflict in Quebec society so that particular language choices in such encounters can symbolize maintenance or loss of collective social power (Bourhis, 1979). Indeed two other studies reported in Genesee & Bourhis (1982) have shown that subsequent language choices in the dialogues were interpreted as a symbolic language duel in which language status and interpersonal accommodation processes played important roles.

Finally the discrepancies between the results obtained in the sociolinguistic study and those obtained from our dialogue experiments beg the question as regards the *actual* language behaviour of QFs and QAs in Montreal. The third study was a field experiment designed to monitor French/English language switches during actual real life encounters between QA and QF pedestrians in downtown Montreal.

Study 3: Field studies of French/English usage in downtown Montreal

The main result to emerge from the sociolinguistic survey in Study 1 was that whereas QF university students overwhelmingly agreed with the promulgation of Bill 101, QA university students were in fundamental disagreement with this law and were opposed to making French the only official language of Quebec. Self reports of language use revealed that QA respondents were more likely to converge to French with QF interlocutors "today" than they were "in the past" prior to the passage of Bill 101. QAs also reported that "today" QFs were less likely to converge to English with them than they had been "in the past". Very different patterns of results emerged for QF respondents who reported being as likely to maintain French with

QA interlocutors "today" as they were "in the past". These post-Bill 101 survey results indicate that QAs seem on the road to accommodating to the "French fact" in Quebec through increased convergence to French with QF interlocutors. This seemed confirmed by QF respondents who reported that QAs were more likely to converge to French "today" than "in the past". These results suggested that Bill 101 is having its effect in increasing the status and use of French in Quebec.

However, the dialogue experiments in Study 2 showed that although situational norms played a major role in the evaluations of language choices made by QF and QA interlocutors, the second major factor determining listeners' responses was the respective status of the French and English language in Quebec. The less transparent method used in Study 2 revealed that despite recent efforts to increase the status of French in Quebec, English seems to maintain its traditional prestige as the language of business transactions in Montreal.

The main purpose of the field experiments (Bourhis, 1984) was to attempt a replication of the main patterns of results obtained in the sociolinguistic survey and the dialogue studies. The field experiments were carried out with pedestrians in downtown Montreal shopping promenades. In these settings a perfectly bilingual QF confederate sought assistance from QA and QF pedestrians by using fluent and non-fluent forms of either French or English. A number of studies in various settings have shown that the language in which a verbal plea is voiced can affect the co-operative behaviour of listeners (Bourhis & Giles, 1976; Harris & Baudin, 1976). In the present field studies pedestrians were approached by the confederate and asked to provide directions to the nearest "metro" station or campus university bookstore. Whether or not pedestrians provided this information and the language(s) in which they replied (French and/or English) constituted the dependent measures for these studies. Two sets of field experiments were designed (Bourhis, 1984). Study 3A consisted of two field experiments carried out in October 1977, two months after the promulgation of Bill 101 and concurrently with the administration of the 1977 sociolinguistic survey (Bourhis, 1983). To monitor the longer term effects of Bill 101, Study 3B consisted of two field experiments carried out in October 1979 at the time the dialogue studies were being conducted (Genesee & Bourhis, 1982).

On the basis of the sociolinguistic survey results (Bourhis, 1983) one could predict the following patterns of results to emerge in the field experiments: 1) the majority of QF pedestrians would maintain French when addressed by the "QA" confederate using English; 2) the majority of QA pedestrians would converge to French when queried in French by the "QF" confederate. However, results from the dialogue studies suggest that English language usage may persist as the preferred language for cross-cultural communications between QAs and QFs despite status language planning in favour of French. The field experiments were specifically designed to explore such possibilities. Since these field experiments are described in detail in Bourhis (1984), main findings only will be discussed in this chapter.

A total of 160 pedestrians served as respondents in Study 3A; 80 were QFs and 80 were QAs. An equal number of male and female respondents were sampled for each linguistic group, and attempts were made to sample mainly "middle class" adults between the ages of 25 and 55 years. If it emerged from the respondent's accent that his or her native language was other than Québécois French or Canadian English the respondent was not included in the analysis.

The pedestrians were addressed during lunch hours on weekdays in either one of two main underground shopping malls situated in downtown Montreal. QF pedestrians were sampled in a predominantly francophone shopping mall situated in east downtown Montreal while QA pedestrians were sampled in a predominantly anglophone shopping mall located in west downtown Montreal (Lieberson, 1970). An equal number of QF and QA pedestrians were randomly assigned to one of four encounter situations. A total of 40 pedestrians were sampled in each situation. A young, discreetly attractive, well dressed QF female bilingual served as the confederate in each of the situations. As in Study 2, the confederate was chosen for her ability to speak both French and English in a native-like fashion. The confederate was also chosen for her ability to adopt a French accent in her English denoting a QF making efforts to speak English (non-fluent English), and to speak French with an English accent denoting a QA making efforts to speak French (non-fluent French).

In each situation pedestrians were approached by the confederate and asked the equivalent of the following: "Excuse me, could you tell me where is the nearest metro station please". The four situations consisted of the plea being voiced in one of the following guises: 1) in fluent French, 2) in fluent English, 3) in non-fluent French with an English accent, and 4) in non-fluent English with a French accent. After the initial plea, the confederate limited her utterances to the minimum and once the information was obtained, the confederate thanked the respondent in the appropriate language. Considering the very recent controversy surrounding the promulgation of the Bill 101 legislation it was considered wiser not to debrief the respondents. After each encounter, the confederate noted the language(s) in which the pedestrians provided the information. As responses are not always exclusively in French or exclusively in English in such circumstances (Giles, Taylor & Bourhis, 1973), the confederate paid special attention to responses that were voiced in a mixture of French and English.

In all cases pedestrians did provide the information requested by the confederate. But the language in which this information was provided did vary depending on the various encounter situations. The first pattern of results to emerge was that all the QF and QA pedestrians responded in their native language when addressed in their own language fluently by the confederate. These results show that the performance of the confederate in fluent French and fluent English was convincing to both the QF and QA pedestrians. However, results showed that QF and QA pedestrians did differ in their response to the "outgroup" interlocutor seeking directions in her native language. The results indicate that whereas 19/20 (95%) QF pedestrians converged to English with the English speaking confederate, only 12/20 (60%) of the QA pedestrians converged to French with the French speaking confederate. Conversely, whereas 8/20 (40%) of the QA pedestrians maintained English in response to the French plea, only 1/20 (5%) of the QF pedestrians was ready to maintain French in response to the English plea.

Do these results indicate that QF pedestrians are more likely to converge to English with QA interlocutors than are QAs to converge to French with QF interlocutors? These findings could be attributed to the fact that in Quebec QAs are usually less fluent in French than QFs are in English (Quebec, 1972). In order to reduce the possible impact of lack of linguistic skills on the results, the criteria adopted for counting a response as a language convergence was to consider any *single* word or phrase uttered in the language of the confederate's plea as a converging response even though the rest of the response was maintained in the pedestrian's native language. Thus, one or more words spoken in French by a QA pedestrian was sufficient to label the response to the French speaking confederate as a "convergence" (e.g. Bonjour, Bienvenue, Excusez-moi je ne parle pas français). These criteria were meant to be charitable in favour of convergent responses. Indeed, of the 12 QAs who converged to French, 4 voiced their responses in a mixture of French and English. Conversely, of the 19 QFs who converged to English, 7 partially converged by using a mixture of English and French. There is little doubt that both QFs and QAs living in Montreal for any appreciable length of time have had the chance to learn at least a few *key* words or sentences in the outgroup language (e.g. Bonjour, Salut, Merci, etc.). Thus there is reason to believe that some QAs did not converge to French with the QF confederate, not because they lacked the linguistic skills to do so, but because they did not wish to do so. These results provide further empirical evidence that language maintenance can be used as a dissociative strategy in cross-cultural encounters (Bourhis, 1979).

Nevertheless, the rate of convergence obtained with QAs in the present study are encouraging when compared with results that emerged in a more rigorously controlled experiment carried out in 1972 by Giles *et al.* (1973). In that study, a QF interlocutor known to be bilingual gave a message in French to QA bilingual McGill undergraduates. In this context only 25% of the QA bilingual students converged to French in their responses, whereas 75% maintained English when returning their message to the QF interlocutor. The contrasting results obtained here suggest that QAs are more likely to converge to French today than they were in the past prior to Bill 101.

The aim of the second 1977 field experiment in Study 3A was to explore a cross-cultural communication in which a QF or QA makes an obvious effort to converge linguistically to a pedestrian by voicing a plea for help in the native language of his/her interlocutor. Results showed that QF and QA pedestrians did react differently when addressed by an "outgroup" interlocutor who made an effort to accommodate by converging to the pedestrian's native language. The findings show that when the QA pedestrians were addressed in non-fluent English only 10% (2/20) of the QAs converged by reciprocating in French, whereas in 90% of the cases (18/20) QAs maintained the conversation in English. Not so for QF pedestrians, who when addressed in non-fluent French, were as likely to converge by reciprocating the effort in English (10/20) as they were to maintain the conversation in French (10/20).

In casual encounters in a bilingual city like Montreal, it does occur that QF and QA interlocutors accidentally address a stranger of their own group in the outgroup language. After one or two such initial utterances one or both interlocutors often realize that both share the same native language and frequently the conversation is pursued by switching back to the speakers' native language. What happened when pedestrians were addressed in the outgroup language by a speaker of their own group? The findings show that the majority of QF (55%) and QA respondents (65%) did prefer to maintain their native language when addressed in a non-fluent form of the outgroup language by an "ingroup" interlocutor. Nevertheless a sizeable number of respondents from both groups "automatically" converged to the language they were addressed in. These results suggest that mutual convergence can be a powerful tendency in the immediacy of face-to-face encounters.

Results from the non-fluent plea situations indicate that QF pedestrians were more likely to use reciprocal convergence (50%) than were QA pedestrians (10%). Indeed when results from both the fluent and non-fluent plea situations are combined, it is noted that when addressed by an "outgroup" interlocutor QA pedestrians were more likely to maintain English (65%) than were QFs likely to maintain French (27%). This general pattern of results was obtained regardless of the language strategy adopted by the "outgroup" confederate. As argued earlier, this effect cannot be attributed solely to the lack of second language skills amongst QA or QF pedestrians.

On the whole the present field study results give greater support to the patterns obtained in Study 2 than to those obtained in the survey results of Study 1. The patterns of results in favour of English language usage obtained with both the QA and QF pedestrians strongly suggest that English is maintaining its historically dominant status position despite recent government efforts to increase the status of French in Quebec. The aim of Study 3B was to examine if by 1979 sustained government efforts to improve the status of French in Quebec had an impact on the language usage patterns of QA and QF pedestrians in Montreal.

To address the above issue two field experiments were carried out in Study 3B. One took place in downtown Montreal as in the 1977 studies and the other took place on the campuses of McGill University and l'Université de Montréal. The procedure used in the 1979 study was similar to the 1977 studies except that pedestrians in the 1979 studies were debriefed and questioned about their linguistic skills in the outgroup language.

A total of 131 pedestrians participated in the downtown Montreal study such that 71 respondents were QFs and 60 QAs. An attempt was made to sample mainly middle class adults between the ages of 25 and 55 years. A total of 173 students participated in the University campus study with 88 QFs sampled from the Université de Montréal campus and 85 QAs sampled from the McGill University Campus. In both experiments roughly equal numbers of male and female students were sampled from each linguistic group. If it emerged from the pedestrian's accent that his or her native language was other than Québécois French or Canadian English, the respondent was not included in the analysis. Also, respondents were not included in the analyses if answers to the debriefing questionnaire showed that the pedestrians had a mother tongue other than English or French.

For the Montreal downtown experiment, pedestrians were sampled in the same locations as in the 1977 study and were queried for directions to the nearest metro station. In the University experiment undergraduate students were encountered on campus and asked to provide directions to the University bookstore. In both experiments the encounters consisted of the plea for directions being voiced in either fluent French or fluent English to QF and

QA pedestrians. After the initial plea the female confederate limited her utterances to the minimum and noted the language(s) in which the pedestrians provided the information. Once the information was obtained participants were debriefed and responded to a series of questions including their mother tongue and self-rated skills in speaking the outgroup language. A five-point Likert scale ranging from not at all to extremely well was used to obtain participants' self ratings of their language skills.

As in the 1977 studies, all pedestrians in the two 1979 experiments of Study 3B provided the information requested by the confederate, but the language in which the responses were voiced differed across the different situations. In downtown Montreal the QF and QA respondents replied in their native language when addressed in their own language by the confederate. As in the 1977 study, these results show that the fluently bilingual confederate was convincing to both groups of pedestrians.

Generally the pattern of results obtained in the 1979 downtown Montreal experiment corroborate results obtained in the 1977 experiment. The 1979 findings indicate that whereas 100% of the QF pedestrians (33/33) converged to the English speaking confederate by responding completely or partially in English, 70% of the QA respondents (21/30) converged by providing responses completely or partially in French. Conversely, whereas 9/30 (30%) of the QA pedestrians maintained English in response to the plea voiced in French, none of the QF pedestrians maintained French in their responses to the English plea voiced by the QA.

Though the 1979 results show a marginal increase in QA convergence to French relative to the 1977 results, these patterns still indicate that QFs are more likely to converge to English with QA interlocutors than are QAs to converge to French with QF interlocutors. Can these patterns of results reflect a lack of French language skills on the part of some QAs rather than QA resistance to French language usage in Quebec? As in the 1977 study one or more words spoken in French by QA respondents in the 1979 study was sufficient to label such responses as convergence to the QF interlocutor. In addition the 1979 study was designed to further explore the linguistic skill hypothesis by including post experimental self-ratings of outgroup language skills (Bourhis, 1984).

Results showed that pedestrians in all four encounter situations reported they had just below average skills in the outgroup language. In addition, QAs who maintained English did not differ much in their French language skills from those who completely or partially converged to French. These results support the notion that QAs who maintained English did so not because they were unable to utter French words but because they chose not to use French in their replies. It is noteworthy that self ratings of French skills could not be obtained from 5 of the 9 QAs who maintained English in their replies to the French plea. In spite of the confederate's further French queries these QA respondents maintained English, refused to provide additional information and rudely walked away from the confederate. These patterns of behaviour provide further support to the notion that language maintenance can be used as a dissociative strategy in cross-cultural encounters (Bourhis, 1979).

Results obtained with University undergraduates in 1979 differed somewhat from those obtained in the downtown Montreal studies of 1977 and 1979. QA students were as likely to converge to French with the French speaking confederate (38/45, 84%) as QFs were of converging to English with the English speaking confederate (34/41, 83%). Conversely, QA students emerged to be as unlikely to maintain English in the French plea encounter (7/41, 17%) as QFs were to maintain French in their replies to the English plea (7/45, 16%). As in previous findings, results show that both QF and QA respondents replied in their own language when addressed in their own language by the confederate.

It is noteworthy that the QAs and QFs in the University setting reported having average skills in the outgroup language. In addition QFs who maintained French did not differ much in their English language skills relative to those who converged to English. Similarly, QAs who maintained English did not differ much in their French language skills from those who converged to French. As in the 1979 downtown Montreal study, lack of skills in the outgroup language could not have played an important role in determining the students' language strategies.

Results obtained with QA undergraduates are particularly interesting since they begin to corroborate attitudinal results obtained from McGill students in Study 1. Indeed, the majority of QA McGill undergraduates surveyed in the 1977 study asserted they *did* converge to French when responding to QFs addressing them in French. This pattern of results was confirmed in the 1979 campus experiment. The language attitudes and behaviour of QA university students indicate that in contrast to earlier studies with McGill students (Giles *et al.*, 1973), this segment of the QA population (all in their early twenties) is indeed more willing to accommodate linguistically to QFs. The lower rate of convergence obtained with QAs in the downtown Montreal field studies of 1977 and 1979 suggests that this older segment of the QA population is adapting less quickly to status planning in favour of French in Quebec. Nevertheless the general pattern of results to emerge from this series of field experiments shows that QAs of all age groups are more and more likely to converge to French with QF interlocutors.

As in the 1977 and 1979 downtown Montreal studies the high rate of convergence to English by QF Université de Montréal undergraduates stands in sharp contrast to the survey results in which this group reported they were more likely to maintain French than converge to English with Quebec anglophones. It could be that in the survey study QFs were under estimating their tendency to converge to English. However, additional recent surveys (Laporte, this volume, chapter 3; Bouchard & Beauchamp, 1980) show that consciously at least, QFs do agree with the notion that Quebec is a francophone province where French should be used as the language of cross-cultural communication with anglophones. In the socio-political climate of the day, a QF who openly admitted he frequently converged to English with QA interlocutors may have feared being viewed as somewhat of a cultural traitor by his peers.

The downtown Montreal field studies did corroborate the pattern of results obtained in favour of English usage in Study 2. These results attest to the validity of the segmented dialogue technique as a method of obtaining respondents' more candid attitudes towards language usage in tense inter-group settings such as Quebec. Despite status planning in favour of French, both studies suggest that QFs may still react to QAs as members of a linguistically superior group with whom they feel they *must* speak English. As such the real life language behaviour of QFs may well lag behind consciously expressed attitudes concerning appropriate use of French and English in Quebec cross-cultural encounters. As regards the language issue at least, QFs were long made to feel inferior to the dominant QA minority in Quebec. In the 1960s, survey and matched guise studies (Lambert, 1967) showed that QFs had internalized the negative views QAs had of them and rated QA English speakers more favourably than French speakers of their *owngroup*. With the rise of the Québécois nationalist movement and re-newed pride in Québécois language and culture in the early 1970s, survey and interview results began to show that consciously at least, QFs felt on a par with QAs both as group members and as French language users (Bourhis, 1982; Quebec, 1972). However, studies using less transparent procedures such as the matched guise technique still showed that QFs downgraded QF speakers relative to QA speakers (Giles & Powesland, 1975). As seen in Study 2, it is only by 1979 that under some circumstances results showed QFs rating French speakers of their owngroup more favourably than outgroup QA English speakers (Genesee & Bourhis, 1982). Consequently, even though survey and interview results show that many QFs consciously state they maintain French when conversing with QA interlocutors, it may take some time before the actual face-to-face language behaviour of QFs catches up with their consciously expressed language attitudes vis-à-vis previously perceived superior QA outgroup speakers.

Concluding Notes

The results of the 1977 sociolinguistic survey (Study 1) showed that attitudinally at least, both QFs and QAs reported using French more frequently "today" than "in the past". However, both the study on evaluative reactions to French/English usage (Study 2) and the field experiments on actual language switching behaviour in downtown Montreal (Study 3) seemed to reflect older patterns favouring English language usage on the part of both QAs and QFs.

Although the aim of Bill 101 was to increase both the status and use of French in Quebec, it may yet take some time for the behavioural consequences of this legislation to be evident in the language switching behaviours of QFs and QAs during cross-cultural encounters. Indeed the present results showed that despite much concern voiced about this linguistic legislation in the English media in Quebec and Canada, QAs in Montreal are still more likely to be helped in English by QFs than are QFs likely to be helped in French by QAs. The persistence of QF respondents in favouring and using the English language may not only reflect the traditionally dominant position of English as the language of business in Quebec but may also reflect the growing attraction of Anglo-American culture for QFs in Montreal. By increasing the status of French in Quebec, Bill 101 may have made QFs more secure in their linguistic and cultural identity. However, Bill 101 may also have had the effect of making English a less threatening language for QFs. QFs may now converge to English not because they feel obliged to show deference to the traditionally dominant QA minority but because they enjoy using English as the lingua franca of Anglo-American culture. Indeed, recent Quebec wide surveys by the Conseil de la langue française have repeatedly shown that as regards the mass media, young QFs are increasingly attracted to Anglo-American radio and TV programming (Beauchamp & Bouchard, 1982; Bédard & Monnier, 1981; Georgeault, 1981). Future studies should investigate the attractiveness of English for QFs not only as the traditional prestige language of the QA minority but also as the lingua franca of Anglo-American culture in North America.

The clearest shift in favour of French convergence amonst QAs was obtained in the 1979 field study with young university undergraduates, while gradual though consistent shifts in favour of French convergence were obtained with the older QAs of the 1977 and 1979 downtown Montreal

200 CONFLICT AND LANGUAGE PLANNING IN QUEBEC

setting. The trends in favour of French usage by QAs may not only reflect
favourable attitudes towards French usage *per se* but may also reflect recent
demographic changes in Quebec. According to the 1981 Canadian Census
interprovincial migration has been greatest from the province of Quebec.
While 18,000 francophones migrated from Quebec between 1971 and 1981,
a total of 106,310 anglophones left Quebec in the last decade. Relative to
1971 figures this anglophone out-migration represents a 13% loss of the
anglophone population of Quebec. Though fiscal policies are recognized to
have been largely responsible for the departure of numerous Anglo-Canadian
business firms from Quebec, the rise of the Quebec nationalist movement
and language planning in favour of French are also recognized as factors
accounting for the out-migration of economically mobile Quebec anglophones. It is reasonable to suggest that some of the socially mobile QAs who
were most hostile against Bill 101 may also have been those QAs most likely
to leave the province. Conversely it is reasonable to expect that the socially
mobile QAs who decided to stay in Quebec may be those most sympathetic
to French usage in Quebec. Indeed, other figures from the 1981 Census
showed that 53% of current QA residents now say they can speak French, a
figure up from 38% obtained with QAs surveyed in the 1971 Census. Recent
figures also show that 15% of QA families now voluntarily send their
children to French medium schools while pressure for more French immersion schools within the English school system mounts yearly. The above
demographic trends, taken together with the growing realization amongst
QAs that language planning in favour of French is "here to stay" regardless
of which political party forms future Quebec governments, suggest that
trends in favour of French language usage amongst QAs will be maintained
in the foreseeable future.

Interestingly, if present trends in favour of QF convergence to English
and QA convergence to French continue well into the 1980s, the climate of
cross-cultural encounters in Montreal could develop harmoniously and
should prove to be increasingly rewarding for both the QF majority and the
QA minority. After all, mutual language convergence at the onset of French-
English cross-cultural encounters may prove a creative strategy for neutral-
izing the potentially divisive consequences of inter-ethnic encounters in
Montreal. Indeed, other results from the Genesee & Bourhis (1982) study
indicated that when speakers showed their goodwill and respect through
mutual language convergence early in the cross-cultural dialogues, subsequent language choices were emptied of their divisive ideological content
and had little impact on listeners' evaluations. It is only by demonstrating
such mutual respect early in conversations that the need to communicate as
efficiently as possible can most clearly emerge as the more important goal of

cross-cultural communication in Montreal. It is perhaps under such favourable circumstances that the French language has the best chances of emerging as the most efficient tool of cross-cultural communication in Quebec.

Finally, the present series of studies show that statements about language behaviour in sociolinguistic surveys should be viewed with caution and when possible should be verified against actual behavioural responses obtained in field settings. Thus, despite language planning in favour of French, results showed that the English language and its speakers still enjoy much status and prestige in Quebec. The present conclusion could not have been reached on the basis of survey questionnaires alone. Language planners who wish to obtain more accurate evaluations of their language planning efforts have much to gain in broadening the range of their monitoring tools to include not only traditional attitude and survey techniques but to also use observational, dialogue evaluation and field experimental procedures which more directly reflect actual language behaviour in real life situations. In the present case a focused question regarding the possible impact of Bill 101 on the language use of QFs and QAs in commercial and public encounters was investigated using three distinct research methodologies. Taken together, discrepancies between self reports of language use, evaluations of language usage and actual language behaviours have proved useful in better understanding the role language planning can have in changing language attitudes and language behaviour. The use of such a combination of research methodologies could be fruitfully extended to monitor the impact of language policies in other "bilingual" urban settings. Follow up studies using the above combination of research methodologies in Montreal should help in better evaluating the long term impact of language planning efforts such as the Charter of the French language in Quebec. In this sense the Quebec setting offers a unique opportunity to investigate the impact of one of the most important and sustained language planning programs ever undertaken in North America.

Acknowledgements

The research presented in this chapter was made possible through a grant from the Canadian Secretary of State, Multiculturalism Directorate, to Richard Y. Bourhis. This research was also made possible through a grant from the Faculty of Graduate Studies and Research at McGill University and from the Arts Research Board at McMaster University. In addition to the above, Study 2 also benefited from grants to Fred Genesee from Le Ministère de l'Education du Québec and from the Canadian Social Sciences and Humanities Research Council.

I wish to thank William Coleman, Ellen Bouchard-Ryan, Itesh Sachdev, Colin Williams and Richard Wood for their valuable comments and suggestions on earlier drafts of this chapter.

References

BEAUCHAMP, S., & BOUCHARD, P. 1982, *Le français et les Médias*. Dossiers du Conseil de la langue française, No. 11. Québec: Editeur Officiel du Québec.

BÉDARD, E., & MONNIER, D. 1981, *Conscience linguistique des jeunes Québécois. Tome I*, Influence de l'environment linguistique chez les élèves francophones de niveau secondaire IV et V. Dossiers du Conseil de la langue française, No. 9. Québec: Editeur Officiel du Québec.

BOUCHARD, P., & BEAUCHAMP, S. 1980, *Le Français langue des commerces et des services publics*. Dossiers du Conseil de la langue française, No. 5. Québec: Editeur Officiel du Québec.

BOURHIS, R. Y. 1979, Language in Ethnic Interaction: A Social Psychological Approach. In: H. GILES & B. SAINT-JACQUES (eds), *Language and Ethnic Relations*. Oxford & New York: Pergamon Press.

— 1982, Language policies and language attitudes: Le monde de la Francophonie. In: E. BOUCHARD-RYAN & H. GILES (eds), *Attitudes towards language variation*. London: Edward Arnold.

— 1983, Language Attitudes and Self Reports of French-English Language Usage in Quebec. *Journal of Multilingual and Multicultural Development*, 4, 163–180.

— 1984, Cross-Cultural Communication in Montreal: Two Field Studies since Bill 101. *International Journal of the Sociology of Language*, in press.

BOURHIS, R. Y., & GILES, H. 1976, The language of co-operation in Wales. *Language Sciences*, 42, 13–16.

— 1977, The Language of Intergroup Distinctiveness. In H. GILES (ed.), *Language, Ethnicity and Intergroup Relations*. London & New York: Academic Press.

BOURHIS, R. Y., GILES, H., & LAMBERT, W. E. 1975, Social consequences of accommodating one's style of speech: a cross-national investigation. *International Journal of the Sociology of Language*, 6, 55–71.

BOURHIS, R. Y., GILES, H., LEYENS, J. P., & TAJFEL, H. 1979, Psycholinguistic Distinctiveness: Language divergence in Belgium. In: H. GILES & R. ST. CLAIR (eds), *Language and Social Psychology*. Oxford: Blackwell.

CAPPON, P. 1978, Nationalism and inter-ethnic and linguistic conflict in Québec. In: L. DRIEDGER (ed.), *The Canadian Ethnic Mosaic*. Toronto: McClelland & Stewart.

CLIFT, D., & ARNOPOULOS, S. MCLEOD. 1979, *Le fait anglais au Québec*. Montréal: Libre Expression.

CORBEIL, J. C. 1980, *L'Aménagement linguistique du Québec*. Montréal: Guérin Editeur.

DOMINGUE, N. 1978, L'usage bilingue dans le centre de Montréal. In M. PARADIS (ed.), *Aspects of Bilingualism*. Columbia: Hornbeam Press.

GENESEE, F. 1981, Bilingualism and biliteracy: A study of cross-cultural contact in a bilingual community. In: J. R. EDWARDS (ed.), *The Social Psychology of Reading*. Silver Spring, Maryland: Institute of Modern Language.

GENESEE, F., & BOURHIS, R. Y. 1982, The social psychological significance of code-switching in cross-cultural communication. *Journal of Language and Social Psychology*, 1, 1–27.

GEORGEAULT, P. 1981, *Conscience linguistique des jeunes Québécois. Tome II*, Influence de l'environment linguistique chez les étudiants francophones de niveau collégial I et II. Dossiers du Conseil de la langue française, No. 10. Québec: Editeur Officiel du Québec.

GILES, H., BOURHIS, R. Y., & TAYLOR, D. M. 1977, Towards a Theory of Language in Ethnic Group Relations. In: H. GILES (ed.), *Language, Ethnicity and Intergroup Relations*. London & New York: Academic Press.

GILES, H., & POWESLAND, P. 1975, *Speech Style and Social Evaluation*. London & New York: Academic Press.

GILES, H., TAYLOR, D. M., & BOURHIS, R. Y. 1973, Towards a theory of interpersonal accommodation through speech: some Canadian data. *Language in Society*, 2, 177–192.

HARRIS, M. B., & BAUDIN, H. 1976, The Language of Altruism: the effects of language, dress and ethnic group. *Journal of Social Psychology*, 97, 37–41.

HERMAN, S. 1961, Explorations in the social psychology of language choice. *Human Relations*, 14, 149–164.

HYMES, D. 1972, Models of the interaction of language and social life. In: J. J. GUMPERZ & D. HYMES (eds), *Directions in Sociolinguistics*. New York: Holt, Rinehart and Winston.

JOY, R. 1972, *Languages in Conflict*. Toronto: McClelland and Stewart.

LAMBERT, W. E. 1967, A Social Psychology of Bilingualism. *The Journal of Social Issues*, 23, 91–109.

LIEBERSON, S. 1970, *Language and Ethnic Relations in Canada*. New York: John Wiley.

LOCHER, U. 1983, *Conscience Linguistique des jeunes Québécois, Tome III*, Le fait français vécu par des élèves étudiants en anglais au 4e et 5e secondaire et en 1re et 2e collegial. Dossiers du Conseil de la langue française, No. 13. Québec: Editeur Officiel du Québec.

LORWIN, V. R. 1972, Linguistic pluralism and political tension in modern Belgium. In J. A. FISHMAN (ed.), *Advances in the Sociology of Language*, II. The Hague: Mouton.

QUEBEC, GOVERNMENT OF, 1972, *Report of the Commission of Inquiry on the Position of the French Language and on Language Rights in Quebec* (Gendron Commission). Québec: Editeur officiel du Québec.

RUBIN, J., & JERNUDD, B. H. 1971, *Can language be planned?* Hawaii: The University Press of Hawaii.

SCOTTON, G. M., & URY, W. 1977, Bilingual Strategies: The social functions of code-switching. *International Journal of Sociology of Language*, 13, 5–20.

SIMARD, L. M. 1981, Intergroup communication. In R. C. GARDNER & R. KALIN (eds), *A Canadian Social Psychology of Intergroup Relations*. London: Methuen.

SIMARD, L. M., & TAYLOR, D. 1973, The potential for bicultural communication in a dyadic situation. *Canadian Journal of Behavioural Science*, 5, 211–217.

TAJFEL, H. 1978, *Differentiation between Social Groups*. London & New York: Academic Press.

TAYLOR, D. M., & SIMARD, L. M. 1975, Social Interaction in a bilingual setting. *Canadian Psychological Review*, 16, 240–254.

TAYLOR, D. M., SIMARD, L. M., & PAPINEAU, D. 1978, Perceptions of cultural differences and language use: A field study in a bilingual environment. *Canadian Journal of Behavioural Science*, 10, 181–191.

WEINSTEIN, B. 1983, *The Civic Tongue: Political Consequences of Language Choices*. New York: Longman.

9 Anglo-Quebec: Demographic realities and options for the future

Gary Caldwell
Institut québécois de recherche sur la culture

1. Introduction

What has not quite dawned on the consciousness of English Quebec in their concern over what academics call "language planning" is the rather obvious fact that English Quebec itself is at the root of much of it. Apart from a certain perception whereby anglophones felt they were the butt of a campaign of revenge in retribution for the sins of long-dead cultural progenitors (see Taylor & Simard, this volume, chapter 7), there is little collective awareness of the fact that language planning in favour of French is a reaction to the nature, shape and evolution of anglophone society in Quebec.

That such is indeed the case is rather succinctly pointed out in Pierre Laporte's overview of the origins of language planning in Quebec (see Laporte, this volume, chapter 3). He makes it abundantly clear that the process was initiated in response to the declining relative demographic position of francophones in Canada and potentially in Quebec itself; and justified as a counterweight to the assimilation of francophones and allophones to English via the influence of the workplace and educational institutions. Indeed, upon review of the history of language planning in Quebec (see d'Anglejan, this volume, chapter 2) one can reasonably postulate that the English of Quebec have been at the source of language planning in Quebec without it being explicitly recognized as such by themselves or the perpetuators of the planning.

205

When the population to which one belongs is the object of language planning, if only indirectly, then it is perhaps time to begin planning oneself; as opposed to simply acquiescing — by default or misguided reaction — in what others are planning for you. Worse yet, one risks becoming the unwilling victim of — from the perspective of those absent, for whatever reason, from the planning process — manipulation.[1] It is from this perspective of the English of Quebec as the object of language planning that we have undertaken the present text.

We begin, then, this chapter with a brief overview of the demographic position, past and present, of the English in Quebec. Following this overview we will address the more difficult question of what exactly is English Quebec today. We shall then proceed to characterize the English population's response to the Charter of the French Language (Bill 101). At that point our descriptive and analytical gleanings give way to series of speculations concerning the range of strategic options open to the anglophone population faced with the challenge of evolving in an increasingly francophone Quebec.

2. Demographic overview

The anglophone population of Quebec reached, in absolute terms, a historical peak in 1976 (see Caldwell 1978a for the period 1844 to 1911 and Caldwell 1974 for the period 1921 to 1971). As reported in the 1976 census, there were in Quebec at that time some three-quarters of a million people who declared themselves to be English mother-tongue, of which four-fifths lived in the Montreal metropolitan area. If one adds to this another quarter million whose mother-tongue is not English but who have adopted English as their lingua franca, one approaches the one-fifth (approximately 18%) of the then overall Quebec population (six million), the number often cited as being the anglophone population in Quebec. There was then some truth to the assertion advanced in the seventies that English Quebec was a million strong. Of the slightly more than a million people who constituted over one sixth of the population of Quebec, approximately two-thirds were of English mother-tongue and one-half of Anglo-Celtic ethnic origin (see Lachapelle & Henripin, 1980 for an excellent overview).

As can be seen in Figure 1 the fact that only half the anglophone population is of English background reflects a process that has been at work for some time. Although anglophones in Quebec have constituted a constant one-fifth of the population since the turn of the century, the English background component has steadily declined from 18% in 1901 to 11% in

FIGURE 1 *The English,[1] the allophone[2] and the total non-francophone[3] population of Quebec in terms of ethnic origin (EO) and mother tongue (MT)[4] as percents of the total population of Quebec from 1901 to 1981. Franco-Québécois (FQ)[5] are represented numerically only, as a percent of the total population of Quebec from 1901 to 1981[6]*

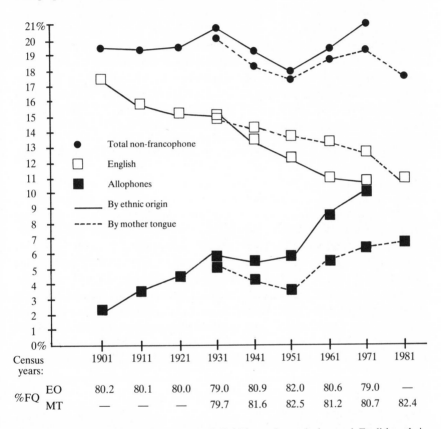

Census years:	1901	1911	1921	1931	1941	1951	1961	1971	1981
%FQ EO	80.2	80.1	80.0	79.0	80.9	82.0	80.6	79.0	—
%FQ MT	—	—	—	79.7	81.6	82.5	81.2	80.7	82.4

Notes: 1. English: all those whose ancestry is British or other and who speak English as their mother tongue.
2. Allophones: Of neither English nor French mother tongue, most of whom adopted English.
3. Total non-francophone: The sum of both English and allophones, note the relatively stable percentage of this total.
4. Data on mother tongue not available before 1931. The 1981 data on ethnic origin is not yet available.
5. Franco Québécois: All those of francophone ancestry and/or who speak French as a mother tongue.
6. This figure is only meant as a rough estimate of the proportion of different ethnic groups in Quebec based on Canadian censuses published by Statistics Canada.

1981, whereas the allophone ethnic component has grown steadily, making up the balance of the anglophone fifth of the population. A further ingredient in the process is the fact that it is the most anglicized elements of the anglophone population which are most inclined to out-migrate (Caldwell, 1978b; Locher, 1982).

Yet one might well ask, can English Quebec maintain its historic demographic position (Caldwell, 1978a), given that anglophones leave Quebec at a faster rate than francophones? Even before the Parti Québécois came to power in 1976 the propensity of anglophones to out-migrate was at least six times that of francophones (Caldwell, 1974). How then, if there has been so much English out-migration, does one account for the fact that the anglophone proportion of the population has maintained itself, at least until 1976, at approximately 20%?

Indeed, the volume and composition of the English-speaking population of Quebec has been, in the post World War II period at least, the consequence of a very particular, very dynamic, and by the same token, very fragile flux of demographic forces, both in the anglophone and the francophone population. Natural increase, births minus deaths, which is obviously the major determinant of the volume of closed populations, has in fact been responsible for only half the growth of the anglophone population (Caldwell, 1974). The other half was the result of a disproportionate anglophone immigration to Quebec, heavy linguistic assimilation to English of francophones and allophones, and finally, a very considerable English-speaking in-migration from the other Canadian provinces. It is the combined action of these factors which contributed to maintaining the English volume of the anglophone population at a level of 20% of the overall Quebec population, despite — until very recently — a very much higher francophone natural increase.

However, in the late sixties it became apparent that the continuation of this historical equilibrium was in jeopardy — an imminent growth in the English-speaking proportion was apprehended (see Laporte, this volume, chapter 3). Notwithstanding, this projected rupture of the demolinguistic equilibrium in Quebec would not have been the result of any dramatic change in the composition and sources of the post World War II anglophone population, but rather by a drastic demographic revolution amongst the francophone population (see in this regard Charbonneau & Maheu, 1973). The collapse of the francophone birth-rate and a renewal of francophone out-migration, provoked by the periodic recessions of the post-war period, first to Ontario and then to western Canada, dramatically reduced the growth rate of francophone Quebec . . . indeed, brought it close to a standstill (Amyot, 1980). Had the trends which prevailed in the sixties and seventies continued unabated, there would have been more children in English than in French elementary schools in Montreal by 1980 (Côté, 1975 and 1982).

Incidentally, the fact that the sudden emergence of the anglophone demographic threat within Quebec was in large part due to demographic changes within the francophone population — drop in birth-rate and out-migration — rather than amongst anglophones, explains in part why anglophones were caught completely by surprise when the francophone community introduced corrective language legislation. Of more consequence, however, is the fact that this language legislation and the political will behind it did in fact change the linguistic situation in Quebec; which it did by acting on the anglophone population dynamic of which we have been speaking. The 1981 census results are eloquent in this regard.

According to these results the English mother-tongue population suffered an absolute decline from the 1976 level of approximately 800,000 to approximately 700,000, with the result that the English mother-tongue proportion of the Quebec population declined from 13% to 11%. We are speaking here of the English mother-tongue, as opposed to the total anglophone population, the size of which in 1981 is, as of yet, unknown. What happened of course was that anglophone international immigration and inter-provincial migration both subsided while anglophone out-migration from Quebec intensified. Consequently, whatever the determining role of language legislation — and particularly Bill 101 — in the complex mix of social political and economic causes, the delicate demographic balance sustaining the anglophone presence in Quebec appears to be broken . . . the demography of anglophone Quebec has definitely entered into a transition phase.

This transition manifests itself in the form of a major population-size shake-down for anglophone Quebec. Of the four sources that have fed the anglophone population base since the war — international immigration, inter-provincial migration, assimilation and natural increase — the contribution of the first two of the four has drastically diminished. The 1981 census results clearly reflect these changes.

However, a smaller shaken-down population will, in all probability, be more stable internally and more capable of self regeneration than has been the case in the past. Nonetheless, the question as to the extent of out-migration hangs in the balance. If, as has been the case (Caldwell, 1980), almost half of the young active population continues to leave Quebec before they reach their middle thirties, any hope of population maintenance by natural increase (excess of births over deaths) would be illusory.

In the present context, not only is the out-migration situation not improving, it appears to be worsening (Locher, 1982). Worn down by years of uncertainty and a loss of confidence in the prospect of a satisfactory future in Quebec, people who, as late as three years ago, had decided that they too were Quebecers and that they were going to stay, "come hell or high water" have experienced a failure of will and many are quite suddenly leaving. If a major haemorrhage is under way it will be difficult to reverse.

A further yet more problematic longer-term demographic threat for anglophone Quebec is that of assimilation. Should francophone Quebec succeed — something which is not at all sure in the light of recent constitutional reversals and the economic plight of Quebec — in its policy of making French the effective language of social communication in Quebec, assimilation of anglophones to francophone society will be inevitable and substantial. Anglophone parents wanting to secure the future of their children in Quebec will be increasingly inclined to send their children to French schools. Presently, approximately one-seventh of English mother-tongue elementary-aged children are in French language schools (see Mallea, this volume, chapter (10). In fact this author's undocumented observation that the entire English élite sends its children of elementary school age to French schools has yet to be contested. Often the strategy involved is to bring the children back to English schools at the high school or CEGEP (junior college) level. Yet, once a young person learns to function well in the, as of now, socially dominant francophone linguistic and cultural environment, the odds of inter-marriage are very high. In a society where French is the dominant vehicle of social intercourse, the children of these marriages in which both partners speak French will have French as their mother tongue. All of this is, of course, a normal demographic process which in the days when English was the dominant language, worked in favour of the anglophone population (Castonguay, 1976).

Several attempts have been made to quantify the influence of some of these factors — the last notable instance having been attempted during the successful supreme court challenge, inspired by the 1982 Canadian Constitution, of the language-of-education provision of Bill 101. However, the demographic situation of the anglophone (and francophone for that matter) population of Quebec is so dynamic that predictions are very quickly dated. Moreover, the condition of the Canadian and Quebec economies in a continental economy based on the mobility of capital and labour is such a major demographic determinant that any prediction which does not take into account economic considerations is quite abstract to say the least. Notwithstanding, for the immediate future two things are definitely on the cards, a much smaller and much stabler anglophone population in Quebec.

3. What is English Quebec today?

To this point in our discussion we have avoided putting the question as to what precisely English Quebec is. Although such a question would not have posed any great difficulty in the nineteenth century — had it even been posed, which is unlikely — it does now. Even the Canadian federal government which administers an "official minorities programme" directed at English or French Canadians living in a minority context has been unable to come up with a satisfactory answer. Is English Quebec constituted by those whose mother-tongue is English, or does it include all anglophones in Quebec? Or, to go further, does English Quebec also include all Quebecers who prefer the English language as their instrument of linguistic interpretation into Canadian society?

Were one to accept the last delimitation, the reality it covers becomes very heterogenous in ethnic and cultural terms. Owing to the high rate of assimilation of allophone immigrants to the English language milieu, and the high turnover in the English mother-tongue population, the anglophone population defined in this extensive sense covers a population of which approximately only two-thirds are English mother-tongue and only one half are remotely of Anglo-Celtic origin; the other being of various cultural heritages, including Jewish, Italian, Greek, etc. Consequently, in terms of what we prefer to call the extensive definition of Anglo-Quebec, the population concerned is extremely heterogenous and geographically mobile. Even in terms of what we call a restrictive definition, those whose initial socialization was in English (the English mother-tongue population) we hypothesize that probably less than half are conscious of being inheritors of the British Anglo-Celtic cultural heritage.

Returning to the population covered by the extensive definition, all those whose language of use is English, the question becomes, what should be held in common, apart from the instrumental use of English? Certainly not the fact of being born in Quebec (only half of the adults were) nor the fact of being socialized in English, nor an adherence to a common religious tradition (apart from Jews, there are almost as many Catholics as Protestants), nor shared ethnic origins (Caldwell & Waddell, 1982).

What members of this wider "anglophone" population have shared since the war, and increasingly so, is participation in a continental anglophone culture. This North American culture imposes itself by its omni-presence and the fact that it is the only common denominator for such a culturally heterogenous population. The question that comes to the mind of the non-Canadian reader is no doubt the following: "Do these Quebec anglophones not share a common participation in English Canadian cul-ture?" For those anglophone Quebecers who were socialized in Canada before the war, such is undoubtedly the case: as reality would have it, this group probably constitutes not more than one-fifth of what now constitute anglophone Quebec. Those are the people and the generation that experi-enced the national affirmation of Anglo-Canada, and who have, in many cases, quite poignant memories of the glories and sacrifices of this era — national independence with the statute of New Westminster and the as-sumption of the responsibilities of a fully sovereign nation during World War II.

However, for the younger members of the population and those who were born elsewhere, English Canada of the pre-war genre is a past to be forgotten or avoided, as the case may be. In many cases, the children of the post-war era passed through educational institutions which were American inspired or even staffed by Americans. Intellectuals of the liberal orthodoxy of the period socialized them to a distaste of WASP (white Anglo-Saxon protestant) anglo-conformity and the cultural particularism of the British tradition which put Anglo-Celtics on the top of the Canadian social mosaic (see Arnopoulos-Clift, 1980, for an instance of the former, and Porter, 1965, for documentation of the latter). The even greater turn-over of educators in Quebec anglophone institutions resulted in the only common cultural de-nominator being the liberalism of America. Consequently, in terms of popular culture and ideology, a whole generation found itself cut off from what was English Canada. Nevertheless, one might well ask, is there not now emerging a new non-wasp, non-American, anglophone Canadian cul-ture to which anglophone Quebec might feel an allegiance? It is possible that this culture exists, but its presence is not readily felt in anglophone Quebec.

Yet all of English Quebec does share the fact of being non-francophone, in the sense that their preferred language of social intercourse is English. In the sense of not being able to speak French the situation has, however, changed dramatically in the last decade: whereas only one-quarter of anglo-phone youth were fluent in French in the early seventies (Caldwell, 1978b), probably three-quarters can now manage in French. Nonetheless, all of anglophone Quebec did live in a social world which had crystallized around the English/French linguistic cleavage (Cappon, 1974); and to this extent found their social position defined accordingly. To the extent that French becomes the common vehicle of social life and of work, and as commerce and public affairs become exclusively French in the wake of this change, the former English/French linguistic cleavage will cease to have the social pertinence it undoubtedly had (Caldwell, 1977).

One of the ineluctable consequences of the cultural make-up of anglophone Quebec, as we have described it, is that it is difficult to find common ground upon which to mobilize, either politically or otherwise. What is held sufficiently dearly by all that is worth defending? One can hardly hold high a banner which reads simply "I am a non-francophone". The result is that the only feasible definition of a greater anglophone Quebec has been that adopted by Alliance Quebec in which it affirms the existence of an anglophone "linguistic community" (Caldwell & Waddell, 1982). Alliance Quebec, issued from the former Council of Quebec Minorities, held a founding convention in May 1982 which was an "Etats généraux" designed to hammer out a programme and substantiate its claim to speak for all of anglophone Quebec.

Yet an alliance founded on no more than a "linguistic" community is a rather fragile alliance. The word "alliance" itself is revealing. Precisely because the individual cultural allies have their own separate interests to protect, they are unwilling to forego what political leverage they have separately in favour of a common cultural cause.

Fortunately, some understanding of the different cultural traditions within anglophone Quebec is beginning to emerge in the academic literature (Arnopoulos & Clift, 1980) and even in popular consciousness, at least as manifested in newspaper coverage. Indeed, behind the anglophone alliance is a series of cultural minorities, each of which has a pre-Quebec cultural experience. This is particularly apparent in the case of the Anglo-Celtic, the Jewish and the native peoples minorities. Furthermore, events have conspired in Quebec to foster a degree of cultural retention amongst members of the individual cultural minorities which appears to surpass that generally experienced elsewhere in Canada (Caldwell, 1983). The "double majority" situation resulting from the social and economic superiority of the English on the one hand, and the numerical and political superiority of the French on the other hand, has made assimilation for allophones more problematic than it was elsewhere. Faced with the ambiguity as to where one should go in terms of assimilation, some groups took recourse and found cultural gratification in their own ethnic milieu, reinforcing the milieu in so doing.

In such a context, anglophone Quebec would appear to have a choice between mobilizing in terms of a "linguistic community" as proposed by Alliance Quebec; or in terms of a number of "cultural minorities", as the Government of Quebec would have it. To date, only the first alternative has been seriously considered by the anglophone leadership. It is of course an ideological and political posture which is not only compatible with, but an expression of the current state of the English/French contradiction in Canadian federalism as manifested by the present Liberal government in Ottawa. Furthermore, the institutional base of Anglo-Quebec was allowed to expand as a function of the non-English population which gravitated to its midst. The largely Anglo-Celtic administrative class who have a vested interest in these organizations are not about to take their cultural distance from their allophone client population.

Yet, the most important factors sustaining the anglophone "linguistic community" option are, on the one hand, an obsession with the political advantage to be gained by being as numerous as possible; and on the other, the facile character, ideologically, of such an option in the context of the Canadian federal political system. Such a posture has no ideological or cultural specificities to be respected other than those that must be borne in mind to placate the francophones of Quebec. There are, consequently, no cultural gods to which reverence must be given. All of this is very convenient in terms of the prevailing liberal pluralistic Anglo-American continental ideology . . . yet it has its risks,

Foremost among these risks is that the population in question becomes deculturated in terms of the Quebec and the Canadian experience. And, as there is no such thing as a cultural vacuum, such a deculturation would, in the circumstances, lead to acculturation into the continental Anglo-American culture. In itself: no harm done; the crux of the matter is that a Quebec anglophone population so acculturated would have no good motive for staying in Quebec, except to administer the colony for Rome . . . not an enviable position.

As for the "cultural minorities" option, it would necessitate abandoning the pretence of an anglophone community — be it linguistic or otherwise — in favour of a number of cultural communities, each with an indigenous Quebec experience. This option has the distinct disadvantage, in the minds of many anglophones, of constituting precisely the position advocated by the present government of Quebec whereby there are a number of cultural minorities in Quebec, some of which happen to be anglophone and one of which is Anglo-Saxon (see Quebec, 1981) although at other times the government has accorded a distinct place and priority to the Anglo-Saxon minority (Quebec, 1978). It would also mean, as we implied earlier, foregoing the political advantage of the larger numbers associated with the "linguistic community" option. Nonetheless, the "cultural minorities" option has advantages that have been, we suggest, largely overlooked.

Among the advantages would be the pride and sense of history associated with identifying with what are, in the case of most of Quebec's cultural minorities, "great" cultural traditions. In addition, as each of these traditions has a history in Quebec, identification with these traditions and re-appropriation of their historical experience would allow an insertion into the history of Quebec which is now sadly lacking: one need only consider the still largely unexplored richness of the Anglo-Celtic and Jewish histories (Rome, 1981) in Quebec.

A further advantage of such a posture would be an attenuation of the English/French linguistic cleavage. This cleavage, now artificially maintained, may well prove in the long run to be very counter-productive for all concerned. The cleavage once transcended in Quebec, the growing empathy and identification with Quebec as a place, and even as a society, now felt by many non-francophones could find expression in fuller participation in one shared yet exclusive linguistic setting . . . francophone Quebec, enriched by the cultural traditions of its cultural minorities.

4. English reponse to being planned

The Saint-Leonard 1967 incident in which anglophone Italians and francophones clashed over an attempt by the French-Catholic school board to terminate English instruction for Italian children was perhaps the first dramatic instance of anglophone reaction to language planning (see d'Anglejan, this volume, chapter 2). However, the rest of the anglophone population — particularly the more secure Anglo-Celtic group — stood somewhat aloof and continued to ignore the language and related demographic issues until Bill 22 descended upon them in 1974.

Having ignored or been indifferent to the debate out of which emerged the political need to pass linguistic legislation, anglophone Quebec was at a loss as to what the problem was. But after the wide awakening of Bill 22 and their unqualified rejection of it (Caldwell & Waddell, 1982), the anglophone world of Quebec rushed to get itself involved, both in the sense of trying to understand what was going on and in protecting its interest. The Bill 22 era marks the effective entry of anglophone Quebec into the language planning controversy. Subsequently, with the emergence of the Parti Québécois, its election to power in 1976, the battle was fully engaged (see d'Anglejan, this volume, chapter 2). In the space of less than a decade, anglophone Quebec moved from a majority mentality, to an embattled minority engaged in strategic political planning (Caldwell & Waddell, 1982). Positive Action and other less substantial groups formed on the spur of the moment gave way to a common front as manifested by the "Council of Quebec Minorities" and, shortly afterwards, its successor, the rather more militant "Alliance Quebec".

To date, the actions undertaken by and the posture adopted by the anglophone common front have been on the whole, reactive: reaction to initiatives taken by the Government of Quebec, be it on language tests for professionals, eligibility for English schools, sign legislation, restriction of the use of English in social service facilities, etc. One notable exception was the Positive Action initiative, pursued by the Council of Quebec Minorities, in identifying with the cause and supporting action taken by the other official minority, the francophone minority outside of Quebec.

Now, it could be argued that this is the Anglo-Saxon method, an *ad hoc* empiricism guided by a certain number of very general principles; as opposed to a more latin method which would have it that particular actions must be legitimized and "logical" with reference to a rational framework or "problématique". I would like to believe this, but Alliance Quebec is not an Anglo-Saxon organization, it represents rather a "linguistic community" which is far from being Anglo-Saxon in cultural inspiration. Furthermore, Alliance Quebec has principles, but its "principles" are of the order of tactics: control and management of educational institutions; presence of English in signs; abolition of French language testing for those educated in Quebec; right to use English as the language of internal communications in organizations serving an anglophone clientele; access of anglophones from elsewhere in Canada to English schools; and, finally, a greater representation of anglophones amongst employees in the public sector (*Montreal Gazette*, November 6, 1982). These are not the kind of general cultural principles one has in mind when one speaks of an Anglo-Saxon way of doing things. For the moment, the anglophone united front action remains very short-term, and without reference to an overall strategy regarding the future of English Quebec. At a very minimum, one would think that there could be some kind of a cultural vision to which reference could be made with a view to providing, in the midst of the manifold pressures and choices which present themselves in the mêlée of practical politics, a sense of direction and perspective.

One suspects that the lack of such a vision or long-term direction is a direct consequence of the cultural incoherence of an "alliance" comprising a population that has very little in common with respect to their cultural traditions and even with respect to experience in Quebec other than the fact that they speak English and are not francophones. A sense of shared direction or a vision is only possible amongst those who already take a lot for granted amongst themselves.

At the level of the individual, as opposed to anglophone Quebec as a group, one sees exemplified another type of reaction to language planning. There are perhaps two extremes of individual-level adaptation to the situation. The first is that of the individual who adapts in terms of learning to speak French sufficiently to work in French, and who creates for himself a French social life. These are the "integrated" individuals about whom Sheila Arnopoulos has written (Arnopoulos & Clift, 1980) and upon which the editors of *The English of Quebec: from Majority to Minority Status* (Caldwell & Waddell, 1982) comment. Incidentally, most of these people send their children to French schools and some become francophiles. A more attenuated, yet more widespread, adaptation is that which consists in sending one's children to French Catholic schools for elementary school education. Such people often continue to be stalwart supporters of and participants in anglophone social and associational life. Whether or not their children will continue to do so is of course quite problematic. As for the other extreme reaction to planned linguistic change in Quebec, it consists in voting with one's feet: the out-migration of which it has been a question several times in the course of this chapter.

5. A cultural strategy for Anglo-Quebec

Against all odds, Quebec has survived as a distinct society to this day, and may even continue to do so, despite the improbability of the maintenance of a distinct urban and industrial society in the shadow of America (Rioux, 1971). Quebec's survival is the fruit of many factors including historical accident, the political and ideological traditions of the British Empire and the sheer determination of the *Québécois* to remain a distinct collective entity in North America.

Indeed, not the least among the host of reasons responsible for the survival of Quebec society has been the existence of a cultural strategy which provided direction as well as confidence in the future. Initially it was the clergy which formulated the vision upon which the strategy was based: a French Catholic civilization in America. The same clergy also created a vehicle for the preservation and perpetuation of this vision, the classical colleges of Quebec out of which came the nationalist élite right down to the founders of the Parti Québécois. Without such an élite there would have been no "nationalist affirmation" in the sixties. When one's society is not the dominant cultural influence of the day, an explicit strategy is required to avoid being swept along by the momentum of the dominant society. Furthermore, the strategy must consist of more than reaction to the hegemony of the dominant society: it must also be sufficiently visionary to stimulate the imagination and win the loyalty of young men and women.

Should Anglo-Quebec wish to survive it must have a strategy, and by implication, a vision. But the vision will have to be such as to give rise to a strategy capable of providing for a cultural experience distinct from two, not one, dominant cultural forces: continental anglophone culture and francophone Quebec. Should Anglo-Quebec fail to become a cultural reality distinct from anglophone North America, it will probably not prevail for two reasons: firstly, it will always be seen as alien to Quebec by francophone Quebec, worse yet, it may be perceived as the enemy within the gates. The second reason is more intrinsic: a culture whose spiritual mainspring is elsewhere — as would be the case with a culture aligned on the anglophone continental culture — could not hope to retain its most active elements who would have no motive to stay in the hinterland. Such a population would simply bleed to death, leaving behind a historically inactive remnant. Anglo-Quebec must find within its collective experience a cultural vision which would justify its existence apart from, on the one hand, francophone Quebec, and on the other, the continental anglophone culture.

From whence might emerge such a vision, and what kind of strategies might it give rise to? The "vision" of what we speak here, to be more pragmatic, is a sense of the significance and worthwhileness of a way of life. Writers of a more latin inspiration speak of a "vouloir vivre collectif" or a "projet collectif". Such a cultural inspiration cannot, of course, be invented or made to measure. It is to be found in the historical experience of a community which has lived and acted together; and it must be distilled and refined by cultural leaders who carry in their historical consciousness the cultural tradition (heritage) of the community.

The question as to where the vision is to be found becomes: "Is there a cultural tradition in Quebec which is both indigenous and sufficiently embracing to serve the purpose for all of anglophone Quebec?" In our opinion the answer is — at least in 1984 — an unequivocal no. However, there are non-francophone cultural traditions in Quebec which do qualify but they do not embrace, now or potentially, all of anglophone Quebec: traditions such as those of Anglo-Celtic Quebec, or Jewish Quebec, or Inuit Quebec.

To take the case of Anglo-Celtic Quebec, it comprises about one-third of anglophone Quebec, somewhere between a fifth and a quarter of a million people; and it has a historical experience in Quebec which is both considerable and integral to the genesis of Quebec society as we know it today. Not only that, this historical experience was both productive and, in many respects, something to be proud of. It is, for instance, not accidental—

far from it — that the statue of James Bruce, the eighth Earl of Elgin, graces the right-hand side of the principal entry of the Quebec National Assembly. The Earl of Elgin was the first British governor of Canada to give the address from the throne in French and to insist that it was incumbent upon him to accept the will of the elected assembly. By doing so he risked his career and, literally, his life. He did so in conformity with his conviction that the purpose of his function was to bestow British liberties on French Canadians; even, as time has shown, the liberty to form an independentist government in Quebec. Passing under Lord Elgin on their way to the National Assembly, those Quebecers who sense themselves to be inheritors of the British tradition ought to experience a special sense of pride in the accomplishments of this Scotsman. As for Lord Elgin himself, a Scottish aristocrat who spent most of the active years of his life away from his beloved Scotland in the service of what he considered to be a great tradition, he might well wonder — if his granite eyes were to come alive — how such a legacy could be forgotten so quickly . . . it is less than 150 years since he sailed away from Quebec City to the cheers of French Canadian well-wishers whose respect and affection he had so deservedly won.

Yet, to have the inspirational character necessary to give rise to a cultural strategy, the cultural traditions in question must be applicable to the trials and tribulations of the contemporary context, Quebec as we know it today. The central contemporary issues in Quebec society — apart from, but not independent of, the issue of the survival of Quebec itself as a distinct cultural entity — are the over-centralization of public life and the need to breathe new vitality into the economic base. The Anglo-Celtic tradition with its special genius for individual and local responsibility — as opposed to control by central regulation — and its historical proclivity for economic activity and initiative could not be more pertinent.

With a view to impressing upon the reader that what we are invoking here is not some ethereal cultural essence relevant only to intellectuals and, at the limit, sociologists, we wish to cite two very specific contemporary controversies, the outcome of which will be crucial to the future of Quebec society. They are the proposed restructuration of elementary and secondary school organization in Quebec (see Mallea, this volume, chapter 10) and the issue of whether Quebec should become a massive exporter of hydro-electric energy. As it happens, anglophones, Anglo-Celtic and otherwise, are inescapably involved in both issues and would have a contribution, both particular and positive, to make to the resolution of both issues. Unfortunately, their present approach to both issues, often one of stubborn and even desperate resistance, risks being interpreted — and perhaps rightly so — as a defence of their own, as opposed to the general, interest.

What is regrettable is that the pursuit, by Anglo-Quebecers, of the very same issues within the framework of a cultural strategy for Anglo-Quebec could, and would, be interpreted as being in the general interest. Without reactivation of civil responsibility on the individual and local government level, and without the re-industrialization of the Quebec economy — possibility by the availability in Quebec of a cheap electrical power — Quebec society as we know it today may well erode under the weight of a bureaucratization become too costly to bear, yet too entrenched to dislodge.

Likewise, the other minority cultural traditions of anglophone Quebec have their particular contributions to make. Obviously, the fragmentation of anglophone political leverage involved in the abandonment of a common anglophone front in favour of a series of cultural minorities is a consideration not easily dismissed. Notwithstanding, we respectfully submit that numbers have not always prevailed in history, and presumably numbers have not been and will not be sufficient: there were only sixty thousand French-speaking inhabitants in New France in 1759; the Boers prevailed against the British until they were outnumbered ten to one; and the British were far from being as numerous as their adversary when hostilities broke out in the Falklands.

Acknowledgements

I would like to express my gratitude to Richard Y. Bourhis for his useful comments on earlier drafts of this chapter.

Notes

1. The oscillating position of the top political authority, notably the Quebec premier, towards the rigour of the application of Law 101 is now being interpreted as manipulation. See the controversy surrounding the premier's long-delayed response to the Alliance Quebec "demands", *Le Devoir*, November 6, 1982.

References

AMYOT, M. 1980, *La situation démolinguistique au Québec et la charte de la langue française*. Québec: Conseil de la langue française.

ARNOPOULOS, S. M., & CLIFT, D. 1980, *The English Fact in Quebec*. Montréal: McGill-Queen's Press.

CALDWELL, G. 1974, *A Demographic Profile of the English-Speaking Population of Quebec 1921–1971*. Québec: Centre International de Recherches sur le Bilinguisme.

— 1977, Minorités et minorité au Québec. In: D. LATOUCHE (ed.), *Premier mandat: une perspective à court terme du gouvernement péquiste*. Montréal: Edition de l'Aurore.

— 1978a, L'histoire des "possédants" anglophones au Québec. *Anthropologie et sociologie*, vol. 2, no. 1.

— 1978b, *Out-Migration of English Mother-Tongue High School Leavers from Quebec 1971–1976*. Lennoxville, Québec: AQEM, March.

— 1980, *Out-Migration of English Mother-Tongue High School Leavers from Quebec 1971–1979*. Lennoxville, Québec: AQEM, December.

— 1983, *Les études ethniques au Québec: bilan et perspective*. Québec: Institut québécois de la recherche sur la culture.

CALDWELL, G., & WADDELL, E. (eds) 1982, *The English of Quebec: From Majority to Minority Status*. Québec: Institut québécois de recherche sur la culture.

CAPPON, P. 1974, *Conflit entre les Néo-Canadiens et les Francophones de Montréal*. Québec: Les Presses de l'Université Laval.

CASTONGUAY, C. 1976, "Les transferts linguistiques au foyer". *Recherches Sociographiques*, 17, 341–351.

CHARBONNEAU, H. & MAHEU, R. 1973, "Les aspects démographiques de la question linguistique". *Commission d'enquête sur la situation de la langue française et sur les droits linguistiques au Québec*, Synthèse S-3. Québec: Editeur officiel du Québec.

CÔTÉ, A. 1975, "Prévision des populations scolaires, francophone et anglophone de l'Ile de Montréal". Conseil scolaire de l'Ile de Montréal. Equipement-Démographie, 20 juin.

— 1982, "Demographie linguistique dans les écoles publiques de l'Ile de Montréal 1970 à 1981, estimation jusqu'en 1985". Communication au congrès *Langue et Société*. Québec: Conseil de la langue française, 12 novembre.

LACHAPELLE, R., & HENRIPIN, J. 1980, *La situation démolinguistique au Canada, évolution passée et prospective*. Montréal: L'institut de recherches politiques.

LOCHER, U. 1982, *La conscience linguistique chez les anglophones du Québec*. Gouvernment du Québec: Conseil de la langue française.

PORTER, J. 1965, *The Vertical Mosaic*. Toronto: University of Toronto Press.

RIOUX, M. 1971, *Quebec in Question*. Toronto: James Lewis & Samuel.

ROME, D. 1981, *Les Juifs du Québec: bibliographie rétrospective annotée*. Québec: Institut québécois de recherche sur la culture.

QUEBEC, GOVERNMENT OF, 1978, Le ministre d'état au développement culturel. *La politique québécois du développement culturel: vol. I, perspective d'ensemble: de quelle culture s'agit-il*. Québec: Editeur officiel du Québec.

— 1981, Développement culturel et scientifique. *Autant de façons d'être québécois. Plan d'action du gouvernement du Québec à l'intention des communautés culturelles*. Québec: Bib. Nationale du Québec, 1er trimestre.

10 Minority language education in Quebec and anglophone Canada

John R. Mallea
The Ontario Institute for Studies in Education

"There have been few policies as volatile in Quebec as those concerned with access to English-language schools. With the implementation of Bill 22 in 1974 and the passage of Bill 101 in 1977, the province has had three different policies of access to English schools in less than a decade. The policy that will apply over the long term will have far-reaching implications for future linguistic, cultural, and social orientation in Quebec. With the emotional as well as practical aspects of so important an issue, it is not surprising that the decision of policy in this area has touched a sensitive public nerve, sparking considerable controversy not only in Quebec, but throughout Canada." (Gordon Robertson in Vanasse, 1980: vii)

Introduction

The phrase minority language education employed in the title refers to those programmes in which the minority language (English in Quebec, French in the other provinces) is used as the language of instruction for all or a large proportion of the school day. Designed to offer instruction in the mother tongue to the minority group, their provision forms a well documented and largely conflictual element in Canadian politics and history.

Efforts to resolve conflicts over the issue of culture and schooling pre-date Confederation. Thus, in 1867, the Fathers of Confederation, in drafting the British North America Act, acknowledged the potentially divisive nature of the issue and responded to it by moving education "out of the national political system and into the sub-systems of the provinces where the differences could flourish" (Mallory, 1976: 2). Their declared intent was to ensure "that all Canadians could retain their historic cultural identities while at the same time sharing economically, militarily and in international affairs in the benefits of a larger nation" (Cook, 1977: 15). Aspirations, however, as is so often the case in the education of minorities, have not been matched by achievement.

Conflict not consensus, controversy not harmony, has more often than not characterized the efforts of Canadian minority language communities to obtain educational services appropriate to their needs and aspirations. The British North America Act, in particular, has not proved equal to the task of dealing adequately or fairly with the minority language education issue. Consequently, Acadians, Franco-Ontarians, Franco-Manitobans, and other French-speaking minorities at various times and in various contexts, have discovered that provincial autonomy in educational matters has worked to their disadvantage.

Over a century later, few would suggest that ideal forms of social justice, consensus or cultural accommodation have been found in the field of education (Johnson, 1968). Until quite recently, far from adopting a positive stance towards differences in language and culture, Canada's English-speaking majority have gone out of their way to eradicate them — especially in the schools. Assimilation, not appreciation of differences, has been the policy, conformity not diversity, the goal (Jaenen, 1972; Palmer, 1978). Two dramatically different histories of the development of Canada are taught in the schools of French and English-speaking Canada.

And, in the latter, "Although we laugh at ourselves for doing so, and perhaps have convinced each other that today things are different, in actual fact we are continuing to teach a white, Anglo-Saxon, Protestant, political and constitutional history of Canada" (Hodgetts, 1968: 20). School textbooks, it has also been pointed out, continue to portray a consensus, non-controversial view of society. At the university level, the study of Canadian issues and conflicts have suffered from widespread omission and neglect — this, moreover, in a context in which, the Taskforce on Canadian Unity concluded: "Instead of being an unquestionable framework within which life's problems are addressed, the country itself has been placed in doubt" (Canada, 1979: 17).

Conflict and struggle over the provision of minorities language education services applies with particular force to situations in which francophone minorities outside Quebec have found themselves since the last century. More recently, in Quebec, conflict has occurred over the provision of minority language education for the anglophone minority and the children of immigrants. Minority language education is a highly volatile, symbolic issue capable of arousing powerful emotions and passions among French and English-speaking Quebecers alike. For the francophone majority in Quebec, conscious of its minority status in an overwhelmingly English-speaking continent, it is a matter of cultural and linguistic survival. For the Quebec anglophone minority, it is a question of rights traditionally enjoyed. To a greater extent than any other single issue — for it affects and is understood by Quebecers from all socio-cultural-linguistic groups — minority language education provisions serve as a barometer of French-English relations in Quebec and by extension the rest of Canada.

The most recent illustration of the power of this issue to arouse deep-seated reactions is the furor touched off in Quebec by the passage of the new Canadian Constitution (Canada, 1982) and the minority language education rights contained in the accompanying Charter of Rights and Freedoms. Quebec was not a signatory to the new constitutional accord. A major reason for the absence of its signature was that the Charter of Rights and Freedoms included minority language education rights intended to apply to all Canadian citizens, irrespective of the province in which they reside.

The Quebec government's position is that the language rights provisions contained in the Charter is an unwelcome intrusion into an area of provincial responsibility, in which traditionally it has exercised sovereignty. The Charter of Rights and Freedoms, Premier Levesque angrily complained, "impinges on and restricts Quebec's exclusive and inalienable rights in linguistics matters . . . once more threatening our demographic and cultural security" (*Globe and Mail*, April 17, 1982: 1/2). More specifically, its provisions over-ride minority language education provisions contained in Quebec's own Charter, the Charter of the French Language (Bill 101). The first, and deliberately symbolic, legislative act introduced by the *Parti Québécois* following its ascension to power in November, 1976.

The conflict over minority language education reveals in clear and unambiguous fashion the larger struggle between at least two competing options: sovereignty-association and renewed federalism. The framework for the latter, the new constitution, notably lacking acceptance by the Quebec government, is now in place. Efforts to apply it in Quebec, there-fore, may well strengthen the sovereignty-association or independence op-tion. The confrontation is quintessentially Canadian, stemming, as it does, from the existence of two competing political cultures emphasizing distinctive political beliefs and values. The survival of the French language is of course a primary objective and *raison d'être* of the political culture of Quebec. Over the past decade and a half, enormous energies have been applied to the development of legislation aimed at its preservation and enhancement. A centrepiece of these efforts has been legislation governing the language of education. If we are to understand the competing claims of the two options cited above, it is important that in the first part of the chapter we examine patterns of linguistic change and minority language education in both the Canadian setting in general and minority language education in the Quebec setting in particular. The second part of the chapter will deal with current issues destined to fuel the controversial debate over minority language education in Quebec and Canada for the next decade and more to come.

Linguistic change and minority language education

The Canadian setting

The complex raft of reasons that have been identified as giving rise to this crisis of confidence in Canadian federalism cannot of course be dealt with in these pages. Our emphasis will be placed on the part played by cultural and linguistic factors and, here too, selection will have to be made.

In terms of importance, the rapid economic development of Canada after World War II, brought widespread social and cultural change. Massive immigration occurred and the ethnic composition of the population changed dramatically, resulting in the aggregate size of the "other" ethnocultural groups approaching that of Francophones. Census statistics from 1871 to 1971 (see Table 1) confirm this development. They also underline the fact that those of British ethnic origin, while falling in overall numerical strength, continue to form the majority. French-Canadians, on the other hand, although not suffering the same overall decline in strength as the British, have seen their overall percentage of the population decline since 1951.

The largest percentage increase in the population has occurred in the category termed the "other" ethnic groups. As early as 1921, these groups formed between 30 and 40% of the Prairie population. By 1951, they formed over 20% of the total population, and in 1971 this figure had risen to over 25%.

Notwithstanding this development, statistics for 1971 on mother tongue and home language confirmed that the overwhelming majority of the Canadian population is still composed of two major linguistic groups: anglo-

TABLE 1 *Number and Composition of Canadian Population According to Ethnic Origin, 1871 to 1971*

	All Origins		British		French		Native		Other	
Year	Number (×1,000)	%	Number (×1,000)	%	Number (×1,000)	%	Number (×1,000)	%	Number (×1,000)	%
1871	3,486	100.0	2,111	60.5	1,083	31.1	23	0.7	269	7.7
1901	4,623	100.0	2,619	56.7	1,606	34.7	38	0.8	360	7.8
1901	5,371	100.0	3,063	57.0	1,649	30.7	128	2.4	531	9.9
1911	7,207	100.0	3,999	55.5	2,062	28.6	106	1.5	1,040	14.4
1921	8,788	100.0	4,869	55.4	2,453	27.9	113	1.3	1,353	15.4
1931	10,377	100.0	5,381	51.9	2,928	28.2	129	1.2	1,939	18.7
1941	11,507	100.0	5,716	49.7	3,483	30.3	126	1.1	2,182	18.9
1951	13,648	100.0	6,372	46.7	4,309	31.6	165	1.2	2,802	20.5
1951	14,009	100.0	6,710	47.9	4,319	30.8	165	1.2	2,815	20.1
1961	18,238	100.0	7,997	43.8	5,540	30.4	220	1.2	4,481	24.6
1971	21,568	100.0	9,624	44.6	6,180	28.7	313	1.4	5,451	25.3

Source: Breton, Reitz & Valentine, 1980, p. 19.

phones and francophones. Territorial duality coincides in large part with linguistic duality. Francophones form the majority in Quebec; anglophones form a massive majority in the rest of Canada. This division, moreover, has become more distinct during the last 25 years. Over 90% of the population claiming English as their mother tongue live *outside* Quebec; while more than 80% of those claiming French as their mother tongue reside *within* Quebec (Breton, Reitz & Valentine, 1980).

A major consequence of English being the predominant language of Canada, as well as North America as a whole, is that it exerts considerable assimilative power among all groups — including the francophones. For example, the extent to which younger French Canadians outside Quebec are being assimilated to English has been vividly documented by Joy (1972). Concern over the increasing marginality of francophone communities has also been vigorously expressed by the Federation of Francophones outside Quebec (FFHQ, 1978). Linguistic transfers among member of the "other" ethnic groups, based on statistics drawn from censuses up to and including that of 1971, have largely been in the direction of English" (O'Bryan *et al.*, 1976). Indeed Breton *et al.* (1980) conclude that "outside Quebec, the situation is very clear. English remains intact, or very nearly, and attracts all. French, as well as the 'other' languages, has a low preservation rate and

TABLE 2 *Percentage Language Transfers (French to English) Among Canadians of French Origin by Province, 1971 Census*

Province	English mother tongue	English spoken at home	Know English and do not know French
Quebec	1.9	2.5	0.6
Alberta	54.1	77.4	49.9
British Columbia	65.4	89.8	59.7
Manitoba	35.5	56.9	33.0
New Brunswick	12.3	18.3	9.2
Newfoundland	80.3	86.9	74.1
Nova Scotia	53.8	67.7	48.2
Ontario	39.3	55.1	32.5
Prince Edward Island	54.6	72.5	47.9
Saskatchewan	47.3	73.4	43.3

Note: Language transfer is defined here as taking place when English is adopted as the main language of the home.

Source: J. Lamontagne, 1975, "Minority Language Education in Ontario and Quebec", following R. Arès, *Les positions — ethniques, linguistiques et religieuses — des Canadiens français à la suite du recensement de 1971.* Montreal: Editions Bellarmin.

attracts nothing. The same situation exists with the 'other' languages in Quebec" (p. 33).

Just how powerful the impact of the anglicization process is on the French-speaking population in the nine English-speaking provinces is dramatically revealed in Table 2.

What these statistics point out, and more recent studies have underscored, is that the threat of linguistic and cultural assimilation is an ever-present, continuing reality for francophone communities. In 1976, as Table 3 confirms, the percentage of the population recording French as their mother tongue had decreased in Quebec as well as in all nine English-speaking provinces.

Although the provision of minority language education is a matter of longstanding controversy and considerable currency, empirical evidence about it remains scarce. Only recently have detailed statistics on the subject been gathered. And these need to be treated with considerable caution as witness the fact that, in school year 1976–77, immersion was still considered

TABLE 3 *Population of Canada by Province and Selected Mother Tongue (English or French) 1971 and 1976*

Province and Year	English		French		Total	
	Number	%	Number	%	Number	%
Quebec						
1971	789,185	13.1	4,867,250	80.8	6,027,765	100
1976	800,680	12.8	4,989,245	80.0	6,234,445	100
Alberta						
1971	1,263,935	77.7	46,495	2.9	1,627,665	100
1976	1,482,720	80.7	44,440	2.4	1,838,040	100
British Columbia						
1971	1,807,250	82.7	38,035	1.7	2,184,625	100
1976	2,037,640	82.6	38,430	1.6	2,466,605	100
Manitoba						
1971	662,725	67.1	60,550	6.1	988,250	100
1976	727,230	71.9	54,745	5.4	1,021,505	100
New Brunswick						
1971	410,400	64.7	215,725	34.0	634,555	100
1976	435,970	64.4	223,785	33.0	677,245	100
Newfoundland						
1971	514,515	98.6	3,635	0.7	522,100	100
1976	545,340	97.8	2,755	0.5	557,725	100
Nova Scotia						
1971	733,555	93.0	39,335	5.0	788,960	100
1976	768,070	92.7	36,870	4.5	828,575	100
Ontario						
1971	5,971,570	77.5	482,040	6.3	7,703,105	100
1976	6,457,650	78.1	462,075	5.6	8,264,465	100
Prince Edward Island						
1971	103,100	92.4	7,360	6.6	111,640	100
1976	109,745	92.8	6,545	5.5	118,230	100
Saskatchewan						
1971	685,920	74.0	31,605	3.4	926,245	100
1976	715,690	77.7	26,705	2.9	921,320	100
Total 10 provinces						
1971	12,942,155	60.2	5,792,030	26.9	21,515,116	100
1976	14,080,735	61.4	5,885,595	25.7	22,928,155	100

Source: Modified table developed from data provided in Council of Ministers of Education, Canada, which in turn were based on Statistics Canada sources.

a minority language programme. Even more instructive, as late as 1981, the province of Alberta still did not provide separate data on minority language and second language immersion programmes (Statistics Canada, 1982). General statements on the subject, therefore, need to be examined carefully. Nevertheless, three points can be made with confidence.

First, since Confederation until relatively recently, *francophones outside Quebec* were systematically denied educational services that adequately reflected their linguistic needs and aspirations. As a noted English-Canadian historian points out:

> "In the 1870s in New Brunswick Catholic school rights were modified in a manner that reduced French language education. In the 1890s in Manitoba, schools which Franco-Manitobans believed had been guaranteed by the Manitoba Act in 1870 were denied any further financial support, and French was abolished as an official language. In 1915 the same province withdrew what little 'bilingual' teaching remained. The other prairie provinces imitated the Manitoba pattern. As for Ontario, where the largest numbers of French Canadians outside Quebec lived, Regulation 17 adopted in 1913, struck down the hopes of Franco-Ontarians that in numbers at least there might be safety. Even when that regulation was repealed in 1927, little change took place. No wonder then that many French Canadians outside Quebec and in Quebec itself, concluded that Henri Bourassa, the great newspaperman and politician, was right when he said that French Canadians, like the Canadian Indians, could only exercise their treaty rights when they remained on 'the reserve' in Quebec." (Cook, 1977: 15)

Seeking solutions to the growing alienation from the rest of Canada of a revitalized Quebec, the federal government established a Royal Commission on Bilingualism and Biculturalism in 1963. Four years later, in 1967, the first of its four volumes drew attention to "grave inequalities in the opportunities for the French-speaking minorities (as compared to Anglophone minorities) to have an education in their mother tongue" (Canada, 1967: 105). The major reason for this, declared the Commissioners, was the unwillingness of the English-speaking majority in Canada to recognize the right of francophones to educate their children in French; the provision made by Quebec for the children of the anglophone minority, on the other hand, was commended and considered worthy of emulation (*Ibid.*: 106). Subsequently, the Commission recommended *that the right of Canadian parents to have their children educated in the official language of their choice be recognized in the educational systems, the degree of implementation to depend on the concentration of the minority population* (*Ibid.*: 107, italics in the original).

The *second* observation that can be made with some confidence is that some liberalization of "what were in 1966 very restrictive policies with respect to minority-language education" has taken place in Ontario, Manitoba and New Brunswick (Ridout, 1977: 132). In 1968, Ontario passed a law guaranteeing education in French for the children of its Franco-Ontarian minority where numbers warranted. New Brunswick, in 1969, passed its own Official Languages Act establishing equality of status for English and French and equal rights in education for these two linguistic groups. A year later, in 1970, Manitoba passed Bill 133 giving francophones the legal right to schooling in French and removing the earlier restriction that French could only be used as a language of instruction for up to half of the school day. In Alberta and Saskatchewan, two provinces which also had very restrictive legislation, changes were also forthcoming. Alberta adopted legislation permitting school boards to provide French-language schools and classes; Saskatchewan opted for a system it termed "designated" French-language schools. Subsequently, in 1978, Saskatchewan's Education Act guaranteed access to education in French where numbers warranted. Prince Edward Island also amended its Education Act in 1980 to provide for French as a language of instruction. No legislation has been passed in Nova Scotia or British Columbia but the latter published a comprehensive policy statement on education in both French and English in 1981.

These changes and others that accompany them are important. Yet, as Canada's Official Languages Commissioner has pointed out, "the bottom line is still the kind of practical improvements that can be wrung from such rights, be they legal, conventional or permissive" (Canada, 1981b: 40, 54). Two questions therefore need to be addressed. What has been the impact of the above changes? And how have they been received by those at whom they have been aimed?

Empirical evidence on the first question is scarce; enrolment statistics before 1976–77 are suspect and even those for the period 1976–77 to 1980–81 are incomplete. The latest Statistics Canada figures underline the difficulty of obtaining data on minority language enrolments. Data are unavailable for Alberta and very recent for British Columbia. Data on participation rates (the proportion of eligible students actually enrolled in minority language education programs) are also unavailable. As can be seen in Table 4, what the figures do reveal is that, in terms of absolute numbers, minority language enrolments fell in every province except Saskatchewan between 1976/77 and

TABLE 4 *Enrolment in Minority Language Education Programs, 1976–77 to 1980–81*

Province	1976–77[1]	1977–78[1]	1978–79[1]	1979–80[1]	1980–81
Alberta					
Total school enrolment	441,070	439,804	437,063	434,383	437,815
Minority language enrolment					
British Columbia					
Total school enrolment	536,237	527,769	517,786	511,671	509,805
Minority language enrolment				213	659
Manitoba					
Total school enrolment	225,698	221,408	215,663	208,770	204,395
Minority language enrolment	8,543	8,203	7,633	7,139	6,501
Newfoundland					
Total school enrolment	157,686	156,168	153,174	150,382	148,533
Minority language enrolment	200	180	208	164	125
New Brunswick					
Total school enrolment	163,520	162,229	159,467	156,385	152,803
Minority language enrolment	53,813	53,101	51,714	50,455	49,316
Nova Scotia					
Total school enrolment	201,279	198,097	194,038	189,225	185,568
Minority language enrolment	5,541	5,896	5,488	5,290	5,184
Ontario					
Total school enrolment	1,973,140	1,943,064	1,909,145	1,866,107	1,835,537
Minority language enrolment	106,099	103,391	100,887	97,485	96,210
Prince Edward Island					
Total school enrolment	27,903	27,628	27,793	27,277	26,850
Minority language enrolment	684	632	621	589	544
Quebec					
Total school enrolment	1,320,724	1,260,983	1,215,133	1,174,552	1,132,648[2]
Minority language enrolment	221,237	207,230	189,257	173,549	158,541[2]
Saskatchewan					
Total school enrolment	219,191	216,248	211,606	208,009	204,974
Minority language enrolment	1,226	1,384	1,735	1,520	1,322
Total school enrolment	5,266,448	5,153,398	5,040,868	4,926,761	4,839,928
Minority language enrolment	397,343	380,017	357,543	336,404	318,412

Notes: 1. Revised figures.
       2. Preliminary figures.

Source: Statistics Canada, 1982, *Minority and second language education, elementary and secondary levels, 1980–81.* Ottawa: Ministry of Supply and Services Canada, February. 36/7.

1980/81. Part of this decline can be accounted for by the overall decline of school enrolments. But it can also be observed that the ratio of total minority language enrolment to total school enrolment for all ten provinces fell during the same period. In 1976/77 it was of the order of 1:22 while in 1980/81 it was 1:23. In only one province, Saskatchewan, did the ratio improve, going from 1:178.8 in 1976/77 to 1:154 in 1980/81. Even more significant is that decreases can be observed within the "bilingual belt" of Ontario, Quebec and New Brunswick. Absolute numbers fell in all three provinces as did ratios in Ontario and Quebec; in New Brunswick, the ratio was barely maintained. All in all, not very encouraging news for official language minority groups.

Evidence on the second question — how francophone minorities have viewed the improvements that have taken place — is more plentiful but far from encouraging. A task force established by the federal department of the Secretary of State reported in 1975 that francophone communities were both disappointed and discouraged with the federal government's support. The report, titled "It's Now or Never", pulled few punches: if catch-up programs for these communities, particularly in education, were not forthcoming, then the federal government should stop talking about bilingualism and national unity altogether.

The *Federation des Francophones hors Québec* (FFHQ) was equally forthright three years later when it described schools for francophone minorities as "centres of assimilation and alienation" (1978: 19). For his part, the Official Languages Commissioner recently commented that the provision of services resembled "a patchwork quilt, a bit ragged at the edges and too thin to be more than cold comfort for the communities involved" (Commissioner of Official Languages, 1981). What was needed, in his view, was "to provide the minorities with as much educational autonomy and control as possible; to augment financial and human resources; and to work towards a comprehensive structure for minority-language education in each province" (Commissioner of Official Languages, 1982).

The *third* point that can be made concerns the situation in Quebec. The provisions of Bill 101 notwithstanding, the actual provision of *minority language education services are far more extensive in Quebec than elsewhere*. Quebec has maintained, since before Confederation, a complete system of English language schools from the primary school level through university (Canada, 1968). Its education system is organized on a confessional basis with the province being divided into 213 Catholic, 31 Protestant and 4 "multiconfessional" school commissions. Ninety-two per cent of the students attending Catholic schools are French-speaking; 98% of those enrolled in Protestant schools are taught in English.

In school year 1976–77, the enrolment in English language elementary and secondary schools, public and private, was 227,438 — approximately 17% of total school enrolment in the province. That same year, at the post-secondary level, three universities and six colleges of general and technical education offered instruction in English; two other colleges offered instruction in French and English; and the universities also provided teacher education programs. Enrolments in English-language programs leading to a college diploma totalled 21,964 full-time students including 1,606 in private colleges. Students enrolled in programs in English-language universities numbered 32,438 full-time equivalent (including 1,802 full-time and 2,224 part-time students enrolled in teacher-training programs) (CMEC, 1978: 35). This brings us to a consideration of linguistic change and minority language education in Quebec.

The Quebec setting and the Charter of the French Language

The high rates of linguistic transfers from French to English among francophones outside Quebec is a commonly known fact among all the citizens of this province. What is more, Quebec demographers have also produced considerable data and analysis to demonstrate that the French language was also threatened inside the province, particularly in Montreal (Arès, 1975; Lieberson, 1965). This threat, it was argued, would grow in strength unless the government intervened with legislation designed to prevent it (Caldwell, 1974). The old demographic equilibrium no longer held. The birthrate of French-Canadians had fallen below that of Canada as a whole and immigrants, in increasing numbers, were integrating with the minority English-speaking community (see d'Anglejan, this volume, chapter 2; Laporte, this volume, chapter 3).

Nowhere was this latter development more obvious than in the educational system. From 1935 on, the trend for allophones (those whose mother tongue was neither French nor English) to enrol their children in English language schools developed into a flood. By 1972, for example, the percentage of language transfers from "other" languages to English in the Montreal Catholic School Board had reached 89%. In addition, a significant proportion of French-Canadian parents were also enrolling their children in these schools. So strong were these trends that in school year 1973–74, francophone and allophone students accounted for 35% of the total English school population of Quebec (Caldwell, 1974).

The reports of two important Commissions of Inquiry only added to the level of anxiety over these developments. The first, the Parent Report

(Quebec, 1966), while recognizing the tendency for immigrants to prefer English schools and expressing concern about it, did not, however, recommend that the government intervene to try to rectify the situation. The second, the Gendron Commission (Quebec, 1972), did advocate intervention. In its view the tendency had reached "alarming proportions", but unlike its predecessor, it queried whether the school was the principal means for integrating the immigrant into the French-speaking community. The proclivity of immigrants to integrate with the anglophone community, it argued, stemmed from broader causes of which economic motivations were by far the most important. The language of work, *not* the language of instruction was the crucial variable for the maintenance and promotion of the French language in Quebec (Mallea, 1977). The conclusions of the Gendron Commission became a focus of controversy within Quebec. Francophone nationalists considered its recommendations to be far too moderate and cautious. The anglophone and immigrant communities, for the most part, accepting the findings of the report and the recommendations it made. What became clear to all was that the political struggle over the language of instruction was intensifying.

Before 1968, in Quebec, no provincial legislation had ever been introduced on the question of minority language education. However, by 1968 controversies over language issues brought successive Quebec governments to legislate on such matters and resulted in the passage of Bill 63 in 1969, Bill 22 in 1974 and Bill 101 in 1977 (see d'Anglejan, this volume, chapter 2).

Bill 63, by providing parents the freedom of choosing either French or English as the language of instruction for their children, received widespread support from anglophones, but was fiercely opposed by francophone nationalists who argued that access to English should be limited to the children of Quebec's anglophone minority, while the children of immigrants should be required to attend French language schools. Bill 63 was short lived since the government fell and was replaced by a Liberal government that promised a new language law following the recommendations of the Gendron Commission. The resulting Bill 22 was passed in 1974 and made French the official language of Quebec. In addressing the issue of minority language rights for immigrant children, Bill 22 made school boards administer language tests to determine whether a child was to be placed in an English or French language school. Bill 22 fell between two poles of public opinion representing two conflicting principles. "The Anglophones and non-Francophone immigrants were committed for the most part to the principle of bilingualism and to the absolute right of parents to choose the language of instruction of their children. The Francophones were devoted to what they regarded as their collective right to exist as a nation and to making French at least the priority language and therefore primary vehicle of integration of immigrants" (Stein, 1977: 253). Francophone unilingualists complained that Bill 22 did not go far enough; minority anglophones complained that their rights (as guaranteed by Bill 63) had been removed; and immigrants spoke bitterly of discrimination (Mallea, 1977).

Despite the introduction of some amendments, Bill 22 pleased no one and by November 15, 1976 the *Parti Québécois* was elected to power in a stunning upset victory over the Liberals. High on the new government's agenda for action was to make good on its promise to repeal Bill 22 — a promise that had formed a major item of its successful campaign platform.

The new session of the National Assembly had hardly begun when the *Parti Québécois* presented its White Paper on the Charter of the French Language. In introducing it, its sponsor, Camille Laurin, Minister of State for Cultural Development, served clear notice of its intentions. "The Government of Quebec has decided to treat the bill on the French language as a priority among the bills to be tabled in the National Assembly. By giving this law the status of a charter, the government seeks to emphasize the special importance and the eminence of the language to which basic rights will now be granted." That language, of course, was French.

The Charter of the French Language (Bill 101) which became law in Quebec on August 26, 1977 recognizes five fundamental language rights, the fifth of which establishes the right of every person eligible for instruction in Quebec to receive that instruction in French. An entire chapter of the law, chapter VIII, consisting of sixteen clauses, is devoted to provisions concerning the language of instruction. Of these sixteen clauses, the first, clause 72, requires that instruction in kindergarten classes and in elementary and secondary schools be in French — except for certain specified exceptions. It applies to all publicly funded educational institutions at these levels and to subsidized instruction provided by institutions declared to be of public interest or recognized for purposes of grants in virtue of the Private Education Act (see "The Charter of the French Language", this volume, Appendix 1).

The major exception to the above is found in clause 73 and concerns access to schools in which English is the language of instruction:

> In derogation of section 72, the following children at the request of their father and mother, may receive their instruction in English:
>
> (a) a child whose father or mother received his or her elementary instruction in English, in Quebec;

(b) a child whose father or mother, domiciled in Quebec on the date of the coming into force of this act, received his or her elementary instruction in English outside Quebec;

(c) a child who, in his last year of school in Quebec, before the coming into force of this act, was lawfully receiving his instruction in English, in a public kindergarten class or in an elementary or secondary school;

(d) the younger brothers and sisters of a child described in paragraph (c).

These constraints on individual access are complemented at the collective level by clause 79. "A school body not already giving instruction in English in its school is not required to introduce it, and shall not introduce it without express and prior authorization of the Ministry of Education". Again, there are exceptions. First, every school body can, where necessary, avail itself of section 496 of the Education Act to arrange for the instruction in English of any child declared eligible thereof. Second, such authorization may be granted if in the Minister's opinion it is warranted by the number of pupils in the jurisdiction of the school body who are eligible for instruction in English under clause 73 (*Ibid.*: 18/19). In addition, as clause 86 points out, the scope of clause 73 may be extended by regulation to include persons covered by any future reciprocity agreement with any of the other nine provinces.

Bill 101's major goal is the preservation and promotion of the French language in Quebec. Its specific educational objectives are three in number. The first is to ensure that the school system reinforces the position of French as the primary language of use. The second and third objectives flow from the first. They involve, in the second instance, the placement of restrictions on admission to English language schools and the establishment of growth limits for the English language education system as a whole. The third objective is to require the children of allophones to enrol in French language schools and eventually to integrate with the francophone not the anglophone community of Quebec.

It is now five years since the passage of Bill 101 and, while this is not a long enough period to provide conclusive answers, it is long enough to gauge how its provisions have been implemented, the consequences that flow from them, and the extent to which the objectives of the law have been achieved.

In general, the francophone population's response to the new law has been one of satisfaction and renewed confidence (see Laporte, this volume, chapter 3). Anglophone arguments that its educational provisions are unduly restrictive have had little impact, due in part to the widespread belief amongst francophones that minority language education services in Quebec are indeed more than comparable to those available to francophone minorities in the rest of Canada. Moreover, as supporters of Bill 101 take pains to point out, the offer to enter into reciprocal agreements with the other provinces on the provision of equivalent minority language education services still stands — an offer that no province has ever taken up.

This response contrasts vividly with those of an increasingly apprehensive anglophone community (see Taylor & Simard, this volume, chapter 7; Caldwell, chapter 9). Its reaction was immediate, vocal and impassioned. Media campaigns were launched protesting the new law, particularly its minority language education provisions. Here opposition has tended to centre on the following seven concerns (CECM, 1979; PSBGM, 1980):

1. The retroactive effects of clause 73, which declared inadmissible to English language education all French Quebecers and all non-francophones, residing in Quebec before August 1977, who for a variety of reasons could not conform to one or other of the provisions contained in the clause.

2. The restrictions placed on the mobility of Canadian citizens in other provinces whose children, on taking up permanent residence in Quebec, would be obliged to undertake their schooling in French.

3. That parents' secondary education in English is excluded as a criterion of eligibility for children to enter English language schools.

4. The effects of the legislation on the English language school boards in the province — especially its impact on enrolments and future growth.

5. The perceived arbitrary, discriminatory and unnecessarily bureaucratic manner in which eligibility and admission to English schools are determined.

6. The fact that, depending upon the financial circumstances of their parents, students declared ineligible to enter public elementary and secondary schools could without let or hindrance attend private English language schools not subsidized by the government.

7. That freedom of choice of language was not a determining factor with respect to francophone children enrolling in English.

Evidence on the last-mentioned point is not extensive but what exists is supportive. Requests for admissibility to the primary level in the English Catholic schools of the Montreal Catholic School Commission, for example, had in fact been diminishing since the beginning of the decade, falling from

11.3% of applications to 5.6% in 1978 (CECM, 1979). Province-wide, as statistics gathered for the *Conseil de la langue française* indicate, the proportion of francophone children enrolled in English language education dropped from 2.2% in 1976–77 to 1.8% in 1977–78. Evidence concerning the enrolment of inadmissible children of allophone parents in private, non-government subsidized English language schools is incomplete but the number of such pupils is not considered significant. Similarly, the number of inadmissible children who clandestinely attend publicly-funded English language schools, while considered significant perhaps by *Le Bureau de l'admissibilité à l'enseignement en anglais* (Proulx, 1980), is not great and has probably been falling each year. Application of the admissibility rules also appears to have improved over time.

Of considerable and continuing significance, on the other hand, are the first four concerns listed above. The first three of these have had their greatest effect on the lives of individual families, while item three impacts at both the individual and systems levels. The following cases illustrate anglophone concern over the retroactive nature of the minority language education provisions of Bill 101 and its restrictive nature.

The first illustration involves children who transferred from an English language school to a French school prior to August 26, 1977, in order to obtain enrichment in French for a year or two. They faced a situation where under Bill 101 both they and their siblings were declared ineligible to return to English language schools. The second pinpoints the major source of anglophone anger over Bill 101 which stems from its denial of access to English language schools to the children of residents of other Canadian provinces taking up residence in Quebec. Thus we have the situation wherein children who have received all their previous education in English in another Canadian province, and have but one or two years of high school remaining, are required by law to complete the remainder of their schooling in French. Several cases are on record where the result has been that students have lost one or more years of schooling (PSBGM, 1980).

The impact of Bill 101 on individual families in a number of instances has unquestionably been severe, and although "two wrongs do not make a right", it is nevertheless worth remembering that the plight of francophone parents and children in Alberta and British Columbia, for example, especially where numbers do not warrant the provision of minority language services, is much worse. On the other hand, while school closures have been going on in *both* francophone and anglophone systems at pretty well the same rate, due to the dramatic fall in French-Canadian birthrates, the impact of Bill 101 has reinforced the effects of decreased enrolments on the English language school system, its schools and personnel.

Enrolments in English language elementary and secondary schools have been dropping since 1968. This decline reflects changes in two major factors determining the size of a school-age population: fertility rates and migration. Quebec's fertility rate continued to fall dramatically throughout this period (falling, for example, from 3.928 in 1957 to 1.740 in 1972) and it is currently among the lowest in North America. Statistics, unfortunately, do not distinguish between French and English language components of the province's population, but the consequences of declining birth rates on the English language school system undoubtedly have been profound. Quebec has also experienced a net loss of population of 16 years and under through inter-provincial migration each year from 1964 to 1979 (Blacklock, 1979). This loss has been considerably greater than the potential enrolment gained from international migration plus there is some evidence to suggest that its impact has been felt more severely in the English language school system (see Caldwell, this volume, chapter 9).

The third causal factor in this decline is Bill 101's restrictions on enrolment in the English language school system. The Bill's eligibility criteria, of course, were intended progressively to decrease the number of allophones and francophones enrolled in these schools and this is what has occurred. "It is generally accepted that from the early 1970s to the passage of the French Language in 1977, enrolments in the French Catholic sector declined faster than in other sectors, and that since 1977 the rate of decline in English schools has been greater. For example, between 1971 and 1979 enrolments in the French Catholic schools on Montreal Island declined by 40%, English Catholic school enrolments by 30.5% and English Protestant by 32%. Between 1976 and 1979 French Catholic enrolments dropped by 17%, while the figure for English Catholic and English Protestant enrolments was about 20%." (Schachter, 1982.)

Since 1978, the year from which Bill 101 can be considered to have begun its effect, enrolments in English schools have been estimated to decline twice as quickly as enrolments in French schools (St-Germain & Maheu, 1981). It is also estimated that enrolments in the English language school system will decline by more than half during the 1980s and that enrolments in the French sector will actually increase (see Table 5 below). One explanation for this is that secondary education enrolment will reflect the increased rates of decline that affected the elementary schools in the late 1970s and early 1980s (Blacklock & Landry, 1982). Another, less important, reason is that there appears to be a small but significant number of children eligible for English instruction enrolling in French language schools. Although figures vary, the government estimated that there were 12,500 of these children in 1980–81 compared to 5,175 in 1977–78 (Schachter, 1982).

TABLE 5 *Enrolments (actual and projected) in public elementary and secondary schools of Quebec by language of instruction 1975–1990*

Year	French	%	English*	%
1975	1,143,589	83.1	231,320	16.8
1980	959,294	85.6	153,951	13.7
1985	1,007,258	90.8	101,608	9.2
1990	1,037,475	93.6	71,125	6.4

The demand for instruction in French among anglophone parents is also increasing inside the English language school system itself. As a consequence of Bill 22, and even more so of Bill 101, anglophone parents are increasingly aware that it is essential their children possess a working knowledge of French. For example, in 1980–81 there were 26 French Protestant schools in Quebec — most located in Montreal — compared to less than 10 before Bill 101 was passed in 1977. Expansion has also taken place in *classes d'accueil* which were originally intended to help children whose mother tongue was neither English nor French to enter French schools and subsequently integrate into the French community. Anglophone parents have also been involved in funding their own French *classes d'accueil* in order that their five-year-olds can receive full-day French language instruction (Schachter, 1982).

This demand for fluency in French among English speaking parents has meant that English schools must improve their instruction in French. Yet this is an extremely sensitive issue when many of the existing teaching staff are unilingual and therefore can only teach in English. If the English school system is to survive, changes will have to be made. It is here perhaps, in its impact on personnel, structures, finance and administrative practices of individual English language school boards that the greatest impact of Bill 101 has occurred. It is within these school boards that the combined effects of the absence of immigrant children, the out-migration of English-speaking pupils, reduced enrolments from in-migration, and the increased demand for instruction in French has been most severely felt.

The Protestant School Board of Greater Montreal (PSBGM), the largest Protestant school board in the province, is a case in point. English language enrolment in Quebec in 1979–80 totalled 173,188 and of these 36,728 were to be found in the classrooms of PSBGM — a 10% decline over the previous year. In 1980 and 1981, enrolments fell by over 9% each year. Overall, enrolments in the period 1977–81 fell from 45,783 to 30,003 — a decline of over a third in five years. English language enrolments in the Montreal Catholic School Commission (CECM) suffered a similar decline falling from 34,414 in 1977 to 22,812 in 1981 (Blacklock & Landry, 1982).

Not only did total enrichment in the PSBGM change in these five years, its composition also underwent change. Parents increasingly opted to enrol their children in French immersion and French classes as Figure 1 graphically reveals. French language enrolments trebled in the period 1977–81 and although the projections are tentative, and therefore suggest caution, they are expected to double again in size by 1986 (Schachter, 1982).

In an effort to ensure the survival of English language schools within the context of contemporary Quebec society, the board is having to offer its services in both English and French. It is also coming to grips with the need for its high school graduates to be fluently bilingual as opposed to possessing a working knowledge of French. If these graduates are to enter and successively compete in a context in which the language of employment is French, this is essential. This increasingly central fact of life in Quebec is reinforced by enrolment statistics in English-language universities and colleges in the province. In 1980, over 20% of the students at McGill University and 25% of the students at John Abbott College (an English language college) were francophone. It is with these bilingual francophone students that those in English language school boards will have to compete for middle and senior level positions in Quebec's increasingly unilingual economy. Anglophone graduates who are not fluently bilingual will not even possess the qualifications to enter the competition (see Miller, this volume, chapter 5).

In summary, therefore, when the above trends are considered together, they offer considerable justification for the expressed fears of the anglophone and allophone communities that, since the promulgation of Bill 101, the long-term survival of English-language instruction in Quebec has been seriously jeopardized.

Current issues

Earlier it was stated that the second part of this chapter would deal with current issues which would provide added fuel to the controversial debate over minority language education provision in the decade ahead. Three major issues can be identified. The first, the application of the minority language educational rights section of the Canadian Charter of Rights and Freedoms, has already been noted. The second, which involves questions of autonomy and control, has received much attention of late in New Brunswick and Ontario. In Quebec, the publication of the government's White Paper

FIGURE 1 *PSBGM: Elementary and Secondary Enrolment and Projections by Language of Instruction, 1977–78 to 1986–87*

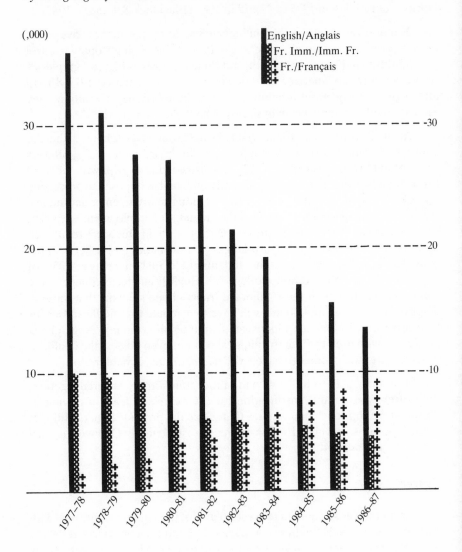

Source: PSBGM Planning Office, 1982.

on the reorganization of the educational system has made it a high profile political issue of considerable import and consequence. The third issue revolves around the funding of minority language education.

Canadian Charter of Rights and Freedoms

In direct contrast to Bill 101, the 1982 Canadian Charter of Rights and Freedoms re-affirms English and French as the official languages of Canada (clauses 16–22). These clauses apply, in the main, to the use of the two official languages in all institutions of the Parliament and government of Canada and those of the legislature and government of New Brunswick. The latter being the only province to have declared both English and French to be the official languages of the province. Minority language education rights are set out in clause 23.

23. (1) Citizens of Canada
    (a) whose first language learned and still understood is that of the English or French linguistic minority population of the province in which they reside, or
    (b) who have received their primary school instruction in Canada in English or French and reside in a province where the language in which they received that instruction is the language of the English or French linguistic minority population of the province,
    have the right to have their children receive primary and secondary school instruction in that language in that province.

(2) Citizens of Canada of whom any child has received or is receiving primary or secondary school instruction in English or French in Canada, have the right to have all their children receive primary and secondary school instruction in the same language.

(3) The right of citizens of Canada under subsections (1) and (2) to have their children receive primary and secondary school instruction in the language of the English or French linguistic minority population of a province
    (a) applies wherever in the province the number of children of citizens who have such a right is sufficient to warrant the provision to them out of public funds of minority language instruction; and

(b) includes, where the number of those children so warrants, the right to have them receive that instruction in minority language facilities provided out of public funds.

A comparison of the above clauses with those of the Charter of the French Language (Bill 101) suggests that both the provisions and their wording were formulated in such a way as to try to make them more palatable to the government of Quebec. In the rough and tumble of constitutional negotiations they underwent a number of revisions with this in mind, but they still failed to get Quebec to accept them. Efforts at compromise, however, did have another result. They reduced the level of protection offered to minority language groups in education and restricted its application. First, and this was always the case of course, the provisions only apply to official language minorities and not to non-official language minorities. Second, and this is an extremely important constraint, they only apply to citizens of Canada. They do not apply to immigrants, even to immigrants whose mother tongue or language of previous education is English.

Clause 23(1)(a) applies in all the provinces *except* Quebec where it shall only come into force after having been authorized by the legislative assembly or the provincial government. No such authorization, of course, will be provided while the *Parti Québécois* is in power. And, should the opposition Liberal Party form the next government, it is also highly unlikely that it would move quickly on the matter for fear of arousing sensitivities it does not wish to offend. The substance of clause 23(1)(b) does not differ to any large extent from that of clause 72 in Bill 101. Its importance lies in the fact that it confirms access to instruction in English for the children of the anglophone minority in Quebec, *as a constitutional right rather than a legal provision subject to legislative change.*

The major target of the *Parti Québécois'* opposition is clause 23(2) or what has become known as the "Canada" clause. In the Quebec context this gives Canadian citizens moving from another province to Quebec, the right to have all their children receive primary and secondary school instruction in English, as long as they or an elder brother or sister received or are receiving primary or secondary school instruction in English in Canada. From the anglophone citizens' point of view, the clause enhances mobility for themselves and their children. It runs directly counter, however, to clause 73 of Bill 101 which restricts access to minority language education in English to children whose father or mother (a) received his/her elementary instruction in English, *in Quebec*; or (b) whose father or mother, domiciled *in Quebec* on the date Bill 101 came into effect, received his/her elementary education in English outside Quebec; or (c) who, in their last year of school *in Quebec* before the Act became law, was lawfully receiving his/her instruction in English; or (d) the younger brothers and sisters of the latter.

A second major problem is the use of two quite different principles of *access* to the two Charters. For example, clause 23(3)(a) and (b) of the Canadian Charter employs the principle "where numbers warrant" to the provision of instruction in French to the children of francophone parents in the English-speaking provinces. Bill 101, on the other hand, employs the principle "any eligible child" in determining access to education in their mother tongue for the children of Quebec's anglophone minority. For example, clause 79 includes the statement that "every school body shall, where necessary, avail itself of section 496 of the Education Act to arrange for the instruction in English of any child declared eligible therefor" (Quebec, 1977). English-speaking provinces, moreover, interpret the phrase "where numbers warrant" differently. The result is that access to instruction in French for francophone minorities varies from province to province and depending on the number of francophones in each area.

A third problem area arises not so much from the provisions of the Canadian Charter as from the rather ambiguous language it employs. How, for example, is one to interpret the phrase "minority language educational facilities"? What constitutes a facility, moreover? Does it refer to class-rooms, buildings, separate institutions or to all three? If interpreted loosely, as seems entirely possible, then it would embrace the widely different provision of facilities in which minority language education is carried on in the ten provinces in their entirety. These range from the use of French as the language of instruction in a single classroom in an otherwise English-speaking school, through programmatically distinct bilingual schools operating in the same building, to homogeneous French language schools and, more recently, in New Brunswick, homogeneous French language school boards. In Quebec, on the other hand, the anglophone minority for the most part has enjoyed a distinct and fully autonomous educational system, elementary through university, for well over a century.

Much more will be heard of these problems in the years ahead. Already, some commentators, for example, are strongly of the opinion that the principle "any eligible child" contained in Bill 101 should apply throughout Canada (Magnet, 1982). It is also worth noting that in Quebec it is possible for an English-speaking student to pursue studies all the way through to a Ph.D., in most of the major disciplines and at a world-ranking university, in English. This is patently *not* the case for francophone students outside Quebec. Moreover, the future of anglophone boards has recently been placed in doubt with the publication of a government White Paper on the re-organization of the school system. Its proposals impinge directly on the issue of local board autonomy for minority groups — a major issue in several other provinces besides Quebec.

Autonomy and control

Evidence is accumulating in Canada on the extent to which linguistic minority groups are engaging (with varying degrees of success) in pressure group politics in the field of education in general, and minority language education in particular (Mallea, 1981). One reason for this is that Canada, as is the case in many other countries, has experienced a remarkable renascence of interest in ethnic and linguistic affairs. Another is that many parents are taking a closer look at the role of publicly-funded schools in transmitting knowledge of their mother tongue to their children, are dissatisfied with what they see, and are making strenuous efforts to change them. As they do so, they are raising basic questions about the role of formal institutions of learning in cultural transmission and development.

Whose culture, whose language are these institutions to transmit? What resources are to be allocated and to what ends? Who should control these resources? Efforts to answer these questions have thrown issues of educational autonomy and control into bold relief in both Canada and Quebec. Paradoxically, however, the present emphasis in Quebec centres on efforts to strengthen and standardize core linguistic and cultural values through the school; whereas, elsewhere, more pluralistic institutional forms are being introduced. The principle involved is nevertheless the same. Minority language groups are seeking increased control over education as a means of assuring their cultural strength and survival. This search has taken on particular force in the provinces of New Brunswick, Ontario and Quebec. In the other seven anglophone provinces some policy changes are in train but francophone numbers are usually below "where numbers warrant" and little action is deemed necessary often in spite of francophone demands (FFHQ, 1978). The vast majority of Canadian francohones reside in these three provinces with the only sizeable Canadian anglophone minority being located in Quebec. Each of the three provinces is aware of developments in minority language education in its sister provinces and each is influenced to some extent by these provisions. Nevertheless, as we shall see, varying demographic, historical and regional settings have led to very different results.

Legislative and structural change according greater control over schooling to minority language education groups, has made the most rapid progress in recent years in *New Brunswick* which is the only officially bilingual province in Canada. Its Official Languages Act was passed in 1974 and four years later a new Schools Act was passed. The following are its major provisions:

(a) School districts, schools and classes shall be organized on one or other of the official languages.

(b) The Minister of Education may establish, on her/his own initiative, with the approval of the Lieutenant-Governor in Council, in any school district in addition to the existing school board, a school board for the official language group in that school district whose language is not the official language on the basis of which the school district is organized.

(c) Alternatively, the Minister shall establish in a school district, where parents
   (i) who reside in that school district,
   (ii) whose language is the official language which is not the official language on the basis of which the school is organized, and
   (iii) who are the parents of not less than thirty children of elementary school age, submit a request in accordance with the regulations, a school board for the official language group in that school district whose language is not the language on the basis of which the school district is organized within six months of receipt by the Minister of such a request.

(d) In any school district where a minority language school board is not in existence, but where there is a minority of persons whose language is one of the official languages, the Minister, with the approval of the Lieutenant-Governor in Council, may establish an advisory committee representative of that minority to advise the school board of that district with respect to the education of the pupils forming a part of that minority of persons (New Brunswick Schools Act, 1978).

The New Brunswick school system enrolled about 150,000 students in Grades 1–12 in 1981. About 100,000 of these are in the English-speaking system and about 50,000 in the French-speaking system. As of September 1, 1981, the school districts were organized on the basis of the official language of the community with their own boards, officials, schools and classes. There were 25 English language boards and 12 French language boards. It was also expected that in the near future four or five minority language boards would be established in particular school districts. Overall, it has been observed, "In the French-speaking districts and schools a full range of instructional and support services is provided which parallels the English system. At the Department (of Education) level two Deputy Ministers are responsible for the provision of services to students in the respective language." (Malmberg, 1981.)

Ontario is the province with the largest francophone population outside Quebec and, in 1976, it numbered 462,075 or 5.6% of the total provincial population. Presently the French-language school population comprises approximately 94,200 students registered in 282 Roman Catholic separate schools, 13 public elementary schools and 63 French or mixed secondary schools. Strenuous and vocal efforts to pressure the province into becoming officially bilingual have been made by the francophone minority in recent years. Some changes have occurred as a result but the province remains officially unilingual and attempts to establish French language school boards, notably in the Ottawa-Carleton region, have to date been unsuccessful.

The most recent manifestation of this lack of success is to be found in the Report of a senior level Joint Committee on Governance of French Language Elementary and Secondary Schools published in April, 1982. Three members were drawn from the government: the assistant deputy minister for French language education in the province (co-chairperson), the secretary of the policy and priorities board of the cabinet Premier's office, and the deputy minister of inter-governmental affairs. The remaining four members were from the Franco-Ontarian community.

First, the Joint Committee recommended that the government recognize the right of each French-speaking student to education in her/his mother tongue from kindergarten to the end of secondary school; second, that the principle of proportional and guaranteed representation of minority language ratepayers on a board of education or separate school board be accepted; third, that there should be a minimum of four trustees from the minority language group on these boards; and, four, that a new administrative structure be established in the Ottawa-Carleton region (Ontario, 1982).

These recommendations represent an attempt at compromise, a means of seeking to accommodate a minority's aspirations and a majority government's wishes. It is doubtful they will satisfy the former. The francophone minority want homogeneous language boards and thus the pressure for them will continue. In the meantime, however, they have attracted the attention of Quebec's anglophone community who feel these proposals compare unfavourably not with existing provisions but with the proposed decrease in anglophone control over their own minority language education (*The Gazette*, June 5, 1982).

In *Quebec* the latest cause of concern is the release of the government White Paper detailing a wide-ranging plan to reorganize and restructure the province's education system (Quebec, 1982). A centrepiece of the White Paper is a radical proposal to do away with Catholic and Protestant school boards, as they are presently constituted, by transforming them into co-ordinating and service bodies for a reformed school organization. Under the latter, individual school councils will manage human, material and financial resources as well as enjoying some increase in powers in specifically educa-tional and pedagogical matters. The government also proposes to reduce the number of school boards, establish regional county municipalities and, where the latter don't exist, define specific districts. For example, if the proposals were adopted, Montreal Island would be divided into thirteen — eight French and five English-language — school boards. The expressed aim of these proposals is to reduce costs and simplify administrative structures by reducing the number of school boards by over a half from 250 to a little more than 100 (each possessing about 30 schools and less than 10,000 pupils). The new boards would be integrated (i.e. contain both elementary and secondary schools) and be classified as either non-denominational, linguistic or unified school boards (*Ibid.*: 60–67).

A key objective of the government's proposals is to make the schools responsible and responsive to the community in which they are located. And in this regard, it points out, it proposes to make schools the key location for the exercise of the linguistic rights of English-speaking Quebecers, by granting English-language status to schools where pupils are admitted to instruction in English in accordance with the provisions of Bill 101. This measure, the government suggests, represents a significant step forward, especially in view of the new status and the new powers assigned to the school. The children concerned will thus be assured of their right to become part of Quebec society, in a learning environment reflecting their own distinctive educational and cultural traditions. And an appropriate number of English schools will be guaranteed stability on the same terms as any other school" (*Ibid.*: 59).

What will not be guaranteed, however, except on Montreal Island, are existing linguistically homogeneous school boards. "Everywhere else where geographical, sociocultural and administrative considerations point clearly in the direction of unified school boards, the partitions which have, up to now, been financially and socially too costly will be broken down . . . In such cases, however, steps will be taken to allow the linguistic minority to be integrated into the school board without being assimilated; the school boards concerned will be given structures designed to guarantee the autonomy required for the linguistic minority's school to flourish" (*Ibid*.: 66).

Such provisions and assurances have not succeeded in removing the very real apprehensions of Quebec's anglophone minority which were initially heightened by the publication in *Le Devoir* in August, 1981, of an earlier and "leaked" working version of the White Paper's proposals. Its initial reaction was that the plan to dis-establish confessional school boards was constitutionally unthinkable because Section 93 of the BNA Act clearly protects the educational rights of Protestant and Catholic minorities (Burgess, 1982). The question is, of course, what rights does the BNA Act protect. The government's answer is it protects those that existed in 1867. That is, under the BNA Act (1867), in the cities of Montreal and Quebec, the duality of religious persuasion was recognized and two school commissions and their boundaries, one Catholic and one Protestant, were established in each city. Few anglophones, however, take comfort from the limited application today of 1867 provisions. Nor are they reassured by the Minister's statement that "those most closely concerned will perhaps realize, after analysis and reflection that these guarantees do not necessarily offer them better arrangements than those proposed by the government plan" (*Ibid*.: 66).

Nevertheless, there is some evidence to suggest that the government may have succeeded in dividing the anglophone minority on the merits or otherwise of the proposed reorganization of the school system. One observer, for example, thought it "unrealistic", another "sensible" and the editorial page of Montreal's only English-language daily, *The Gazette*, deemed it a "risky experiment". Alliance Quebec, the anglophone minority's umbrella organization (successor organization to the Council of Quebec Minorities) originally advocated a "wait and see" approach to the White Paper. On publication of its contents, however, Alliance Quebec immediately went on the attack. Its President was quoted as accusing the Minister of Education of having "ignored every bit of advice given to him throughout his many consultations in the preparation of the white paper . . . All English Quebecers off the Island of Montreal have been written off." The President of the Quebec Association of Protestant School Boards expressed his organization's fears regarding increased centralization and standardization, a view, incidentally, shared by a number of Quebec francophone groups and the danger of the educational system being taken over by the civil service. And, in the view of an English-speaking member of the National Assembly, "the white paper shows the government's real objective is the disappearance of the English community in Quebec" (*The Gazette*, June 22, 1982: 2).

Already the main outlines of opposition among the anglophone minority community are clear. It believes that the reform proposal is a device for the further centralization of power in the hands of the Ministry of Education (a view shared by many francophones as well). It is afraid that in practice individual school councils will possess little choice or flexibility in teaching the government's required curriculum. It expects that schools will have to administer their budgets according to strict government guidelines. Most of all it fears the loss of control and management of school councils off the Island of Montreal. "What a minority linguistic community needs is control and management of a network of schools with both administrative and pedagogical support services. Linguistic committees, where they exist, are totally inadequate" (*The Gazette*, June 23: 2).

The picture that emerges then regarding autonomy and control over educational resources is that while francophones in New Brunswick have made considerable gains, and will likely obtain some improvements in Ontario, the autonomy traditionally enjoyed by anglophones in Quebec is threatened by proposals advanced in its White Paper on education by the Quebec government. Herein lies a major paradox in minority language education provision in the overall Canadian context. It is part of a larger dilemma and it is one to which we shall return in some detail in the final section. But first we must examine the funding of minority language education provision.

Funding

The third major issue currently arousing controversy in Canada involves the federal government's support programme for minority language education. The controversy straddles a whole range of issues, in addition to those of costs, involving matters of national unity, linguistic rights, and questions of jurisdiction, accountability and political credit. It also reflects the climate of confrontation that has grown up between the federal and provincial governments in recent years. Nowhere, of course, is the confrontation more intense than with Quebec.

The federal programme for the support of minority language education is administered by the department of the Secretary of State. It provides financial assistance, by way of formula funding agreements, to provincial and territorial governments to support the expansion of opportunities for education in the minority official languages. The major beneficiaries to date have been New Brunswick, Quebec and Ontario, with Quebec receiving by far the largest amount (see Table 6).

Federal support for minority language education was introduced in 1970 (the year following passage of Canada's Official Languages Act).

TABLE 6 *Total Contributions Under the Elementary, Secondary and Post-Secondary Levels Minority Official Language Education Formulas, 1970–71 to 1980–81*

Province	First Agreement 1970–71 to 1973–74	Second Agreement 1974–75 to 1978–79	First Interim Year 1979–80	Second Interim Year 1980–81	Total 1970–71 to 1980–81
Newfoundland	39,934	216,434	48,873	62,808	368,049
Prince Edward Island	280,703	842,008	190,515	209,892	1,523,118
Nova Scotia	1,800,415	4,304,877	687,213	728,789	1,521,294
New Brunswick	21,204,167	44,703,425	9,117,713	9,870,148	84,895,453
Quebec	130,931,665	380,427,257	77,447,429	74,000,383	662,806,734
Ontario	55,182,560	117,385,361	23,715,227	23,773,542	220,056,690
Manitoba	2,354,016	6,958,663	1,404,358	1,642,047	12,359,084
Saskatchewan	525,236	1,694,005	370,391	355,618	2,945,250
Alberta	1,344,108	3,839,381	1,210,979	1,436,926	7,831,394
British Columbia	279,552	1,443,027	493,905	670,792	2,887,276
Total	213,942,356	561,814,438	114,686,603	112,750,945	1,003,194,342

However, due to federal sensitivities over the fact that the provinces possess constitutional jurisdiction over education, strict accounting guidelines were not applied. The funds in effect flowed directly into the general revenues of the ten provinces. And this, in turn, has meant that the provinces have not felt it necessary to render a precise accounting of expenditures of these funds on minority language education.

The absence of adequate accounting procedures has aroused considerable concern among both francophone and anglophone minorities. Francophone minorities in the majority English-speaking provinces have expressed concern over whether or not the transfer monies received were actually expended on the programmes for which they were received (FFHQ, 1978). In much the same vein, the anglophone minority in Quebec has argued vehemently that they have not been spent on the programmes for which they were intended (QFHSA, 1976). For their part, the provincial governments have paid little heed to these complaints. Nowhere, perhaps, is this more true than in Quebec. From the outset, successive Quebec governments have considered federal transfer funds for minority language education to be a "reimbursement" for the province's extensive support for educational services in the English language (QFHSA, 1975a). The anglophone minority, on the other hand, has consistently viewed the transfer funds as "supplementary" monies specifically earmarked for minority language education programmes (QFHSA, 1975b).

In the past couple of years the federal government has assumed a more aggressive posture and pressed for greater provincial accountability (Canada, 1981a). It has, for example, tried without success to transfer the cost of *maintaining* minority language education programmes to the provinces so as to concentrate future transfer payments on their *expansion*. What future success it will have in its demands for improved and extended forms of provincial reporting remains to be seen. The same applies to its efforts to obtain systematic evaluations of the effectiveness of minority language education programmes. Progress is likely to be slow and piecemeal given the present state of federal-provincial relations. Thus the funding issue, while not as sharply contentious as the issue of minority language educational rights and that of autonomy and control over minority language educational institutions, will continue to be a focus of complaint and a staging area for continued minority concern and complaint.

Conclusion

Considerable ground has been traversed in this chapter and so it will come as no surprise to the reader to discover in the conclusion that there are no simple answers to the complex issues of minority language education provision in Quebec and Canada. It is possible, however, to identify key factors that will materially effect this provision in the future. A number of these appear overly obvious, perhaps; others less so. All are important, as are their inter-relationships and cumulative impact.

The over-riding linguistic fact in North America is that English is, overwhelmingly, the dominant language of economics, politics and social relations. Its drawing power in Canada is so powerful and pervasive that major doubts must be raised as to the adequacy of current efforts to protect and support the French language in well over half of the provinces. Even in the three provinces of Ontario, Quebec and New Brunswick, which together form Canada's so-called "bilingual belt", serious questions have been raised as to its long-term health and prospects for survival. Nowhere, of course, have these questions been more searchingly analysed and appraised than in Quebec. Here, as we have seen, they form the underlying rationale for the province's language policies and legislation. The consequence is that, even among many anglophones, most of Bill 101 is now accepted as being a fundamentally necessary means of protection for the French language and culture. So strong is this belief that even if its sponsor, the *Parti Québécois* government of Premier Levesque, were defeated in the next election, the legislation would probably be left virtually intact by its successor.

These realities have important consequences for minority language groups throughout Canada. It becomes crucial, if they are to survive, that they do not falter in their hard-fought struggle for constitutional, legislative, and structural change. In Quebec, where anglophones are gradually grasping the realities of their minority status, this will require continued vigilance and the development of a wide range of expertise and skills in pressure group politics. Outside Quebec, where francophone minorities possess less power and fewer advantages, conflicts over increased control of educational resources will continue. The number of legal challenges to existing language legislation will likely increase. And the Supreme Court of Canada will likely be called upon to consider and pass judgement on the issues they represent.

Legal judgements are no substitute for constitutional guarantees of rights and freedoms, however. In some provinces minority language educational rights, as contained in the new constitution, will have little more effect than to confirm the *status quo*. In others, they may serve to enhance the struggle for improved access to minority language education. Where further debate and controversy are certain to arise is over the criteria of eligibility governing access. For example, the principle of "where numbers warrant" will be increasingly and pejoratively compared to that of "guaranteed access" for individual students. Comparisons will focus on differences between Quebec and the other nine provinces and will involve discussions of school transportation allowances, subsistence monies and boarding school education. Much more will be heard of this issue in the years ahead. Its resolution will have a major impact on what seems to be the trend in Quebec toward reducing minority language education provision.

Anyone familiar with the history and current status of eligibility, access and provision of minority language education in Canada recognizes that acrimonious confrontation and conflict will continue to characterize relations between the provincial government of Quebec and the federal government of Canada in the years ahead. Moreover, the reason for this is not hard to find — for conflict over minority language education in Quebec and Canada is quintessentially representative of much broader divisions over the nature of Canadian society and Canadian federalism. Often such conflict has served as a surrogate, at the local and regional as well as national level, for these divisions. That it continues to do so is starkly revealed by the fact that fundamental disagreement over minority language education rights was a major reason for the absence of Quebec's signature on the new constitutional accord. Its absence from a document, whose declared purpose was that of enhancing national integration, recalls vividly to mind divisions over earlier attempts to achieve the same goal.

Lord Durham recommended the gradual assimilation of the franco-phone minorities into the English-speaking majority in 1841 (Craig, 1969). As part of the agreement over Confederation this approach was explicitly rejected by the British North America Act of 1867. However, although this Act embraced the principle of Canadian dualism, it was more often than not eschewed in practice. Implicit and, in a number of cases, explicit support for the assimilation of francophones became the norm over the next hundred years — especially in education.

Not until the effects of Quebec's Quiet Revolution made themselves felt in fact were the contradictions between these diametrically opposed principles of majority-minority group relations subjected to broadly-based scholarly review and analysis.

The most ambitious attempt to rectify this unfortunate state of affairs, which was so injurious to national health and well-being, was carried out by the Royal Commission on Bilingualism and Biculturalism, established in 1963. Significantly, the entire contents of one of its four volumes was devoted to education (Canada, 1968). The Commission's task, as its title reveals, was "to inquire into and report upon the existing state of bilingual-ism and biculturalism in Canada and to recommend what steps should be taken to develop the Canadian Confederation over the basis of equal part-nership between the two founding races . . ." (Canada, 1967: 173–4). Not long after the Commission began its work, however, it discovered that the very assumptions on which it was established did not adequately describe Canada's cultural make-up. In brief, demographic, economic and political changes since Confederation, and particularly since World War II, had brought into being a far more plural society. This central, fundamental fact, allied to strong vestiges of support for the vision of Canada as a unilingual society, helps explain why the Official Languages Act of 1969 met with the opposition that it did — especially in the Western provinces. Many second and third generation Canadians in these provinces were of neither British nor French backgrounds, and for them official bilingualism often had little social relevance or meaning. Moreover, they were of the opinion that their contribution to the building of Canadian society had been grossly under-estimated. In their view, and that of the Native Peoples (the first inhabitants of the country) Canada was a plural society not a bicultural one. They made their voice and presence felt with the result that the fourth and final volume of the RCBB was devoted in its entirety to *The Contributions of Other Ethnic Groups* (Canada, 1970). In 1971 the federal government announced its new policy of "Multiculturalism Within a Bilingual Framework". According to it, Canada had two official languages but no official culture.

The francophone minority's response, especially in Quebec, to this characterization of Canada as a plural society was strongly negative. Here, according to Quebec nationalists, was further evidence of anglophone perfidy and lack of support for dualism. The federal government may have roundly rejected assimilation and the "melting pot" metaphor of majority-minority relations, but its endorsement of multiculturalism not biculturalism as the *leitmotiv* of Canadian society led many in Quebec to look more closely at a third option, that of cultural nationalism leading ultimately perhaps to the status of an independent nation.

It is in this context — one in which fundamental divisions over the nature of Canadian federalism, its core political values, and an increasingly uncertain economy dominate all other considerations — that linguistic policies and the future of minority language education in Quebec and Canada will be decided. It is a context, moreover, in which modern Quebec society is also becoming more, rather than less, plural (see d'Anglejan, this volume, chapter 2; Quebec, 1982). In the rest of Canada, meanwhile, non-official as well as official language minorities are voicing their aspirations and making their presence felt. They, too, are demanding that their sense of collectivity find expression in educational terms (Mallea, 1981). Among the most explicit set of demands for autonomy and control over the linguistic and cultural education of their children are those made by Canada's original peoples (Couture, 1979). And these demands, backed by political action and legal challenge, are part of a much broader movement of ethnic revitalization that is likely to increase rather than decrease in the foreseeable future.

This is the crux of the Canadian dilemma: how to develop a form of revised federalism that reconciles the historic principle of dualism with the realities of contemporary Canadian pluralism. At the national level, the new Canadian constitution is but the first of many steps that will need to be taken if the dilemma is to be successfully resolved. Further changes, especially in the area of minority language education rights, must be forthcoming. And these will need to include additional safeguards for the French language and culture — especially in Quebec — while at the same time maintaining the rights of Canadian citizens to guaranteed access to schooling in the official language of their choice.

Policies and practices at the provincial and local levels must also undergo change. And it is here that the realities of contemporary pluralism can probably best be addressed. The legitimate linguistic and cultural aspirations of non-official, as well as official, language groups will need to be reflected in institutional and structural as well as normative terms. And this will involve granting a greater degree of autonomy and control over educational decision-making to all minority language groups — especially as it relates to the allocation of resources (Mallea & Young, forthcoming).

Local or municipal levels of government also have an important contribution to make towards the resolution of the Canadian dilemma. They can do so, for example, by adopting a far more responsive attitude in policy and practice towards minority group requests for alternative forms of schooling. Local boards of education need to understand that there is no *a priori* reason to believe that introduction of instruction in a non-official language is incompatible with good citizenship, social cohesion or identificaton with the larger collectivity. To the contrary, in the increasingly complex, impersonal and often alienating environment of contemporary society, such instruction may help provide a much-needed antidote to the negative effects of such an environment — one that emphasizes positive inter-personal and inter-generational relationships and fosters a well-developed sense of identity and personal well-being. Finally, one expects democratic societies, almost by definition, to provide a wide range of educational alternatives that help mediate the influence of the state, prevent the growth of bureaucratic, monopolistic power, and contribute to the development of those essential attitudes and skills required by a democratic citizenry if it and the Canadian political process is to meet successfully the challenge of unity in diversity within the framework of a modern nation-state.

Acknowledgements

I wish to acknowledge the generous donation of time, information and criticism made by individuals in various school boards and government offices, as well as colleagues at the Ontario Institute for Studies in Education and Queen's University in the preparation of this chapter.

References

ARÈS, R. 1975, *Les positions — ethniques, linguistiques et religieuses — des Canadiens français à la suite du recensement de 1971*. Montréal: Editions Bellarmin.
BLACKLOCK, T. 1979, "Enrolment Changes and the Implications for English Language Education". Unpublished paper, January, 46 pp.
BLACKLOCK, T., & LANDRY, B. 1982, "Enrolment Analysis for the Province of Quebec and each Administrative Region". Unpublished paper, February.

BRETON, R., REITZ, J. G., & VALENTINE, V. 1980, *Cultural Boundaries and the Cohesion of Canada*. Montreal: The Institute for Research on Public Policy.

BURGESS, D. A. 1982, "School Board Reorganization in Quebec: An Introduction". Unpublished paper presented at the annual conference of the Canadian Society for the Study of Education. Ottawa, June. 6pp.

CALDWELL, G. 1974, *A Demographic Profile of the English-Speaking Population of Quebec 1921–1971*. Quebec City: International Center for Research on Bilingualism.

CANADA 1967, Report of the Royal Commission on Bilingualism and Biculturalism. Book I. *The Official Languages*. Ottawa: Queen's Printer.

— 1968, Book II. *Education*. Ottawa: Queen's Printer.

— 1970, Book IV. *The Cultural Contribution of the Other Ethnic Groups*. Ottawa: Queen's Printer.

— 1979, The Task Force on Canadian Unity. *A Future Together*. Ottawa: Ministry of Supply and Services Canada.

— 1981a, Secretary of State. *Descriptive and Financial Summary of Federal-Provincial Programmes for the Official Languages in Education, 1970–1971 to 1980–81*. Ottawa: Language Programmes Directorate, Education Support Programmes Branch. November.

— 1981b, Secretary of State Communiqué, "Federal Support for Official Language Education to Continue". January 27.

— 1982, *The Canadian Constitution 1981. A resolution adopted by the Parliament of Canada, December, 1981*. Ottawa: Government of Canada.

CANADA, COUNCIL OF MINISTER OF EDUCATION (CMEC) 1978. *The State of Minority Language Education in the Ten Provinces of Canada*. Toronto: CMEC.

COMMISSION DES ECOLES CATHOLIQUES DE MONTREAL (CECM) 1979, *A Rationale for Changing Bill 101*. Montreal: English Sector Parents Co-ordinating Committee. October 5.

COMMISSIONER OF OFFICIAL LANGUAGES 1981, *Annual Report, 1980*. Ottawa: Ministry of Supply and Services Canada.

— 1982, *Annual Report, 1981*. Ottawa: Ministry of Supply and Services Canada.

COOK, R. 1977, Presentation to First Session, Destiny Canada Conference Final Report. Toronto: York University. Mimeographed, 19pp.

COUNCIL OF MINISTERS OF EDUCATION, CANADA (CMEC) 1978, *The State of Minority Language Education in the Ten Provinces in Canada*. Toronto.

COUTURE, J. E. 1979, *Secondary Education for Canadian Registered Indians, Past, Present and Future: A Commentary*. Ottawa: Department of Indian and Northern Affairs.

CRAIG, G. M. 1969, *Lord Durham's Report*. Toronto: McClelland and Steward.

FEDERATION OF FRANCOPHONES OUTSIDE QUEBEC (FFHQ) 1978, *The Heirs of Lord Durham, Manifesto of a Vanishing People*. Ottawa: La Fédération des Francophones hors Québec.

HODGETTS, A. B. 1968, *What Culture? What Heritage?* Toronto: The Ontario Institute for Studies in Education.

JAENEN, C. J. 1972, "Canadian Education and Minority Rights", *Slavs in Canada*. Vol. 3, 191–208.

JOHNSON, F. H. 1968, *A Brief History of Canadian Education*. Toronto: McGraw Hill Company of Canada Limited.

JOY, R. J. 1972, *Languages in Conflict*. Toronto: McClelland and Steward.

LAMONTAGNE, J. 1975, "Minority Language Education in Ontario and Quebec". In: R. ARÈS (ed.), *Les positions ethniques, linguistiques et religieuses des Canadiens français à la suite du recensement de 1971*. Montreal: Editions Bellarmin.

LIEBERSON, S. 1965, "Bilingualism in Montreal: A Demographic Analysis". *American Journal of Sociology*, LXXI, July, 10–25.

MAGNET, J. E. 1982, "The myth of equality in minority language rights", April 13. 7.

MALLEA, J. R. 1977, *Quebec's Language Policies: background and responses*. Quebec: CIRB, Les Presses de l'Université Laval.

— 1981, "Cultural Diversity and Canadian Education". In: J. W. GEORGE IVANY & M. E. MANLEY-CASIMER (eds), *Federal-Provincial Relations: Education Canada*. Toronto: OISE Press. pp. 91–104.

MALLEA, J. R., & YOUNG, J. C. (eds), *Cultural Diversity and Schooling in Canada: Issues and Innovations*. Ottawa: Oxford University Press (forthcoming).

MALLORY, J. R. 1976, The Evolution of Federalism in Canada. Paper presented as part of a Seminar on Federal Provincial Relations, Ottawa. Mimeographed, 15pp.

NEW BRUNSWICK *Schools Act* 1978. New Brunswick: Queen's Printer for New Brunswick, February.

O'BRYAN, K. G., REITZ, J. G., & KUPLOWSKA, O. 1976, *Non-Official Languages, A Study in Canadian Multiculturalism*. Ottawa: Ministry of Supply and Services Canada.

ONTARIO 1982, *Report of the Joint Committee on the Governance of French Language Elementary and Secondary Schools*. Toronto: Government of Ontario, April.

PALMER, H. 1978, *Immigration and the Rise of Multiculturalism*. Toronto: Copp Clark Publishing.

PROTESTANT SCHOOL BOARD OF GREATER MONTREAL 1980, *The Effect of Bill 101 on English Education and the Inherent Inequities in the Language Provisions of the Law*. October.

PROULX, J-P. 1980, *Rapport statistique sur l'activité du bureau de l'admissibilité à l'enseignement en Anglais*. Montréal.

QUEBEC 1966, Report of the Royal Commission of Inquiry in the Province of Quebec on Education. 4 vols. Quebec: Government of the Province of Quebec (Parent Report).

— 1972, *Report of the Commission of Inquiry on the Position of the French Language and on Language Rights in Quebec* (Gendron Commission). Québec: Editeur officiel du Québec.

— 1977, *Charte de la Langue Française*, LRQ, du c-11.

— 1982, *The Québec School: A Responsible Force in the Community*. Quebec: Ministry of Education.

QUEBEC FEDERATION OF HOME AND SCHOOL ASSOCIATIONS (QFHSA), 1975a, Summary of meeting with Department of Education of Quebec re Federal Provincial Programme on Bilingualism in Education. May 23, 1975.

— 1975b, Fact sheet — on Grants being received by the Province of Québec under the Federal-Provincial Programme for the Development of Bilingualism in Education. Mimeo. October 7, 1975.

— 1976, Brief to the Minister of Education on the use being made by the Government of Québec of the Formula Payments received by Québec under the terms of the Federal-Provincial Programme for the Development of Bilingualism in Education. Mimeo. April 19, 1976.

RIDOUT, E. B. 1977, *Policy Changes of the Ten Canadian Provinces Between 1967 and 1976 with respect to Second-Language Learning and Minority Language Education as expressed in Acts, Regulations, Directives, Memoranda, and Policy Statements of Provincial Departments and Ministries of Education*. Research Project funded by the Department of the Secretary of State. Mimeographed, 135pp.

SCHACHTER, S. (ed.) 1982, *Working Papers on English Language Institutions in Quebec*. Montreal: Alliance Quebec. March.

STATISTICS CANADA, 1982, *Minority and second language education, elementary and secondary levels 1980−81*. Ottawa: Minister of Supply and Services Canada.

STEIN, M. B., 1975, "Bill 22 and the Non-Francophone Population in Québec: A Case Study of Minority Group Attitudes on Language Legislation". In J. R. MALLEA, *Québec's Language Policies: Background and Response*. Québec: CIRB, Les Presses de l'Université Laval.

ST-GERMAIN, C., & MAHEU, R. 1981, *Mother Tongue and Language of Instruction in Quebec's Public Schools: Recent Evolution*. Quebec City: Ministry of Education of Quebec.

VANASSE, D. 1980, *L'évolution de la population scolaire du Québec*. Montreal: L'Institut de recherches politiques.

Appendix 1

SECOND SESSION

THIRTY-FIRST LEGISLATURE

ASSEMBLÉE NATIONALE DU QUÉBEC

Bill 101

Charter of the French language

ASSENTED TO 26 AUGUST 1977

CHARLES-HENRI DUBÉ, ÉDITEUR OFFICIEL DU QUÉBEC

1977

❧

Chapter C-11

CHARTER OF THE FRENCH LANGUAGE

PREAMBLE

Preamble.   Whereas the French language, the distinctive language of a people that is in the majority French-speaking, is the instrument by which that people has articulated its identity;

Whereas the Assemblée Nationale du Québec recognizes that Quebecers wish to see the quality and influence of the French language assured, and is resolved therefore to make of French the language of Gouvernement and the Law, as well as the normal and everyday language of work, instruction, communication, commerce and business;

Whereas the Assemblée Nationale du Québec intends in this pursuit to deal fairly and openly with the ethnic minorities, whose valuable contribution to the development of Québec it readily acknowledges;

Whereas the Assemblée Nationale du Québec recognizes the right of the Amerinds and the Inuit of Québec, the first inhabitants of this land, to preserve and develop their original language and culture;

Whereas these observations and intentions are in keeping with a new perception of the worth of national cultures in all parts of the earth, and of the obligation of every people to contribute in its special way to the international community;

Therefore, Her Majesty, with the advice and consent of the Assemblée nationale du Québec, enacts as follows:

TITLE I

STATUS OF THE FRENCH LANGUAGE

CHAPTER I

THE OFFICIAL LANGUAGE OF QUÉBEC

Official language.   **1.** French is the official language of Québec.

1977, c. 5, s. 1.

FRENCH LANGUAGE

CHAPTER II
FUNDAMENTAL LANGUAGE RIGHTS

Communications with public and private sectors.   **2.** Every person has a right to have the civil administration, the health services and social services, the public utility firms, the professional corporations, the associations of employees and all business firms doing business in Québec communicate with him in French.

1977, c. 5, s. 2.

In deliberative assembly.   **3.** In deliberative assembly, every person has a right to speak in French.

1977, c. 5, s. 3.

Workers.   **4.** Workers have a right to carry on their activities in French.

1977, c. 5, s. 4.

Consumers.   **5.** Consumers of goods and services have a right to be informed and served in French.

1977, c. 5, s. 5.

Instruction.   **6.** Every person eligible for instruction in Québec has a right to receive that instruction in French.

1977, c. 5, s. 6.

CHAPTER III
THE LANGUAGE OF THE LEGISLATURE AND THE COURTS

Legislature and courts.   **7.** French is the language of the legislature and the courts in Québec.

1977, c. 5, s. 7.

Bills.   **8.** Legislative bills shall be drafted in the official language. They shall also be tabled in the Assemblée nationale, passed and assented to in that language.

1977, c. 5, s. 8.

FRENCH LANGUAGE

Statutes and regulations.
9. Only the French text of the statutes and regulations is official.
1977, c. 5, s. 9.

English version.
10. An English version of every legislative bill, statute and regulation shall be printed and published by the civil administration.
1977, c. 5, s. 10.

Artificial persons before the courts.
11. Artificial persons addressing themselves to the courts and to bodies discharging judicial or quasi-judicial functions shall do so in the official language, and shall use the official language in pleading before them unless all the parties to the action agree to their pleading in English.
1977, c. 5, s. 11.

Procedural documents.
12. Procedural documents issued by bodies discharging judicial or quasi-judicial functions or drawn up and sent by the advocates practising before them shall be drawn up in the official language. Such documents may, however, be drawn up in another language if the natural person for whose intention they are issued expressly consents thereto.
1977, c. 5, s. 12.

Judgments.
13. The judgments rendered in Québec by the courts and by bodies discharging judicial or quasi-judicial functions must be drawn up in French or be accompanied with a duly authenticated French version. Only the French version of the judgment is official.
1977, c. 5, s. 13.

CHAPTER IV
THE LANGUAGE OF THE CIVIL ADMINISTRATION

Designation.
14. The Gouvernement, the government departments, the other agencies of the civil administration and the services thereof shall be designated by their French names alone.
1977, c. 5, s. 14.

Texts and documents.
15. The civil administration shall draw up and publish its texts and documents in the official language.

Exceptions.
This section does not apply to relations with persons outside Québec, to publicity and communiqués carried by news media that publish in a language other than French or to correspondence between the civil administration and natural persons when the latter address it in a language other than French.
1977, c. 5, s. 15.

Communication with other governments and artificial persons.
16. The civil administration shall use only the official language in its written communications with other governments and with artificial persons established in Québec.
1977, c. 5, s. 16.

Interdepartmental communications.
17. The Gouvernement, the government departments and the other agencies of the civil administration shall use only the official language in their written communications with each other.
1977, c. 5, s. 17, s. 14.

Internal communications.
18. French is the language of written internal communications in the Gouvernement, the government departments, and the other agencies of the civil administration.
1977, c. 5, s. 18, s. 14.

Notices of meeting.
19. The notices of meeting, agendas and minutes of all deliberative assemblies in the civil administration shall be drawn up in the official language.
1977, c. 5, s. 19.

Knowledge of French for appointment or promotion.
20. In order to be appointed, transferred or promoted to an office in the civil administration, a knowledge of the official language appropriate to the office applied for is required.

Criteria and procedures.
For the application of the preceding paragraph, each agency of the civil administration shall establish criteria and procedures of verification and submit them to the Office de la langue française for approval, failing which the Office may establish them itself. If the Office considers the criteria and procedures unsatisfactory, it may either request the agency concerned to modify them or establish them itself.
1977, c. 5, s. 20.

Contracts.
21. Contracts entered into by the civil administration, including the related sub-contracts, shall be drawn up in the official language. Such contracts and the related documents may be drawn up in

FRENCH LANGUAGE

another language when the civil administration enters into a contract with a party outside Québec.
1977, c. 5, s. 21.

Signs and posters. **22.** The civil administration shall use only French in signs and posters, except where reasons of public health or safety require the use of another language as well.
1977, c. 5, s. 22.

Health services and social services. Notices. Notices. **23.** The health services and the social services must ensure that their services are available in the official language.
They must draw up their notices, communications and printed matter intended for the public in the official language.
1977, c. 5, s. 23.

Recognized bodies and services: bilingual signs and posters. **24.** The municipal and school bodies, the health services and social services and the other services recognized under paragraph *f* of section 113 may erect signs and posters in both French and another language, the French text predominating.
1977, c. 5, s. 24.

Delay to comply. **25.** The municipal and school bodies, the health services and the social services recognized under paragraph *f* of section 113 must comply with sections 15 to 23 before the end of 1983 and, upon 26 August 1977, must take the required measures to attain that objective.
1977, c. 5, s. 25.

Bilingual names and internal communications. **26.** The school bodies, the health services and the social services recognized under paragraph *f* of section 113 may use both the official language and another language in their names and in their internal communications.
1977, c. 5, s. 26.

Clinical records in health services and social services. **27.** In the health services and the social services, the documents filed in the clinical records shall be drafted in French or in English, as the person drafting them sees fit. However, each health service or social service may require such documents to be drafted in French

FRENCH LANGUAGE

alone. Resumés of clinical records must be furnished in French on demand to any person authorized to obtain them.
1977, c. 5, s. 27.

Internal communication in school bodies. **28.** In the school bodies, the official language and the language of instruction may be used as the language of internal communication in departments entrusted with organizing or giving instruction in a language other than French.
1977, c. 5, s. 28.

Traffic signs. **29.** Only the official language shall be used on traffic signs. The French inscription may be complemented or replaced by symbols or pictographs.
1977, c. 5, s. 29.

CHAPTER V
THE LANGUAGE OF THE SEMIPUBLIC AGENCIES

Public utilities and professional corporations: services. **30.** The public utility firms, the professional corporations and the members of the professional corporations must arrange to make their services available in the official language.
Notices, tickets. They must draw up their notices, communications and printed matter intended for the public, including public transportation tickets, in the official language.
1977, c. 5, s. 30.

Written communications. **31.** The public utility firms and the professional corporations shall use the official language in their written communications with the civil administration and with artificial persons.
1977, c. 5, s. 31.

With general membership. **32.** The professional corporations shall use the official language in their written communications with their general membership.
Option: with individual member. They may, however, in communicating with an individual member, reply in his language.
1977, c. 5, s. 32.

Exceptions. **33.** Sections 30 and 31 do not apply to communiqués or publicity

FRENCH LANGUAGE

intended for news media that publish in a language other than French.

1977, c. 5, s. 33.

Professional corporations: designation.
34. The professional corporations shall be designated by their French names alone.

1977, c. 5, s. 34.

Appropriate knowledge of French.
35. The professional corporations shall not issue permits in Quebec except to persons whose knowledge of the official language is appropriate to the practice of their profession.

Proof.
Proof of that knowledge must be given in accordance with the regulations of the Office de la langue française, which may provide for the holding of examinations and the issuance of certificates.

1977, c. 5, s. 35.

Proof before diploma is obtained.
36. Within the last two years before obtaining a qualifying diploma for a permit to practise, every person enrolled in an educational institution that issues such diploma may give proof that his knowledge of the official language meets the requirements of section 35.

1977, c. 5, s. 36.

Temporary permit for outsiders.
37. The professional corporations may issue temporary permits valid for not more than one year to persons from outside Quebec who are declared qualified to practise their profession but whose knowledge of the official language does not meet the requirements of section 35.

1977, c. 5, s. 37.

Renewal.
38. The permits envisaged in section 37 may be renewed, only twice, with the authorization of the Office de la langue française and if the public interest warrants it. For each renewal, the persons concerned must sit for examinations held according to the regulations of the Office de la langue française.

1977, c. 5, s. 38.

Temporary permit for Quebec graduates.
39. Persons having obtained, in Quebec, a diploma referred to in section 36 may, until the end of 1980, avail themselves of sections 37 and 38.

1977, c. 5, s. 39.

FRENCH LANGUAGE

Restricted permit.
40. Where it is in the public interest, a professional corporation, with the prior authorization of the Office de la langue française, may issue a restricted permit to a person already authorized under the laws of another province or another country to practise his profession. This restricted permit authorizes its holder to practise his profession for the exclusive account of a single employer, in a position that does not involve his dealing with the public.

1977, c. 5, s. 40.

CHAPTER VI
THE LANGUAGE OF LABOUR RELATIONS

Employer's notices, offers.
41. Every employer shall draw up his written communications to his staff in the official language. He shall draw up and publish his offers of employment or promotion in French.

1977, c. 5, s. 41.

Offer of employment in newspaper.
42. Where an offer of employment regards employment in the civil administration, a semipublic agency or a firm required under section 136, 146 or 151 to have a francization certificate, establish a francization committee or apply a francization programme, as the case may be, the employer publishing this offer of employment in a daily newspaper published in a language other than French must publish it simultaneously in a daily newspaper published in French, with at least equivalent display.

1977, c. 5, s. 42.

Collective agreements.
43. Collective agreements and the schedules to them must be drafted in the official language, including those which must be filed pursuant to section 72 of the Labour Code (chapter C-27).

1977, c. 5, s. 43.

Arbitration awards.
44. Where a grievance or dispute regarding the negotiation, renewal or review of a collective labour agreement is the subject of arbitration, the arbitration award shall be drawn up in the official language or be accompanied with a duly authenticated French version. Only the French version of the award is official.

Decisions under Labour Code.
The same rule applies to decisions rendered under the Labour Code by investigators, investigation-commissioners and the Labour Court.

1977, c. 5, s. 44.

FRENCH LANGUAGE

Prohibition: dismissal, or demote for ignorance of other language.

45. An employer is prohibited from dismissing, laying off, demoting or transferring a member of his staff for the sole reason that he is exclusively French-speaking or that he has insufficient knowledge of a particular language other than French.

1977, c. 5, s. 45.

Prohibition: knowledge of other language as condition of employment.

Onus.

46. An employer is prohibited from making the obtaining of an employment or office dependent upon the knowledge of a language other than the official language, unless the nature of the duties requires the knowledge of that other language.

The burden of proof that the knowledge of the other language is necessary is on the employer, at the demand of the person or the association of employees concerned or, as the case may be, the Office de la langue française. The Office de la langue française has the power to decide any dispute.

1977, c. 5, s. 46.

Vindication of worker's rights under Labour code.

47. Any contravention of section 45 or 46, in addition to being an offence against this act, gives a worker not governed by a collective agreement the same entitlement to vindicate his rights through an investigation-commissioner appointed under the Labour Code as if he were dismissed for union activities. Sections 15 to 20 of the Labour Code then apply, *mutatis mutandis*.

Arbitration of grievance.

If the worker is governed by a collective agreement, he has the same entitlement to submit his grievance for arbitration as his association, if the latter fails to act. Section 16 of the Labour Code applies, *mutatis mutandis*, for the arbitration of this grievance.

1977, c. 5, s. 47.

Juridical acts null.

48. Except as they regard the vested rights of employees and their associations, juridical acts, decisions and other documents not in conformity to this chapter are null. The use of a language other than that prescribed in this chapter shall not be considered a defect of form within the meaning of section 151 of the Labour Code.

1977, c. 5, s. 48.

Associations of employees' written communications.

49. Every association of employees shall use the official language in written communications with its members. It may use the language of an individual member in its correspondence with him.

1977, c. 5, s. 49.

FRENCH LANGUAGE

Ss. 41 to 49 integral to all collective agreements.

50. Sections 41 to 49 of this act are deemed an integral part of every collective agreement. Any stipulation in the agreement contrary to any provision of this act is void.

1977, c. 5, s. 50.

CHAPTER VII

THE LANGUAGE OF COMMERCE AND BUSINESS

Labels, directions, warranties, menus: in French.

51. Every inscription on a product, on its container or on its wrapping, or on a leaflet, brochure or card supplied with it, including the directions for use and the warranty certificates, must be drafted in French. This rule applies also to menus and wine lists.

Other languages.

The French inscription may be accompanied with a translation or translations, but no inscription in another language may be given greater prominence than that in French.

1977, c. 5, s. 51.

Exceptions.

52. The Office de la langue française may, by regulation, indicate exceptions to the application of section 51.

1977, c. 5, s. 52.

Catalogues, brochures.

53. Catalogues, brochures, folders and similar publications must be drawn up in French.

1977, c. 5, s. 53.

Toys and games.

54. Except as provided by regulation of the Office de la langue française, it is forbidden to offer toys or games to the public which require the use of a non-French vocabulary for their operation, unless a French version of the toy or game is available on no less favourable terms on the Quebec market.

1977, c. 5, s. 54.

Contracts pre-determined by one party.

55. Contracts pre-determined by one party, contracts containing printed standard clauses, and the related documents, must be drawn up in French. They may be drawn up in another language as well at the express wish of the parties.

1977, c. 5, s. 55.

Exception.

56. If the documents referred to in section 51 are required by any act, order in council or government regulation, they may be excepted

FRENCH LANGUAGE

from the rule enunciated in that section, provided that the languages in which they are drafted are the subject of a federal-provincial, interprovincial or international agreement.

1977, c. 5, s. 56.

Application forms for employment.
57. Application forms for employment, order forms, invoices, receipts and quittances shall be drawn up in French.

1977, c. 5, s. 57.

Signs and posters.
58. Except as may be provided under this act or the regulations of the Office de la langue française, signs and posters and commercial advertising shall be solely in the official language.

1977, c. 5, s. 58.

Exceptions.
59. Sections 58 does not apply to advertising carried in news media that publish in a language other than French, or to messages of a religious, political, ideological or humanitarian nature, if not for a profit motive.

1977, c. 5, s. 59.

Firms employing not over four persons.
60. Firms employing not over four persons' including the employer may erect signs and posters in both French and another language in their establishments. However, the inscriptions in French must be given at least as prominent display as those in the other language.

1977, c. 5, s. 60.

Ethnic groups.
61. Signs and posters respecting the cultural activities of a particular ethnic group in any way may be in both French and the language of that ethnic group.

1977, c. 5, s. 61.

Foreign national specialities.
62. In commercial establishments specializing in foreign national specialities or the specialities of a particular ethnic group, signs and posters may be both in French and in the relevant foreign national language or the language of that ethnic group.

1977, c. 5, s. 62.

Firm names.
63. Firms names must be in French.

1977, c. 5, s. 63.

C-11 / 11

FRENCH LANGUAGE

Juridical personality.
64. To obtain juridical personality, it is necessary to have a firm name in French.

1977, c. 5, s. 64.

Delay to comply.
65. Every firm name that is not in French must be changed before 31 December 1980, unless the act under which the firm is incorporated does not allow it.

1977, c. 5, s. 65.

Firms registered under Companies and Partnerships Declaration Act.
66. Sections 63, 64 and 65 also apply to firm names registered under the Companies and Partnerships Declaration Act (chapter D-1).

1977, c. 5, s. 66.

Family names in firm names.
67. Family names, place names, expressions formed by the artificial combination of letters, syllables or figures, and expressions taken from other languages may appear in firm names to specify them, in accordance with the other acts and with the regulations of the Office de la langue française.

1977, c. 5, s. 67.

Firm names outside Quebec.
68. A firm name may be accompanied with a version in another language for use outside Québec. That version may be used together with the French version of the firm name in the inscriptions referred to in section 51, if the products in question are offered both in and outside Québec.

1977, c. 5, s. 68.

Firm names in Quebec.
69. Subject to section 68, only the French version of a firm name may be used in Québec.

1977, c. 5, s. 69.

Health services and social services.
70. Health services and social services the firm names of which, adopted before 26 August 1977, are in a language other than French may continue to use such names provided they add a French version.

1977, c. 5, s. 70.

Non-profit organizations.
71. A non-profit organization devoted exclusively to the cultural development or to the defense of the peculiar interests of a particular

C-11 / 12

FRENCH LANGUAGE

ethnic group may adopt a firm name in the language of the group, provided that it adds a French version.

1977, c. 5, s. 71.

CHAPTER VIII
THE LANGUAGE OF INSTRUCTION

Language of instruction. **72.** Instruction in the kindergarten classes and in the elementary and secondary schools shall be in French, except where this chapter allows otherwise.

Scope. This rule obtains in school bodies within the meaning of the Schedule and also applies to subsidized instruction provided by institutions declared to be of public interest or recognized for purposes of grants in virtue of the Act respecting private education (chapter E-9).

1977, c. 5, s. 72.

Derogation. **73.** In derogation of section 72, the following children, at the request of their father and mother, may receive their instruction in English:

(a) a child whose father or mother received his or her elementary instruction in English, in Québec;

(b) a child whose father or mother domiciled in Québec on 26 August 1977, received his or her elementary instruction in English outside Québec;

(c) a child who, in his last year of school in Québec before 26 August 1977, was lawfully receiving his instruction in English, in a public kindergarten class or in an elementary or secondary school;

(d) the younger brothers and sisters of a child described in paragraph c.

1977, c. 5, s. 73.

Request by parent or tutor. **74.** Where a child is in the custody of only one of his parents, or of a tutor, the request provided for in section 73 must be made by that parent or by the tutor.

1977, c. 5, s. 74.

Verification of eligibility. **75.** The Minister of Education may empower such persons as he may designate to verify and decide on children's eligibility for instruction in English.

1977, c. 5, s. 75.

FRENCH LANGUAGE

Verification of eligibility. **76.** The persons designated by the Minister of Education under section 75 may verify the eligibility of children to receive their elementary instruction in English even if they are already receiving or are about to receive their instruction in French.

Effect of confirmation of eligibility. Children whose eligibility has been confirmed in accordance with the preceding paragraph are deemed to receive their instruction in English for the purposes of section 73.

1977, c. 5, s. 76.

Fraud. **77.** A certificate of eligibility obtained fraudulently or on the basis of a false representation is void.

1977, c. 5, s. 77.

Revocation of certificate. **78.** The Minister of Education may revoke a certificate of eligibility issued in error.

1977, c. 5, s. 78.

Authorization to introduce instruction in English. **79.** A school body not already giving instruction in English in its schools is not required to introduce it and shall not introduce it without express and prior authorization of the Minister of Education.

Arrangements for eligible children. However, every school body shall, where necessary, avail itself of section 450 of the Education Act to arrange for the instruction in English of any child declared eligible therefor.

Authorization at Minister's discretion. The Minister of Education shall grant the authorization referred to in the first paragraph if, in his opinion, it is warranted by the number of pupils in the jurisdiction of the school body who are eligible for instruction in English under section 73.

1977, c. 5, s. 79.

Procedure and proof. **80.** The Gouvernement may, by regulation, prescribe the procedure to be followed where parents invoke section 73, and the elements of proof they must furnish in support of their request.

1977, c. 5, s. 80, s. 14.

Exempt children. **81.** Children having serious learning disabilities must be exempted from the application of this chapter.

Regulation: exemption. The Gouvernement, by regulation, may define the classes of children envisaged in the preceding paragraph and determine the procedure to be followed in view of obtaining such an exemption.

1977, c. 5, s. 81, s. 14.

FRENCH LANGUAGE

Appeal.
82. An appeal lies from the decisions of the school bodies, the institutions mentioned in the second paragraph of section 72, and the persons designated by the Minister of Education, dealing with the application of section 73, and from the decisions of the Minister of Education taken under section 78.
1977, c. 5, s. 82.

Appeals committee.
83. An appeals committee is established to hear appeals provided for in section 82. This committee consists of three members appointed by the Gouvernement. Appeals are brought in accordance with the procedure established by regulation. The decisions of this committee are final.
1977, c. 5, s. 83, s. 14.

Secondary school leaving certificate.
84. No secondary school leaving certificate may be issued to a student who does not have the speaking and writing knowledge of French required by the curricula of the Ministère de l'éducation.
1977, c. 5, s. 84.

Temporary residents.
85. The Gouvernement, by regulation, may determine the conditions on which certain persons or categories of persons staying in Quebec temporarily, or their children, may be exempted from the application of this chapter.
1977, c. 5, s. 85, s. 14.

Reciprocity agreement.
86. The Gouvernement may make regulations extending the scope of section 73 to include such persons as may be contemplated in any reciprocity agreement that may be concluded between the Gouvernement of Quebec and another province.

Coming into force.
Notwithstanding section 94, such regulations may come into force from their date of publication in the *Gazette officielle du Québec*.
1977, c. 5, s. 86, s. 14.

Instruction to the Amerinds.
87. Nothing in this act prevents the use of an Amerindic language in providing instruction to the Amerinds.
1977, c. 5, s. 87.

Instruction to the Cree and Inuit.
88. Notwithstanding sections 72 to 86, in the schools under the jurisdiction of the Cree School Board or the Kativik School Board, according to the Education Act, the languages of instruction shall be Cree and Inutituut, respectively, and the other languages of instruction in use in the Cree and Inuit communities in Québec on the date of the signing of the Agreement indicated in section 1 of the Act approving the Agreement concerning James Bay and Northern Québec (chapter C-67), namely, 11 November 1975.

Cree School Board and the Kativik School Board.
The Cree School Board and the Kativik School Board shall pursue as an objective the use of French as a language of instruction so that pupils graduating from their schools will in future be capable of continuing their studies in a French school, college or university elsewhere in Quebec, if they so desire.

Rate of introduction of French and English.
After consultation with the school committees, in the case of the Crees, and with the parents' committees, in the case of the Inuit, the commissioners shall determine the rate of introduction of French and English as languages of instruction.

Non-qualifying Crees or Inuit.
With the assistance of the Ministère de l'éducation, the Cree School Board and the Kativik School Board shall take the necessary measures to have sections 72 to 86 apply to children whose parents are not Crees or Inuit qualifying for benefit under the Agreement.

Naskapi of Schefferville.
This section, with the necessary changes, applies to the Naskapi of Schefferville.
1977, c. 5, s. 88.

CHAPTER IX
MISCELLANEOUS

French use exclusive only if specified.
89. Where this act does not require the use of the official language exclusively, the official language and another language may be used together.
1977, c. 5, s. 89.

Statutory publication may be in French only.
90. Subject to section 10, anything that, by prescription of an act of Québec or an act of the British Parliament having application to Quebec in a field of provincial jurisdiction, or of a regulation or an order, must be published in French and English may be published in French alone.

Publication in French newspaper.
Similarly, anything that, by prescription of an act, a regulation or an order, must be published in a French newspaper and in an English newspaper, may be published in a French newspaper alone.
1977, c. 5, s. 90.

Prominence of French version.
91. Where this act authorizes the drafting of texts or documents both in French and in one or more other languages, the French

FRENCH LANGUAGE

version must be displayed at least as prominently as every other language.

1977, c. 5, s. 91.

International organizations.

92. Nothing prevents the use of a language in derogation of this act by international organizations designated by the Gouvernement or where international usage requires it.

1977, c. 5, s. 92, s. 14.

Regulations.

93. In addition to its other regulation-making powers under this act, the Gouvernement may make regulations to facilitate the administration of the act, including regulations specifying the scope of the terms and expressions used in the act.

1977, c. 5, s. 93, s. 14.

Coming into force.

94. The regulations of the Office de la langue française or of the Gouvernement made under this act come into force from their publication in the *Gazette officielle du Québec* together with a notice of the date of their approval or adoption by the Gouvernement, whichever applies.

Prior notice of draft regulations.

The Gouvernement, before adopting or approving a regulation under this act, must publish the draft regulation in the *Gazette officielle du Québec* at least sixty days previously, except regulations tabled in the Assemblée nationale before 26 August 1977.

Amendments.

If a regulation of the Office de la langue française or of the Gouvernement is amended, the amended text comes into force on its publication in full in the *Gazette officielle du Québec*.

Regulations of the Office.

Regulations ascribed by this act to the Office de la langue française, approved and tabled before 26 August 1977, are deemed regulations of the Office de la langue française.

1977, c. 5, s. 94, s. 14.

Right to use Cree and Inuttuut.

95. The following persons and bodies have the right to use Cree and Inuttuut and are exempt from the application of this act, except sections 87, 88 and 96:

(a) persons qualified for benefit under the Agreement indicated in section 1 of the Act approving the Agreement concerning James Bay and Northern Québec (chapter C-67), in the territories envisaged by the said Agreement;

(b) bodies to be created under the said Agreement, within the territories envisaged by the Agreement;

(c) bodies of which the members are in the majority persons

FRENCH LANGUAGE

Naskapi of Schefferville.

referred to in subparagraph a, within the territories envisaged by the Agreement.

This section, with the necessary changes, applies to the Naskapi of Schefferville.

1977, c. 5, s. 95.

Introduction of French.

96. The bodies envisaged in section 95 must introduce the use of French into their administration, both to communicate in French with the rest of Québec and with those persons under their administration who are not contemplated in subparagraph a of that section, and to provide their services in French to those persons.

Transitional period.

During a transitional period of such duration as the Gouvernement may fix after consultation with the persons concerned, sections 16 and 17 of this act do not apply to communications of the civil administration with the bodies envisaged in section 95.

Naskapi of Schefferville.

This section, with the necessary changes, applies to the Naskapi of Schefferville.

1977, c. 5, s. 96, s. 14.

Indian reserves.

97. The Indian reserves are not subject to this act.

1977, c. 5, s. 97.

Agencies contemplated.

98. The various agencies of the civil administration, and the health services and social services, the public utility firms and the professional corporations referred to in this act are listed in the Schedule.

1977, c. 5, s. 98.

TITLE II

THE OFFICE DE LA LANGUE FRANÇAISE AND FRANCIZATION

CHAPTER I

INTERPRETATION

Interpretation: "Commission"; "Minister".

99. In this title,

(a) "Commission" means the Commission de toponymie established by this title;

(b) "Minister" means the Minister responsible for the application of this act;

FRENCH LANGUAGE

"Office"

(c) "Office" means the Office de la langue française established by this title.

1977, c. 5, s. 99.

CHAPTER II
THE OFFICE DE LA LANGUE FRANÇAISE

Office established.

100. An Office de la langue française is established to define and conduct Québec policy on linguistics research and terminology and to see that the French language becomes, as soon as possible, the language of communication, work, commerce and business in the civil administration and business firms.

1977, c. 5, s. 100.

Members and terms.

101. The Office is composed of five members, including a president, appointed by the Gouvernement for not more than five years.

1977, c. 5, s. 101, 14.

Staff

102. The staff of the Office shall be appointed and remunerated under the Civil Service Act (chapter F-3).

1977, c. 5, s. 102.

President's powers.

103. The president shall exercise in regard to the members of the staff of the Office the powers vested by the Civil Service Act in the deputy-heads of departments.

1977, c. 5, s. 103.

Emoluments.

104. The Gouvernement shall fix the fees, allowances or salary of the president and of the other members of the Office or, as the case may be, their additional salary.

1977, c. 5, s. 104, s. 14.

No plurality of offices.

105. The duties of president of the Office are incompatible with any other duties.

1977, c. 5, s. 105.

FRENCH LANGUAGE

Replacement of president.

106. If the president is unable to act, he shall be replaced by another member appointed by the Gouvernement.

1977, c. 5, s. 106, s. 14.

Personal interest.
At discretion of Office.

107. No member of the Office shall participate in the discussion of a question in which he has a personal interest. The Office shall decide if he has a personal interest. The member concerned shall not participate in that decision.

1977, c. 5, s. 107.

Quorum.

108. Three members shall constitute a quorum of the Office. In case of a tie-vote, the president shall have a casting vote.

1977, c. 5, s. 108.

Term continued.

109. At the expiry of their term, the president and the other members of the Office shall remain in office until they are reappointed or replaced.

1977, c. 5, s. 109.

Head office.
Other office.
Place of sittings.

110. The seat of the Office shall be in the City of Québec or in the City of Montréal, as the Gouvernement may decide.
The Office shall have an office in both cities.
The Office may hold its sittings at any place in Québec.

1977, c. 5, s. 110, s. 14.

Minutes authentic:

111. The minutes of the sittings approved by the Office and certified true by the president or the secretary are authentic. The same applies to documents or copies emanating from the Office or forming part of its records when they are signed by the president or the secretary of the Office.

1977, c. 5, s. 111.

Immunity.

112. The members and staff of the Office cannot be prosecuted by reason of official acts done in good faith by them in the performance of their duties.

1977, c. 5, s. 112.

Duties of the Office.

113. The Office shall
(a) standardize and publicize the terms and expressions approved by it;

FRENCH LANGUAGE

(b) establish the research programmes necessary for the application of this act;

(c) draft the regulations within its competence that are necessary for the application of this act and submit them for consideration to the Conseil de la langue française, in accordance with section 188;

(d) define, by regulation, the procedure for the issue, suspension or cancellation of the francization certificate;

(e) assist in defining and preparing the francization programmes provided for by this act and oversee the application thereof;

(f) recognize, on the one hand, the municipal bodies, school bodies, health services and social services that provide services to persons who, in the majority, speak a language other than French, and, on the other hand, the departments that have charge or organizing and giving instruction in a language other than French in the school bodies.

1977, c. 5, s. 113.

Powers. **114.** The Office may

(a) adopt regulations within its competence under this act, which shall be submitted for examination to the Conseil de la langue française;

(b) establish terminology committees and determine their composition and their terms and conditions of operation and, as may be required, delegate such committees to the departments and agencies of the civil administration;

(c) adopt internal management by-laws subject to approval by the Gouvernement;

(d) establish by by-law the services and committees necessary for the attainment of its purposes;

(e) subject to the Act respecting the Ministère des affaires intergouvernementales (chapter M-21), make agreements with any other agency or any government to facilitate the application of this act;

(f) require every teaching institution at the college or university level to file a report on the language used in its manuals and state its observations in that respect in its annual report;

(g) assist the agencies of the civil administration, the semi-public agencies, business firms, the different associations, and individuals, in refining and enriching spoken and written French in Québec.

1977, c. 5, s. 114, s. 14.

Co-operation by departments. **115.** The Gouvernement may, by regulation, prescribe the measures of co-operation with the Office that must be taken by the departments and other agencies of the civil administration.

1977, c. 5, s. 115, s. 14.

FRENCH LANGUAGE

Mandate of terminology committees. **116.** The mandate of the terminology committees established by the Office shall be to make an inventory of the technical words and expressions in use in the sector assigned to them, to indicate any lacunae that become apparent, and to prepare a list of the technical words and expressions they recommend.

1977, c. 5, s. 116.

Approval of conclusions. **117.** Once their work has been completed, the terminology committees shall submit their conclusions to the Office for approval.

1977, c. 5, s. 117.

Use of terms obligatory. **118.** Upon publication in the *Gazette officielle du Québec* the terms and expressions standardized by the Office, their use becomes obligatory in texts and documents emanating from the civil administration, in contracts to which it is a party, in teaching manuals and educational and research works published in French in Québec and approved by the Minister of Education, and in signs and posters.

1977, c. 5, s. 118.

Annual report. **119.** Not later than 31 October every year, the Office must submit a report of its activities for the preceding fiscal year to the Minister.

1977, c. 5, s. 119.

Tabling. **120.** The Minister shall table such report in the Assemblée nationale within thirty days following its receipt. If he receives it while the Assemblée nationale is not sitting, he shall table it within thirty days after the opening of the next session or after resumption.

1977, c. 5, s. 120.

Immunity. **121.** No civil action may be brought by reason of the publication in good faith of the whole or a part of the reports of the Office, or of resumés of such reports.

1977, c. 5, s. 121.

CHAPTER III

THE COMMISSION DE TOPONYMIE

Commission established. **122.** A Commission de toponymie is established at the Office de

FRENCH LANGUAGE

la langue française and is incorporated into it for administrative purposes.

1977, c. 5, s. 122.

Composition. **123.** The Commission is composed of seven persons appointed by the Gouvernement, at least four of whom, including the chairman and secretary, are members of the permanent staff of the Office. The Gouvernement shall fix the remuneration and indemnities of the non-permanent members of the Commission.

1977, c. 5, s. 123, s. 14.

Competence. **124.** The Commission has competence to establish the criteria of selection and rules of spelling of all place names and to make the final decision on the assignment of names to places not already named and to approve any change of place names.

1977, c. 5, s. 124.

Duties. **125.** The Commission shall:

(a) establish the standards and rules of spelling to be followed in place names;

(b) catalogue and preserve place names;

(c) establish and standardize geographical terminology, in cooperation with the Office;

(d) officialize place names;

(e) publicize the official geographical nomenclature of Québec;

(f) advise the Gouvernement on any question submitted by it to the Commission relating to toponymy.

1977, c. 5, s. 125, s. 14.

Powers. **126.** The Commission may:

(a) advise the Gouvernement and other agencies of the civil administration on any question relating to toponymy;

(b) make regulations on the criteria of selection of place names, on the rules of spelling to be followed in the matter of toponymy and on the method to be followed in naming places and approving the names given them;

(c) in unorganised territories, name geographical places or change their names;

(d) with the consent of the agency of the civil administration having concurrent jurisdiction over the place name, determine or change the name of any place in an organized territory.

The regulations of the Commission shall be submitted to the requirements of section 94 as if they were regulations of the Office.

1977, c. 5, s. 126, s. 14.

FRENCH LANGUAGE

Publication. **127.** The names approved by the Commission during the year must be published at least once a year in the *Gazette officielle du Québec*.

1977, c. 5, s. 127.

Use of names obligatory. **128.** Upon the publication in the *Gazette officielle du Québec* of the names chosen or approved by the Commission, the use of such names becomes obligatory in texts and documents of the civil administration and the semipublic agencies, in traffic signs, in public signs and posters and in teaching manuals and educational and research works published in Québec and approved by the Minister of Education.

1977, c. 5, s. 128.

CHAPTER IV

FRANCIZATION OF THE CIVIL ADMINISTRATION

Francization programme. **129.** Every agency of the civil administration requiring a delay to comply with certain provisions of this act or to ensure the generalized use of French in its domain must as soon as possible adopt a francization programme under the authority and with the assistance of the Office.

1977, c. 5, s. 129.

Near retirement, long service. **130.** The francization programmes must take into account the situation of persons nearing retirement or having a long record of service with the civil administration.

1977, c. 5, s. 130.

Report. **131.** Every agency of the civil administration must, before 31 December 1978, submit to the Office a report including an analysis of the language situation in that agency and an account of the measures it has adopted in view of complying with this act.

Form and content. The Office shall determine the form of such report and the information it must furnish.

1977, c. 5, s. 131.

Hearing. **132.** If the Office considers the adopted or envisaged measures insufficient, it shall hear the persons concerned and have the documents and information it considers essential forwarded to it.

Correctives. It shall prescribe appropriate correctives, if needed.

FRENCH LANGUAGE

Offence.	Any agency refusing to implement such correctives is guilty of an offence. 1977, c. 5, s. 132.
Exemption.	**133.** For a period of not more than one year, the Office may exempt from the application of any provision of this act any service or agency of the civil administration that requests it, if it is satisfied with the measures taken by that service or agency towards the objectives set by this act and the regulations. 1977, c. 5, s. 133.
Action authorized by the Office.	**134.** No action may be instituted, without the express authorization of the Office, against any agency of the civil administration for an offence against sections 14 to 29 and 129 to 132 committed before 31 December 1978. 1977, c. 5, s. 134.

CHAPTER V
FRANCIZATION OF BUSINESS FIRMS

Scope.	**135.** This chapter also applies to public utility firms. 1977, c. 5, s. 135.
Fifty or more employees: certificate.	**136.** Business firms employing fifty or more employees must, from the date determined under section 152, which shall not be later than 31 December 1983, hold a francization certificate issued by the Office. 1977, c. 5, s. 136.
Offence.	**137.** From 3 January 1979, any firm required to hold a francization certificate is guilty of an offence if it does not hold one. 1977, c. 5, s. 137.
Francization certificate.	**138.** A francization certificate attests that the business firm is applying a francization programme approved by the Office, or that French already enjoys the status in the firm that such programmes are designed to ensure. 1977, c. 5, s. 138.

FRENCH LANGUAGE

Provisional certificate.	**139.** The Office may, by regulation, provide for the issue of francization certificates, provisionally, to business firms that plan to adopt a francization programme, if they show that they have made the appropriate arrangements. 1977, c. 5, s. 139.
Certification.	**140.** The Office shall grant a francization certificate to a business firm if it is of opinion that such firm complies with the requirements provided for in section 138 or 139. 1977, c. 5, s. 140.
Object of francization programme. Objectives of francization programme.	**141.** The francization programme is intended to generalize the use of French at all levels of the business firm. This implies: (a) the knowledge of the official language on the part of management, the members of the professional corporations and the other members of the staff; (b) an increase at all levels of the business firm, including the board of directors, in the number of persons having a good knowledge of the French language so as to generalize its use; (c) the use of French as the language of work and as the language of internal communication; (d) the use of French in the working documents of the business firm, especially in manuals and catalogues; (e) the use of French in communications with clients, suppliers and the public; (f) the use of French terminology; (g) the use of French in advertising; (h) appropriate policies for hiring, promotion and transfer. 1977, c. 5, s. 141.
Near retirement, long service.	**142.** Francization programmes must take account of the situation of persons who are near retirement or of persons who have long records of service with the business firm. 1977, c. 5, s. 142.
Extra-provincial dealings.	**143.** Francization programmes must take account of the situation relations of business firms with the exterior and of the particular case of head offices established in Québec by business firms whose activities extend outside Québec. 1977, c. 5, s. 143.

FRENCH LANGUAGE

Head offices: Special agreements.

144. The manner of applying francization programmes in head offices may be decided by special agreements with the Office. While any such agreement remains in force, the head office concerned is deemed to be observing sections 136 to 156. The Office, by regulation, shall define "head office" and recognize such head offices as may avail themselves of this section.

1977, c. 5, s. 144.

Cultural goods: Language content.

145. In business firms producing cultural goods having a language content, francization programmes must take account of the particular situation of production units whose work is directly related to such language content.

1977, c. 5, s. 145.

One hundred or more employees: Francization committee.

146. Business firms employing one hundred or more employees must, before 30 November 1977, form a francization committee composed of at least six persons to which at least one-third of the members are appointed in accordance with section 147 to represent the workers of the firm.

1977, c. 5, s. 146.

Designation of workers' representatives.

147. Where one association of employees only is certified to represent the majority of the workers of a business firm, that association shall designate the workers' representatives contemplated in section 146.

Designation of workers' representatives.

Where several associations of employees are certified to represent, together, the majority of the workers of a business firm, such associations may, by agreement, designate the workers' representatives contemplated in section 146.

Designation of workers' representatives.

In the absence of an agreement, or in other cases, such representatives shall be elected by the whole body of the workers of the business firm in accordance with the terms and conditions determined by the management of the firm.

1977, c. 5, s. 147.

Subcommittees.

148. The francization committee of the business firm may form subcommittees operating under its authority.

1977, c. 5, s. 148.

Analysis.

149. Using the forms and questionnaires furnished by the Office, the francization committee shall analyse the language situation in the

FRENCH LANGUAGE

firm and make a return to the management of the firm, for forwarding to the Office.

1977, c. 5, s. 149.

Decision.

150. After studying the return referred to in section 149, the Office shall decide whether or not the business firm must adopt and apply a francization programme. If the decision is that it must, the firm shall entrust the drafting of the appropriate programme, and the supervision of its application, to its francization committee.

1977, c. 5, s. 150.

Under fifty employees.

151. The Office may, with the approval of the Minister, and on condition of a notice in the *Gazette officielle du Québec*, require a business firm employing less than fifty persons to analyse its language situation and to prepare and implement a francization programme.

Under fifty employees.

The Office must make a return to the Minister every year of the representations it has made in this regard and of the measures taken by the business firms.

1977, c. 5, s. 151.

Regulation: classification of firms.

152. The Office may, by regulation, establish classes of business firms according to the nature of their activities and the number of persons they employ. For each class so established, it may fix the date on which francization certificates become exigible, set the terms on which certificates are issued and prescribe the obligations of the firms holding certificates.

Criteria.

The Office may, in the same manner, establish criteria for recognizing firms as belonging to the class of business firms employing fifty or more persons or to that of business firms employing one hundred or more persons and for the purposes of this chapter define the expression "business firm".

1977, c. 5, s. 152.

Temporary exemption.

153. When granting a francization certificate, even provisionally, the Office may temporarily exempt the business firm from the application of any provision of this act. It shall notify the Commission de surveillance de la langue française established in Title III.

1977, c. 5, s. 153.

Suspension or cancellation of certificate.

154. The Office may suspend or cancel the certificate of every business firm failing to comply with the francization programme it

FRENCH LANGUAGE

has undertaken to follow, or no longer observing its obligations under this act and the regulations.
1977, c. 5, s. 154.

Appeal. **155.** An appeal lies from a decision of the Office refusing, suspending or cancelling a francization certificate.

Appeals committee. The appeal is brought before an appeals committee established by the Gouvernement for such purpose, following the procedure it may establish.

Composition. The appeals committee consists of three members appointed by the Gouvernement.
1977, c. 5, s. 155, s. 14.

Return of cancellations. **156.** In its annual return, the Office shall indicate the cancellations of certificates it has declared, and the business firms having failed to obtain francization certificates within the prescribed delay or to form the francization committee provided for in section 146.
1977, c. 5, s. 156.

TITLE III
THE COMMISSION DE SURVEILLANCE AND INQUIRIES

Interpretation: **157.** In this title,
"*Commission de surveillance*": (a) "Commission de surveillance" means the Commission de surveillance de la langue française established by this title;
"*Minister*": (b) "Minister" designates the Minister responsible for the application of this act;
"*Office*": (c) "Office" means the Office de la langue française;
"*chairman*": (d) "chairman" designates the chairman of the Commission de surveillance.
1977, c. 5, s. 157.

Commission established. **158.** A Commission de surveillance is established to deal with questions relating to failures to comply with this act.
1977, c. 5, s. 158.

Composition. **159.** The Commission de surveillance is under the direction of a

FRENCH LANGUAGE

chairman and is composed of investigation commissioners, inspectors and the other necessary staff.
1977, c. 5, s. 159.

Term of chairman. **160.** The chairman of the Commission de surveillance shall be appointed by the Gouvernement for not more than five years.
1977, c. 5, s. 160, s. 14.

Investigation commissioners, inspectors, staff. **161.** The investigation commissioners, inspectors and the other members of the staff of the Commission de surveillance shall be appointed and remunerated under the Civil Service Act.
1977, c. 5, s. 161.

Chairman's powers. **162.** The chairman shall exercise in regard to the investigation-commissioners, inspectors and the other members of the staff of the Commission de surveillance the powers granted by the Civil Service Act to the deputy-heads of departments.
1977, c. 5, s. 162.

Chairman's emoluments. **163.** The Gouvernement shall fix the fees, allowances or salary of the chairman or, as the case may be, his additional salary.
1977, c. 5, s. 163, s. 14.

No plurality of offices. **164.** The duties of chairman of the Commission de surveillance are incompatible with any other duties.
1977, c. 5, s. 164.

Replacement of chairman. **165.** If the chairman is unable to act, his powers shall be exercised by a person appointed by the Gouvernement.
1977, c. 5, s. 165, s. 14.

Term continued. **166.** At the expiry of his term, the chairman shall remain in office until he is reappointed or replaced.
1977, c. 5, s. 166.

Chairman's functions. **167.** In addition to his attributions under section 162, the chairman shall direct, coordinate and assign the work of the investigation commissioners, inspectors and other members of the

FRENCH LANGUAGE

staff of the Commission de surveillance. He may himself exercise the functions of an investigation commissioner.
1977, c. 5, s. 167.

Immunity. **168.** The investigation commissioners and the staff of the Commission de surveillance cannot be prosecuted for acts done in good faith in the performance of their duties.
1977, c. 5, s. 168.

Inquiries. **169.** The investigation commissioners shall make the inquiries provided for by this act.
1977, c. 5, s. 169.

Inspectors. **170.** The inspectors shall assist the investigation commissioners in the performance of their duties, verify and establish facts that may constitute offences against this act and submit reports and recommendations to the investigation commissioners on the facts established.
1977, c. 5, s. 170.

Inquiries. **171.** The investigation commissioners shall make an inquiry whenever they have reason to believe that this act has not been observed.
1977, c. 5, s. 171.

Inquiries. **172.** Business firms to which the Office has issued or is about to issue a francization certificate are subject to an inquiry where so requested by the Office.
1977, c. 5, s. 172.

Petition for inquiry. **173.** Any person or group of persons may petition for an inquiry.
1977, c. 5, s. 173.

Petitions in writing. **174.** Petitions for inquiry must be in writing and be accompanied with indications of the grounds on which they are based and identification of the petitioners. The identity of a petitioner may be disclosed only with his express authorization.
1977, c. 5, s. 174.

FRENCH LANGUAGE

Assistance of investigation commissioners. **175.** The petitioners are entitled to the assistance of the investigation commissioners and their staff to draw up their petitions.
1977, c. 5, s. 175.

Refusing inquiry. **176.** The investigation commissioners must refuse to make an inquiry
(a) if they do not have the required competence under the terms of this act;
(b) if the question is within the jurisdiction of the Public Protector or the Commission des droits de la personne;
(c) if the grounds for a petition no longer exist at the time it is filed;
(d) if the petition is frivolous or in bad faith.
In the case contemplated in subparagraph b, the investigation commissioners shall forward the record to the Public Protector or to the Commission des droits de la personne, as the case may be.
1977, c. 5, s. 176.

Record to Public Protector.

Refusing inquiry. **177.** The investigation commissioners may refuse to make an inquiry if, in their opinion,
(a) the petitioner disposes of an appeal or of an appropriate recourse;
(b) the ground for complaint will no longer exist at the time the inquiry is to begin;
(c) the circumstances do not justify it.
1977, c. 5, s. 177.

Notice of refusal. **178.** If they refuse the petition, the investigation commissioners must notify the petitioners, giving them the reasons for their refusal and advising them of their right of recourse, if any.
1977, c. 5, s. 178.

Powers and immunity of commissioners. **179.** For their inquiries, the investigation commissioners and the inspectors delegated by them are vested with the powers and immunity granted commissioners appointed under the Act respecting public inquiry commissions (chapter C-37).
1977, c. 5, s. 179.

Certificate of office. **180.** Investigation commissioners and the inspectors delegated by

FRENCH LANGUAGE

them must on demand produce a certificate of office signed by the chairman of the Commission de surveillance.

1977, c. 5, s. 180.

Code of Civil Procedure applies.
181. Articles 307, 308 and 309 of the Code of Civil Procedure apply to witnesses heard by the investigation commissioners and the inspectors delegated by them.

1977, c. 5, s. 181.

Putting in default.
182. When, after an inquiry, an investigation commissioner considers that this act or the regulations hereunder have been contravened, he may put the alleged offender in default to conform within a given delay.

Record to Attorney-General.
If the investigation commissioner considers that the offence has continued beyond such delay, he shall forward the record to the Attorney-General for his consideration and, if necessary, institution by him of appropriate penal proceedings.

1977, c. 5, s. 182.

Annual report.
183. Not later than 31 October each year, the Commission de surveillance must submit to the Minister a report of its activities for the preceding fiscal year.

Content.
The report of the Commission de surveillance shall indicate the inquiries made, the proceedings instituted and the results obtained.

1977, c. 5, s. 183.

Tabling.
184. The Minister shall table the report of the Commission de surveillance in the Assemblée nationale within thirty days after he receives it. If he receives it while the Assemblée nationale is not sitting, he shall table it within thirty days after the opening of the next session or after resumption.

1977, c. 5, s. 184.

TITLE IV

THE CONSEIL DE LA LANGUE FRANÇAISE

Interpretation: "Conseil"; "Minister":
185. In this title,
(a) "Conseil" means the Conseil de la langue française;
(b) "Minister" designates the Minister entrusted with the application of this act;

FRENCH LANGUAGE

"Office":
(c) "Office" means the Office de la langue française.

1977, c. 5, s. 185.

Conseil established.
186. A Conseil de la langue française is established to advise the Minister on Quebec language policy with regard to the French language and on any question relating to the interpretation and application of this act.

1977, c. 5, s. 186.

Composition.
187. The Conseil shall be composed of twelve members, appointed by the Gouvernement, namely:
(a) the chairman and a secretary;
(b) two persons chosen after consultation with the representative socio-cultural associations;
(c) two persons chosen after consultation with the representative union bodies;
(d) two persons chosen after consultation with the representative management groups;
(e) two persons chosen after consultation with the universities;
(f) two persons chosen after consultation with the representative associations of the ethnic groups.

1977, c. 5, s. 187, s. 14.

Duties.
188. The Conseil shall:
(a) advise the Minister on the questions he submits to it relating to the situation of the French language in Quebec and the interpretation or application of this act;
(b) keep a watch on language developments in Quebec with respect to the status and quality of the French language and communicate its findings and conclusions to the Minister;
(c) apprise the Minister of the questions pertaining to language that in its opinion require attention or action by the Gouvernement;
(d) advise the Minister on the regulations prepared by the Office.

1977, c. 5, s. 188, s. 14.

Powers.
189. The Conseil may:
(a) receive and hear observations of and suggestions from individuals or groups on questions relating to the status and quality of the French language;
(b) with the approval of the Minister, undertake the study of any question pertaining to language and carry out or have others carry out any appropriate research;
(c) receive the observations of any agency of the civil

FRENCH LANGUAGE

administration or business firm on the difficulties encountered in the application of this act and report to the Minister;

(d) inform the public on questions regarding the French language in Québec;

(e) adopt internal management by-laws, subject to approval by the Gouvernement.

1977, c. 5, s. 189, s. 14.

Term of office.
Term of office.
190. The chairman and the secretary shall be appointed for not more than five years and the other members for four years.

However, three of the first members other than the chairman shall be appointed for one year, three for two years, two for three years and two for four years.

Renewal.
The term of office of the members of the Conseil may be renewed.

1977, c. 5, s. 190.

Continuation.
191. At the expiry of their term, the members of the Conseil shall remain in office until they are reappointed or replaced.

1977, c. 5, s. 191.

Replacement of member.
192. In the case where a member does not complete his term, the Gouvernement shall replace him, in the mode prescribed in section 187, for the remainder of his term.

1977, c. 5, s. 192, s. 14.

Chairman's functions.
193. The chairman shall direct the activities of the Conseil and coordinate its work; he shall be responsible for liaison between the Conseil and the Minister.

1977, c. 5, s. 193.

No plurality of offices.
194. The duties of chairman or secretary of the Conseil are incompatible with any other duties.

1977, c. 5, s. 194.

Chairman's emoluments.
195. The Gouvernement shall fix the fees, allowances or salary of the chairman or, as the case may be, his additional salary.

1977, c. 5, s. 195, s. 14.

FRENCH LANGUAGE

Other members: no emoluments expenses reimburses.
196. The members of the Conseil other than the chairman and the secretary shall not be remunerated. They are entitled, however, to reimbursement of their expenses incurred in the exercise of their functions and to an attendance allowance fixed by the Gouvernement.

1977, c. 5, s. 196, s. 14.

Staff.
197. The staff of the Conseil are appointed and remunerated in accordance with the Civil Service Act.

Chairman's powers.
The chairman shall exercise in regard to the members of the staff of the Conseil the powers vested by the said act in the deputy-heads of departments.

1977, c. 5, s. 197.

Special committees.
198. The Conseil may, with the approval of the Minister, establish special committees for the study of specific questions and commission them to collect the relevant information and report their findings and recommendations to it.

Composition, allowances, fees.
Such committees may, with the prior approval of the Minister, consist in whole or in part of persons who are not members of the Conseil. The attendance allowances and fees of such persons shall be determined by the Conseil in accordance with the standards established for that purpose by the Gouvernement.

1977, c. 5, s. 198, s. 14.

Additional staff.
199. In addition to the staff contemplated in section 197, the Conseil, with the approval of the Minister, may employ the persons required to carry out the duly authorized work.

1977, c. 5, s. 199.

Seat.
200. The seat of the Conseil shall be in a municipality of the territory of the Communauté urbaine de Québec. It may hold its sittings at any place in Québec. It shall meet as often as necessary.

1977, c. 5, s. 200, s. 14.

Quorum.
201. Six members are a quorum of the Conseil. In the case of a tie-vote, the chairman has a casting vote.

1977, c. 5, s. 201.

FRENCH LANGUAGE

Replacement of chairman. **202.** If the chairman is temporarily absent or unable to act, he shall be replaced by the secretary.

1977, c. 5, s. 202.

Annual report. **203.** Not later than 31 October each year, the Conseil must submit to the Minister a report of its activities for the preceding fiscal year.

1977, c. 5, s. 203.

Tabling. **204.** The Minister shall table the report of the Conseil in the Assemblée Nationale if he receives it during a session. If he receives it while the Assemblée Nationale is not sitting, he shall table it within thirty days after the opening of the next session or after resumption.

1977, c. 5, s. 204.

TITLE V
OFFENCES AND PENALTIES

Offences and penalties. **205.** Every person who contravenes a provision of this act other than section 136 or of a regulation made under this act by the Gouvernement or by the Office de la langue française is guilty of an offence and liable, in addition to costs,

(a) for each offence, to a fine of $25 to $500 in the case of a natural person, and of $50 to $1,000 in the case of an artificial person;

(b) for any subsequent offence within two years of a first offence, to a fine of $50 to $1,000 in the case of a natural person, and of $500 to $5,000 in the case of an artificial person.

1977, c. 5, s. 205, s. 14.

Offences and penalties. **206.** A business firm guilty of an offence contemplated in section 136 is liable, in addition to costs, to a fine of $100 to $2,000 for each day during which it carries on its business without a certificate.

1977, c. 5, s. 206.

Summary proceedings. **207.** The Attorney-General or the person authorized by him shall institute, by way of summary proceedings, the prosecutions provided for by this act and shall exercise the recourses necessary for its application.

1977, c. 5, s. 207.

FRENCH LANGUAGE

Court order to remove or destroy sign, poster. **208.** Any court of civil jurisdiction, on a motion by the Attorney-General, may order the removal or destruction at the expense of the defendant, within eight days of the judgment, of any poster, sign, advertisement, bill-board or illuminated sign not in conformity with this act.

Person affected. The motion may be directed against the owner of the advertising equipment or against whoever placed the poster, sign, advertisement, bill-board or illuminated sign or had it placed.

1977, c. 5, s. 208.

TITLE VI
TRANSITIONAL AND MISCELLANEOUS PROVISIONS

Coming into force, s. 11. **209.** Section 11 shall come into force on 3 January 1979 and shall not affect cases pending on that date.

Coming into force, s. 13. Section 13 shall come into force on 3 January 1980 and shall not affect cases pending on that date.

Coming into force, ss. 34, 58 and 208. Section 34, 58 and 208 shall come into force on 3 July 1978, subject to section 211.

1977, c. 5, s. 209.

Delay to comply: signs. **210.** Owners of bill-boards or illuminated signs erected before 31 July 1974 must comply with section 58 from its coming into force.

1977, c. 5, s. 210.

Delay to comply. **211.** Every person who has complied with the requirements of section 35 of the Official Language Act (1974, chapter 6) in respect of bilingual public signs shall have until 1 September 1981 to make the required changes, in particular to change his bill-boards and illuminated signs, in order to comply with this act.

1977, c. 5, s. 211.

Minister responsible. **212.** The Gouvernement shall entrust a minister with the application of this act. Such minister shall exercise in regard to the staff of the Office de la langue française, that of the Commission de surveillance and that of the Conseil de la langue française the powers of a department head.

1977, c. 5, s. 230, s. 14.

FRENCH LANGUAGE

Scope　**213.** This act applies to the Gouvernement.

1977, c. 5, s. 231, s. 14.

Section 11 of this act shall come into force on 3 January 1979.
Section 13 of this act shall come into force on 3 January 1980.
Sections 34, 58 and 208 of this act shall come into force on 3 July 1978, subject to section 211.

FRENCH LANGUAGE

SCHEDULE

A. *The civil administration*

1. The Gouvernement and the government departments.

2. The government agencies:
Agencies to which the Gouvernement or a minister appoints the majority of the members, to which, by law, the officers or employees are appointed or remunerated in accordance with the Civil Service Act (chapter F-3), or at least half of whose capital stock is derived from the consolidated revenue fund except, however, health services and social services, general and vocational colleges and the University of Québec.

3. The municipal and school bodies:
(*a*) the urban communities:
The Communauté urbaine de Québec, the Communauté urbaine de Montréal and the Communauté régionale de l'Outaouais, the Commission de transport de la Communauté urbaine de Québec, the Bureau d'assainissement des eaux du Québec métropolitain, the Commission de transport de la Communauté urbaine de Montréal, the Commission de transport de la Communauté régionale de l'Outaouais, the Société d'aménagement de l'Outaouais, the Commission de transport de la Ville de Laval and the Commission de transport de la Rive Sud de Montréal;

(*b*) the municipalities:
The city, town, village, country and county corporations, whether incorporated under a general law or a special act, and the agencies under the jurisdiction of such corporations which participate in the administration of their territory;

(*c*) the school bodies:
The regional school boards, the school boards and the corporations of school trustees governed by the Education Act (chapter I-14), the Conseil scolaire de l'île de Montréal.

4. The health services and the social services:
Establishments within the meaning of the Act respecting health services and social services (chapter S-5).

FRENCH LANGUAGE

B. *Semipublic agencies*

1. Public utility firms:
If they are not already government agencies, the telephone, telegraph and cable-delivery companies, the air, ship, autobus and rail transport companies, the companies which produce, transport, distribute or sell gas, water or electricity, and business firms holding authorizations from the Commission des transports.

2. Professional corporations:
The professional corporations listed in Schedule I to the Professional Code (chapter C-26) under the designation "Corporation professionnelle", or established in accordance with that Code.

1977, c. 5, Schedule.

FRENCH LANGUAGE

REPEAL SCHEDULE

In accordance with section 17 of the Act respecting the consolidation of the statutes (chapter R-3), chapter 5 of the annual statutes of 1977, in force on 31 December 1977, is repealed, except sections 224 to 229 and 232, effective from the coming into force of chapter C-11 of the Revised Statutes.

ᴱ Editeur officiel du Québec, 1979

CONCORDANCE TABLE

STATUTES OF QUEBEC, 1977	REVISED STATUTES, 1977	
Chapter 5	Chapter C-11	
CHARTER OF THE FRENCH LANGUAGE	CHARTER OF THE FRENCH LANGUAGE	
SECTIONS	SECTIONS	REMARKS
Preamble	Preamble	
1 - 211	1 - 211	
212		Amendment integrated into c. I-16, s. 14
213		Amendment integrated into c. I-16, s. 40
214 - 216		Omitted
217		Amendment integrated into c. D-1, s. 3
218		Amendment integrated into c. I-14, s. 189
219		Omitted
220		Amendment integrated into c. E-9, s. 22
221		Amendment integrated into c. P-40, s. 4
222		Amendment integrated into c. C-26, s. 1
223		Amendment integrated into c. C-26, s. 41
224 - 229		Omitted
230	212	

FRENCH LANGUAGE

S.Q. 1977, c. 5	R.S. 1977, c. C-11	
SECTIONS	SECTIONS	REMARKS
231	213	·
232		Omitted
Schedule	Schedule	

The Concordance Table indicates all section numbers, whether or not they have been renumbered. Other divisions (i.e. Part, Chapter, Division, Subdivision, Paragraph, etc.), where applicable, are indicated only where they have been renumbered.

The term "Omitted" in the "Remarks" column refers to a section that does not appear in the consolidation because it is without effect, not in force, or of a temporary, transitory, local or private character, or because its object has been accomplished or it is a repealing or replacing section.

Appendix 2
Selected historical and linguistic events in Quebec and Canada[1]

1750   French Rule: "La Nouvelle France" (Quebec) is populated by 65 thousand francophones.

1755 to Following their refusal to swear allegiance to the British Crown, the
1762   francophone Acadians are deported from Nova Scotia and New Brunswick while their land is distributed amongst British settlers.

1763   Anglo-French rivalry in Europe results in the loss of French control over "La Nouvelle France" following the battle of the "plains of Abraham" in Quebec city. British rule is established in the Province of Quebec through the instoration of the British Common Law system.

1774   The *Quebec Act* guarantees the maintenance of French civil laws and customs as well as freedom of worship and education in Quebec. These actions help secure the allegiance of Canada to Britain during the American War of Independence. Empire loyalists from New England states emigrate north to Canada.

1791   The *Constitutional Act* divides Lower Canada with its francophone majority (Quebec) from Upper Canada with its anglophone majority (Ontario) and establishes limited self-government to both provinces.

1837 to Francophones in Lower Canada and anglophones in Upper Canada
1838   rebel against British control and demand responsible government in the two Canadas. Both rebellions are crushed by the British Army.

1839   *Lord Durham* tables his report to the British House of Commons concerning the rebellions in the two Canadas. It is proposed that the French problem can be solved by the union of the two Canadas in a single Assembly in which francophones could become a minority. The Assembly would have control over the budget thus satisfying Upper Canada demands for greater autonomy in the colony.

1840   The *Act of Union* establishes the Province of Canada with an Assembly made up of an equal number of members elected from Upper and Lower Canada. However, the only official language of the Assembly is English while Lower Canada absorbs the financial debts of Upper Canada through the Act of Union. At this time the francophone population of Lower Canada numbers 650,000 while the anglophone population of Upper Canada numbers 450,000.

1864   A law stipulates that both English and French can be used in the parliament of the Province of Canada as well as in the legislature of Lower Canada.

1867   The *British North America* (BNA) Act declares the Dominion of Canada to be composed of four provinces: Ontario, Quebec, Nova Scotia and New Brunswick. The House of Commons is established in the capital city of Ottawa. Federal Deputies to the House of Commons are elected from districts in all the provinces. The Federal Government holds key powers such as trade, commerce, taxes, the judiciary and defence. Provincial legislatures have control over education, the courts and social affairs and can levy provincial taxes. Article 133 of the BNA act recognizes English and French as official languages in Federal laws and within the Federal Assembly. Article 80 of the BNA act declares "permanent" anglophone districts of Quebec to guarantee their representation in the Quebec legislature. This clause remained in effect until 1970 when all districts were put on an equal footing in Quebec.

1868   The Canadian Federal Government buys the North West territories (today's Manitoba, Saskatchewan, Alberta and Yukon) from the Hudson Bay Company for the sum of £300,000 sterling. However, the francophone Metis led by Louis Riel resist the annexation to Canada by establishing a provisional government and force negotiations with Ottawa.

1869   A Quebec school law insures anglophone Protestant control over their own school system.

1870   Negotiations between Riel and Ottawa result in the creation of the
        Province of Manitoba. The *Manitoba Act* declares French and
        English as official languages and guarantees the existence of French
        Catholic and English Protestant schools. In 1870 the population of
        Manitoba consists of francophone Metis (5,700), anglophone Metis
        (4,000), British (1,100) plus native peoples. Immediately following
        the Manitoba Act, anglophone Protestants from Ontario establish
        settlements in Manitoba. Metis refers to the progeny of mixed
        couples consisting of native Indians and white settlers.

1871   A New Brunswick government law restricts funding only to non-
        confessional schools, forcing francophone Catholics to support
        their own schools or attend anglophone majority schools.

1884 to Louis Riel establishes another Metis provisional government, this
1885   one for the Metis and native people whose lands and hunting
        customs are being eroded by the advance of Canadian settlers and
        the Canadian Pacific Railway. Riel advocates the creation of the
        provinces of Saskatchewan and Alberta where the property rights
        of the Metis and native Indians would be guaranteed. However this
        time the Canadian forces crush the Metis rebellion.

1885   Riel is "tried" and found guilty of high treason. Metis and many
        francophones plea for clemency. Anglophones, especially in
        Ontario, rally for his execution. A Toronto paper headlines: "Riel
        should be strangled with a French flag". In Ottawa the Prime
        Minister John A. MacDonald asserts "Riel must swing". Riel is
        executed in November 1885.

1890   The Manitoba legislature abolishes confessional schools forcing
        francophone Catholics to subsidize their own school. Francophone
        minorities contest the law up to the Canadian Supreme Court but to
        no avail. French is also banned from the Manitoba legislature, and
        the judicial system. Laws are only passed in English.

1912   In Ontario Regulation 17 bans the teaching of French from all
        public schools in the province while efforts are also made to curb the
        development of French Catholic private schools, hospitals and even
        parishes that functioned in French. This at a time when franco-
        phone Ontarians form 20% of the Ontario population.

1914 to The conscription issue further deepens the linguistic rift between
1918   francophones in Quebec and the anglophone majority in Canada.
        Francophones resist conscription to serve in a 'British Imperial'
        war.

1916   In Manitoba, the teaching of French in all public schools is banned.

1927   In Ontario, Regulation 17 is withdrawn and is removed from the registers in 1944.

1929   In Saskatchewan the teaching of French is abolished in anglophone school boards.

1940 to Francophones in Quebec join the war effort voluntarily but remain
1945   opposed to conscription.

1942 to Saskatchewan draws new school districts which result in franco-
1946   phones losing control of their educational system and schools.

1948   The Quebec Asbestos strike has a major impact on the development of the Quebec labour movement.

1950s   In post-WWII Quebec, rural French Canadian Catholic social patterns are breaking down through the industrialization of Quebec society. A conservative nationalistic ideology fades away along with the death of the Quebec Premier, Maurice Duplessis in 1959.

1960s   The Quebec "Quiet Revolution" is based on the notion of "rattrapage" which consists of modernizing every aspect of Quebec society (education, energy, transport, etc.) to better participate in the Canadian and American "way of life" and economy. The Quiet Revolution also coincided with the emergence of a distinctive Québécois cultural revival. The Quiet Revolution fostered high expectations which, when not met, helped the rise of the Quebec Independence Movement.

1960   The Quebec Liberal Party is swept to power as the bearer of Quebec's secular "Quiet Revolution".

1962   René Lévesque, a cabinet member of the Quebec Liberal government, nationalizes Quebec electricity under the new "Hydro Québec".

1963   Québécois francophone engineers design and build a hydro-electric power dam in Northern Quebec for Hydro Québec, This is heralded as a symbolic demonstration that Québécois francophones can also excel in science and technology.

Creation of the Canadian *Royal Commission on Bilingualism and Biculturalism*, which tables its final reports in 1969. Demonstrates the extent of the anglicization of francophone minorities beyond Quebec and the dearth of federal government services offered in

French across the country except Quebec. Also "discovers" multi-cultural Canada.

1964   Creation of the Quebec Ministry of Education.

1965   Publication of John Porter's *Vertical Mosaic* in which it is argued that Canada's cultural mosaic is simply a division of labour by means of which the British-stock anglophones maintained a privileged position in Canada.

Beginning of Québécois "Joual" literature.

1967   Montreal hosts "Expo 67". The President of France, General de Gaulle, proclaims his famous "Vive le Québec Libre" to a huge enthusiastic francophone crowd in Montreal.

1968   Publication of Pierre Valliere's influential book, *White Niggers of America*, discussing the subordinate position of French Canadians within Quebec, itself a double colony of Canada and the USA.

Quebec's independence movements rally under a single political party: Le Parti Québécois.

In Montreal, the trustees of the Saint-Leonard School Board adopt a resolution making French the only language of schooling for immigrant children within the board's district. Francophones and Italian Canadians clash in the streets of Montreal over the matter.

Creation of the *Gendron Commission* to investigate the position of the French language and linguistic rights in Quebec. This report is tabled in 1972.

In Ontario, the government passes a law recognizing the right to French schooling in the province, "where numbers warrant" in the opinion of the school boards.

1969   Inspired by the recommendations of the *Royal Commission on Bilingualism and Biculturalism*, the Canadian federal parliament adopts the *Official Languages Act*. This act guarantees federal government services in the mother tongue of francophones and anglophones whose group concentration exceeds 10% of the regional population. The Act also enshrined French/English bilingualism in federal government documents and laws.

The Quebec government promulgates *Bill 63* in reponse to the Saint-Leonard School Board controversy. The Language Bill enshrines freedom of language choice in French or English for parents of all children in Quebec. The Bill also promotes French as the language of work and as a necessary second language in non-French schools. The Office de la langue française is given watchdog functions. The Bill is vehemently opposed by francophone nationalists who feel it will further erode the demographic position of Quebec francophones to the advantage of anglophones.

1970   *The Quebec October Crisis.* The "Front de Libération du Québec" (FLQ), an organization modelled after urban guerrilla groups in Latin America, kidnaps both a British High Commission commercial attaché and Quebec's Labour Minister. Canada's Prime Minister, Pierre E. Trudeau, declares the *War Measures Act* which suspends civil rights in all Canada. The Canadian army occupies Quebec. The Quebec Labour Minister is killed and the British Commissioner is exchanged for the FLQ safe passage to Cuba. Though the FLQ tactics were disclaimed by most, the Prime Minister's handling of the crisis most likely promoted the cause of the Quebec Independence Movement. The promulgation of the War Measures Act as applied in Quebec was overwhelmingly approved in anglophone Canada.

In Manitoba, the government passes a law which restores the right to French schooling in the province, "where numbers warrant" in the opinion of the school boards.

1971   The federal government proclaims a policy of *Canadian Multiculturalism* within a bilingual framework. The policy supports the activities of "non-official language" ethnic groups in spheres such as ethnic press, ethnic cultural events and assisted programs of linguistic instruction.

1974   The Liberal Quebec government adopts *Bill 22* making French the official language of Quebec. Immigrant children must pass a language test to determine if they have a right to English schooling. The Bill is vehemently opposed by anglophones for being too restrictive and is opposed by francophones for not going far enough in the promotion of French.

1975   Foundation of the "Fédération des Francophones hors Quebec" based in Ottawa (FFHQ). Francophone minorities beyond Quebec mobilize to more effectively fight for their rights.

1976   The Quebec *"Air War"* further exacerbates the linguistic tension between francophones and anglophones. Francophone Quebec air controllers and pilots demand French/English bilingualism in ground to air communications over Quebec air space. They base their claim on Article 2 of the 1969 Official Languages Act. The use of French in aerial communications is declared safe by a commission of enquiry in 1979.

M. George Forest, a francophone of Manitoba, declines to pay a unilingual English parking ticket on the ground that English unilingualism enshrined in the Manitoba legislature and laws since 1890 is unconstitutional. The case is settled in his favour by the Canadian Supreme Court in 1979.

The pro-independence Parti Québécois, led by René Lévesque, is elected to power in November 1976. The overwhelming majority of Quebec anglophones voted for the federalist Quebec Liberal party.

1977   The Quebec government adopts *Bill 101*, the *Charter of the French Language*, making French the official language of Quebec society (this volume).

New Brunswick declares both English and French as official languages in the province.

1978   The "Fédération des Francophones hors Québec" (FFHQ) publishes *The Heirs of Lord Durham: Manifesto of a Vanishing People*. This volume documents and compares the demographic and legal position of francophone minorities across Canada. The findings are evident from the title.

1979   The Canadian Supreme Court of Canada declares unconstitutional the sections of Bill 101 which state that only the French version of Quebec laws is official. Consequently the Quebec government must translate and declare official both versions of all its laws. The same Supreme Court ruling declared unconstitutional the 1890 Manitoba law declaring English unilingualism in the legislature and laws (Forest case). In both cases the Supreme Court of Canada based its judgment on article 133 of the 1867 BNA act. The only difference between these two cases is that the ruling on the Manitoba case came 90 years "after the fact" whereas the Quebec ruling came 2 years "after the fact".

1980   The Parti Québécois government proposes a *referendum on "sovereignty-association"* which would give Quebec greater self-government while maintaining economic ties with the rest of Canada. The *no* forces win with 60% of the votes and the *yes* forces lose with 40%. A slim majority of francophones also voted for the *no* option on the promise of a renewed Canadian federalism.

1981   The Parti Québécois under the Lévesque leadership is re-elected to power in a decisive victory in the April general elections.

1982   The Quebec government is out-manoeuvred by both the anglophone provinces and the federal government in the negotiations for the patriation of the *Canadian Constitution* and the adoption of the new 1982 *Canadian Charter of Rights and Freedoms*. The new Canadian *Charter* declares the use of English and French as official languages but these sections (16–22) are adopted only by New Brunswick and the federal government while Ontario refuses to adopt them. The deal reached by the federal government and the anglophone provinces means that Quebec lost out on its traditional demands for a veto on all constitutional changes. Consequently the Quebec government refused to sign the *Charter* though it remains subject to its provisions.

1982 to Camille Laurin, the Minister of Education, drops one of the contro-
1983   versial clauses in his *White Paper on Education* regarding the anglophone school system. Quebec anglophones both within Montreal *and* in other parts of the province will keep control of their schools and school boards.

1983   Through a one month Parliamentary Commission the Quebec Government invites all sectors of Quebec society to propose amendments to Bill 101. Minor changes to Bill 101 are adopted by the Quebec National Assembly as Bill 57. The most interesting change makes English schooling available to anglophone children coming from Canadian provinces where school services for the francophone minority are deemed comparable to those offered the anglophone minority in Quebec. For Quebec anglophones Bill 57 is seen as a positive first step but is found to fall far short of anglophone expectations.

1983 to The Manitoba Government attempts to re-establish the language
1984   rights of the Province's 50,000 francophones by declaring English and French official languages of Manitoba. The Government's Bill 115 proposes to give its francophone minority of 5% the right to deal in French with Government offices in areas where francophones comprise 8% or more of the population. Bill 115 is also a political compromise which would avoid the translation to French of all the English only laws passed since the 1890 banning of French in Manitoba. However a wide spread anti-French backlash lead by the Conservatives blocks Parliamentary procedures and forces the

closure of the Parliamentary session thus killing the French Right Bill 115. The Federal Government responds by asking the Canadian Supreme Court to declare invalid all English only laws passed in Manitoba since 1890.

Note to Appendix 2

1. Perhaps the best historical account of the francophone presence in Canada produced in the English language remains that of Professor Mason Wade entitled *The French Canadians: 1760–1967*, Laurentian Library, Macmillan, Toronto, 1968. The present overview concentrating on French/English linguistic conflicts cannot do justice to the broad range of events that have shaped Canadian history. (*The Editor*)

Contributors

ALISON D'ANGLEJAN, Faculté des Sciences de l'Education, Université de Montréal, C.P. 6128 Succursale "A", Montréal H3C 3J7, Québec.

RICHARD Y. BOURHIS, Department of Psychology, McMaster University, 1280 Main Street West, Hamilton, Ontario, L8S 4K1, Canada.

GARY CALDWELL, Institut Québécois de Recherche sur la culture, 77 Belvidère, Suite 201, Lennoxville J1M 2E5, Québec.

WILLIAM COLEMAN, Department of Political Science, McMaster University, 1280 Main Street West, Hamilton, Ontario, L8S 4K1, Canada.

DENISE DAOUST, Service de la recherche Socio-Linguistique, Office de la langue française, 800 Place Victoria, C.P. 316, Tour de la Bourse, Montréal H4Z 1G8, Québec.

LISE DUBE-SIMARD, Département de Psychologie, Université de Montréal, C.P. 6128 Succursale "A", Montréal H3C 3J7, Québec.

PIERRE LAPORTE, Directeur, Direction de la recherche et de l'évaluation, Office de la langue française, 800 Place Victoria, C.P. 316, Tour de la Bourse, Montréal H4Z 1G8, Québec.

WILLIAM F. MACKEY, Centre International de recherche sur le bilinguisme, Université Laval, Cité Universitaire G1K 7P4, Québec, Québec.

JOHN MALLEA, Department of Sociology in Education, Ontario Institute for Studies in Education, 252 Bloor Street West, Toronto, Ontario, M5S 1V6, Canada.

ROGER MILLER, Etudes d'Administration, Université du Québec à Montréal, c/o 555 Dorchester West, Suite 922, Montréal H2Z 1B1, Québec.

DONALD E. TAYLOR, Department of Psychology, McGill University, 1205 Ave. Dr Penfield, Montréal H3A 1B1, Québec.

Notes on Contributors

Alison d'Anglejan is Associate Professor in the Faculty of Education at the Université de Montréal. Born in Montreal, her own childhood experience of being educated in a second language (French) stimulated an interest in bilingualism which led to a Ph.D. in Psychology at McGill University. Her published work includes studies in the cognitive and social aspects of language learning and in language policy and language education.

Richard Y. Bourhis was born and raised in the French-speaking part of Montreal and received his education in both French and English. After completing a B.Sc. in Psychology at McGill University he obtained his Ph.D. in Social Psychology at the University of Bristol in England. His main research interests are the Social Psychology of Intergroup Relations, Language Attitudes, the Dynamics of Cross-Cultural Communication in Multiethnic Settings and issues related to Language Policies and Language Planning. Richard Y. Bourhis has pursued his research interests in numerous cultural settings including Quebec, Wales, England, Belgium, Switzerland and Canada. Along with numerous book chapter contributions, Richard Y. Bourhis has published articles in journals such as the *European Journal of Social Psychology, The International Journal of the Sociology of Language, Ethnicity* and the *Journal of Language and Social Psychology*. Dr Bourhis joined the Psychology Department at McMaster Universty in 1978 where he is now an Associate Professor.

Gary Caldwell is a native of Ontario and has resided in the Eastern Townships of Quebec since 1971. He studied at the University of Toronto before obtaining his Masters degree at Laval University in Quebec City. One of his research interests deals with social change in post-war Quebec, see for example "Rattrapage raté" in *Recherches Sociographiques*. His current research focuses on the anglophone population of Quebec especially as it relates to demographic and social demographic issues. He and Professor Eric Waddell are the co-editors of *The English of Quebec: From Majority to Minority Status*, published in 1982 by the Institut québécois de recherche sur la culture (IQRC). Since 1980 Gary Caldwell has been associated with the IQRC, first in a part-time capacity and subsequently in a full-time capacity. At the Institut he directs a research group interested in the non-francophone population of Quebec.

William Coleman is Assistant Professor of Political Science at McMaster University in Hamilton. Born in British Columbia, he earned his B.A. at Carleton University and then completed his M.A. and Ph.D. degrees at the University of Chicago. He has written several articles on language policy in Quebec and has just completed a book on Quebec politics entitled *The Independantiste Coalition in Quebec*, to be published by the University of Toronto Press in 1984. William Coleman is currently taking part in a cross-national research project on the role of business interest associations in Canada and Europe, sponsored by the Canadian SSHRC and the Volkswagen Foundation.

Denise Daoust was born in Ottawa where she received her B.A. at the Université d'Ottawa. She then studied at the Université de Montréal and obtained a Licence Es Lettres in French Literature and Art History. Subsequently Denise Daoust specialized in Linguistics at the Université de Montréal where she obtained her Ph.D. in 1975. Using a sociolinguistic perspective her thesis work has dealt with syntactic aspects of Quebec French. Her current research interests are in syntax, sociolinguistics, language planning and terminology change. Denise Daoust has published several articles on issues related to language problems and language planning in Quebec. Since 1975 she has been Chief Research Officer of the Sociolinguistic Research Division of the Office de la Langue Française (OLF). Currently Denise Daoust is responsible for the OLF Research Program on French terminology implementation in Quebec.

Lise Dubé-Simard is Associate Professor of Psychology at the Université de Montréal. She obtained her Ph.D. in Social Psychology at McGill University. Lise Dubé-Simard published numerous articles on interpersonal and intergroup relations in journals such as the *Canadian Journal of Behavioral Science*, the *Journal of Personality and Social Psychology*, the *Journal of Social Psychology*, and *Revue Québécoise de Psychologie*. Her current research interest is concerned with processes involved in perceptions of inequality, injustice and relative deprivation with disadvantaged groups such as francophones in Quebec and women at work. She is co-author (with D. M. Taylor) of *Les relations intergroupes au Quebec et la loi 101: les réactions des francophones et des anglophones*, published by l'Office de la langue française in 1981.

Pierre-Etienne Laporte has studied at Laval, Berkeley and McGill Universities. Before joining the Office de la langue française, in 1975, he taught at McGill and the University of Sherbrooke. From 1970 to 1972, he was Director of Research for the *Commission on the situation of the French language and linguistic rights in Quebec* (Gendron Commission, Quebec, 1972). In 1977, he was a lecturer on language planning at the American Linguistic Summer Institute in Hawaii. Pierre E. Laporte has been a consultant for several government enquiries on ethnic relations and health problems, and is the author of numerous articles on these subjects. Pierre E. Laporte is the current Director of Research of l'Office de la langue française in Montreal.

William Francis Mackey was born in English-speaking Winnipeg and educated, first in the bilingual schools of French-speaking St Boniface, and later at the Universities of Manitoba, Columbia, Laval, Harvard, and Geneva. After teaching at the Universities of London, Cambridge, California, Texas, Nice, and Laval, Dr Mackey served on government language commissions in Australia, Canada, Ireland, and Quebec. A fellow of both the Royal Society of Canada and the Royal Academy of Belgium, he is the author of over two dozen books and some two hundred articles on bilingualism, language didactics and language contact, and has been a collaborator on the *Encyclopaedia Britannica*, the BBC, and the editorial boards of several journals. He is currently Research Professor in Laval University's International Centre for Research on Bilingualism, which he founded in 1967.

John Mallea is Professor of Sociology at the Ontario Institute for Studies in Education (OISE) in Toronto. In addition to publishing widely on issues related to cultural diversity and education, John Mallea edited the only English language volume on Bill 22, the language law preceding the current Charter of the French Language. This volume is entitled *Quebec's Language Policies: Background and Response*, and was published by Laval University Press in 1977. Assistant Director (Academic) of OISE (1977–81) and President of the Comparative and International Education Society of Canada (1974–76), John Mallea is currently working on a comparative study of multi-racial, multi-cultural education in Canada, Australia and the UK.

Roger Miller is Professor of Management at l'Université du Québec à Montréal. He is also an associate in Secor Inc., a strategic management consulting firm based in Montreal. Roger Miller obtained an M.Sc. in Engineering at the University of Stanford and also completed an M.B.A. degree at Columbia University. In Belgium, Roger Miller obtained a D.Sc. in Applied Economics at l'Université Catholique de Louvain. Professor Miller has been a member of the Canadian Royal Commission on Corporate

Concentration (Brice Commission, 1977) and was also involved in the Canadian Royal Commission on Financial Management (Lambert Commission, 1980). Roger Miller's most recent publication is a volume entitled *Corporate Strategy and Technology*, Montreal: Innovation Centre, 1983.

Donald M. Taylor is Associate Professor in the Psychology Department of McGill University. He obtained his Ph.D. in Social Psychology from the University of Western Ontario in 1969, where, with the assistance of a Canada Council doctoral fellowship he studied cross-cultural communication. Dr Taylor's research interests are in aspects of intergroup relations, including such topics as language and ethnic relations, ethnic identity, intergroup stereotypes, language legislation and cultural diversity. He has taught and conducted research in a wide variety of settings including Canada, the Philippines (Ford Foundation), India (Ford Foundation), Europe and the United States. Dr Taylor has contributed numerous articles to journals in social psychology and sociolinguistics. As well, he has co-authored a number of books in the area of cultural diversity and language policies, including *The Individual Language and Society in Canada* and *Multiculturalism and Ethnic Attitudes in Canada*.

Index

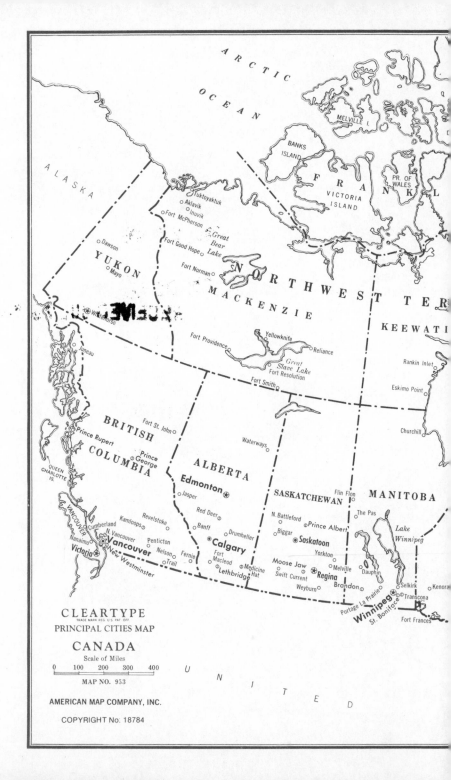

ARCTIC OCEAN

MELVILLE I.

BANKS ISLAND

F R A N K L

PR. OF WALES

VICTORIA ISLAND

A L A S K A

Tuktoyaktuk
Aklavik
Inuvik
Fort McPherson
Fort Good Hope
Great Bear Lake
Fort Norman

Dawson

Y U K O N
Mayo

N O R T H W E S T   T E R

M A C K E N Z I E

KEEWATI

Whitehorse

Fort Providence
Yellowknife
Reliance
Great Slave Lake
Fort Resolution
Fort Smith

Rankin Inlet

Eskimo Point

Juneau

Fort St. John

B R I T I S H

Prince Rupert

QUEEN CHARLOTTE IS.

C O L U M B I A
Prince George

Waterways

Churchill

A L B E R T A

Edmonton

Jasper

Flin Flon

M A N I T O B A

Revelstoke
Kamloops
Cumberland
N. Vancouver
Nanaimo
Vancouver
Victoria
New Westminster
Penticton
Nelson
Fernie
Trail

Red Deer
Banff
Drumheller

Calgary

Fort Macleod
Lethbridge
Medicine Hat

S A S K A T C H E W A N

N. Battleford
Biggar
Prince Albert

Saskatoon

Yorkton

Moose Jaw
Swift Current
Regina
Weyburn

The Pas

Lake Winnipeg

Melville
Dauphin
Brandon
Portage La Prairie
Winnipeg
St. Boniface
Selkirk
Transcona
Kenora
Fort Frances

CLEARTYPE
TRADE MARK REG. U.S. PAT. OFF.
PRINCIPAL CITIES MAP

CANADA
Scale of Miles
0   100   200   300   400

MAP NO. 953

AMERICAN MAP COMPANY, INC.

COPYRIGHT No: 18784

U   N   I   T   E   D